Ajay M. Rambhia

XML Distributed Systems Design

SAMS

201 West 103rd Street, Indianapolis, Indiana 46290

XML Distributed Systems Design

International Standard Book Number: 0672323281

Library of Congress Catalog Card Number: 2001094820

Printed in the United States of America

First Printing: March 2002

04 03 02 4 3 2 1

Trademarks

All terms mentioned in this book that are known to be trademarks or service marks have been appropriately capitalized. Sams cannot attest to the accuracy of this information. Use of a term in this book should not be regarded as affecting the validity of any trademark or service mark.

Warning and Disclaimer

Every effort has been made to make this book as complete and as accurate as possible, but no warranty or fitness is implied. The information provided is on an "as is" basis. The author and the publisher shall have neither liability nor responsibility to any person or entity with respect to any loss or damages arising from the information contained in this book or from the use of the CD or programs accompanying it.

Executive Editor
Michael Stephens

Acquisitions Editor
Carol Ackerman

Development Editor
Michael Watson

Managing Editor
Matt Purcell

Project Editor
Natalie Harris

Indexer
Erika Millen

Production Editor
Rhonda Tinch-Mize

Technical Editor
Mahesh Panchwagh

Team Coordinator
Pamalee Nelson

Interior Designer
Dan Armstrong

Cover Designer
Alan Clements

Contents at a Glance

Table of Contents

Appendixes

About the Author

Ajay M R, also known as Ajay Manoj Rambhia, is chief technology officer of EvolveWare, a company that offers systems architecture and development services. The company's Web site offers more information at `http://www.evolveware.com`

Ajay is involved in the design of high-end systems that integrate with and extend legacy systems via XML and other automation methods. His application design and development has been focused toward banking and finance industries, network monitoring, and ERP systems integration.

Ajay also has expertise in knowledge-based systems, has authored papers on Artificial Neural Networks and fuzzy logic, and has worked on KB based system architectures.

Ajay has supported various companies, including Fortune 500 companies, as project manager, systems architect, and system integration specialist.

He can be contacted at `ajaymr@evolveware.com`.

Dedication

For Nita, my wife and friend

My parents, Manjula and Manoj

My in-laws, Shirish and Anju

This book is devoted to

Keshavaji, my Grandpa, for his inspiration and support

Acknowledgments

Although there are several contributors—directly and indirectly—to this effort, the following list reflects only a few of them:

- Miten Marfatia, CEO of EvolveWare, Inc
- Raymond Ennis, First Vice President, Information Systems Group, Prudential Securities
- Richard Henderson, VP Business Development, EvolveWare, Inc
- Mahesh Panchwagh, Sr. Consultant and Architect, NY State
- Hemant Puranik, Inxight, Inc

My special thanks to Carol Ackerman, acquisitions editor, for her suggestions and support from time to time; without her the book would have been not possible. Furthermore, I am also thankful to Michael Stephens, executive editor, for his timely attention to the proposal and his effort to get it going.

I would also take this opportunity to thank Michael Watson, development editor, for his timely attention and responses.

Finally, my special thanks to the entire EvolveWare team: Without their support, this effort would not have been successful.

Tell Us What You Think!

As the reader of this book, *you* are our most important critic and commentator. We value your opinion and want to know what we're doing right, what we could do better, what areas you'd like to see us publish in, and any other words of wisdom you're willing to pass our way.

As an executive editor for Sams, I welcome your comments. You can fax, email, or write me directly to let me know what you did or didn't like about this book—as well as what we can do to make our books stronger.

Please note that I cannot help you with technical problems related to the topic of this book, and that due to the high volume of mail I receive, I might not be able to reply to every message.

When you write, please be sure to include this book's title and author as well as your name and phone or fax number. I will carefully review your comments and share them with the author and editors who worked on the book.

Fax: 317-581-4770

Email: `feedback@samspublishing.com`

Mail: Michael Stephens
Sams Publishing
201 West 103rd Street
Indianapolis, IN 46290 USA

PART I

XML Concepts and Design

Extensible Markup Language, or XML, is everywhere! XML is today's buzzword for tech savvy guys.

This section of the book concentrates on getting the theory and the concepts right. As required in any system's construction approach, the concepts are important and the understanding needs to be sound to architect and arrive at model. I will concentrate in teaching XML and its applications with an architectural approach throughout this book.

Chapter 1 is a general systems architecture overview. I have tried to keep it brief and concise.

Chapters 2–4 are introduction chapters to XML and related technologies. They cover the basics of XML and parsers. The chapters are not rigorous in terms of code examples because readers should be intermediate. The theories are treated with reference to design concepts. Furthermore, some workings of XML-RPC (XML Remote Procedure Call) and SOAP (Simple Object Access Protocol) are addressed, which are used extensively in the discussions.

Chapters 5–6 introduce the concept of open-end systems. For a distributed system, modeling "open-ended-ness" is an important concept. The chapters cover the theory of integrating different systems. They also cover the concept of using the Web as a transport medium for communicating over wide area networks. The concept of frameworks is also introduced in these chapters. For modeling and architecting flexible distributed systems, it is important to have the basic architecture defined. The flexibility of the model would further allow you to extend the system and make it distributed. Hence, frameworks are treated extensively, with common methodology references. The coverage of open-ended systems and frameworks is from a practical application perspective.

Chapter 8 covers the principles of middleware. In it, I define the middleware and try to construct a model for the same. It introduces you to some recent middleware concepts, especially that of Message-Oriented Middleware (MOM).

Chapter 9 covers the data exchange scenarios. I treat XML as a protocol for all data transfer mediums. Various industry standard protocols, such as the EDI (Electronic Data Interchange), are treated. I discuss the possible transformation of the standard protocols to XML and various methods to do it.

Chapter 10 deals with XML from a data storage perspective. Various approaches to databases and other related mechanisms, such as data warehousing, are discussed. It also presents some basic theory on the same, for those who are not conversant with the concept of warehousing and inference engines or data mining. I have composed the chapter to include possible alternatives to the approach and knowledge gathering and utilization. Finally, I have covered possible approaches for wrapping a SQL query in XML format.

It is worth mentioning that the writing style of the book and the examples are visualized and expressed from a systems architecture perspective. You will find many possible analogies and suggested theories for utilizing the concepts in a variety of forms. My major goal throughout the book has been to provide enough of a conceptual base so that you will be in a better position to utilize and apply XML thinking in your design and development.

1

Introduction to Design Systems

If builders built buildings the way programmers wrote programs, the first woodpecker that came along would destroy civilization.

—*Murphy's Laws*

No offense intended! Everybody reading this book is a programmer-cum-designer, or at least ought to be one!

Systems design has came a long way in the past decade or two. We have gone through classical system design phases where we had functions and procedures. Various programs then used this code by including the code, itself. This was further modified by the concept of calling programs and using them as procedures. Later, we used the concept of compiled code libraries.

Finally, languages got "smarter" in their approaches, and we ended with the use of objects. Object-oriented programming shook almost everyone in the programming arena. I won't go into classical definitions and models of system design here, but I will focus on real-world cases.

The conceptual changes in writing code, to some extent, affected the way we designed and modeled systems. These aspects are often neglected: hence, I feel the important thing for a system architect to do is to arrive at a model based on preferred languages and platform interactions. In some cases this would affect a very small fragment of the model, but that would be significant in the long run.

Classic methodology is old, but could still be applied to model the interfacing systems code because the system to be interfaced would be using old coupling mechanisms. A typical example would be to design a Web-based interface that interacts with a "legacy" system.

To be more specific, you could assume that a legacy banking system provides the ability to interact with a set of "flat" ASCII files, which have to be FTPed to a specific directory or folder. So, for example, if you need to inquire about a user account balance, you need to create a file with the following definitions and FTP it to a specific directory:

```
055NITA    AJAY    GETACCOUNTBALANCE   012761276172
```

The file structure could be interpreted using the following syntax:

```
Activity Code [3 chars]:      055 Program call
                              000 Return data set
Username [8 chars]
Password [8 chars]
Data segment [n chars] [max 255K chars]
For activity code 055:
Data segment [n chars]
Program name [20 chars]
Parameters [| delimited]
For return data [n chars]
Field / Value pairs separated by | as delimiter
```

The interpretation of the preceding structure is straightforward because it specifies the description of the various elements in a flat file record. This starts with the activity code, which has length of three characters and two possible values. The special case is for the data segments, which represent information in name/value pairs. Because our sample has only one parameter, we do not use any delimiters like the comma or vertical bar character. The `Data segment` is the entire part that follows the user authentication information. There can be two types of data segments, which correspond to two types of activity code types.

Sorry for giving you so much detail in the first chapter, but this provides you with a clear understanding of what we are trying to achieve with this information!

The legacy system imposes the requirement of FTPing the request and reading the information back through the same folder. At this moment we would not worry about how we would know that the information received from FTP is meant for us, which in the real world would involve a token generator coupled with the read cycle.

My intention, for this example, is to develop a Web site that will allow users to inquire about their account balances. The Web interface would allow the user to type in the account number and click a button, or link. The middle-tier logic would do the primary validation on the account number format and construct the flat file in the format specified previously. This would then trigger the FTP module, which would read the host configuration from a file, log in to the FTP server, and upload the file.

Once uploaded, the middle-tier would spawn a "wait" thread that would check for the presence of a file on the server by FTPing into the server. Once a file is determined to be present, the process would download the file and pass it on to the business logic stage. The business logic would check for a valid amount, deduct the minimum, and display the available balance. Essentially, this model also shows how a synchronous request can be served with an asynchronous coupling.

I have included a lot of schematics and case studies in this book. Real world applications, especially distributed applications, will always require some coupling mechanism for older systems. When we apply XML in such cases, we will always deal with the basic data format in XML. This means that in the preceding example, the business tier would generate the resultant file format as an XML document, and the actual file formatter, or legacy system adapter, would parse the XML and generate the ASCII flat file.

In systems design, it is always good to have a common, native protocol supporting all system interfaces. Using XML for this protocol would make life easier due to its advantages, which you will learn in the course of reading this book. Few examples of XML could be described as an easy-to-read data format, or self-describing data with the capability to describe the nested (hierarchical) data in a simplistic fashion.

System architecture would also largely depend on the type of system used. What I really mean is that whether the system is for a product or a custom solution like a service or a process, modeling and design are common. For example, if you were modeling a shopping cart purchase system, you would need to worry about the "back office" database a client might have. The client might require interfacing the system to their specific existing system, like an *ERP* (*Enterprise Resource Planning*) system, but generally this requires a generic system that is highly-customizable in terms of configuration. The interface logic needs to be configurable by settings in a file and needs to be dynamic. For a custom solution, the challenge would be limited to designing the interface with a fixed system and the ultimate solution would be less dynamic and flexible.

The general system time-frame rule applies to all designs, which states that the more the system needs to be flexible, the more development time it requires. As seen from the previous example, our initial custom system would not involve the step of writing the file as XML and again parsing it to derive the flat file. Adding this would be advantageous in the long run, though because the legacy system would typically have an RDBMS backup system or archive system and we would not need to generate transaction history data from it. Therefore, we would not have to re-write the business tier. Rather, we can pick up the XML file, package it for RDBMS requirement, and still use it.

The general approach to systems design in distributed computing involves the following:

- Determine basic system protocol
- Define interface strategies
- Define middle-tiers for interfacing with existing systems
- Identify the data transformation needs
- Define base or core business process and model it

I didn't illustrate the second item in the list in our previous examples because I have assumed that our business model would exist on the same system that has Web services running. What if our business tier grows with added functionality, and we need to move it to the second system or secured server? We have, rather luckily, considered that the legacy system would be on a network with the FTP service available.

If our application needs to reside on a different server, we need to divide the rendering logic on the Web side and the business logic on the other side. The rendering logic would simply pass the `POST` method data to the business tier over the network. It would use some mechanism, or rather a interface layer, to talk between this system on the network. Effectively, or logically, the rendering system would trigger a method in the business tier from the remote end. In theory, this mechanism is defined as *Remote Procedure Call*, or *RPC*. RPC is a boon to the distributed world and makes many new methods possible now.

Previously, I thought about dividing the logic that resides on a given computer or system. Now, I think about the same system distributed over the network and that's exactly what we will be exploring throughout this book. RPC mechanisms were included in many platforms and languages before many years had passed, but, because of the unavailability of proper networking infrastructure and associated costs, it never became popular. Because of the availability of the Internet, the network became accessible from any point with an access to an Internet service provider and many things changed.

In addition to this is the concept of the central name server. To understand the concept of the central name sever, it's necessary to consider the concept of systems interacting over a network. For example, system A uses system B for getting information for financial processing. Now, system C offers similar functionality with some additions. System A has the option to use either system B or system C. Again, many more systems might be located on a network that could provide functionality. We could then imagine that system C and others are secondary sources. We could then have system A look for system B and, in case it could not reach it, it could then try system C, and so on. This concept is similar to the Domain Name Service we use, with the TCP/IP protocol, which uses primary and secondary DNS server addresses. Moving one step ahead, what if we account for the services provided by applications on systems A, B, C, and others in some sort of registry? This registry can again be located on the network as a separate system and could act as a central registry or "lookup" server. The various systems then broadcast or register their availability by registering themselves with this central server. The systems could also broadcast the services they provide, like financial, purchase, inventory, and so on. Any system that needs some sort of service would inquire with the central server and specify the type of service it requires. The central server will search through its registry database and accordingly provide the system that is inquiring with either the address of the matching system or an error specifying that no system (or service) exists.

Recently, many distributed systems have been designed from the preceding ideology, and hence we could say the mode works. Jini is an example that offers a discovery protocol to hunt for lookup services and then inquire for the type of services required.

The system model should be robust for providing concurrent services and the capability to attend to multiple requests. Further separate systems need to be provided with some isolation so that they can still interact with each other. Hence, there has to be some sort of middle-tier that could receive requests and forward them to another system. This concept is referred to as *middleware*. Again, many models for middleware design exist, but the most popular one is the message-oriented one. Such a middleware model works on the simplistic concept of receiving the message, which could be a procedure call, and passing it to another other system. Similarly, the remote system could process the request and package it as a message to pass back to the calling system.

In establishing models like the preceding, we definitely need to standardize on protocol and packet formats. This standardization also allows us to create a general repository of standards. Business "members" could then design collaborative systems that could use such repositories.

We know the advantages of including more tiers in code. The distributed approach for systems design requires more elaboration of specific tiers, specifically the interface tiers. New mechanisms and models coupled with these tiers would make the system distributed and more flexible. Because of the requirement of dynamism in the systems, throughout this book, I will concentrate on generic system models. Generic system models will include a basic workflow and methodology to support processing requests. The process is more like designing interfaces and then adding the procedural code.

From a distributed system perspective, the advantages of including multiple tiers would be ease of de-localization. This means that including multiple tiers you create enough couplings within the workflow pattern that you could co-locate or re-locate the modules on the network. Of course, this requires the system to be designed with that in mind.

Workflow and low-level model definitions can be represented using *UML* (*Unified Modeling Language*). Even development methodologies are advancing with the need to accommodate faster design and coding. *XP* (*Extreme Programming*) is one such novel method. Equally true is the argument that simplistic paper-pen workflow diagrams might prove to be more productive. The representation of tasks is important and the question is: "How do you do it?" Though use case diagrams are useful tools, the only reason you would use modeling techniques like UML is to allow for automation tools to analyze and interpret the problem.

Today, maximum effort is spent in systems integration. The system, on cross-platforms and on cross-languages, needs to interact to make electronic collaboration possible. This creates tremendous savings in time and money for the business. Vendor/Supplier system integration had been the dream of major corporations. EDI was the result of such a dream. *EDI* (*Electronic Data Interchange*) did allow and still allows major corporate houses to transfer data electronically and inquire about materials in stock throughout global locations, but it is complex and has a huge learning curve associated with it. This is because EDI messages are not easy to create and read. Because it is more like a flat file representation of data, the nesting is not clearly represented and requires some proprietary interpretation.

Summary

As distributed systems architects, we need to break down barriers and use available resources for implementing a given system. With the next chapter I begin using simple tools, like XML and Web services, to create some real-world systems that offer future extensibility. These systems are open-ended to allow accessibility and scalablity to the greatest extent.

I end this chapter with a goal, which you should bear in mind throughout this book. The book is not intended to teach you how to code; rather it teaches you the imagination to design and create the system.

2

XML Overview

IN THIS CHAPTER

- What Is XML?
- What Is Document Object Model?
- Simple API for XML—SAX
- XML Style Sheets—XSL
- Validation Document

Imagination is more important than knowledge.

—Albert Einstein

What Is XML?

XML stands for *Extensible Markup Language.* A markup language is usually a language of *tagsets.* For a typical software developer, the most used tag today is `<HTML>`.

Is HTML even a tagged or markup language similar to XML? Yes, it is. Over past few years, HTML became a standard language to present the data on Web interfaces. We have seen advances in HTML tags and additions to their set of attributes several times over the last year. These advancements and additions were either global (as specified by the W3C committee) or proprietary (specified by browser supplier). The Microsoft versus Netscape browser war was the main aspect, which is still the case today. It would require a complete chapter to describe the differences and advantages.

Coming back to HTML, we have set of tags, which are used to lay out the text or images in formatted fashion. HTML gives us the ability to adjust text size, font, and color. It also has special format tags such as the `<TABLE>` tag, which makes the formatting tailored to the exact requirement in terms of placing elements on the user browser.

So HTML is essentially a Web presentation markup language. Then what about XML? XML consists of tags, but they are not predefined as HTML. XML allows you to invent and use your own tags. This is important. Consider an example of the HTML representation of a table as shown in Listing 2.1.

LISTING 2.1 HTML Page with Employee Contact List Data

```
<HTML>
<TITLE>Employee Contact List</TITLE>
<BODY BGCOLOR="#FFFFFF" TOPMARGIN="0">
<TABLE CELLPADDIN="0" CELLSPACING="0" BORDER="1">
<TR>
    <TD><B>Sr#</B></TD>
    <TD><B>Employee Name</B></TD>
    <TD><B>Telephone</B></TD>
    <TD><B>Email Address</B></TD>
</TR>
<TR>
    <TD>1.</TD>
    <TD>Nita Barve</TD>
    <TD>408-732-0824</TD>
    <TD>nitabarve@hotmail.com</TD>
</TR>
<TR>
    <TD>2.</TD>
    <TD>Shirish Barve</TD>
    <TD>408-738-1399</TD>
    <TD>shirishbarve@hotmail.com</TD>
</TR>
<TR>
    <TD>3.</TD>
    <TD>Leena Panchwagh</TD>
    <TD>732-750-4086</TD>
    <TD>leenauma@hotmail.com</TD>
</TR>
<TR>
    <TD>4.</TD>
    <TD>Miten Marfatia</TD>
    <TD>408-733-1451</TD>
    <TD>mitenmarfatia@hotmail.com</TD>
</TR>
</TABLE>
</BODY>
</HTML>
```

Sorry to make so many rows in the listing, but it will be helpful to have a lot of data to use in later examples.

In the listing, you can see that the page would display a table with an employee contact list. The point to observe is that the table tags contain the data and the page title tells us what the data is about. Alternatively, we could have included a statement on top of the table that specifies what this listing is.

Now if the `<TITLE>` tag and the table headers, especially the first row, were lost, there is no way to easily say what the table is all about. So we lose the data description. Also, for a simple HTML page such as the one in the listing, the main purpose is to display the data and not describe it. This is where XML comes in. XML is not a presentation language; rather, it is a data description language.

So let us try to gather some points about tag markup languages. Before we list the requirements, or rather feature list, let's talk about tags. Tags used in describing a document have a specific start and end indication. As shown in the preceding simple HTML document, note that we have `<HTML>` and `</HTML>`. This rule would be applicable to all tags in terms of using the `</>` convention for closing. So any tag that opens with <> should essentially close with `</>`.

Note that not all tags used in HTML have an open and close tag. Certain exceptions to this rule exist: `<P>` or `<BR>` tags. For such format tags, we normally use the same concept.

Let us consider nesting. In Listing 2.1, you can observe that first the `<HTML>` tag and then the `<BODY>` tag were opened . The closing tags have been placed for `<BODY>`, which is `</BODY>`, and then for `<HTML>`, which is `</HTML>`. This means that the `<BODY>` tag is nested within the `<HTML>` tag. This is important because a standard parser would throw an error if this is not true or you switched the end positions of the tags at the end of the document. This concept is similar to nested loops found in code.

The important aspects of a tag or markup language are as follows:

- Every start tag should normally have an end tag. This is true for all XML tags, but not for HTML (as described previously).
- Tags should be properly nested, without any crossing over. Nesting means including a subset into a higher level set, and crossing over would mean the inner subset growing out of main set, which is not permissible.
- All tags should be embedded within one main element or root tag, such as `<HTML>`.
- Empty or formatting tags should use the syntax `<tag_name/>` for completeness in XML.

That's all! These are the only four main points for a tagged language. Now let's consider XML. Being a tagged language, XML follows the preceding points rather closely. HTML documents can still have missing end tags, but an XML cannot have one because they would be malformed and unparseable.

Still, you might be wondering what XML is. Let us try to reformat Listing 2.1 from the XML perspective. The result is shown in Listing 2.2.

LISTING 2.2 HTML Version of the Employee Contact List from Listing 2.1

```
<? XML version="1.0" ?>
<EMPLOYEECONTACTLIST>
    <RECORDS>
<SERIAL>1</SERIAL>
    <EMPLOYEENAME>Nita Barve</EMPLOYEENAME>
    <TELEPHONE>408-732-0824</TELEPHONE>
    <EMAIL>nitabarve@hotmail.com</EMAIL>
</RECORDS>
    <RECORDS>
<SERIAL>2</SERIAL>
    <EMPLOYEENAME>Shirish Barve</EMPLOYEENAME>
    <TELEPHONE>408-732-1399</TELEPHONE>
    <EMAIL>shirishbarve@hotmail.com</EMAIL>
</RECORDS>
    <RECORDS>
<SERIAL>3</SERIAL>
    <EMPLOYEENAME>Leena Panchwagh</EMPLOYEENAME>
    <TELEPHONE>732-750-4086</TELEPHONE>
    <EMAIL>leenauma@hotmail.com</EMAIL>
</RECORDS>
    <RECORDS>
<SERIAL>4</SERIAL>
    <EMPLOYEENAME>Miten Marfatia</EMPLOYEENAME>
    <TELEPHONE>408-733-1451</TELEPHONE>
    <EMAIL>mitenmarfatia@hotmail.com</EMAIL>
</RECORDS>
</EMPLOYEECONTACTLIST>
```

From Listing 2.2, you should have guessed why XML is more of a data representation language rather than a presentation language. The first important aspect is that all the presentation tags of HTML have been eliminated. Second, we have (sort of) replaced the `<TR>` tags or row tags with `<RECORDS>` tags. Finally, we have replaced the `<TD>` tags with a respective column name or field name.

Also, it is worth noting that all XML documents should start with

```
<? xml version="1.0" ?>
```

which specifies that the document is an XML file and has a particular version number. Moreover, the representation is human readable and understandable. Without any extra information, you could interpret the listing and—because of the indenting used for formatting it—visualize each record. The indenting used in tagged languages is for readability and has nothing to do with the requirement.

If you were to generate a quick view or a list using the preceding listing as the input string, you would write a string parsing logic and look for `<RECORD>` tags and then individual tags to arrive at the data. Finally, put the data in the respective grid cell. You could also populate the grid heading with the tag names such as `EMPLOYEENAME` by removing start and end signs. This is exactly what an XML parser does.

But the parser just described has a limitation that if we represent data in a different manner—for example, if we introduce two sub-levels under the `<TELEPHONE>` tag, one for `<OFFICE>` and another for `<HOME>`—the parsing would fail or at least give an error. However, with a slight modification, you could definitely write a good parser that would understand the concept of root element and subelements. So, we need a generic parser, which is an XML parser.

Now that you know what an XML document looks like, you can learn more about it. The tag names as they appear in Listing 2.2 are just simple column or field names. In an XML stream, the tag can have any names, except that they could not have spaces and, of course, <, >, or / signs. Hence, we could safely say that XML contains (at least a majority of) metadata within its layout. By metadata we mean that the field descriptions, such as `EMPLOYEENAME`, are present with the data itself. Hence, the data contained in the document is self describing. This makes it easier for us to read it directly and also represent data using it. Still, some potion of data is not contained in the preceding document: For example, the field related information such as data type is not present. Also, the representation controllers, such as how many maximum `<RECORDS>`, could be contained within a `<EMPLOYEECONTACTLIST>` tag. Such crucial and related data can be represented in a different way, which you will learn in the following sections.

Try to visualize an XML document or stream. An XML document has a main element or document root, such as `<EMPLOYEECONTACTLIST>` shown in Listing 2.2. The root is the parent of entire document, which has various child elements or nodes such as `<RECORDS>`. A node can be parent to another child node, and so on. Essentially, the XML document is hierarchical. It is a hierarchy of elements arranged in a specific way depending on the relationship between the elements.

Essentially, we could imagine an XML document to be a tree similar to your file manager or explorer. We could represent the document from Listing 2.2 as a hierarchy or tree as shown in Figure 2.1.

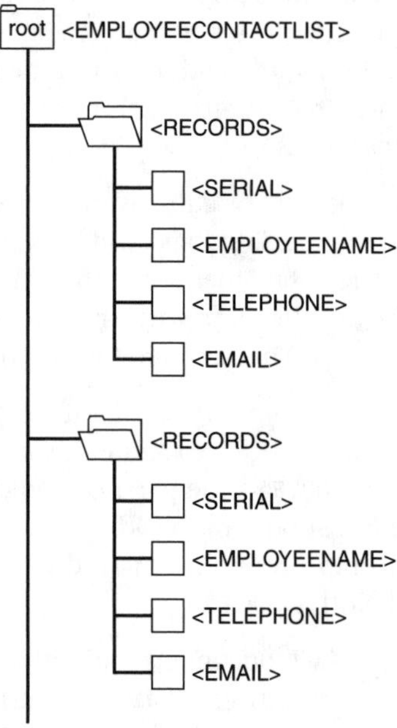

FIGURE 2.1 A hierarchical/tree like description of the XML document shown in Listing 2.2.

Because XML stream is capable of containing metadata to some extent, it can be a very powerful way to present data from within two different systems. It could form an ideal protocol.

The *protocol* is a language or a standard agreement to communicate between two systems. People often get confused when specifying and understanding this term. Over the Internet and in typical networks these days, TCP/IP is the protocol of choice. For e-mail, SMTP (Simple Message Transfer Protocol) and POP3 (Post Office Protocol) are used. To connect to a DSL service, you could normally use PPP (Point-to-Point Protocol) or possibly SLIP.

It would be simpler if we consider our domain of reference. For example, when talking about communication over wires, it makes sense to talk about TCP/IP and OSI. But, when TCP/IP is your protocol for communicating over the network that is in place and you are talking about receiving mails over that network protocol, you would arrive at SMTP and POP3. Again, in the e-mail that you receive, if you consider the data formatted in some protocol, it can have one more protocol, such as EDI. Generally, there can be a data formatting protocol and a carrier one. This is a broad differentiation, but would suffice for most of your needs. XML belongs to data packaging. It cannot replace TCP/IP. And it might still use HTTP over TCP/IP to come to you. This might sound confusing: well, it is. This probably should have been named something else. It is like calling your PC and phone by a single name: system.

So, we could say that XML would be ideal for data packaging. This itself opens tremendous potential for its application. A data packet can describe anything from commands to database data itself. Various systems could use XML as a standard for exchanging information and then provide some sort of validation rules to decode and use it.

You could learn more about the validation and supporting documents, but for now assume that the XML parser could parse the XML stream depending on some supporting document that specifies the rules.

Looking back in the history of computing, we are faced with the need to exchange data several times and for variety of purposes. Let's review the situations and conclude the use of XML in those situations.

A typical vendor end system would require data, such as invoice details, to be transferred back to the corporate house. A corporate house would require interacting with vendors and their zonal stores for inquiring about the material and placing purchase orders. All these are typical electronic commerce requirements. Although the latest buzzword is e-commerce, before the word itself existed, these transactions were made in the form of EDI. EDI was perhaps the most successful and widely accepted standard for communicating and exchanging data. Hence, I have devoted a whole section of a chapter to it in this book (refer to Chapter 5, "Open-Ended Systems").

In a corporate house and vendor scenario, you would need to establish a data exchange protocol to transfer invoices and purchase orders. All business documents usually have a structure similar to the following:

- Header—Contains company related information, such as the company name and date of invoice
- Details—Itemized view, such as a list of products and their pricing
- Footer (Trailer)—Summary, such as the total amount

A typical invoice for example would look like the one shown in Figure 2.2. The invoice has a header, which contains fields such as company invoiced, invoice date, and invoice address. The body consists of fields such as serial number, item name, item quantity, item rate, and amount. The footer consists of fields such as total and a message of terms and conditions. This structure and schematic could be applicable to any invoice, with small variations. Try to arrive at the packaging of such a document in the form of XML. This would allow you to visualize and construct XML message packets from the representation itself.

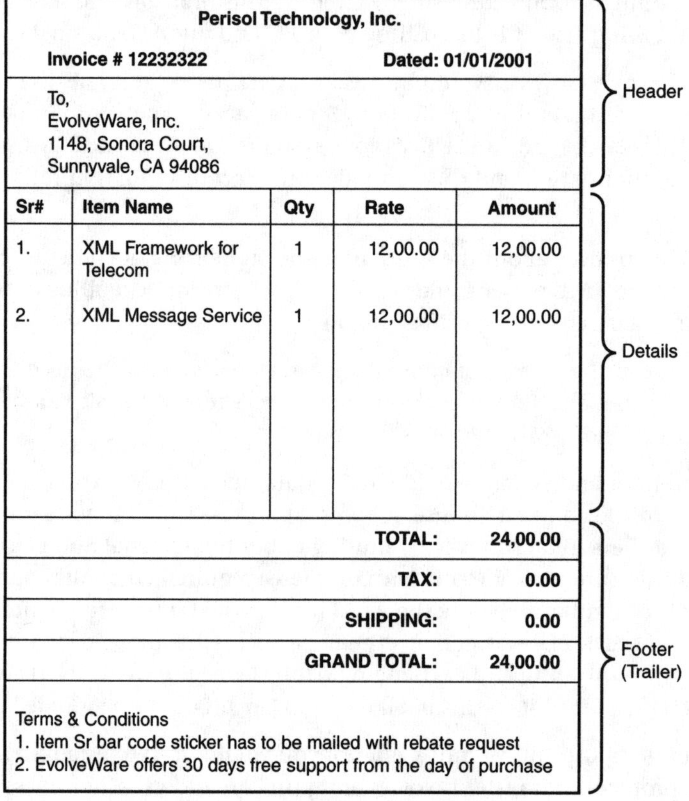

Perisol Technology, Inc.

Invoice # 12232322 **Dated: 01/01/2001**

To,
EvolveWare, Inc.
1148, Sonora Court,
Sunnyvale, CA 94086

Sr#	Item Name	Qty	Rate	Amount
1.	XML Framework for Telecom	1	12,00.00	12,00.00
2.	XML Message Service	1	12,00.00	12,00.00

TOTAL:	**24,00.00**
TAX:	**0.00**
SHIPPING:	**0.00**
GRAND TOTAL:	**24,00.00**

Terms & Conditions
1. Item Sr bar code sticker has to be mailed with rebate request
2. EvolveWare offers 30 days free support from the day of purchase

FIGURE 2.2 Invoice example.

The skeleton of the XML representation for this invoice would be as shown in Listing 2.3.

LISTING 2.3 Skeleton of an Invoice in XML Format

```
<?xml version="1.0"?>
<INVOICE>
    <HEADER>


    </HEADER>
    <DETAILS>
```

LISTING 2.3 Continued

```
    </DETAILS>
    <FOOTER>

    </FOOTER>
</INVOICE>
```

The listing shows the division of the invoice in terms of XML tags. The root node is named `<INVOICE>`.

Let's put other elements in the skeleton and see how the XML representation would look. The listing for the complete invoice is shown in Listing 2.4.

LISTING 2.4 Complete XML Representation of the Invoice in Figure 2.2

```
<?xml version="1.0"?>
<INVOICE>
    <HEADER>
        <INVOICINGCOMPANY>Perisol Technology, Inc</INVOICINGCOMPANY>
        <DATE>01/01/2001</DATE>
        <INVOICENUMBER>12232322</INVOICENUMBER>
        <INVOICETO>
            <TO>EvolveWare, Inc</TO>
            <ADDRESS>
                <ADDRESS1>1148, Sonora Court</ADDRESS1>
                <ADDRESS2></ADDRESS2>
                <CITY>Sunnyvale</CITY>
                <STATE>CA</STATE>
                <ZIP>94086</ZIP>
            </ADDRESS>
            <TITLE>EvolveWare, Inc</TITLE>
        </INVOICETO>
    </HEADER>
    <DETAILS>
            <ITEM>
                <SR>1</SR>
                <ITEMNAME>XML Framework for Telecom</ITEMNAME>
                <QUANTITY>1</QUANTITY>
                <RATE>1200</RATE>
                <AMOUNT>1200</AMOUNT>
            </ITEM>
            <ITEM>
```

LISTING 2.4 Continued

```
                <SR>2</SR>
                <ITEMNAME>XML Messaging Service</ITEMNAME>
                <QUANTITY>1</QUANTITY>
                <RATE>1200</RATE>
                <AMOUNT>1200</AMOUNT>
            </ITEM>
    </DETAILS>
    <FOOTER>
            <AMOUNT>
                <TOTAL>2400</TOTAL>
                <TAXPERCENT>0.00</TAXPERCENT>
                <TAXAMOUNT>0.00</TAXAMOUNT>
                <SHIPPING>0.00</SHIPPING>
                <GRANDTOTAL>2400</GRANDTOTAL>
            </AMOUNT>
            <TERMS>
1. Item Sr bar code sticker has to be mailed with rebate request
2. EvolveWare offers 30 days free support from the day of purchase
            </TERMS>
    </FOOTER>
</INVOICE>
```

The XML stream shown in Listing 2.4 is long, but simple. I have divided the sections into sub-sections to accommodate the various bits of information. I want to point to some aspect of how I arrived at the XML stream.

Note that I have added additional tags wherever possible. For example, the `<ADDRESS>` tag is broken into a typical set of Address1, Address2, City, State, and ZIP Code. It is always a good idea to add as much description to data in a file as possible. In case of latter situations in which a company might need it that way for the application to insert data in the database, they have it. Also in case the database stores addresses as a single field, the application could concatenate all the strings together.

Let's look at the details. The details section could have multiple items of products listed that are sold to the customer. Hence, we have a second level child node to the `<DETAILS>` tag called `<ITEMS>`. This helps us to place as many items as we want to. When I talk about DTDs and schemas, you will see how we can specify as many items and maximum items allowable in this file.

We could have improved the invoice listing by further including some sort of data types within the XML document. This is a debatable issue because I have already said that we can write a validation document to validate the XML document. But in some cases, it would be sufficient for a system to have the data type defined right in the document—a sample case is SOAP, which is a rather new protocol formed above XML to invoke methods on a remote machine. You will read about it in Chapter 4, "SOAP."

With the inclusion of data types, Listing 2.4 would appear as shown in Listing 2.5.

LISTING 2.5 XML Representation of Listing 2.4 with Data Type Additions

```
<?xml version="1.0"?>
<INVOICE>
    <HEADER>
        <INVOICINGCOMPANY><string>Perisol Technology,
        ➥ Inc</string></INVOICINGCOMPANY>
        <DATE><date>01/01/2001</date></DATE>
        <INVOICENUMBER><id>12232322</id></INVOICENUMBER>
        <INVOICETO>
            <TO><string>EvolveWare, Inc</string></TO>
            <ADDRESS>
                <ADDRESS1><string>1148, Sonora Court</string></ADDRESS1>
                <ADDRESS2><string></string></ADDRESS2>
                <CITY><string>Sunnyvale</string></CITY>
                <STATE><string>CA</string></STATE>
                <ZIP><number>94086</number></ZIP>
            </ADDRESS>
            <TITLE><string>EvolveWare, Inc</string></TITLE>
        </INVOICETO>
    </HEADER>
    <DETAILS>
            <ITEM>
                <SR><number>1</number></SR>
                <ITEMNAME><string>XML Framework for Telecom</string></ITEMNAME>
                <QUANTITY><number>1</number></QUANTITY>
                <RATE><currency>1200</currency></RATE>
                <AMOUNT><currency>1200</currency></AMOUNT>
            </ITEM>
            <ITEM>
                <SR><number>2</number></SR>
                <ITEMNAME><string>XML Messaging Service</string></ITEMNAME>
                <QUANTITY><number>1</number></QUANTITY>
                <RATE><currency>1200</currency></RATE>
                <AMOUNT><currency>1200</currency></AMOUNT>
            </ITEM>
```

LISTING 2.5 Continued

```
    </DETAILS>
    <FOOTER>
            <AMOUNT>
                <TOTAL><currency>2400</currency></TOTAL>
                <TAXPERCENT><number>0.00</number></TAXPERCENT>
                <TAXAMOUNT><currency>0.00</currency></TAXAMOUNT>
                <SHIPPING><currency>0.00</currency></SHIPPING>
                <GRANDTOTAL><currency>2400</currency></GRANDTOTAL>
            </AMOUNT>
            <TERMS><string>
1. Item Sr bar code sticker has to be mailed with rebate request
2. EvolveWare offers 30 days free support from the day of purchase
            </string></TERMS>
    </FOOTER>
</INVOICE>
```

As seen in Listing 2.5, I just added few data type tags. It is important to note that I invented some types here, such as `<id>` and `<currency>`. Even though they are numbers, they are special data types, and hence the application might treat them in a special way. There is no standard used to arrive at the preceding definition. I just invented them and showed it in there. That's the beauty of the extensiveness you could add to the XML data stream. The possibilities are endless. Depending on your application need, you could accordingly formulate or code the encoder so that it would result in the respective XML stream output. You will learn more about placing data type tags in an XML stream when I cover SOAP.

Before going further, I want to mention the concept of attributes. Attributes are common in all tag languages. An attribute can have important effects in the way that an XML document is formatted.

Technically speaking, you could reduce elements and replace them with attributes. Before seeing why and how, let's see few examples of attributes. Attributes are used almost everywhere in HTML. A typical image tag would resemble the following:

```
<IMG SRC="myphoto.jpg" BORDER="0">
```

Here, the tag name is `<IMG>`. The attributes of the `<IMG>` tag are `SRC` and `BORDER`. Note that attributes essentially define a set of parameters or supply values for the tag to behave and show up in a certain way. The attribute values might or might not be included within `""`.

Similarly, you could use the concept in XML. The effect of attribute usage in an XML document is that it reduces the elements. Consider the XML example in Listing 2.6.

LISTING 2.6 Sample Contact List

```
<?xml version="1.0"?>
<CONTACTLIST>
    <CONTACT>
        <SR>1</SR>
        <NAME>Nita Barve</NAME>
        <EMAIL>nitabarve@hotmail.com</EMAIL>
        <TEL>408-732-0824</TEL>
    </CONTACT>
    <CONTACT>
        <SR>2</SR>
        <NAME>Richard Henderson</NAME>
        <EMAIL>rhson@hotmail.com</EMAIL>
        <TEL>408-738-1399</TEL>
    </CONTACT>
</CONTACTLIST>
```

The listing shows contact book export or dump in XML format. We have two contacts in our contact list. Now look at how the listing looks with attributes (see Listing 2.7).

LISTING 2.7 Sample Contact List with Attributes

```
<?xml version="1.0"?>
<CONTACTLIST>
    <CONTACT SR="1" NAME="Nita Barve">
        <EMAIL>nitabarve@hotmail.com</EMAIL>
        <TEL>408-732-0824</TEL>
    </CONTACT>
    <CONTACT SR="2" NAME=" Richard Henderson</">
        <EMAIL>rhson@hotmail.com</EMAIL>
        <TEL>408-738-1399</TEL>
    </CONTACT>
</CONTACTLIST>
```

So, you see that the two elements `<SR>` and `<NAME>` are dropped and they are added to attributes of `<CONTACT>` tag. Hence, XML also allows you to have your own set of attributes.

When using a standard XML parser, the parser would provide you with an attribute name/value for each element. Then, when should you use elements and when should you use attributes? This is a matter of the designer's choice! But usually you group sensible elements into attributes. For example, you would not have something like

```
<AMOUNT TOTALAMOUNT="100.00" TAXAMOUNT="20.00">
        <GRANDTOTAL>120.00</GRANDTOTAL>
</AMOUNT>
```

Although this is a valid XML fragment, it's not a good way to do things! Why? First, although the TOTALAMOUNT and TAXAMOUNT are types of amounts, they should have been presented as elements. Because they are specifying the declaration of some major composite part, the report generation would be required to pick up only TOTALAMOUNT and show the addition amount without taxes. Now, if the entire data were available as an XML stream, you would need to parse each element and then each attribute to arrive at the TOTALAMOUNT in the <AMOUNT> tag. This is not only a bad design, but also inefficient in terms of parsing the document and making sense.

By making sense what I mean is the document would then distribute the metadata in terms of elements and attributes and would no longer be a useful collection. For example, if you have a intelligent parser, which is coupled with a resolution business rule or knowledge base system, it could fail for searching a critical set of information in the document. Maybe I have sped up too much. Let's see what I meant by knowledge base or rule based.

Consider that you have various sets of the preceding tags included in an XML document, which represents a collection of reports. You save all such reports every week on a disk. Now, your manager needs you to write a simple agent program, which would look out among the reports (that can be of different types and having different elements) and generate an aggregate report. This means that you would have to create a business rule mechanism. The simplest rule engine would be the one that converts the business entity into its equivalent synonym. So, the cost would give the output as amount, price, and rate. The reporting engine would then parse all the reports and search for the element names having the occurrence of the keywords. As soon as it finds one, it would pull the data and collect it with related details. It would repeat the process for all the reports on the disk and present an aggregate report.

What Is Document Object Model?

To parse an XML document, you need to parse tags and form a hierarchy—a tree of nodes. This operation requires you to understand some existing concepts used in the latest eWorld.

The *Document Object Model (DOM)* is one such concept. DOM is not new, and Web developers have been using it for quite a while to access objects on an HTML document. All browsers support and use DOM to present HTML on the screen. And the developer could use the same model to access the various contents of the page. A typical browser program would use the DOM as codified model to provide access to various objects in the browser. Hence, all the documents, which are shown in the browser, can be represented using a DOM model.

This is the same mode as used by the scripting languages, which form the arena of DHTML. A DOM model is a tree like hierarchical set of various objects placed under the browser. It is used extensively with scripting and is used for front-end Web page programming under DHTML. A high level listing is shown in Listing 2.8.

LISTING 2.8 Brief Listing of Top Level Objects in DOM

```
window
    location
    frames
    history
    navigator
    event
    screen
    document
        links
        anchors
        images
        filters
        forms
        applets
        embeds
        plug-ins
        frames
        scripts
        all
        selection
        stylesheets
        body
```

The simple description of Listing 2.8 would be that the complete document you see in your browser is referred to as *window*. Each window can have a document, which in turn can have a form in it. The form might have additional text boxes and other objects.

As you can see, the entire HTML document received by the browser is divided into the preceding set of hierarchical elements and presented on the user interface. Each node in the preceding hierarchy can have a number of attributes, which could specify their representation details. To reference the 23rd element on the page and change its color to red, you have to use the following statement:

```
document.all(23).style.color = 'red';
```

The `all` collection or array is used to reference the 23rd element. The `style` is a property of that element in the collection, which in turn has `color` as its property.

The DOM as defined by W3C is a platform- and language-neutral interface that will allow programs and scripts to dynamically access and update the content, structure, and style of documents. The document can be further processed and the results of that processing can be incorporated back into the presented page.

DOM provides a standard set of objects for representing HTML and XML documents, a standard model of how these objects can be combined, and a standard interface for accessing and manipulating them. Vendors can support the DOM as an interface to their proprietary data structures and APIs, and content authors can write to the standard DOM interfaces rather than product-specific APIs, thus increasing interoperability on the Web.

DOM is being designed at the several levels specified as follows:

- Level 1—Concentrates on the actual core, HTML, and XML document models. It contains functionality for document navigation and manipulation.
- Level 2—Includes a style sheet object model and defines functionality for manipulating the style information attached to a document. It also enables traversals on the document, defines an event model, and provides support for XML namespaces.
- Level 3—Addresses document loading and saving, as well as content models (such as DTDs and schemas) with document validation support. In addition, it also addresses document views and formatting, key events, and event groups. First public working drafts are available.
- Further Levels—Might specify some interface with the possibly underlying window system, including some ways to prompt the user. They might also contain a query language interface and address multithreading and synchronization, security, and repository.

DOM is the most popular API for manipulating XML in use today. It presents an XML document in an object-based form, making it simple to manipulate for Java programmers and other developers who are already familiar with objects. Hence, we could say that DOM is an object-oriented presentation and chiefly to present an XML document.

In other words, you could produce even a stream of strings from an XML document. But major vendors, per W3C specifications, have developed generic XML parsers that give DOM representation (and accessibility) to an XML document or stream. This is useful and important because most programmers are familiar with using DOM to code, designing a parser to produce a similar form of output would allow leveraging their existing knowledge to use XML.

DOM represents a parsed XML document as an abstract tree. It is abstract because only the interfaces reflect a tree structure. The actual data structures and algorithms implementing the abstract tree need not be a tree.

So you need to use some parser to parse and hence read the XML document. This parser would present the document in some accessible format so that the program could reference the various elements (nodes) and their values in the document. DOM is one way to represent XML as an object-oriented model. It uses a tree-like structure to represent the entire document. The accessibility of elements is simple because they follow our familiar object concepts.

Consider a simple XML document as shown here:

```
<?xml version="1.0"?>
<SimpleDoc>
    <Name>
        Nita Ajay Rambhia
    </Name>
</SimpleDoc>
```

If you assume that we have parsed this document using a DOM based parser and the reference object, which stores this document, is `objSimpleDoc`, you could get the value of the `<Name>` tag using a simple statement as shown here:

```
valName = objSimpleDoc.Node("Name")(0).value
```

The preceding statement is a sample statement and does not represent any specific DOM parser. But it is shown here to present the idea of a reference in a DOM based parser.

From the preceding statement, you see that we are referring to the high-level object and its node that has the name `Name`. There might be several nodes of type `Name` in a single XML document. We are interested in getting the first value, hence the element number is `0`. The `value` is a property of the `Node` object, which would return the value of that node.

You will see some sample code of using DOM parsers in the DTD section later.

Simple API for XML—SAX

As I have mentioned in previous sections, the parsers are programs that allow the XML document to be programmatically accessible. This allows the programs and system to parse the document and extract data from it.

Another recently popular parser is *Simple API for XML (SAX)*. SAX is an event-based parser. In a typical programming model, an event is a asynchronous method call. For example, if you have a form or panel with a button and you code for the click event of that button, you are writing an asynchronous event method. The user could invoke the method by clicking the button with a mouse or keyboard, and the program doesn't know when the user clicks. The code exists in the program to attend the event in case it occurs.

So what are the advantages of an event driven parser? Why do we need another parser at all? SAX, being an event-based parser, has some advantages over DOM. The SAX parser goes through all the nodes and triggers an event, passing it the relevant node information (including attributes and values). It does not create a memory image of the document as DOM does, which means that it has a less working memory requirement.

Consider a situation in which you are interested in searching an XML document for some value in some node, and that document has over 100,000 nodes. Using DOM would require memory to create and reassemble the whole document, which can be resource hungry. Here it would be efficient to use the SAX approach.

So depending on the application, you have a choice of using either DOM or SAX.

Listing 2.9 shows sample code that implements parsing using the SAX parser by AElfred (`http://www.microstar.com/XML/AElfred/`). This parser, as all SAX parsers do, offers a Handler interface to handle events. This is the basic interface for getting the XML document element details in an SAX based program. Listing 2.9 shows the simple class that extends the `HandlerBase` class.

LISTING 2.9 Class `SAXEeventHandler` Code Extending `HandlerBase`

```
import org.xml.sax.HandlerBase;
import org.xml.sax.AttributeList;

//SAX Event handler written by Ravinder Khokhar

public class SAXEventHandler extends HandlerBase {

  public void startElement (String name, AttributeList atts)
  {
```

LISTING 2.9 Continued

```
    System.out.println("Element Starts with name: " + name);
  }

  public void endElement (String name)
  {
    System.out.println("Element Ends with name: " + name);
  }

}
```

The code in Listing 2.9 extends the `HandlerBase` and will get the SAX parser events. It will show a message on the console every time the parser is at the start and end of an element.

The code in Listing 2.10 will invoke SAX and parse a document using your handler.

LISTING 2.10 Class `SAXParserApp` Using `SAXEventHandler`

```
import org.xml.sax.Parser;
import org.xml.sax.DocumentHandler;
import org.xml.sax.helpers.ParserFactory;

//SAX Parser written by Ravinder Khokhar & Jatinder Singh

public class SAXParserApp {

  static final String parserClass = "com.microstar.xml.SAXDriver";

  public static void main (String args[])
    throws Exception
  {
    Parser parser = ParserFactory.makeParser(parserClass);
    DocumentHandler handler = new SAXEventHandler();
    parser.setDocumentHandler(handler);
    for (int i = 0; i < args.length; i++) {
      parser.parse(args[i]);
    }
  }
}
```

You create a parser using the `ParserFactory` class method. You set the parser document handler to your handler, which you created in Listing 2.9.

The sample SAX parsing application in Listing 2.10 gets the URL reference to the XML document as command-line arguments supplied with the program.

Before ending this section on SAX, a few more important points must be noted. SAX reports parsing events (such as the start and end of elements) directly to the application through callbacks and does not usually build an internal tree, like DOM.

DOM could be useful for the application that requires a tree to be built for the elements, but at times the application needs to model its own set of trees; in which case, SAX could be useful.

Consider for example that you have an XML document that specifies the Web site map. You need to represent the site map in the form of zones and spaces, depending on user interest. This means that depending on cookies stored at the user end, which specifies user interest on a particular subject, the navigation pattern should represent the tree derived from the actual site map. The system would then have to generate or at least filter the XML site map representation with respect to the keyword element appearing under each node. This calls for a new tree formed for every user. Hence, SAX comes to the rescue, and it is easier in this case to build dynamic trees or rather custom trees from actual XML representation.

To further look into the XML model discussed in the previous paragraph, take a look at Listing 2.11, which shows the Site Map XML file.

LISTING 2.11 Site Map XML File

```
<SiteContentMap>
    <Section title="News">
        <Keywords>
            <Key>
                Java
            <Key>
            <Key>
                XML Parsers in Java
            <Key>
        </Keywords>
        <Link>
            http://www.mysite.com/newspage?id=N1232
        </Link>
    </Section>
    <Section title="News">
        <Keywords>
```

LISTING 2.11 Continued

```
            <Key>
                Java
            </Key>
            <Key>
                Framework
            </Key>
            <Key>
                Sun
            </Key>
        </Keywords>
        <Link>
            http://www.mysite.com/newspage?id=N1332
        </Link>
    </Section>
    <Section title="Developer">
        <Keywords>
            <Key>
                Java
            </Key>
            <Key>
                Remote Invokation
            </Key>
            <Key>
                XML-RPC
            </Key>
        </Keywords>
        <Link>
            http://www.mysite.com/newspage?id=N1312
        </Link>
    </Section>
    <Section title="Developer">
        <Keywords>
            <Key>
                .Net
            </Key>
            <Key>
                BizTalk
            </Key>
            <Key>
                Microsoft
            </Key>
        </Keywords>
```

LISTING 2.11 Continued

```
        <Link>
            http://www.mysite.com/newspage?id=N1512
        </Link>
    </Section>
</SiteContentMap>
```

The sample site map XML representation in the listing has a generic tag for specifying a section, with an attribute name specifying the major category. We assume that the site is a general programming site and has audience interest groups of a wide variety.

Say that one of the users has customized the site to view everything appearing as News because he might be interested in only changes in technology. Then the preceding listing could be easily parsed to filter that out.

But consider a more involved situation. You want to present the user with an ability to navigate on your site using domain-oriented specification. The domains could be specific to user interest in a wide variety of ways. Say that the user likes the categorization of site content per the technology dealt with in its contents—for example Java and Microsoft. This requires the system to reconfigure the previous files and generate derived map files that the front end can use to display the site map in the desired way. The two derived sets are shown in Listings 2.12 and 2.13.

LISTING 2.12 Derived XML Document for Microsoft as the Domain Keyword

```
<DerivedContentMap>
    <Section title="Microsoft">
        <Keywords>
            <Key>
                News
            <Key>
            <Key>
                .Net
            <Key>
            <Key>
                BizTalk
            </Key>
        </Keywords>
        <Link>
            http://www.mysite.com/newspage?id=N1512
        </Link>
    </Section>
</DerivedContentMap>
```

LISTING 2.13 Derived XML Document for Java as the Domain Keyword

```
<DerivedContentMap>
    <Section title="Java">
        <Keywords>
            <Key>
                News
            <Key>
            <Key>
                XML Parsers in Java
            <Key>
        </Keywords>
        <Link>
            http://www.mysite.com/newspage?id=N1232
        </Link>
    </Section>
    <Section title="Java">
        <Keywords>
            <Key>
                News
            </Key>
            <Key>
                Framework
            </Key>
            <Key>
                Sun
            </Key>
        </Keywords>
        <Link>
            http://www.mysite.com/newspage?id=N1332
        </Link>
    </Section>
    <Section title="Java">
        <Keywords>
            <Key>
                Developer
            </Key>
            <Key>
                Remote Invokation
            </Key>
            <Key>
```

LISTING 2.13 Continued

```
                XML-RPC
            </Key>
        </Keywords>
        <Link>
            http://www.mysite.com/newspage?id=N1312
        </Link>
    </Section>
</DerivedContentMap>
```

You could easily see how flexible navigation could be by using some more intelligent code. Also, a similar approach would be to have a graphical interface that allows the user to select the domain and show the entire navigation per domain representation spaces on the screen.

A schematic of the preceding approach is shown in Figure 2.3. This figure represents the basic site map in terms of graphical representation. Note how each node is represented so that it can be mapped to the actual URL for clarity. On such an interface, if a user selects or clicks on some node, the representation adjusts itself to show the derived map as shown in Figure 2.4. Note how the old domain reference is shown alongside the derived map, thus allowing the user to return to the previous view.

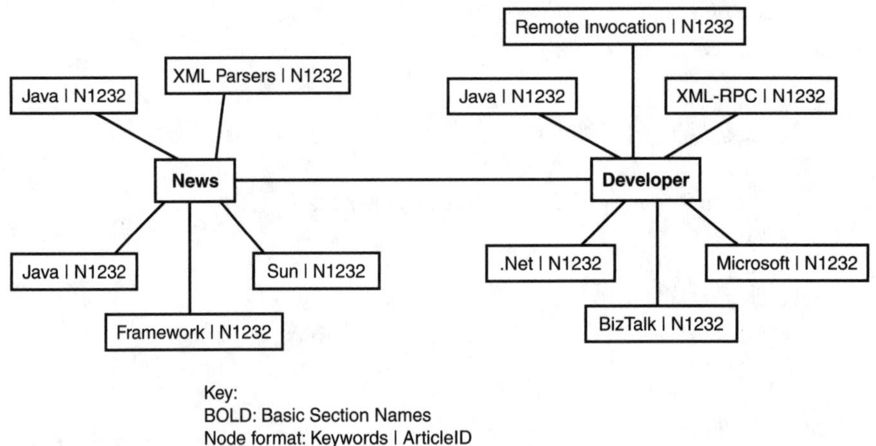

FIGURE 2.3 A schematic representation of a basic site map.

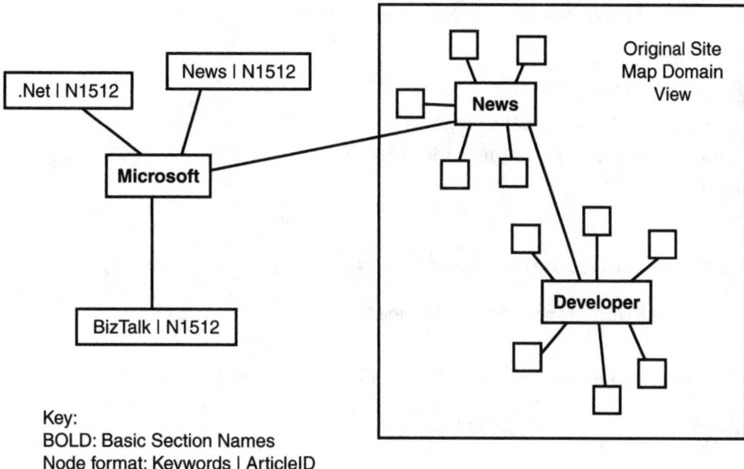

FIGURE 2.4 A schematic representation of a derived site map for Microsoft.

Many derivations of representational maps and references can be derived from simple combinations as the preceding.

XML Style Sheets—XSL

Style sheets are common these days because of Web influence on developers. They are used to presenting the content to the user. Similarly, XSL is used for styling XML so that it could be transformed and presented to the users or some other application.

XSL is used for styling XML and is processed by XSL engine. Combined with XSL, and a sort of extension to it, is XSLT (XSL Transformation). XSLT is used to transform, and XSL is used to render it on user end.

An XSL skeleton would resemble

```
<xsl:stylesheet xmlns:xsl="http://www.w3.org/1999/XSL/Transform" version="1.0">
.
</xsl:stylesheet>
```

The information is referenced and filtered using a set of *patterns* in the style sheet. The patterns are formed by specifying the node and using a / as a separator for the elements.

Consider a few examples of representing XSL for an XML document shown in Listing 2.14.

LISTING 2.14 Employee Details XML Document

```
<?xml version="1.0"?>
<employees empid="0452">
  <empname>Richard Henderson</empname>
  <designation>Business Manager</designation>
</employees>
```

To select the employee name using XSL syntax, use the following syntax:

```
<xsl:value-of select="employees/empname"/>
```

To get the employee designation, the code would be as follows:

```
<xsl:value-of select="employees/designation"/>
```

To select an attribute (`empid`), the syntax would be `employees/@empid`. Also, you could access a group of nodes: altogether, you can use `employees/*`. A specific employee could be referenced as `employees/@empid = '0452'`. Consider the usage of the preceding syntax in XSL as shown in the following syntaxes:

```
<xsl:value-of select="employees/empname"/>
```

which would result in the value `'Richard Henderson'`.

```
<xsl:value-of select="employees/@empid"/>
```

which would result in the value `'0452'`.

To match and process nodes, you could use *templates*. The template is applied on the node name and can be called using the `apply-templates` command. A sample template would resemble

```
<xsl:template match="empname"
  <xsl:value-of select="."/>
</xsl:template>
```

This template could be called as shown in the following statement:

```
<xsl:apply-templates select="empname"/>
```

Besides this, XSL provides a set of control elements in the form of logical conditions. One such condition is the `choose` command:

```
<xsl:choose>
  <xsl:when test="test situation">
    XSL syntaxes
```

```
  </xsl:when>
  <xsl:otherwise>
    XSL syntaxes
  </xsl:otherwise>
</xsl:choose>
```

The `otherwise` tag is executed if all tests fail and to represent an empty `otherwise`. We can represent it as

```
  <xsl:otherwise/>
```

The `If` condition would be represented using the following syntax:

```
<xls:if test="test situation">
    XSL syntaxes
</xsl:if>
```

The `for-each` command would be represented using the following syntax:

```
<xsl:for-each select="select statement">
    XSL syntaxes
</xsl:for-each>
```

To aggregate the preceding syntax, let us write a transform code to generate Listing 2.15.

LISTING 2.15 Required Output HTML Document

```
<html>
  <body>
    <p><b>Richard Henderson</b>: 0452</p>
  </body>
</html>
```

It would generate the previous document after filtering all business managers from the document. The XSL version would resemble the one shown in Listing 2.16.

LISTING 2.16 XSL Code for Generating the HTML Document in Listing 2.15

```
<xsl:stylesheet xmlns:xsl="">
  <xsl:template match="/">
    <html>
      <body>
          <xsl:for-each select="employees[designation='Business Manager']">
          <p>
```

LISTING 2.16 Continued

```
          <b>
            <xsl:value-of select="employees/empname"/>
          </b>
          <xsl:text>: </xsl:text>
          <xsl:value-of select="employees/@empid"/>
        </p>
        </xsl:for-each>
      </body>
    </html>
  </xsl:template>
</xsl:stylesheet>
```

A few things can be observed in Listing 2.15. Note how the XSL code is embedded in HTML. Note that the pattern matching the filter used `employees[designation='Business Manager']`.

In XSL, you could even define variables as shown here:

```
<xsl:variable name="loopcounter">10</xsl:variable>
```

To access the variable name, you can use `$loopcounter` in XSL code.

A style sheet can have parameters defined in it as follows:

```
<xsl:param name="ParamName" select="'DefaultValue'"/>
```

The parameter value can be passed through the XSLT processing engine and many allow doing it.

Some prebuilt methods are available in the style sheet as shown in the following list:

- `sum()`—Sums up the values in designated nodes
- `count()`—Counts the number of nodes
- `position()`—Returns current node position in a loop
- `last()`—Checks to see if this is the last node of the document; returns a Boolean

XSL allows creating extensions in many languages, such as Java. In order to use Java, you need to include a Java namespace in your document as shown here:

```
xmlns:java=http://xml.apache.org/xslt/java
```

The preceding declaration, for example, points to the Apache XSLT processor namespace declaration.

The various methods typically useful in XSL implementations are summarized in the following:

To instantiate a class,

```
prefix:class.new (args)
```

Example:

```
variable sampleVector select"java:java.util.Vector.new()"
```

To call a method on an object,

```
prefix:methodName (object, args)
```

Example:

```
variable sampleAddEmployee select="java:addElement($sampleVector,
➥ string(@empid))"
```

To call a static method,

```
prefix:class.methodName (args)
```

Example:

```
variable sampleString select="java:java.lang.String.valueOf(@qty))"
```

Validation—DTD

As discussed before, *Document Type Definition (DTD)* can be used to present a validating stream for a set of XML documents. Here's what I mean by validating an XML document.

XML documents would need validation or checks for the following reasons:

- To define the element data types
- To specify the number of times a sub-element can occur
- To specify what is nested below or rather the parent-child relationship between various elements

DTD does well for the last two points, and the latest validation scheme for covering all the three aspects are XML Schemas. Still I will cover DTD because many XML validation parsers still support it, and a lot of documents use them.

DTD are hard to read and are not at all manually readable. Let's start with a simple XML document in Listing 2.17.

LISTING 2.17 Simple XML Document

```
<?xml version="1.0"?>
<DETAILS>
    <ITEM>
        <SR>1</SR>
        <ITEMNAME>XML Framework for Telecom</ITEMNAME>
        <QUANTITY>1</QUANTITY>
        <RATE>1200</RATE>
        <AMOUNT>1200</AMOUNT>
    </ITEM>
    <ITEM>
        <SR>2</SR>
        <ITEMNAME>XML Messaging Service</ITEMNAME>
        <QUANTITY>1</QUANTITY>
        <RATE>1200</RATE>
        <AMOUNT>1200</AMOUNT>
    </ITEM>
</DETAILS>
```

As you can see, I have just shrunk the invoice representation in XML format and picked up the details portion here. Now you will see what a DTD for such a document would look like. The complete DTD is given in Listing 2.18.

LISTING 2.18 DTD for Listing 2.17

```
<!DOCTYPE list [
<!ELEMENT DETAILS (ITEM)+>
       <!ELEMENT ITEM (SR, ITEMNAME, QUANTITY, RATE, AMOUNT)>
      <!ELEMENT SR (#PCDATA)>
<!ELEMENT ITEMNAME (#PCDATA)>
       <!ELEMENT QUANTITY (#PCDATA)>
       <!ELEMENT RATE (#PCDATA)>
       <!ELEMENT AMOUNT (#PCDATA)>
]>
```

Let's see how the preceding file was put together.

```
<!DOCTYPE list [
```

This line says that whatever is inside the brackets is the DTD for a document with the root element `<list>`. As mentioned earlier, the root element contains all other elements.

```
<!ELEMENT ITEM (SR, ITEMNAME, QUANTITY, RATE, AMOUNT)>
```

This line defines the `<ITEM>` tag. The parentheses say that these four other sets of tags must appear inside the `<ITEM>` tags, in that particular order.

```
<!ELEMENT DETAILS (ITEM)+>
```

This line specifies that each `<DETAILS>` tag can have one or more `<ITEM>` tag, specified by a + sign. For specifying that either zero or more elements could occur, we have to use the following:

```
<!ELEMENT DETAILS (ITEM)*>
```

Note the `*`, which specifies zero or more.

```
<!ELEMENT SR (#PCDATA)>
```

This specifies that the element `SR` is having `#PCDATA`, which stands for parsed character data (that is, anything other than binary data, such as a image).

Now for some strange XML document as follows:

```
<TERMS>
30 day warranty period from day of purchase
30 day free support from day of purchase
<SPECIALCONDITIONS>
No support can be provided for an unregistered product
</SPECIALCONDITIONS>
</TERMS>
```

Also, it has to specify that the `<SPECIALCONDITIONS>` tag might or might not appear. The DTD for such a representation would be as follows:

```
<!ELEMENT TERMS (#PCDATA|SPECIALCONDITIONS)*>
```

The item within, which might or might not be present, is specified with `*` (zero or more), and the item tag itself is indicated as shown after the `|` sign.

The occurrence indicators are summarized in Table 2.1.

TABLE 2.1 XML Occurrence Indicators

Indicator	Meaning
?	The content must appear either once, or not at all.
*	The content can appear one or more times, or not at all.
+	The content must appear at least once and might appear more than once.
[none]	The content must appear once, exactly as described.

DTDs can also be used to represent attribute types occurring in the XML document. Consider the following simple XML example:

```
<Product Price="10.12" Units="Lbs">Sugar</Product>
```

Before you see the DTD representation of the attributes, consider the following variation of the previous example:

```
<Product>
    <Price>10.12</Price>
    <Units>Lbs</Units>
</Product>
```

The preceding variation forms a valid XML representation of the same thing, So which one should you choose? Let's reason it out.

In the application, which is for displaying the product list, the tag items `<Price>` and `<Units>` are meaningful only with the product name. Hence, the previous representation would be better, having `Price` and `Units` as attributes rather than separate tags.

```
<!ELEMENT Product #PCDATA>
<!ATTLIST Product Price CDATA #REQUIRED>
<!ATTLIST Product Units CDATA #REQUIRED>
```

The DTD specification specifies `#REQUIRED` as one of the tokens, which specifies that the data is required for this tag. The DTD also has a token called `#FIXED`, which specifies that the values specified in this attribute is fixed (or static) and would not change throughout the document. If the value can be optional, it can be specified by using `#IMPLIED`.

Enumeration can also be specified easily in an attribute, as shown in the following code:

```
<!ATTLIST Subscribe (yes | no) #REQUIRED>
```

In the preceding example, `Subscribe` can have either of the two values `yes` or `no`.

As we define aliases, we can define the same called *entities* using DTD representation. For example `>` is an entity representation for >, as used in an XML document. But, it is a predefined entity in both XML and HTML. XML allows us to set up and define our own entities, as in the following code example:

```
<!ENTITY ew "EvolveWare">
```

Now if we want to use the full terms in our document, we can use `&ew`.

The most recent specification for scripting a validation scheme is that of *schemas*.

XML Schema is a more convenient way to represent the validation scheme for an XML document. The working group defines the schema as follows.

Although XML 1.0 supplies a mechanism, the *Document Type Definition (DTD)* for declaring constraints on the use of markup, the automated processing of XML documents requires more rigorous and comprehensive facilities in this area. Requirements are for constraints on how the component parts of an application fit together, the document structure, attributes, data typing, and so on. The XML Schema Working Group is addressing a means for defining the structure, content, and semantics of XML documents.

To better understand how to write a schema, we will arrive at one. Consider the sample XML document shown in Listing 2.19.

LISTING 2.19 Sample Order XML Document

```
<?xml version="1.0"?>
<order oid="13215462">
 <company>EvolveWare Incorporation</company>
 <contact>Miten Marfatia</contact>
 <item>
  <name>XML Framework</name>
  <productid>EW-XML-0998</productid>
  <qty>4</qty>
  <description>
   Customizable XML framework for financial system
  </description>
 </item>
<item>
  <name>Accounting System</name>
  <productid>EW-XML-0999</productid>
  <qty>1</qty>
  <description>
   Company Accounting system
```

LISTING 2.19 Continued

```
  </description>
 </item>
</order>
```

The schema definition should start with the following code:

```
<?xml version="1.0" encoding="utf-8"?>
<xsd:schema xmlns:xsd="http://www.w3.org/2000/10/XMLSchema">
```

The declaration of target namespace is shown. I start the schema for the document with a starting element called `order`. This element has attributes and non-text children: Thus, it is a `complexType` because the other data type, `simpleType`, is reserved for data types holding only values and no element or attribute sub-nodes. The list of children of the order element is described by a sequence element.

```
<xsd:element name="order">
 <xsd:complexType>
  <xsd:sequence>
```

The company and contact elements are simple types because they don't have attributes or non-text children and can be described directly within a degenerate element element. The type (`xsd:string`) is prefixed by the namespace prefix associated with XML Schema, indicating a predefined XML Schema data type.

```
   <xsd:element name="company" type="xsd:string"/>
   <xsd:element name="contact" type="xsd:string"/>
```

The item element is of a complex type and is defined as follows:

```
    <xsd:element name="item" minOccurs="0" maxOccurs="unbounded">
    <xsd:complexType>
     <xsd:sequence>
```

The element occurrences (number of) are defined as shown previously (also called *cardinality*). The `unbounded` value specifications for `maxOccurs` means that there are as many occurrences of the item element.

The list of children are listed as follows:

```
      <xsd:element name="name" type="xsd:string"/>
      <xsd:element name="productid" type="xsd:string" minOccurs="0"
      ➥maxOccurs="unbounded"/>
      <xsd:element name="qty" type="xsd:string"/>
      <xsd:element name="description" type="xsd:string"/>
```

Finally, I terminate its description by closing the `complexType` and element elements.

```
    </xsd:sequence>
   </xsd:complexType>
  </xsd:element>
```

The sequence of elements for the document element (order) is now complete.

```
  </xsd:sequence>
```

I can now declare the attributes of the document elements, which must always come last (per W3C recommendations).

```
  <xsd:attribute name="oid" type="xsd:string"/>
```

and close all the remaining elements, as follows:

```
 </xsd:complexType>
</xsd:element>
</xsd:schema>
```

The complete schema now appears as shown in Listing 2.20.

LISTING 2.20 Schema for the XML Document in Listing 2.19

```
<?xml version="1.0" encoding="utf-8"?>
<xsd:schema xmlns:xsd="http://www.w3.org/2000/10/XMLSchema">

<xsd:element name="order">
 <xsd:complexType>
  <xsd:sequence>
   <xsd:element name="company" type="xsd:string"/>
   <xsd:element name="contact" type="xsd:string"/>
   <xsd:element name="item"minOccurs="0" maxOccurs="unbounded">
    <xsd:complexType>
     <xsd:sequence>
      <xsd:element name="name" type="xsd:string"/>
      <xsd:element name="productid" type="xsd:string" minOccurs="0"
      ➥maxOccurs="unbounded"/>
      <xsd:element name="qty" type="xsd:string"/>
      <xsd:element name="description" type="xsd:string"/>
     </xsd:sequence>
    </xsd:complexType>
   </xsd:element>
```

LISTING 2.20 Continued

```
  </xsd:sequence>
  <xsd:attribute name="oid" type="xsd:string"/>
 </xsd:complexType>
</xsd:element>

</xsd:schema>
```

As seen, XML Schema is more XML-like and hence is a more convenient way to specify the validation rules for an XML document.

Many explicit declaration types are available in XML schemas. Consider the following declaration of *types* in XML schemas:

```
<xsd:simpleType name="likeType">
  <xsd:restriction base="xsd:string">
   <xsd:maxLength value="35"/>
  </xsd:restriction>
 </xsd:simpleType>
```

The sample `likeType` element defined previously shows a convenient way to define `simpleTypes` in XML schemas. Notice that a `restriction` was applied to the element that it has to be of type `string` and its maximum length can be `35`.

Even *patterns* can be included in the schema element definitions. Consider the following example, which specifies that the `orderid` element can have only numbers from `0` to `9` and be of a maximum length of `12`.

```
<xsd:simpleType name="orderid">
  <xsd:restriction base="xsd:string">
   <xsd:pattern value="[0-9]{12}"/>
  </xsd:restriction>
 </xsd:simpleType>
```

One nice addition to definitions in XML schemas is the ability to specify constraints as you do in database design. For example, in a typical relational database model, you specify a *key* or an *index* field, which has to contain a unique value. We have similar concept of constraints in schema declaration. But it uses XPath syntax to specify the constraint. XPath is a path language specified by W3C specifications and is useful to define a path within an XML document. For example, if we have an `order` element as parent with `company` as its child and another `alternatecompany` child that has `company` as a tag, using XPath we could provide a guideline to the parsing mechanism so that it would consider the `company` under `order` tag and not the other one. Hence, it has ability to specify a relative reference. Let's jump to the constraint definition and see how it looks in schema syntax.

```
<xsd:unique name="charCompanymustbeUnique">
  <xsd:selector xpath="company"/>
  <xsd:field xpath="order"/>
</xsd:unique
```

The preceding specifies that the `orderid` must be unique. This location of the `xsd:unique` element in the schema gives the context node in which the constraint holds. By inserting `xsd:unique` under our `order` element, we specify that the `company` has to be unique in the context of an `order` only.

The two XPaths defined in the uniqueness constraint are evaluated relative to the context node. The first of these paths is defined by the selector element. The purpose is to define the element, which has the uniqueness constraint—the node to which the selector points must be an element node.

The second path, specified in the `xsd:field` element, is evaluated relative to the element identified by the `xsd:selector` and can be an element or an attribute node. This is the node whose value will be checked for uniqueness. Uniqueness over a combination of several values can be specified by adding other `xsd:field` elements within `xsd:unique`.

Another constraint construct is the `xsd:key`, which is similar to `xsd:unique` but specifies the additional condition that the element cannot be null. This is closer to the database Index Key definitions.

XML schema also has some important documentation specifications such as `xsd:annotation`. The following example shows the use of the same:

```
<xsd:element name="order">
  <xsd:annotation>
    <xsd:documentation xml:lang="en">
      Topmost element.
    </xsd:documentation>
    <xsd:appinfo source="http://mysample.com/">
      <bind xmlns="http://mysample.com/ns/">
        <class name="Order"/>
      </bind>
    </xsd:appinfo>
  </xsd:annotation>
```

The documentation information is included in `xsd:documentation`. The `xsd:appinfo` specifies a URL to the application information online.

There is also an `xsd:include` tag to include schemas in another document. The effect of the tag is the same as copying and pasting the schema in place of the tag.

```
<xsd:include schemaLocation="order.xsd"/>
```

XSLT could play an important role in user end data representation and formatting, but more importantly it could be used as a transformation engine.

Consider a simple case of converting XML document into a flat-file format, typically required for sending the data to a back-end system such as a mainframe. Such a transformation could prove useful as a middle-tier.

Consider for example a typical system that feeds the data into back-end systems using an XSLT processor as a core block. The Data Interface and Transform gateway receives the XML packet through the network and passes it to the XSLT engine with some transform initiative. The XSLT engine, based on the transform requirement parameter, would initiate a suitable XSL document from the XSL bank sitting on the Web server.

The Data Output Validation gateway could then deliver the data to respective back-end systems. Hence, we could imagine that for each back-end data, we would need a unique XSL document to process the request. So for extending this system to accommodate more support to data sources, we could include the respective XSL document as and when required.

Summary

Now that you know what an XML stream or a document looks like, we will further look into how you can derive useful information from an XML document. The next chapter looks into some common mechanisms available for parsing the information and utilizing it in the code. We will also look into some popular parsing mechanisms and their use.

3

Parsing an XML Document

IN THIS CHAPTER

The whole is more than the sum of its parts.

—Aristotle

Parsing an XML Document

Parsing is the act of reading an XML document to use the data in another application.

Parsing is a way to formulate and compose XML so that it can be accessible for use. Many interesting mechanisms can be developed to parse an XML document. The simplest one would be the plain string parser, which would treat the XML document as string content and return element values by sensing the presence of < and /> within that string.

An application might have varied usage for the data in the document. For example, some applications might use the XML document to present an explorer-like tree view so that the user could navigate through the system. Some other applications might use the XML document data values to plot a 2D graphic onscreen, representing a top view plan.

Each application has a specific need for interpreting the XML data stream and hence has a specific parsing mechanism associated with it. It is not practical to write a new parser for every application, however. Besides the amount of effort, in terms of achieving efficient parsing by using specialized algorithms and techniques, it is not efficient to do so.

Hence, we have generic parsers for parsing the document and feeding it to our applications.

Popular Parsers

As discussed before, two popular mechanisms representing a parser are DOM and SAX. SAX cannot be a representation of an XML document, but still it can be said to be a way to parse it. A parser is usually any utility that allows you to reach the respective element by linking through a parent-child relationship.

DOM presents a hierarchical way to represent the elements in an XML document and access them like a tree. The user programmatically accesses them using simple, implied statements.

SAX opens innumerable possibilities for using the XML document. As each element, or node occurrence, is parsed and triggered as a resulting event in the application, it can be interpreted in the way the application requires. This increases the representation flexibility for an XML document.

DOM ties the parsed document to a tree-like view, whereas SAX is used to create your own custom views: Both are useful.

As seen in most of our real-world applications, the need to represent data in tree-like hierarchical fashion is a major one. Hence, DOM is a useful and efficient way to do this.

As a guideline, it is advisable to use DOM wherever a tree-like memory image of the XML data is required. SAX, on the other hand, is better wherever a special representation method is to be used, being created within applications.

Between DOM and SAX, there are many parser types available from different sources. Some of the most popular parsers in use today are as follows:

- Megginson—Java based SAX parser
- Aelfred—Java based SAX parser
- IBM's DOM and SAX parsers
- Microsoft's DOM parser

An extensive list of XML tools and parsers is found at

`http://www.garshol.priv.no/download/xmltools/cat_ix.html.`

Using Parsers

We have seen a previous code example that uses a SAX parser. This section presents some more code examples.

Let's look at an example in Listing 3.1.

LISTING 3.1 Java Code Using a SAX Parser

```
import org.xml.sax.*;
import org.xml.sax.helpers.*;
import java.io.*;
import java.util.*;
import common.*;

public class SAXSample extends DefaultHandler {

   // The following variable stores the XML string in sort of stack
   private Stack tagStack = new Stack();

   // List of item names stored as Vector
   private Vector items = new Vector();

   // Client name
   private String client;

   // Collecting data in the buffer from
   // the "characters" SAX event.
   private CharArrayWriter contents = new CharArrayWriter();

   // Override methods of the DefaultHandler class
   // to receive of SAX Events.

   public void startElement( String namespaceURI,
               String localName,
              String qName,
              Attributes attr ) throws SAXException {

      contents.reset();

      // push the tag name in the stack
      tagStack.push( localName );

      // display the current path that has been found...
      System.out.println( "Path: [" + getTagPath() + "]" );

   }
```

LISTING 3.1 Continued

```
public void endElement( String namespaceURI,
            String localName,
           String qName ) throws SAXException {

   if ( getTagPath().equals( "/Order/Customer/Name" ) ) {
      client = contents.toString().trim();
   }
   else if ( getTagPath().equals( "/Order/Items/Item/Name" ) ) {
      items.addElement( contents.toString().trim() );
   }

   // clean the stack
   tagStack.pop();
}


public void characters( char[] ch, int start, int length )
              throws SAXException {
   // collect the contents into a buffer.
   contents.write( ch, start, length );

}




// Build the path string from the current stack
private String getTagPath( ){

   //  construct path string
   String buffer = "";
   Enumeration e = tagStack.elements();
   while( e.hasMoreElements()){
            buffer  = buffer + "/" + (String) e.nextElement();
   }
   return buffer;
}
```

LISTING 3.1 Continued

```
public Vector getItems() {
        return items;
}

public String getClientName() {
      return client;
}

public static void main( String[] argv ){

   System.out.println( "SAXExample:" );
   try {

      // Start using SAX 2 parser
      XMLReader xr = XMLReaderFactory.createXMLReader();

      // Set ContentHandler
      SAXExample ex1 = new SAXExample();
      xr.setContentHandler( ex1 );

      System.out.println();
      System.out.println("Tag Paths:");

      // File parsing
      xr.parse( new InputSource(new FileReader( "Sample.xml" )) );

      System.out.println();
      System.out.println("Names:");

      // Display Client
      System.out.println( "Client Name: " + ex1.getClientName() );


      // Display all item names
      System.out.println( "Order Items list: " );
      String itemName;
      Vector items = ex1.getItems();
      Enumeration e = items.elements();
      while( e.hasMoreElements()){
```

LISTING 3.1 Continued

```
                itemName = (String) e.nextElement();
             System.out.println( itemName );
          }


       }catch ( Exception e )  {
          System.out.println( "ERROR: Stack Trace: ");
          e.printStackTrace();
       }


    }

}
```

The XML file used to test the preceding code is shown in Listing 3.2.

LISTING 3.2 XML Input File for Code Example in Listing 3.1

```
<?xml version="1.0"?>
<Order>
   <Customer>
      <Name>EvolveWare Inc</Name>
      <Address>Sunnyvale</Address>
   </Customer>
   <Items>
      <Item>
         <ProductCode>098</ProductCode>
         <Name>XML Framework</Name>
         <Price>1232.99</Price>
      </Item>
      <Item>
         <ProductCode>4093</ProductCode>
         <Name>XMLUI 4x</Name>
         <Price>90.88</Price>
      </Item>
   </Items>
</Order>
```

Unlike a previous example, the code in Listing 3.1 includes all the handlers within one class, as seen by noting that the default class itself extends `DefaultHandler`. The rest of the code pushes all the retrieved elements on to a simple plain string variable. This is referred to as the stack in the code.

Let's look at the DOM example code in Java using IBM's XML DOM Parser (IBM XML4J). To begin with, consider the XML document to be parsed, as shown in Listing 3.3 (the DTD for the same in Listing 3.4 for reference).

LISTING 3.3 Product XML Document

```
<?xml version="1.0">
<catalog category="software">
    <name>EvolveWare Software Products></name>
    <itemlist>
        <item>
            <itemname>XML Framework</itemname>
            <cost>1230.34</cost>
            <description>Framework for financial enterprise
            ➥solution</description>
            <id>N12323</id>
        </item>
    </itemlist>
</catalog>
```

LISTING 3.4 DTD for XML Document in Listing 3.2

```
<!DOCTYPE catalog [
<!ELEMENT catalog (category, itemlist*) >
  <!ELEMENT category (#PCDATA) >
    <!ATTLIST catalog category(software|hardware|network) #REQUIRED>
  <!ELEMENT itemlist (itemname,cost,description,id) >
    <!ELEMENT itemname (#PCDATA) >
    <!ELEMENT cost  (#PCDATA) >
    <!ELEMENT description (#PCDATA) >
    <!ELEMENT id (#PCDATA) >
]>
```

The DOM representation of the XML document is shown in Figure 3.1.

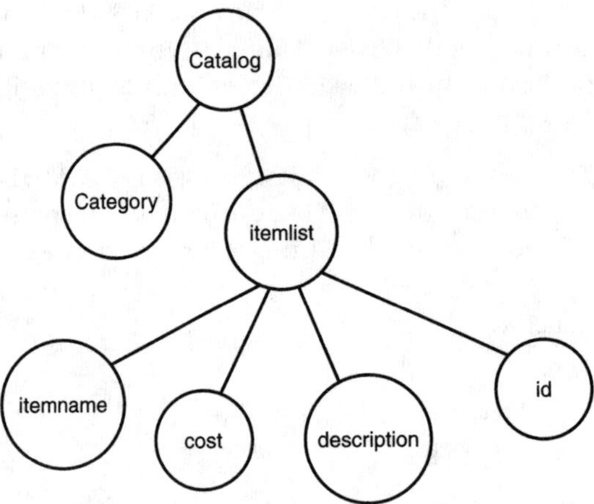

FIGURE 3.1 DOM representation of Listing 3.2.

The following needs to be imported for use by the IBM parser:

```
import com.ibm.xml.parsers.DOMParser;
import org.w3c.dom.Document;
import org.w3c.dom.NodeList;
import org.w3c.dom.Element;import org.w3c.dom.NamedNodeMap;
```

The following code parses the source XML string and returns the DOM object pointing to it:

```
public static Document parseDOM(String sourceFile) throws Exception{
    try {
        // Get a new parser and attach an error handler
        DOMParser objParser = new DOMParser();
        // Parse the source file
        objParser.parse(sourceFile);
        // Return the document
        return objParser.getDocument();
    } catch (Exception ex) {
        System.err.println("Failed with exception: " + ex);
    }
    return null;
}
```

As shown, the code creates the instance of the parser, parses the XML source, and returns the DOM object reference to it.

The following code resides in the `main()` method call of the Java code: it simply calls the `printXMLfromDOM()` method:

```
if (document != null) {
    System.out.println("*******Print XML document from DOM Tree**************");
    printXMLfromDOM(document.getDocumentElement());
   } else{
           System.out.println("*********In main()*****");
       }
}
```

The `printXMLfromDOM()` method is as follows:

```
private static void printXMLfromDOMt(Element element) {
 int k;
 NamedNodeMap attributes;
 NodeList children = element.getChildNodes();
 //  Start from this element
 System.out.print("<" + element.getNodeName());
 //  print attibutes inside the element start tag
 attributes = element.getAttributes();
 if (attributes != null) {
    for (k = 0; k < attributes.getLength(); k++) {
        System.out.print(" " + attributes.item(k).getNodeName());
        System.out.print("=" + attributes.item(k).getNodeValue());
    }
}
//  check for element value or sub-elements
 if (element.hasChildNodes()) {
  System.out.print(">");

 // print all child elements in the DOM tree

  for (k = 0; k < children.getLength(); k++) {
   if (children.item(k).getNodeType() == org.w3c.dom.Node.ELEMENT_NODE) {
    printElement((Element) children.item(k));
   } else if (children.item(k).getNodeType() == org.w3c.dom.Node.TEXT_NODE) {
    System.out.print(children.item(k).getNodeValue());
    }
  }    // for loop ends here
```

```
    // print end tag
    System.out.print("</" + element.getNodeName() + ">");

  } else {
      // element seems to be empty
      System.out.print(" />");
  }// else ends here
  }// printXMLfromDOM ends here
```

The preceding code is simple because it loops through the child elements and prints the entire XML document to the console.

DOM Versus SAX

DOM uses the principle of reading the entire XML document into memory, as described before. SAX, however, is more like an event parsing mechanism because it fires or triggers events depending on where it is in the course of parsing the document.

Because DOM stores the entire document as a memory map, it is not resource friendly, and hence we need to be careful in deciding when to use it. Ideally, if there is need for referring to the parameter or configuration variable values in most transactions, DOM is the answer. Consider, for example, that you have a typical need to refer to a mapping that might correlate a URI with actual IP addresses. Whenever the user triggers a request, the system has to look up in this map file and go to that IP accordingly. A DOM model is best suited for this application. The trade-off is that even though we would have thousands of such mappings defined, they must be readily available to go to the right IP. This typical requirement is a must for some designs in the distributed world, like a lookup server as described in Chapter 13, "Cross-Platform and Diverse System Integration," and Chapter 14, "Implementing an ERP System," of Part II, "Case Studies."

SAX, on the other hand, creates no such memory map and hence has a smaller memory "footprint." A typical application dynamically reads an XML file and represents coordinates that plot on a white board. This would be a requirement for a typical graphics view program or chat application supporting a white board type of interface. Then, the requirement narrows to plotting only the graphic from the sets of coordinates. Hence, SAX is ideal for such an application.

Summary

XML is very flexible and represents one data set in numerous formats, which creates the usability crisis. Also, the way information is bundled has to be specified and essentially needs to follow a standard so that the receiving system will know how to locate information within the stream. This calls for some specialized standard message formats like SOAP.

Further, as XML has diminished as a cross system protocol for maximum flexibility, we will look into aspects of using XML for connecting and communicating with remote systems.

4 SOAP

IN THIS CHAPTER

- SOAP
- XML-RPC

I must create a system, or be enslaved by another man's.

- *William Blake*

SOAP

Packaging data in the XML format opened many possibilities for generic communication. The need was for generic packets that form message layouts. Once the message layout was fixed it could be standardized, and multiple systems could use it as a standard information interchange format.

Such message packets were then utilized to connect to and interact with remote systems. They formed the anchor for interconnecting two systems over a network. This technique of interacting and utilizing the remote system was termed a *Remote Procedure Call* (*RPC*).

The W3C defined a new set of standards called *SOAP* for effectively using XML to invoke and execute methods on remote objects. The W3C description of SOAP is given here:

> SOAP is a lightweight protocol for exchange of information in a decentralized, distributed environment. It is an XML based protocol that consists of three parts: an envelope that defines a framework for describing what is in a message and how to process it, a set of encoding rules for expressing instances of application-defined data types, and a convention for representing remote procedure calls and responses.

Additional SOAP information is found at `http://www.w3c.org/`.

XML-RPC

Before dealing with SOAP, I would like to discuss XML-RPC. RPC is of special interest to the distributed computing world because it allows the invoking of a remote object and the executing of any of its public methods. RPC also allows the returned data to be passed back to the calling method. RPC is not a new concept and many organizations have deployed it in proprietary formats. For example, both DCOM from Microsoft and RMI from Sun Microsystems have some type of RPC support package. So far, all RPC implementations have been tightly coupled to languages and hence have been language and platform dependent. A typical RPC mechanism is as illustrated in Figure 4.1.

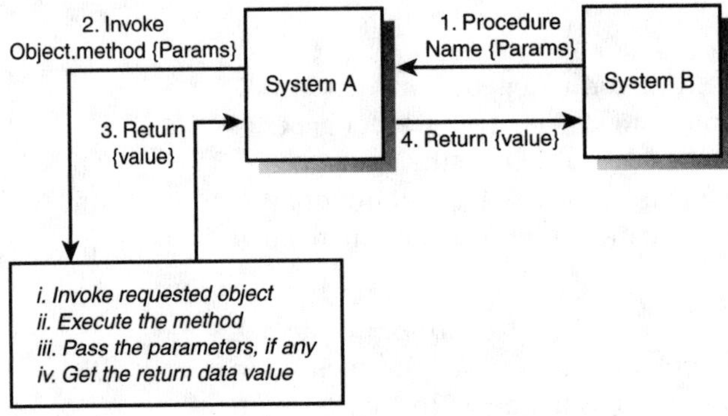

Figure 4.1 Schematic of an RPC mechanism.

XML-RPC is a new way to deal with RPC. Most importantly, it is language neutral because XML is used for defining the protocol of calling methods on the remote end. XML-RPC allows a program to execute a procedure or method on the remote end, over the Internet, and is easy to use. It employs HTTP for transport and XML for encoding calls. For the RPC schematic shown in Figure 4.1, the protocol used to transfer the method name and parameter from System B to A would be XML. The return value would be supplied back to System B from A using an XML stream. XML-RPC implementation provides the system to be deployed on both ends so that the respective objects and their methods can be invoked and the parameters passed to them. Essentially, XML-RPC allows the system deployed on the remote end to be invoked by a third-party system and returns the value. The caller receives the return value.

XML-RPC is simple, straightforward, and has wide acceptance in industry today. I'm showing an example demonstrating the use of XML-RPC. Consider a simple method call XML stream shown in Listing 4.1.

LISTING 4.1 Sample XML-RPC Method Call XML Stream

```
POST /RPC2 HTTP/1.0
User-Agent: EvolveWare/5.1.2 (Win2000)
Host: perisol.evolveware.com
Content-Type: text/xml
Content-length: 163

<?xml version="1.0"?>
<methodCall>
   <methodName>expenses.getStatePerDiem</methodName>
   <params>
      <param>
         <value><string>CA</string></value>
         </param>
      </params>
   </methodCall>
```

The top few lines are the header, which your Web server should transfer with the message. Note the important information in the header is the `POST` keyword and the content-type specification, which is `text/xml`. To better understand the concept of a header, let me elaborate on a few things.

When a Web browser receives any Web document, it receives a header that is not displayed in the browser window. This header tells the browser how to render, or display, this page in the window. For example, a typical Web page would be plain HTML and the content-type would be `text/html`. Hence, the browser uses its parser to decode and display the HTML document. Similarly, when you click a button in a search form, your browser passes information back to the Web server. If the `form` tag `method` attribute specifies `POST`, the browser returns the information with a header similar to the one previously shown in Listing 2.14. The XML-RPC requires you to `POST` the information to the server where you want to invoke the method.

I'll describe the XML stream. It has a `<methodCall>` tag, which contains an embedded method and parameters. This is the syntax of calling a remote method using the XML-RPC specification. The name of the method to call is specified in the `<methodName>` tag. Note that the method name is specified as a fully-qualified method reference, denoted by `object_name.method_name` syntax. This defines, at the server end, which object to invoke and which method to call with that object.

A method might have several parameters that are placed under the `<params>` tag. Each parameter occurrence is specified by the `<param>` tag. The value of a parameter can be a specific data type, and XML-RPC allows the data type to be specified under tags. This makes the message packet complete and more readable. In the listing, the parameter is of the type *string*, though XML-RPC supports various data types as follows:

- string—ASCII string type
- i4 (or int)—4-byte signed integer
- boolean—0 for false or 1 for true
- double—double-precision signed floating point number
- base64—base64-encoded binary
- datetime.iso8601—date/time

By default, the data type is *string* unless specified by using the preceding indicators.

The parameter passed can be a complex type like an array or structure. Sample code, using an array, is as follows:

```
<array>
   <data>
      <value><int>22</int></value>
      <value><boolean>0</boolean></value>
      <value><string>Nita</string></value>
   </data>
   </array>
```

As shown, each array can have multiple data elements with different values. The array elements do not have names, but they can be of different data types.

The sample code for a structure is as follows:

```
<struct>
   <member>
      <name>open</name>
      <value><double>18.32</double></value>
      </member>
   <member>
      <name>close</name>
      <value><double>139.12</double></value>
      </member>
   </struct>
```

Each structure has a member and each member can have some name and value.

The XML-RPC response received from the server is again in XML format. A typical response is shown in Listing 4.2.

LISTING 4.2 XML-RPC Response Example

```
HTTP/1.1 200 OK
Connection: close
Content-Length: 158
Content-Type: text/xml
Date: Sat, 12 Jul 2001 19:55:08 GMT
Server: Frontier/5.1.2-Win2000

<?xml version="1.0"?>
<methodResponse>
   <params>
      <param>
         <value><double>61.23</double></value>
         </param>
      </params>
   </methodResponse>
```

If the request is successful, the response header specifies `200 OK` as shown in the listing. The response message packet is indicated by `<methodResponse>` tag in the response message. The returned values are again specified as parameters shown in the request example.

If the request failed and the server responded with an error or fault, this condition would return a specific fault code and message as shown in Listing 4.3.

LISTING 4.3 Response Message in Case of Error

```
HTTP/1.1 200 OK
Connection: close
Content-Length: 158
Content-Type: text/xml
Date: Sat, 12 Jul 2001 19:55:08 GMT
Server: Userland Frontier/5.1.2-Win2000

<?xml version="1.0"?>
<methodResponse>
   <fault>
      <value>
         <struct>
            <member>
               <name>faultCode</name>
               <value><int>322</int></value>
```

LISTING 4.3 Continued

```
            </member>
          <member>
             <name>faultString</name>
             <value><string>Wrong State Code specified.</string></value>
             </member>
          </struct>
        </value>
      </fault>
   </methodResponse>
```

Various XML-RPC implementations could be used, and an exhaustive list exists at `http://www.xml-rpc.org`.

Many XML-RPC Java based implementations allow the deployment and use of a library for *Handler* methods in code and this can also be applied to Web servers. The Helma XML-RPC library is quite good and is implemented in Java. Information is available at `http://xmlrpc.helma.org/`. This library provides an easy way to add the XML-RPC handlers to code, as shown here:

```
addHandler (String name, Object handler);
removeHandler (String name);
```

This object can be *any* Java object. The library incorporates the `helma.xmlrpc.WebServer` Web server that is small and sufficient for adding XML-RPC support to your application. The library incorporates the `XMLRPCServer` object, which can be instantiated to use XML-RPC. On the client side, the `execute()` method is used to execute the XML-RPC request.

The Java data types are mapped to XML-RPC representations with the additional data type (`nil`) represented as `<nil/>` to specify the Java *null* type object.

Various implementations of the XML-RPC mechanism are found at `http://www.xmlrpc.com/directory/1568/implementations`.

Code will vary, depending on the implementation. The important aspect is the use of specifications to learn the mechanism. The following list is a typical sequence of server end actions for handling an XML-RPC request:

- Read the `POST` request and verify the header.
- Decode XML-RPC XML stream and get method name and parameter values (if any).
- Invoke the object with the method dynamically (or through late binding in terms of Microsoft code).
- Pass the parameters and get the return values.

- If an error (or exception) occurs, get the error code and error description.
- Format an XML-RPC response packet and route it back to the caller.

Late binding involves invoking the objects at runtime. This means that only at runtime does the system know the object name, or reference, and can use the runtime invoking mechanism to instantiate and use the name. This process is called *late binding* because the object is instantiated only at runtime.

The initialization of the service involves various objects having the XML-RPC Handlers specified within and the receptive objects registering themselves with the *central registrar*. This ensures that when a method is invoked, the dynamic invoker knows where the object is.

The use of XML-RPC in distributed computing is clear because it allows the flexibility of placing objects anywhere on a network and provides the capability of access for calls. The most important aspect is the use of the readily available Web backbone for this service.

I'll explain SOAP, which is a more recent methodology related to RPC.

SOAP Overview

SOAP can be thought of as very close to XML-RPC because it is also used for remote method call invocation. Although SOAP has a formal draft of its specification, located on the W3C Web site, and has industry-wide use, it is equally true that XML-RPC is popular among developers. However, some additional aspects make SOAP useful.

SOAP is not specifically for RPC implementation, but provides a generic messaging mechanism for transfer over the Web or between systems. This is an important point because it is often believed that SOAP is a direct alternative and replacement for RPC!

A SOAP message has an *envelope*, a *header*, and a *body*. The message can describe anything. Typically, a SOAP message is an XML document that consists of a mandatory SOAP `Envelope`, an optional SOAP `Header`, and a mandatory SOAP `Body`. The contents for these parts are listed here:

- SOAP `Envelope`—This is the top element of the XML document representing the SOAP message.
- SOAP `Header`—This is a generic mechanism for adding features to a SOAP message in a decentralized manner without prior agreement between the communicating parties: a SOAP sender, a SOAP receiver, and possibly one or more SOAP intermediaries.
- SOAP `Body`—This holds information for the final SOAP receiver.

Later in this chapter, I will demonstrate that SOAP can define a SOAP fault for reporting errors. Listing 4.4 shows a typical SOAP message.

LISTING 4.4 SOAP Message Example

```
POST /StockQuote HTTP/1.1
Host: www.stockquoteserver.com
Content-Type: text/xml; charset="utf-8"
Content-Length: 198
SOAPAction: "http://myquoteserver.com/2001/06/quotes"

<env:Envelope xmlns:env="http://www.w3.org/2001/06/soap-envelope" >
 <env:Body>
  <m:GetStockPrice
        env:encodingStyle="http://www.w3.org/2001/06/soap-encoding"
        xmlns:m="http://myquoteserver.com/2001/06/quotes">
    <symbol>EW</symbol>
  </m:GetStockPrice>
 </env:Body>
</env:Envelope>
```

This looks similar to an XML-RPC representation, with some additions. The similarities include the `POST` method used for posting the message to the server.

The message includes the `SOAPAction` URL reference marking the final destination of the SOAP packet. Note that the SOAP message does not have a message header, but implements the concept of an envelope. The envelope is specified as an opening tag with the body as child element. This is per the SOAP specification. The envelope has `http://www.w3.org/2001/06/soap-envelope` as the namespace identifier, which is, again, a standard defined by the SOAP specification. The namespace identifier is a simple pointer to a URI and serves to distinguish between duplicate elements and attribute types within the same XML document. The `encodingStyle` attribute specifies the serialization rules to be used when transferring the message.

A typical SOAP header would look like this:

```
<env:Header xmlns:env="http://www.w3.org/2001/06/soap-envelope" >
  <s:Securitylevel xmlns:t="http://mysample.com/sec" env:mustUnderstand="1" >
    2
  </s:Securitylevel>
</env:Header>
```

There are significant things to note, here. The header, again, has a namespace pointer to `http://www.w3.org/2001/06/soap-envelope`. The element level namespace points to a user-set value. A `mustUnderstand` attribute specifies if the receiver must understand the header to process the message. A value of `1` indicates it should. If the header is not important, the value is typically `0` or the `mustUnderstand` attribute is ignored. A typical SOAP response message with the body element and fault element tags is as follows:

```
<env:Body>
  <env:Fault>
    <faultcode>MustUnderstand</faultcode>
    <faultstring>Some mandatory headers not understood</faultstring>
  </env:Fault>
</env:Body>
```

The preceding fault error specifies that the receiver did not understand the `mustUnderstand` header specification and therefore generated a fault message.

A typical RPC SOAP request is shown in Listing 4.5.

LISTING 4.5 SOAP RPC Request Packet

```
POST /examples HTTP/1.1
User-Agent: EW/7.0 (WinNT)
Host: localhost:81
Content-Type: text/xml; charset=utf-8
Content-length: 474
SOAPAction: "/examples"

<?xml version="1.0"?>
<SOAP-ENV:Envelope SOAP-ENV:encodingStyle="http://schemas.xmlsoap.org/
➥soap/encoding/" xmlns:SOAP-ENC="http://schemas.xmlsoap.org/
➥soap/encoding/" xmlns:SOAP-ENV="http://schemas.xmlsoap.org/
➥soap/envelope/" xmlns:xsd=
➥"http://www.w3.org/1999/XMLSchema" xmlns:xsi=
➥"http://www.w3.org/1999/XMLSchema-instance">
   <SOAP-ENV:Body>
      <m:getStatePerDiem xmlns:m="http://www.evolveware.org/">
         <stateshort xsi:type="xsd:string">CA</stateshort>
         </m:getStatePerDiem>
      </SOAP-ENV:Body>
   </SOAP-ENV:Envelope>
```

To allow for a better comparison, I have used the same method call as in Listing 4.1 for XML-RPC. The representation is changed only in the namespaces referred to. Unlike XML-RPC, SOAP includes parameter names. Again, it has the action path and hostname specification, in the header, for directing the request to the respective server.

Recently, the concept of `M-POST` came into existence. Technically an `M-POST` mechanism functions the same as `POST` except that you see the `M-POST` string in the HTTP header. This method was introduced to differentiate between forms of `POST` requests issued over the Web. Hence, it makes the receiver's work easier because it can interpret the header and know beforehand that `M-POST` is a special messaging request from a SOAP client. This mechanism also enables firewalls to allow or disallow any specific request type.

The `M-POST` request would be represented like the one shown previously, except that the header would specify a changed method type as shown here:

```
M-POST /examples HTTP/1.1
User-Agent: EW/7.0 (WinNT)
Host: localhost:81
Content-Type: text/xml; charset=utf-8
Content-length: 474
SOAPAction: "/examples"
```

The body is the same as before. Please note that a method name `M-POST` appears in the header enabling the client end to recognize the method. This method allows administrators to set firewalls appropriately because such requests are guaranteed to be originating from a trusted RPC source.

The `charset` can be specified: If not specified, the default is US-ASCII. Other acceptable `charsets` are UTF-8 and UTF-16. UTF-8 is recommended for maximum interoperability.

The SOAP receiver uses the required header information, although, in many cases, the URI and the `SOAPAction` header will have the same value. Here, the string following `POST` is `/examples`.

As shown in Listing 4.5, all attributes of the `<SOAP-ENV:Envelope>` are required. Data types, or scalar values, supported by SOAP are as follows:

- `xsd:string`—ASCII string of characters
- `xsd:int`—32-byte signed integer
- `xsd:boolean`—0 for false or 1 for true
- `xsd:double or xsd:float`—signed floating point number
- `SOAP-ENC:base64`—base64-encoded binary
- `xsd:timeInstant`—date/time

These types approximate the XML-RPC supported types, except they refer to namespaces.

Structures can be passed as parameters, as in the following example:

```
<param>
   <lowest xsi:type="xsd:int">60</lowerBound>
   <highest xsi:type="xsd:int">180</upperBound>
</param>
```

The parameter can also contain an array, which is specified by an XML element with a `SOAP-ENC:arrayType` attribute whose value begins with `ur-type[`, followed by the number of array elements, followed by `]`. The following shows the definition of a three-element array:

```
<param SOAP-ENC:arrayType="xsd:ur-type[3]" xsi:type="SOAP-ENC:Array">
   <item xsi:type="xsd:string">Pune</item>
   <item xsi:type="xsd:int">18</item>
   <item xsi:type="xsd:boolean">1</item>
</param>
```

This array contains mixed types. SOAP array definitions also allow the specification of the type, as shown in this example:

```
<param SOAP-ENC:arrayType="xsd:string[3]" xsi:type="SOAP-ENC:Array">
   <item>Nita Barve</item>
   <item>Raymond Ennis</item>
   <item>Anju Barve</item>
</param>
```

The response example for the request in Listing 2.18 is shown in Listing 4.6.

LISTING 4.6 SOAP RPC Response Packet

```
HTTP/1.1 200 OK
Connection: close
Content-Length: 499
Content-Type: text/xml; charset=utf-8
Date: Wed, 28 Mar 2001 05:05:04 GMT
Server: EW/7.0-WinNT

<?xml version="1.0"?>
<SOAP-ENV:Envelope SOAP-ENV:encodingStyle="http://schemas.xmlsoap.
➥org/soap/encoding/" xmlns:SOAP-ENC="http://schemas.xmlsoap.
➥org/soap/encoding/" xmlns:SOAP-ENV="http://schemas.xmlsoap.
```

LISTING 4.6 Continued

```
➥org/soap/envelope/" xmlns:xsd="http://www.w3.org/1999/XMLSchema"
➥xmlns:xsi="http://www.w3.org/1999/XMLSchema-instance">
  <SOAP-ENV:Body>
     <m:getStatePerDiemResponse xmlns:m="http://www.soapware.org/">
        <Result xsi:type="xsd:float">61.24</Result>
        </m:getStatePerDiemResponse>
     </SOAP-ENV:Body>
  </SOAP-ENV:Envelope>
```

As with XML-RPC, the `200 OK` code is returned. In the body element, the tag name has a method name followed by the keyword `Response`.

The fault or error condition can be represented by returning a fault code packet as shown in Listing 4.7. Please note that in the SOAP (and even in the case of XML-RPC) response process, the error is delivered through both the returned message packet and the header. The dispatcher sends back the header with a suitable error message, and the message body, or load, is the XML stream representing the message that can be parsed for errors. Hence, the error is propagated through the header and body contents in the case of remote delivery over Web services.

Listing 4.7 SOAP Fault Message Packet Example

```
HTTP/1.1 500 Server Error
Connection: close
Content-Length: 511
Content-Type: text/xml; charset=utf-8
Date: Wed, 10 Mar 2001 05:06:32 GMT
Server: EW/7.0-WinNT

<?xml version="1.0"?>
<SOAP-ENV:Envelope SOAP-ENV:encodingStyle="http://schemas.
➥xmlsoap.org/soap/encoding/" xmlns:SOAP-ENV=
➥"http://schemas.xmlsoap.org/soap/envelope/"
➥xmlns:xsd="http://www.w3.org/1999/XMLSchema"
➥xmlns:xsi="http://www.w3.org/1999/XMLSchema-instance">
  <SOAP-ENV:Body>
     <SOAP-ENV:Fault>
        <faultcode>SOAP-ENV:Client</faultcode>
        <faultstring>Can't call getStatePerDiem because
        ➥there are too many parameters.</faultstring>
        </SOAP-ENV:Fault>
     </SOAP-ENV:Body>
  </SOAP-ENV:Envelope>
```

For all errors, the header contains `500 Server Error`. This means that all errors occurring at the SOAP handler result in A `500 Server error` that is returned as part of the HTTPd header. With the `mustUnderstand` attribute set to `1`, the server will return a `500` error if the header cannot be understood.

Using SOAP

Using SOAP is the same as using XML-RPC. The Apache Software Foundation's implementation of the SOAP specification is based on IBM's SOAP4J and is quite simple to use. Information is available at `http://xml.apache.org/`.

Creating a service using Apache SOAP is easy. A simple service is shown in Listing 4.8.

LISTING 4.8 Simple SOAP Service in Apache

```
package myservice;
public class HelloService
{
   public String greetTo(String name)
   {
      System.out.println("***In method greetTo()");
      return "Hello " + name + "!";
   }
}
```

Specific settings are required because each service under Apache has a unique Object ID that is required for a client to call the service. The client uses the `org.apache.soap.rpc.Call` object to call a service. This method accepts the Object ID and method name with any parameters. To execute the method, the client calls the `invoke()` method after setting the `Call` object. This method accepts two parameters: one is the URL for the `rpcrouter` servlet, usually `webserver/apache-soap/servlet/rpcrouter`, and the other is the `SOAPAction` header, which is the SOAP header previously discussed. The `invoke()` method converts the `Call` object into a SOAP request and executes the method: This always returns a `org.apache.soap.rpc.Response` object. Apache SOAP has interfaces defined to *marshallers* and *unmarshallers* on its side, which help in serializing and de-serializing the object types. The Apache administration tool is used to create the object ID, method names, and service type (Java in our case). In this example, I will assume the ID to be `myhelloservice`.

The client code appears in Listing 4.9.

LISTING 4.9 Client Code for Apache SOAP Service in Listing 4.8

```
package myservice;

import java.net.URL;
import java.util.Vector;
import org.apache.soap.SOAPException;
import org.apache.soap.Constants;
import org.apache.soap.Fault;
import org.apache.soap.rpc.Call;
import org.apache.soap.rpc.Parameter;
import org.apache.soap.rpc.Response;

public class mySOAPClient
{
   public static void main(String[] args) throws Exception
   {
      if(args.length == 0)
      {
         System.err.println("Usage: java myhelloservice.
         ➥mySOAPClient [SOAP-router-URL] ");
         System.exit (1);
      }

      try
      {
         URL url = null;
         String name = null;
         if(args.length == 2)
         {
            url = new URL(args[0]);
            name = args[1];
         }
         else
         {
            url = new URL("http://Apache_SOAP_RPC_Webserver_here/
            ➥apache-soap/servlet/rpcrouter");
            name = args[0];
         }

         // Cosntruct the Call
         Call call = new Call();
         call.setTargetObjectURI("urn:myHelloService");
         call.setMethodName("greetTo");
```

LISTING 4.9 Continued

```
        call.setEncodingStyleURI(Constants.NS_URI_SOAP_ENC);
        Vector params = new Vector();
        params.addElement(new Parameter("name", String.class, name, null));
        call.setParams(params);

        // Execute the SOAP call using invoke() call.
        Response resp = null;
        try
        {
           resp = call.invoke(url, "");
        }
        catch( SOAPException e )
        {
           System.err.println("Exception Occured SOAP
           ➥ (" + e.getFaultCode() + "): " + e.getMessage());
           System.exit(-1);
        }

        // verify response for any faults
        if( !resp.generatedFault() )
        {
           Parameter ret = resp.getReturnValue();
           Object value = ret.getValue();
           System.out.println(value);
        }
        else
        {
            // if fault occurred then print the fault details on the console....
           Fault fault = resp.getFault();
           System.err.println("Generated fault: ");
           System.out.println ("  Fault ID    = " + fault.getFaultCode());
           System.out.println ("  Fault Message = " + fault.getFaultString());
        }
     }
     catch(Exception e)
     {
         // Display the error stack on console....
        e.printStackTrace();
     }
   }
}
```

The client code sets the Object ID using the `setTargetObjectURI()` method. The method name is set using `setMethodName()`. The encoding style is chosen as a standard SOAP encoding type. Finally, the parameters are passed as `Vector` and set using `setParams()`. Each element in the vector is of type `org.apache.soap.rpc.Parameter`, which takes the parameter's name, value, and encoding style.

By checking the value returned by `generatedFault()`, it was determined that the call, which returned true and printed the hello message to the console, was successful. Otherwise, the fault message would be printed.

Using SOAP with Microsoft components is interesting, too. An example is a simple SOAP client in the form of an ASP page. The complete code is shown in Listing 4.10.

LISTING 4.10 ASP Based SOAP Client

```
<%
  ' Create the desired DOM and HTTP objects
  set xmldom = server.CreateObject("Microsoft.XMLDOM")
  set xmlhttp = server.CreateObject("Microsoft.XMLHTTP")

  ' Set the SOAP envelope packet
  SampleSoap = SampleSoap & "<SOAP:Envelope   xmlns:
➥SOAP=""urn:schemas-xmlsoap-org:soap.v1"">"
  SampleSoap = SampleSoap & "<SOAP:Body>"
  SampleSoap = SampleSoap & "<sampleRequest>"
  SampleSoap = SampleSoap & "<pw>NitaAjay</pw>"
  SampleSoap = SampleSoap & "<msg>Are you there?</msg>"
  SampleSoap = SampleSoap & "</sampleRequest>"
  SampleSoap = SampleSoap & "</SOAP:Body>"
  SampleSoap = SampleSoap & "</SOAP:Envelope>"

  ' Sent the request as POST type to the server
  xmlhttp.open "POST", "http://localhost/SOAP/SOAPServer.asp", false
  xmlhttp.setRequestHeader "Man", POST & " " & http://localhost/
➥SOAP/SOAPServer.asp & " HTTP/1.1"
  xmlhttp.setRequestHeader "MessageType", "CALL"
  xmlhttp.setRequestHeader "ContentType", "text/xml"
  xmlhttp.send(SampleSoap)
  'Only 200 means no error
  if xmlhttp.Status = 200 then
  'collects the data returned.
  Set xmldom = xmlhttp.responseXML
```

LISTING 4.10 Continued

```
  'print it to see the response, as to what we have got
  Response.write(xmldom.xml)

  'Check for errors and print them what are they
Else
  Response.Write("Some Error Occurred")

 'Show the error code returned by the server
  Response.Write("status=" & xmlhttp.status)

  'Show associated description text
  Response.write("" & xmlhttp.statusText)
  Response.Write("" & Request.ServerVariables("ALL_HTTP"))
End if
  ' Set the objects to nothing..to kill them
  set xmlhttp = nothing
  set xmldom = nothing
%>
```

The preceding code is quite straightforward. Notice how I am using `XMLDOM` and `XMLHTTP` objects to send the requests. Please note that I have used ASP (Active Server Pages) over PWS (Personal Web Server) or IIS (Internet Information Server) and the MSXML parser to code the previous example.

The example forms the `SampleSoap` string resembling the SOAP request. The SOAP request is a message sent, with an embedded password, and `POST`ed to the server side URL for processing. The response is displayed if successful; otherwise an error message is displayed.

The SOAP server side code is shown in Listing 4.11.

LISTING 4.11 SOAP Server Side Code for the Client in Listing 4.10

```
<%
Response.Buffer=true

' set response type
Response.ContentType = "text/xml"
set xmldom = server.CreateObject("Microsoft.XMLDOM")
set xmlhttp = server.CreateObject("Microsoft.XMLHTTP")
```

LISTING 4.11 Continued

```
' Get the SOAP request from client
xmldom.load(Request)

' form the return SOAP message
returnSOAP = returnSOAP & "<SOAP:Envelope xmlns:
➥SOAP=""urn:schemas-xmlsoap-org:soap.v1"">"
returnSOAP = returnSOAP & "<SOAP:Body>"
returnSOAP = returnSOAP & "<msg>"
returnSOAP = returnSOAP & "<presence>Yes I am here!</presence>"
returnSOAP = returnSOAP & "</msg>"
returnSOAP = returnSOAP & "</SOAP:Body>"
returnSOAP = returnSOAP & "</SOAP:Envelope>"

' lets get the pw
set pw = xmldom.documentElement.childNodes.item(0).childNodes.item(0)

' validate the pw and get the request
if pw.childNodes.item(0).text = "NitaAjay" and _
  msg.childNodes.item(0).text = "Are you there?" then

   ' write the response
  Response.Write(returnSOAP)

   ' and close
end if

' and clean up
set xmldom = nothing
set xmlhttp = nothing
%>
```

The server is straightforward, too! Again, it receives the SOAP message from the client, validates the password, and returns the SOAP message.

The server uses the XML DOM-based parser from Microsoft to read the child nodes and get both message and password.

As seen from the preceding examples, the use of SOAP is quite straightforward, just like XML-RPC, and these methodologies could provide important ways to form and model distributed frameworks.

Summary

The next chapter deals with the open-ended systems design approach. For the distributed systems engineer and designer, the open-ended approach is an important foundation for the design of successful systems. These systems form the basis of large-scale systems. I will discuss their modules and describe their inter-connections.

In the chapter I will explain some important facts, put specific XML knowledge to use, and design models. We would evolve at most generic frameworks for architecting the real world systems.

I will also put different models to use, forming scalable and extendible models. The open-ended capability will be treated as the primary, important aspect.

5

Open-Ended Systems

IN THIS CHAPTER

- Overview
- What Are Open-Ended Systems?
- How to Accommodate Open-End in System Architecture
- Queuing—Processing Large Chunks of Data

The king looked puzzled—he wasn't a very heavy weight, intellectually. His head was an hourglass. It could show an idea, but it had to do it a grain at a time, not the whole idea at once.

—*Mark Twain*

This chapter introduces the open-ended systems and covers the topic in greater detail. The chapter describes the architectural requisites for implementing such systems.

Web fundamentals are explained with respect to open-ended systems and how it can be used to provide a gateway for distributed computing.

Finally, the chapter deals with designing and implementing a generic framework. It defines the model requisites and details for implementing the same. It provides a rigorous treatment on the model, which is applied from the open-ended perspective using XML. It also elaborates and explains possible security options, which could be incorporated for making the system secure by discussing common security requirements and providing for the same.

Overview

This chapter advocates Web technologies and treats them as a basic platform for forming the practical open-ended system. It explains using Web services and XML to devise a high-end distributed system.

Finally, the chapter concludes by presenting an open-ended system framework. It shows and explains how a generic framework approach could help you solve connectivity problems and apply the same for forming an open-ended system. It is important for you to have a basic knowledge of XML and hence, I suggest that you read the previous chapter before starting this one.

In systems today, more challenging are the tasks of integrating with existing systems and making sure that the systems developed are able to talk freely with future systems. Particularly in the systems world, it is essentially becoming important that you architecture the system in the most scalable manner. What is making the system scalable? Making the system scalable can be extended into numerous modules: self or external. For example, you are devising an architecture for a financial system and provide some module, which would let some external system integrate with the financial system and exchange information seamlessly. As of now, any developer team could develop a supporting module that could provide input to get output from these systems. Now if you need to provide some bank data to serve as input to this module, it can be done easily by using the interfaces provided with these modules.

Often the extendibility for the modules is provided in the previous description, but then such systems are not always open-ended. The reason is that the system or module, which is written to extend the existing system, has to be in the same language (in terms of computer language or technology) and many times is platform dependant. So, not all extendable or scalable systems are open-ended. A typical scalable system would be able to deploy itself over multi-server environment due to load balancing, but would still not offer any option for third-party systems to talk to it and hence are not open-ended.

To achieve a truly open-ended system, the most important aspect is the platform neutral protocol for command and data transfer. XML provides both of this and, because of its advantages, it is the protocol of choice for implementing such systems.

What Are Open-Ended Systems?

Open-ended systems, by definition, are those systems that provide an easy and generic way for extendibility.

Systems, in general, refer to any architecture defining collection of modules (or objects) that serve the overall solution for an application. I will cover the subject of open-ended systems after we deal with generic systems.

What we are trying to arrive at is a notion of an open-ended system. Consider a generic system, with typical building blocks as shown in Figure 5.1. The figure specifies an over-simplified system, typical of many environments. An *input process* is typically a user interface or a data file on the mainframe system. The *intermediate process*, also called a *middle-tier*, in modern n-tier systems design, serves the purpose of the processing/interfacing engine. This stage includes business logic, and can have pointers to back-end systems and interaction code with another system. Finally, the *output process* block is where the output is presented or dumped. So, essentially this simplified version of the system signifies that any system can be broken into these three basic blocks.

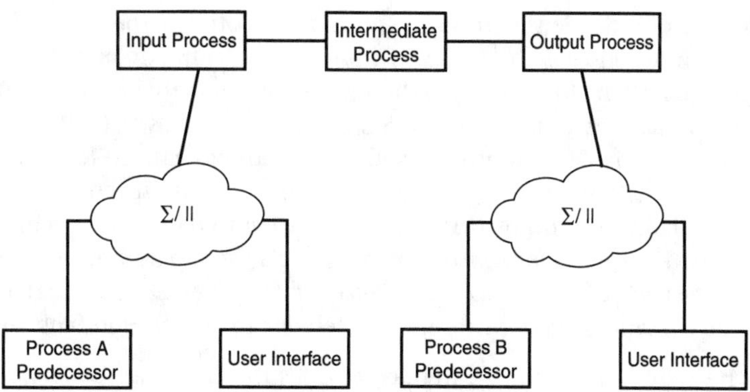

FIGURE 5.1 Generic system—block schematic.

Now, let's reason out the open-ended quality of a system. To extend the preceding system, there can be many ways. For example, you can design a system so that it broadcasts, stores, or dumps intermediate data. You can provide an output in different formats so that the data is available for a third-party system. The approach can be quite dependent on a number of factors including what data you have to share and at what point it has to be shared in the processing time and cycle.

Again, many approaches are available for devising this output and communicating with other systems. Essentially, it depends on how you devise the design.

So, by providing the capability for the system to make the data available, from intermediate or final output process, you can make it extendable. If a system is extendable, it can be scalable. Scalability is a different issue when viewed from within the same system. This aspect should be considered when devising the system. Designers and developers worry about this issue. So, to make their system scalable, they need to introduce a model that allows multiple copies of the systems to be deployed and replicated over multiple servers and run on different machines (as a single integrated system).

Even though the system is extendable and scalable, there still might be some issues. Say that, for example, the development platforms for the system are fixed; if anyone has to extend the system, the platform requirement is a restriction. Because of platform dependency, the system extension would require specified skills and can be a limiting factor. Even if the project manager has planned enough in the future, you cannot rely on platforms and languages. We have all learned enough from our past experiences that the more the system is independent, the better the chances are of futuristic extensibility. When talking about language and platform dependency issues, one model that comes to mind is CORBA. CORBA has been around for many years and is still a language of choice. It is platform independent and has a strong support for the object-oriented model. Say that you solve the problem of platform and language independence by using CORBA or some similar concept, but still the major issue is data transformability. When programming languages and platforms are in the scenario, data types matter a lot. So, even if you choose CORBA and use a data type that is not available in another language (or can be mapped to), it's the same problem again. CORBA is the most widely used and popular specification for constructing a language and platform neutral system to date. The specifications are defined by *OMG (Object Management Group)*, and all the program interfaces are required to be specified in terms of *IDL (Interface Definition Language)*. Hence, you have to code IDL and then use those to implement in any chosen language.

After all, the systems need to be extended and it's the data that matters. Reliable data transfer is the one final requirement for all systems to work in harmony (not a philosophy). Thus, the system can be truly open only if it allows for the ease of data transfer and representation. Hence, the data can be traded in a generic and an open manner—termed *Open Data*.

This concept could even be extended to distribute computing. As the load increases, the system can be deployed on *n* number of machines and still perform. This challenge is also one of the important requirements for an open system.

Then an open-ended system would be the one that

- allows extendibility using diverse languages and platforms
- allows ease of data transfer and mapping—Open Data
- could be easily deployable in a distributed environment
- allows deploying the systems over multiple machines for load sharing

You will learn how to accommodate open-end in architecture in the next section. From the preceding, you could easily conclude that the only real way to make a system open-ended is to provide a generic protocol. This protocol would provide data in a universal representation format. Try to arrive at what could really be a solution of choice.

Before I reason out and give examples for using XML for open-ended system design, one important consideration is the term *extendibility*. It also applies to all those systems that require talking to third-party systems and offer data trading services.

One typical example is the banking system. A banking system design should accommodate huge flexibility and extendibility because of the requirement of data sharing or trading. The system usually needs to exchange data with third-party systems such as freelance loan agents, government bureaus, and other banks. Such a system would require you to provide the data-on-demand capability if a bank is offering gateway services for third-party systems to read transaction data.

XML is the protocol of choice for many reasons. The most important is the capability to represent data in a self-descriptive way.

XML allows you to include data descriptors, (called *metadata,*) and data values, both in the same stream. The term *stream* means a series of characters or a *string* in programming terms. The inherent flexibility provided by the approach of representing data hierarchically with the capability to have a validating document supporting the data document (such as Document Type Definition, DTD, or Schemas) and the fact that it is self-documenting make it a protocol of choice.

Using XML Streams

Instead of glorifying a technology, let's take a look at how it really helps. Consider the banking system that provides a gateway service to its clients so that they can read the transaction from the system. Assume that the middle-tier for the system provides an option to use the internal methods such as

```
QueryUserTransaction(lUserID, lUPassword, lUSecurityKey, dtFromDate, dtToDate)
```

This method is enough for our current sample scope. The parameters are assumed to be as follows:

- `lUserID` is user-id for the user account with the bank.
- `lUPassword` is the associated public domain password for that user.
- `lUSecurityKey` is the security key provided by the bank for third-party systems to interact. It can be a decryption key.
- `dtFromDate` is the date from which the transaction data is needed.
- `dtToDate` is the date to which the transaction data is needed.

It would be further assumed that the system is capable of generating a resultset in XML format.

For this discussion to be complete, assume that the third-party system has an interface, which would trigger the respective object to execute this method. (This is covered in the following Web services section.)

The interaction would then be programmed in a third-party end. The third party would request for the transaction data to give suitable parameters to the interface layer and to get the response back in the form of XML (see Figure 5.2).

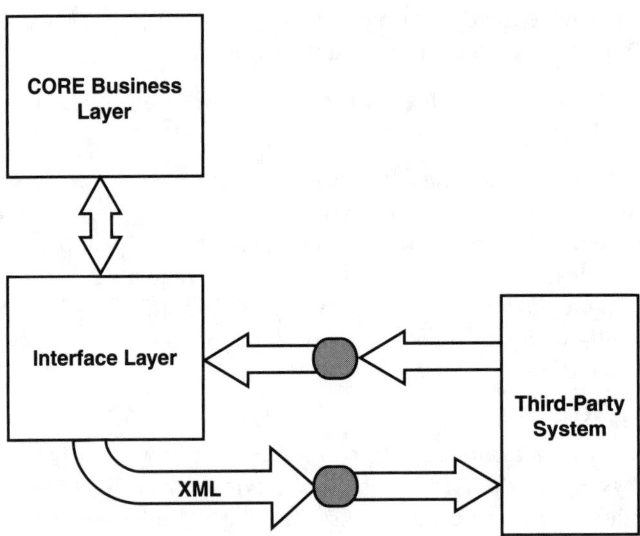

FIGURE 5.2 A Bank system sample.

That was simple. Now think about it from a practical perspective. One link missing here is the understanding of data representation in the XML string. Consider the following XML data stream, which we assume would be the output given by the banking system in response to the `QueryUserTransaction()` call.

LISTING 5.1 A Transaction XML Document

```
<?xml version="1.0"?>
<!-- transaction data sample from bank -->
<transactionledger>
        <transid>NN01012000-007</transid>
        <transdate>20000101</transdate>
        <transdescription>Purchase at Nita's Gift Shop</transdescription>
        <transcode>1111222233334444</transcode>
        <transtype>debit</transtype>
        <transamount>123.65</transamount>
        <transauthorize>SIG</transauthorize>
</transactionledger>
```

As you can see, the transaction stream is as shown in Listing 5.1. Although it's self descriptive, there might be confusion if you include and combine different data in a single stream (like, for example, when you combine this stream with HTML or other raw data).

A better approach is to define a namespace. The namespace is just a *URI (unified resource identifier)* that might point to nothing. This also would make the document reference easier and tailored for client-ends. This would also change the preceding representation. Consider, for example, that the namespace is on `bank.com` server and you name it `banktrans`. Then the preceding XML file would resemble Listing 5.2.

LISTING 5.2 A Transaction XML Document with the Namespace Included

```
<?xml version="1.0"?>
<!-- transaction data sample from bank -->
<transactionledger xmlns="urn:bank.com:banktrans">
    <transid>NN01012000-007</transid>
    <transdate>20000101</transdate>
    <transdescription>Purchase at Nita's Gift Shop</transdescription>
    <transcode>1111222233334444</transcode>
    <transtype>debit</transtype>
    <transamount>123.65</transamount>
    <transauthorize>SIG</transauthorize>
</transactionledger>
```

The use of namespaces would be more evident if you were to extract data from a combined document that also has a combination of some HTML tags or XML data.

To make the use of namespaces more prominent, look at the following listing:

```
<?xml version="1.0"?>
<!-- transaction data sample from bank -->
<transactionledger xmlns="urn:bank.com:banktrans">
    <transid>NN01012000-007</transid>
    <udt:transdate xmlns:udt="urn:mybank.trans.com">20000101</transdate>
    <transdescription>Purchase at Nita's Gift Shop</transdescription>
    <transcode>1111222233334444</transcode>
    <transtype>debit</transtype>
    <transamount>123.65</transamount>
    <transauthorize>SIG</transauthorize>
</transactionledger>
```

Note that I have designated the `<transdate>` as belonging to a namespace different from the entire document. This allows you to include an additional element or attribute with the same name in the document, and they can still be interpreted as different ones.

Another addition to the concept would be DTDs and schemas. Both are explained in initial chapters of this book, and they could form the validation check rules for the third-party engine to decode the preceding XML stream.

You will now learn how to extend the system and make it open-ended in the following sections.

How to Accommodate Open-End in System Architecture

In terms of extensibility, accommodating the open-ended quality in a system design could prove very useful. The previous section gives an overview of what can be achieved by using a uniform protocol approach to make the system open-ended.

Open-end has to be the vision of the system designer and architect. For making the system open-ended, you need to go through the process of reasoning out something like what data would be useful for the to future systems and also decide how can that be provided. Note that although we have agreed that the protocol of choice is XML, we still require some design objective to include the methods that would invoke the whole data exchange process.

Before we delve deeper into the issues of a perfect design approach, we will take a look at various approaches adopted for making a system extendable and open.

General System Architectures

The coverage of system architectures can be extensive, but we will revise some of the system architectures, which are commonly used and have existed for years. We will overview these architectures in light of making the systems open-ended.

Any system can prove to be extendable by using various approaches. Some of these approaches, which occur in major systems existing today, are listed in the following:

- Extending using a database
- Extending using interfaces
- Extending using a generic query engine

Extending Using a Database

Extending a system using a database is perhaps the oldest, since classical days. Note that using a database essentially means some sort of map file and a data structure to transpose and transform the data into the resulting system. It can use temporary data stores such as disk files. The data structures provided a way to understand the format of the data and hence made it easier for it to be transformed in resultant layout. Old systems often used the concept of Copybooks (as in COBOL) for achieving the same. This scheme can be presented as shown in Figure 5.3.

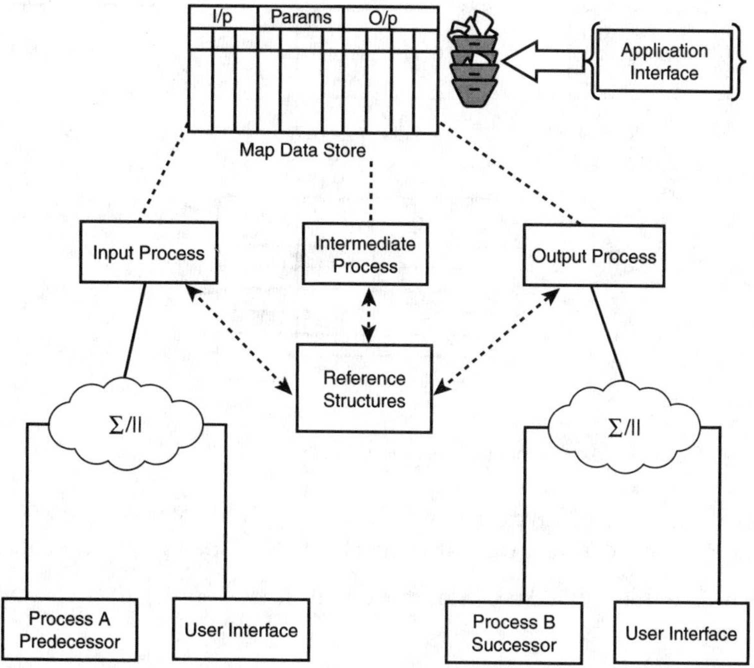

FIGURE 5.3 System architecture—Extendibility using Database for Mapping.

As shown in the figure, each block is associated with an interaction with a map store or a database and the reference structures. Each module dumps the final output data in the database. The data stored in this database is the one that would be of interest for third-party system interactions. Further, each block can also pick up the data from the database, which could serve as input to that module (process).

The module understands the data stored in the database and interprets the mappings by using a reference structure. Usually, the approach used in these systems is pretty simple and generic. Let's consider a typical case.

Consider a production support system used for monitoring inventory, purchases, and accounts. Consider this system to be using the database approach for extendability (see Figure 5.4). Assume that the system should be able to generate purchase orders automatically and make amount entries into the accounting system so that suitable payments could be appended to accounts payable.

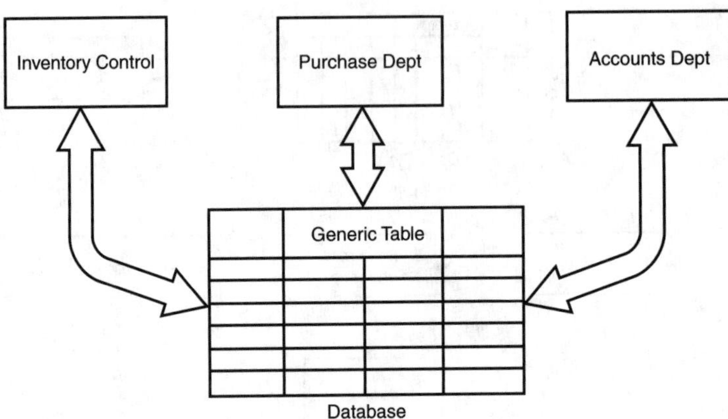

FIGURE 5.4 Database connected sample system.

The preceding three modules are connected to a central database storing all the information. Now consider the following process and their respective data sets:

- For Inventory (Process: Out of stock items to be re-ordered) the set of fields is as follows:

  ItemCode—Item code for each item

  ReorderQty—Minimum quantity at which the item needs to be re-ordered

  RequirementDate—Date specifying when the item would be required

- For Purchase (Process: Releases purchase order and forwards order details) the set of fields is as follows:

  ItemCode—Item code for each item

  VendorCode—Vendor code specifying the vendor referred from Vendor master table

  VendorRate—Vendor Rate for the item

  QtyOrdered—Quantity ordered in units

  ShipAddress—Shipping address stream

  PODate—Purchase order date

  RequestedDeliveryDate—Delivery date requested

- For Accounts (Process: Appends to Accounts Receivable) the set of fields is as follows:

  ItemCode—Item code for each item

  VendorCode—Vendor code specifying the vendor referred from Vendor master table

AmountPayable—Amount in decimal

PayDate—Invoice date

TransDate—Date on which transaction occurred

PayByDate—Final pay date for the invoice

As you can see, the fields are related, and they should flow through the process to complete the cycle (see Figure 5.5).

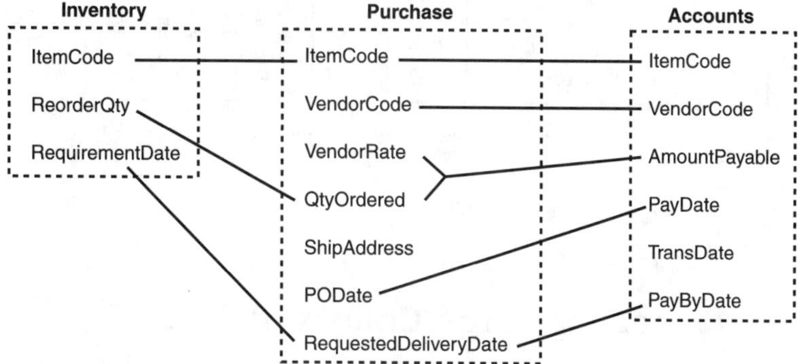

FIGURE 5.5 Database connected sample system.

The bifurcated markings in the flow means that the resultant data is because of some process on the dependent entities. For example,

```
AmountPayable = (VendorRate) * (QtyOrdered)
```

So, the process flow would be dependent on each of the stages executed in the required sequence. In a particular environment, with reference to old systems, the sequence can be maintained by specifying the job order in something called a *process queue*. Process queue is simply a queue; or rather an *array* (hash table in Java, or collection in Visual Basic) in which you assign the jobs with suitable reference tags. The reference tags would specify the job-id, which in turn specifies when the job was shown in time stamp. The dependent-on is the job-id of the job that needs to be completed before the job can be executed. In theory, this would be predecessor job-id (see Figure 5.6). By predecessor job-id, what I mean is that in a simple queue based approach, it is necessary that the processes be executed in logical sequence. For example, you do not want to debit the accounts payable register before you actually cut the check. Hence, the sequence should be that you first cut the check and then specify the entry in accounts as debit or payables. Similarly, it is necessary to execute the jobs not only with a reference to their position in the queue, but also depending on whether their predecessor or the required jobs to be executed before this one are executed. Most widely used queues are the MQ Series in IBM mainframes.

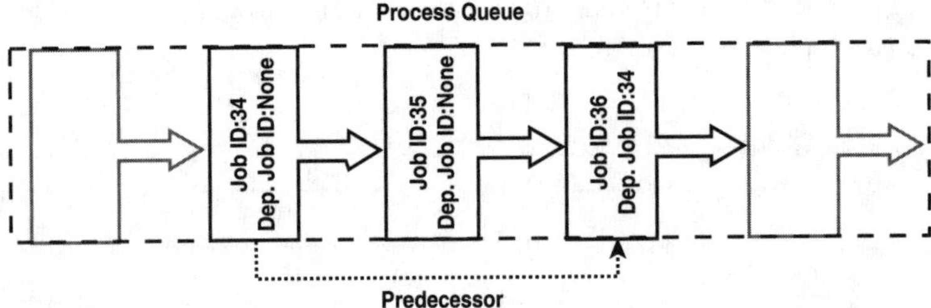

FIGURE 5.6 Process queue schematic.

Queuing—Processing Large Chunks of Data

As we arrive at the important concept of queuing, I will explain briefly how this concept could help in architecting distributed and large-scale systems.

In a system having *n* number of modules, there would (almost always) be interdependency. Also, the large systems would have distributed control centers (or servers executing the code on separate systems), where the Central Queue Manager would route the jobs to a respective processing machine. Sounds good, doesn't it? Quite interestingly, many high-end distributed systems existing today follow and use these simple concepts.

So, you have a Central Queue Manager that interprets a job in the queue and accordingly redirects it to a suitable computer (over the network) for processing. A concept of Response Queue holds the return responses from the jobs, if there are any.

With the advancement in technology, we could arrive at a very simplistic, but important architecture (see Figure 5.7). The jobs in this case would be viewed as messages or message packets. They represent the tasks to be performed and carry any data to be provided to perform the task. And the choice of representation for this message packet is XML.

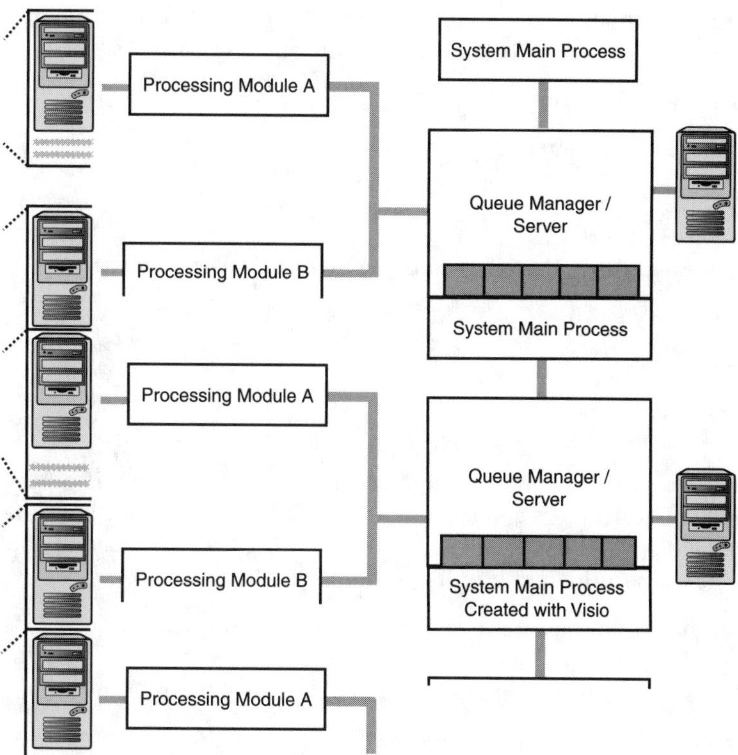

FIGURE 5.7 Queue-based distributed processing schematic.

The simple architecture relies entirely on a Central Queue Manager, which monitors and controls the message routing. The various modules—such as A, B, and N—would place their processing result request on the queue as directed by the main process. The queue manager would decode the message and accordingly compose a message to be redirected toward the respective module.

Various message formats can be derived for the purpose:

- Packet format for placing the job in queue
- Packet for receiving the job and processing the request from the queue
- Packet for placing the job return data to the queue

We can easily derive the message packet formats as follows.

For a message packet definition, note that certain information has to be present always in the packet and would be the same for most of the system. We would classify this information as <MessageHeader>. A message header would usually have the following information fixed in most of the application types:

- Packet Date and Time
- Message From reference
- Message To reference

Additional examples of data that could be included are as follows:

- Message Type
- Security Key
- User ID

Note that Message To/From references could be hostnames or an IP address as used here. (You will learn more about these terms in the following sections.) In this example, message packets are given in the following listings. I have dropped some aspects such as security and user ID for simplicity.

A message packet for placing the job in the queue is shown in Listing 5.3.

LISTING 5.3 Message Packet Example for Placing the Job in a Queue

```
<?xml version="1.0"?>
<!-- message for placing the job in the queue -->
<MessagePacket>
    <MessageHeader>
    <MessageDate>01012001</MessageDate>
    <MessageFrom>192.168.168.10</MessageFrom>
    <MessageTo>192.168.168.7</MessageTo>
    <MessageTime>12:02:22</MessageTime>
    <MessageType>JOBDEFINITION</MessageType>
</MessageHeader>
    <MessageDetails>
        <JobType>PROCESSREQUEST</JobType>
        <JobDetails>
            <ExecuteType>PROCEDURE</ExecuteType>
            <ExecuteName>GETVENDORS</ExecuteName>
            <ParametersData>
                <ParamName>ProductCode</ParamName>
                <ParamValue>SADF1234</ParamValue>
            </ParametersData>
        </JobDetails>
</MessageDetails>
</MessagePacket>
```

A message packet for receiving the job in the queue is shown in Listing 5.4.

LISTING 5.4 Message Packet Example for Receiving the Job in a Queue

```
<?xml version="1.0"?>
<!-- message for receiving the job from the queue -->
<MessagePacket>
    <MessageHeader>
    <MessageDate>01012001</MessageDate>
    <MessageFrom>192.168.168.10</MessageFrom>
    <MessageTo>192.168.168.7</MessageTo>
    <MessageTime>12:02:22</MessageTime>
    <MessageType>JOBPERFORMREQUEST</MessageType>
</MessageHeader>
    <MessageDetails>
        <JobType>PROCESSREQUEST</JobType>
        <JobDetails>
            <ExecuteType>PROCEDURE</ExecuteType>
            <ExecuteName>GETVENDORS</ExecuteName>
            <ParametersData>
                <ParamName>ProductCode</ParamName>
                <ParamValue>SADF1234</ParamValue>
            </ParametersData>
        </JobDetails>
</MessageDetails>
</MessagePacket>
```

This message looks similar to the previous one, except that the `<MessageType>` has changed.

A message packet for placing the job return data in the queue is shown in Listing 5.5

LISTING 5.5 Message Packet with Example Returned Data from a Method

```
<?xml version="1.0"?>
<!-- message for placing the job return data in the queue -->
<MessagePacket>
    <MessageHeader>
    <MessageDate>01012001</MessageDate>
    <MessageFrom>192.168.168.10</MessageFrom>
    <MessageTo>192.168.168.7</MessageTo>
```

LISTING 5.5 Continued

```
    <MessageTime>12:02:22</MessageTime>
    <MessageType>JOBRETURNREQUEST</MessageType>
</MessageHeader>
    <MessageDetails>
        <JobType>PROCESSRETURN</JobType>
        <JobDetails>
            <ExecuteType>PROCEDURE</ExecuteType>
            <ExecuteName>GETVENDORS</ExecuteName>
            <ResultSet>
                <FieldName>VendorCode</FieldName>
                <FieldValue>VEND1234</FieldValue>
                <FieldName>VendorName</FieldName>
                <FieldValue>XYZ Corporation</FieldValue>
            </ResultSet>
        </JobDetails>
</MessageDetails>
</MessagePacket>
```

Note in the preceding packet that the only change is in `<MessageType>`, and `<Job.Details>` has changed to represent a resultset.

The beauty of extendibility in terms of XML is that you can have separate namespace resources and parse rules predefined in the parser engine for all possible occurrences. In this case, the parsing logic needs to interpret the `<JobDetails>` tag depending on the `<MessageType>` or `<ExecuteType>` tag values.

Extending Using Interfaces

Another variation of incorporating extendibility in the system is to use interfaces. Using an interface is not new for CORBA users. CORBA uses an interface language to derive objects that are used for client and server end interactions. The terminology used is stub and skeletons. The *stub* is a client-side version of the *skeleton*, which is the server-side implementation. They are also referred to as *proxies* for client and server. The client needs only the stub to reside on its end. The client could talk to the stub, which acts as a proxy for the server-side skeleton. The beauty of the system is that the client calls the object methods as if it were locally residing on the same system and the actual object is executing on some remote machine located on network. Another such service, with slight variation, is the *Remote Method Invocation (RMI)* for Java. RMI uses the same principle of stubs and skeletons. The concept of the naming service is used in the context of a CORBA and RMI setup. The naming service is something similar to our central queue manager as shown previously, which redirects the request to a suitable skeleton on the network.

Microsoft has DCOM in place for distributed COM objects, and has extended its framework to COM+ environments recently. COM stands for Component Object Model, a Microsoft invented and provided extension. It allows using a single component in different Windows based languages. DCOM is an extension of COM and stands for Distributed COM. It provides the ability to interact with the COM components over a network—that is remotely. Although not platform neutral, these system approaches could be your choice if you look for distributed support, which would be platform and language dependent.

We could still term the usage type as interfaces. By using the preceding approaches, we merely extend this interface over the network.

A typical schematic of an interface-based system is shown in Figure 5.8. All processes or modules have their skeletons loaded on their end, and the stubs can reside on client machines. (I am continually specifying that a divided system could be a process or a module so that no confusion is held at any point in time.) A third-party application can use this interface to tap data from the process. From a simplistic view, in the world of design based on interfaces, the only key is to make all those methods/members public, which would possibly be used by third-party applications.

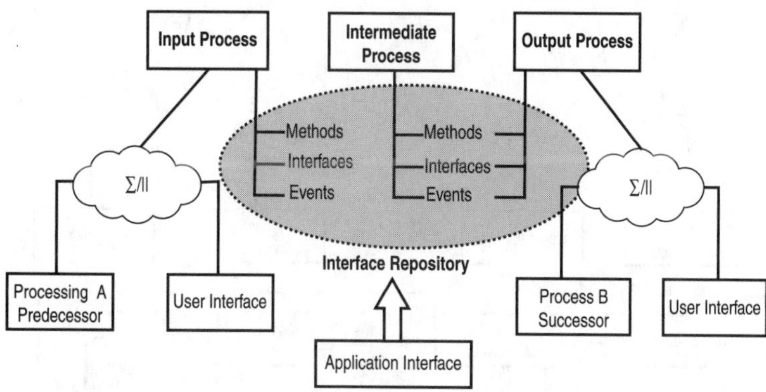

FIGURE 5.8 System architecture—extendibility using interfaces.

The system could create an interface repository, which would have all the skeletons loaded in a pool and referenced in naming service. The clients can access the interfaces by simply referring to the stubs on their end and exchanging the data, thereby allowing for system extendibility. I will cover the principle of connection pooling later in this chapter. The term *naming service* is the central server that keeps the various services or stubs available for use on the network as a database. Any client who wants to use the service (rather, the proxy at the client end) would use the service to locate the actual server where the component is located and hence use it.

Extending Using Generic Query Engine

Finally, let's look at a query engine approach for designing a highly scalable system. The concept of query engine oriented design is not new, and you could relate them with systems as old as mainframe or Unix based systems. But, the concept of having a centrally located service to serve the clients makes it easier to add more modules in the system and provide extendibility.

The schematic approach is shown in Figure 5.9. The basic modules of the system remain the same, except that they use the central query engine to process all their requests. The actual tier objects are isolated from the system modules.

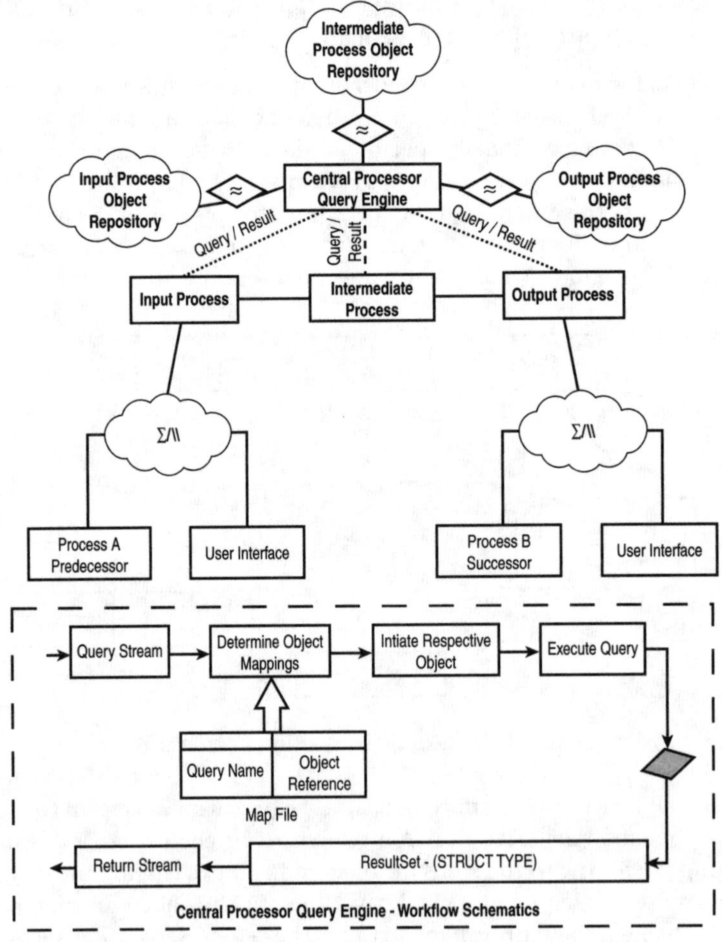

FIGURE 5.9 System architecture—extendibility using a generic query engine (central processor) approach.

The entire logic can reside on either the same or different systems on the network and has suitable interfaces for interacting with the central processor (or *query engine*). The term *central processor* is suitable for query engine because it works similar to a CPU in controller systems. All the methods residing in the blocks of the main system are dummy methods, which means methods with no functional code. The dummy methods pass the method calls with parameters to the query engine, which parses the calls and accordingly interacts with the actual objects.

The database approach given at the start of this section followed with a queue manager approach, as you could see, can be easily reworked into the central query engine type of architecture. Consider for example the queue manager approach; the Central Queue Manager can process the query results by posting the request central query engine. Further, the singular queue concept could be extended to a networked queue, where a number of queues exist on the network and there is one single master or central queue keeping into account and synchronizing all of them. Again, the Central Processor architecture could be used to feed the jobs from the queue and post the responses on the Response Queue.

The query engine approach is flexible in numerous ways for the following reasons:

- Objects are isolated from actual modules and hence can be easily upgraded and changed.
- Pre-existing objects or systems could be plugged in (with limited modifications including middle-tier, as talked about in Chapter 6, "Open-Ended Web Systems: Providing Ease of Extendibility").
- The entire system could be made truly distributed by incorporating a definite framework (as described in the next section).
- Repositories can be *pooled* and hence save resources.
- Varied systems residing on a large network or the Internet could take part in the process, which includes systems using different operating systems.
- The system could be easily modified to include fallback support and load sharing, which means that the current processor jobs can be relocated on a different set of processor, depending on the load. The queue could specify the current jobs pending and hence provide the job sharing feedback.
- Using generic protocol for intra and inter communications, such as XML, could make the system truly distributed.

Although not all the advantages are listed here, they cover major advantages, which are required for creating flexible systems.

Because the actual process is isolated from the object taking part in the workflow, the system could easily extend to incorporate other systems. Imagine that you need to provide an additional process to be included in the workflow. Using the query engine, this could be easy and could be matter of setting some preset files. Let's see how.

Using the previous Inventory, Purchase, and Accounts modules example, assume that the government has introduced a new regulation affecting the tax calculations on the goods purchased. For the system to automatically append an entry in accounts receivable after generating a purchase order, it must be able to calculate tax very accurately.

Imagine that your code is deployed and there will be havoc if you shut down the system. So you need to upgrade a running system. By running system, what I mean is that the system cannot be shut down and restarted because the process might be mission critical. However, you still want the users using the component to be plugged out—not to use it. Hence, you effectively need to replace the component while other users are using the system.

The accounts module would have a method call that resembles the following:

```
GetTotalTaxes(ItemCode, SourceCode, DestinationCode, ItemCost, ItemQty,
➥ DiscountPercentage, ShipDate)
```

Note that *Source* and *Destination* refer to zones or geographical locations for the product movement.

This call would be dispatched to the query engine using XML message protocol as in previous sections.

The query engine would probably have a look-up chart. The look-up chart would be an XML stream that specifies what method is mapped to which object. A sample format of such an `Method::Object` mapping file would be as shown in Listing 5.6.

LISTING 5.6 Sample `Method::Object` Mapping File

```
<?xml version="1.0"?>
<!-- Method::Object Reference file-->
<MethodObjectMap>
    <MapRecord>
        <Methodname>GetTotalTaxes</Methodname>
        <ObjectReference>objTaxCalculator</ObjectReference>
        <LocationDetails>
            <PrimaryLocation>
                <ServerName>192.168.168.7</ServerName>
            </PrimaryLocation>
```

LISTING 5.6 Continued

```
        <SecondarLocation>
            <ServerName>192.168.168.70</ServerName>
        </SecondarLocation>
    </LocationDetails>
    <ChainInterface>addTaxPerGovtChanges</ChainInterface>
  </MapRecord>
</MethodObjectMap>
```

The query engine would refer to the preceding stream to arrive at the object mapped to the method in question. Note that the preceding stream of XML is written with `<Methodname>` as the base element. The query engine also gets the object location and chaining information from the file. For all major developers out there, *chaining* refers to sequencing the events or processes. Most recently we chained servlets. In the example, the chaining tag specifies whether the query engine, once it receives the returned value or stream from the object, passes the returned stream back to the object as-is or it has to be processed with the dependent object.

In the previous sample map snapshot, I have included one `<ChainInterface>` element. This element refers to a method. The query engine in this case would perform the following steps to process the example in Listing 5.6:

1. The engine would refer to the map file and invoke the particular object on a specified primary location.
2. If unsuccessful, it would try to invoke the object from a secondary location.
3. After it receives a response back from the object, it would refer to the map file for the `<ChainInterface>` element.
4. If any such element exists, it would refer to the stream and get the object mapped to this chain method.
5. It would follow the first two steps to invoke the object and pass it the returned value by the first method.
6. After it receives the response back from the chain reference object, it will refer to the map file again for more `<ChainInterface>` elements.
7. If there are more, it would sequentially repeat the preceding process.
8. Finally, when it's done, it will return the response back to the module or accounts block.

This is one of the several ways in which you can extend your query engine architecture. Because of the map file, it's easy to include new objects on modules.

One major advantage in the central query engine system is it facilitates (and supports) true monitoring. Every transaction in the system will take place through the engine. Further, you could introduce keywords for each module so that you know which modules made the call at what time, and hence develop a robust control monitoring utility.

Ideas are extendable. One other use of such a system is that you can introduce tracking framework. Tracking is a process by which the system logs all actions—including transactions, method calls, major database calls, and many more. Tracking serves the useful purpose of introducing a concept of security and auditing in the system.

For example, in a CSR system for a financial company, tracking is very important. As in the event of any malicious usage of the system, the system administrator could audit the system. He could determine the exact path of the system usage by various CSR members and discover the culprit.

Keeping an End Open

To provide an open-end, you have to allow for enough open nodes, as in the banking system, which allows third-party systems to easily plug-in to the architecture and seamlessly integrate with it. Let's review the same system from the open-end perspective. For the system to be open-ended, you have to make sure that the third-party systems are able to interact freely. We can provide a generic interface layer for accommodating this. The purpose of this interface would be to accept invocation calls from other systems and accordingly trigger suitable methods within the system to get the required data.

There is one another important consideration to make—to provide the capability of a system being switched to open-ended, which means what if you deploy the modules within the system over a network and distribute them? This is the intra-system communication. Let's discuss the strategy for the communication layer, which would make the system more flexible and generic.

Usually, in systems design methodologies, we insist on dividing the functionality in terms of modules or small blocks. We try to develop these blocks as separate individual systems and then worry about integrating it with other modules and perform integrated testing. At the module level, you would use object-oriented design models to design and code; including specific approach techniques such as UML.

But, how do you arrive at these minor blocks or modules in the first place? As you have seen from the generic system schematic in the previous section, a system can essentially have three functional blocks—the exact representation of input and output blocks might vary, but the stages and workflow is the same. This is from a very high-level perspective. Theoretically, systems can be divided into n number of modules, but we need to stop at some point of time when we are dividing it. How and where do we stop? This can depend on several factors—for a commercial project manager, the stop sign would appear as soon as he sees that the division has gone far enough that he could relate modules to existing team groupings. For some other managers, it would be when further division would essentially mean breaking the system in terms of the functionality it's going to perform. Many previous books have probably covered various approaches.

But the truth is, somewhere down the line you stop, and at that point of time, you have modules. Essentially, this division of systems into modules would be in the middle-tier because of the availability of previous libraries or code.

For all applications, dealing in a real-world database is the major aspect. And it is always preferred to have one Data Manager module within the system. This way, from our principles of designing entire system in terms of isolated modules, we could make sure that sudden changes in data access policies won't affect the system as a whole.

Putting the system together would essentially mean dealing with module level interfaces. An output interface of a module would invoke the input interface of the next module and so on. Here is where intra-modular or intra-process communication comes up. Let's take a closer look at this aspect.

Consider the simple banking system, which has following modules:

- User Interface and Data Validation
- Data Manager
- Account Services
- Output Interface and Reporting

The Account Services module would essentially interact with the Data Manager and User and Output interfaces, and hence is kind of a core module for this system.

The User Interface would worry about interactions with the user. The user enters account number and then clicks some menu option titled Get Transaction History. This invokes a method in Account Services, which would then go to the Data Manager and get the data back. The data would be formatted and returned back to the User Interface through the Output Interface. This is a typical process flow for a banking system exhibiting an account inquiry.

Consider the intercommunication links involved:

- Link between User Interface and Account Services
- Link between Account Services and Data Manager
- Link between Account Services and Output Interface

How can you make sure that the inquiry for accounts can be made even through the third-party interface? If you realize that, we are arriving at our previous scenario. Hence, when we say that a third-party system wants to get transaction data set from our system, it's the same as visualizing that a User Interface is requesting that data. And, the Output Interface is now not the User End Interface, but is rather another system. Note that the transaction reference in the previous discussion is related to a financial or business transaction and not the database transaction.

Developing Open-end Systems with Extendibility

So, from a system extendibility and open-ended perspective, you need to make sure that you are able to tap data between the first and last interactions in the preceding list.

Imagine for a moment that the intra-process communication is carried out using some generic protocol, rather than direct code based linkages. This means that the entire request made from one module to another has a definite *set* and *get* pattern. Wouldn't it make things much easier? Now you can directly have this interface exposed off the methods to a third party by using standard protocol calling instead of referring to tedious code calls. Further, the most important aspect of this system is that it can be isolated from the third party.

The third-party systems, instead of dealing with invoking the objects and getting the return data, now use a middle-tier or interface layer to talk to your system. They would never know the results of how your system translates their message calls. Isn't that nice? So, you also get some privacy and security. What this means is that the interface methods could be generic process methods. For example, all input interfacing methods could be called `inputInterface()` and output interfacing methods could be `outputInterface()`. So all the modules would have these methods to accept and process input. The actual method names would not be exposed to the external module or code at all.

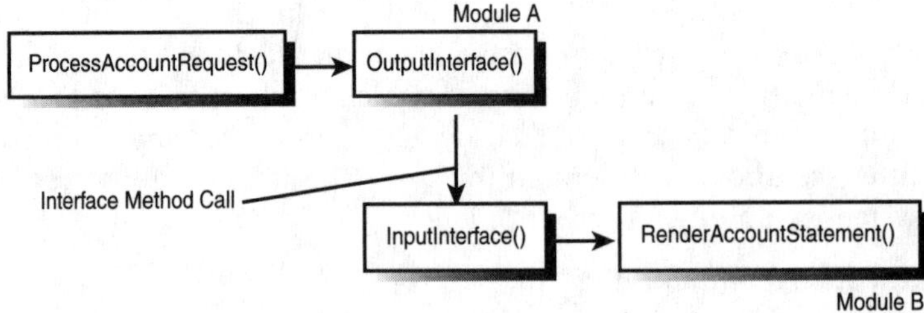

FIGURE 5.10 Module wise interface schematic—`OutputInterface()` of module A calls `InputInterface()` of module B.

This intra-process protocol would be XML. The XML stream would now be serving the intra-process link as command packets or message packets.

This approach simplifies the system extensibility and usage aspect, but now the modules need to be more than dumb (or non-intelligent) code. They need to decode and understand the message and process the request accordingly. We can build some utility module in our system offering XML Services, which will provide XML coding and decoding services to internal system.

Also, we need to decide the message packet formats; both for set and get patterns in the system.

A sample message packet XML stream for a get pattern is shown in Listing 5.7.

LISTING 5.7 Sample Message Packet for Get

```
<?xml version="1.0"?>
<!---intra-communication message packet xml stream -->
<message>
    <senddate>0101200</senddate>
    <sendtime>12:00:02</sendtime>
    <messagetype>QUERY</messagetype>
    <messagetypedescriptor>TRANSACTION DETAILS FOR A/C#NNAA-010101
    ➥</messagetypedescriptor>
    <messagedetails>
        <detailstype>PARAMS</detailstype>
        <parameters>
            <paramname>lUserID</paramname>
            <paramvalue>NNAA-010101</paramvalue>
            <paramname>lUPassword</paramname>
            <paramvalue>NITA123</paramvalue>
            <paramname>lUSecurityKey</paramname>
            <paramvalue>AQWERFT91829</paramvalue>
            <paramname>dtFromDate</paramname>
            <paramvalue>01012000</paramvalue>
            <paramname>dtToDate</paramname>
            <paramvalue>03012000</paramvalue>
        </parameters>
    </messagedetails>
</message>
```

A sample message packet XML stream for a set pattern is shown in Listing 5.8.

LISTING 5.8 Sample Message Packet for Set

```
<?xml version="1.0"?>
<!--intra-communication message packet xml stream -->
<message>
    <senddate>0101200</senddate>
    <sendtime>12:00:02</sendtime>
    <messagetype>RESULT</messagetype>
    <messagetypedescriptor>TRANSACTION DETIALS FOR A/C#NNAA-010101
    ➥</messagetypedescriptor>
    <messagedetails>
        <detailstype>RESULTSET</detailstype>
        <resultset>
            <record>
                <fieldname>TransDate</fieldname>
                <fieldvalue>01012000</fieldvalue>
                <fieldname>TransType</fieldname>
                <fieldvalue>WITHDRAW</fieldvalue>
                <fieldname>Amount</fieldname>
                <fieldvalue>123.65</fieldvalue>
            </record>
        </resultset>
    </messagedetails>
</message>
```

Certain points to be noted about the approach are as follows:

- The `<detailtype>` specifies what is contained in the `<messagedetails>` tag. The value in this tag would always be `PARAMS` for method calls, and for the return packet it can be either `VALUE` or `RESULTSET`.
- The `<parameters>` tag holds the parameter name/value pairs.
- The `<resultset>` tag holds the record tag.
- Each `<record>` is further broken into name/value pairs.

The `<resultset>` and `<parameters>` tags in preceding sample packets are a bit over-simplified, but would do in most practical cases. In the real world, you can have even field data type specified as a tag (as in XML-RPC, for example), which would make the data more self descriptive. The key to ideal packet design is to make it as self descriptive as possible.

After reviewing the message packet approach, the next thing that comes to mind is the use of utility classes as specified previously. Every module has to receive a message packet, parse it, and accordingly invoke a suitable method within its interface. The utility module, which would extend throughout the system and be available to the entire system, would help all these modules to parse the data and return them in some sort of hash table (in terms of Java) or collections (in terms of Visual Basic). A real-world case study application highlighting the use of this concept is listed in Chapter 11, "Extending Existing Close-Ended Systems."

Take a look at the various methods you could use for passing these message packets within the modules. One simplistic approach would be to incorporate generic methods such as `GetMessageStreamPacket()` and `SetMessageStreamPacket()` so that every module in the system would have support for these methods. Rather, an easy suggestion and cleaner way to do this, in Java, would be to have an interface of type `MessagePacket` with the preceding methods that let the system modules or classes implement it (see Figure 5.11).

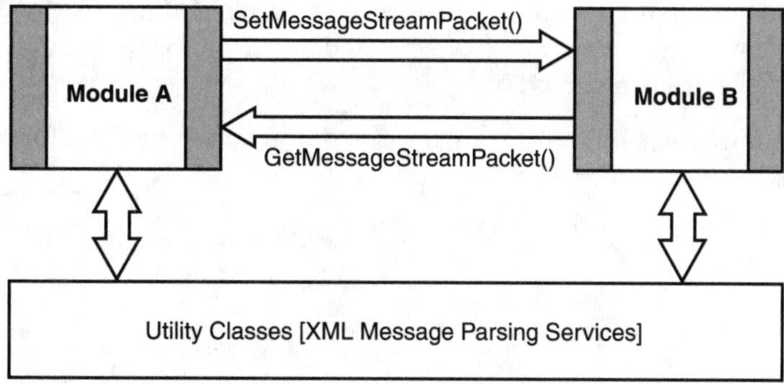

FIGURE 5.11 Message Packet based system schematic.

Although the preceding approach can be implemented easily, it has certain limitations. Imagine that the system modules demand more scalability, or they need to be truly distributed. This would essentially mean using, say, a separate server for each module or block and hence greatly share the load between systems. Another reason for doing this could be that one of the modules is secured and deals with crucial legacy data, and hence has to be developed and deployed on specific co-located servers at a different location. This would lead to deploying your modules on separate machines as separate applications and integrated through some connectivity (interface) layer.

The concept of load balancing should not be considered the same as distributed processing. In load balancing, the single or same system is deployed completely on different systems. In case of distributed processing, the various system modules (subcomponents or sub-systems) are deployed over different systems (computers).

Another interconnection problem is having a common reservoir for processing the requests. Imagine where you would locate generic stuff such as utility classes in distributed environment. This issue is dealt in greater detail in Chapter 7, "Framework-Based Systems," where you will learn how to devise the most competing models and architectures for a system.

Considering the cost associated with connectivity approaches and the complexity, the best approach is to use Web-based services. We will take a look at Web-based systems and how they could be utilized for cost-effective and better connectivity solutions.

Summary

Although open-ended systems are the most flexible way to architect various systems, we need some practical mode of connecting them. This means using the most common connectivity mechanism to effectively design and deploy the system. The Web can provide such a network, which could be used effectively and is also the most available mechanism today.

Chapter 6 introduces basic Web principles and how to use the Web for connecting distributed systems.

6

Open-Ended Web Systems: Providing Ease of Extendibility

IN THIS CHAPTER

- Overview
- Web Server Engine: Providing Ease of Extendibility
- Providing Flexibility and Scalability

Oh, what a tangled web we weave when first we practice to believe.

—Laurence J. Peter

Overview

The Web might be today's most widely-used technology, primarily as a connectivity mechanism. Over the past few years, the Web has evolved through various phases and is a mature technology.

Regarding distributed computing, the main problem of the past was that of interconnectivity. Connecting remote systems was a costly and tedious job until recently. Currently, the Web provides an easy and cost-effective way for distributed computing. Today, the developer can utilize advancements in this technology for creating fully-distributed systems.

Web Server Engine: Providing Ease of Extendibility

In recent years nothing has emphasized the way that systems should be designed more than the Web. The advent of the Internet has introduced us to the best-available network for constructing massive distributed systems around the globe.

Users employed traditional WANs for intra-office and network connections, and these WANs were effective, but costly. Small businesses could not afford these WAN connections and stayed with their small, internal networks. Slowly, the networked world we live in changed, and we are now instantly communicating with computers separated by huge distances. Isn't this quite remarkable?

Still, the perfect use of the available network and cost-effectiveness has yet to be discovered and tailored. We do not have enough systems in place to use the available network bandwidth to the fullest extent.

Web Server: General Principles

Web servers are ideal resources, and one could term them as distributed, computing servers. Let's talk about some basic practical terms used in Web server world.

Each Web server must have an *IP (Internet Protocol)* address with which it can be located on the global Internet or a *local area network (LAN)*. This is true for any machine on a TCP/IP network. The IP helps to identify a system on a TCP/IP network, and the typical protocol used for information transfer via the Web is *HTTP (Hypertext Transfer Protocol)*.

Consider a simple network server in an office, serving 10 users. Also assume that the network is TCP/IP, Windows NT, Windows 2000, or Windows XP. Assume that the name of the server machine is XYZ and IP is `192.168.168.1`. You install Web server software like Microsoft IIS (Internet Information Server) or PWS (Personal Web Server) on the server machine. This service allows network users to browse the Web site's content on XYZ, and typically you would access this by entering `http://XYZ` or `http://192.168.168.1`. Note that the name appearing after `http://` is either the domain name or the IP of the server instance. The default Web server document, or *page*, is downloaded and displayed by your browser. Usually, the document name is `default.htm`, `default.html`, or `default.asp` for Microsoft-based Web servers; index.html for Unix or Linux Web servers; and `index.jsp` for Java-enabled Web servers. You might set the default page to any filename by defining it accordingly in the Web server configuration.

The default port for a Web server is 80. If you enter `http://XYZ:80`, the default page should be displayed. This string is called a *URL (uniform resource locator)* by techies or *Web address* by other users. This address is limited to your internal network and would not be available outside that network. If you go to your home and connect to the Internet through dial-up or broadband, the same URL will not be reachable and will produce some error like "Page cannot be found." You are able to browse the Web site from within its local network: In other words, it is your *intranet* site. Hence, the IP is accessible and *resolvable* only on the private network and is not accessible from the outside. For the IP to be accessible from outside the intranet, it has to be on a publicly accessible network.

How can it be made publicly accessible? For a Web address to be available on the Internet, it needs a *static* or fixed IP. A static IP is constructed like private IP used internally, but the IP range is controlled by a standards organization like InterNIC (Internet Network Information Center) that maintains a database or registry of domains and IPs. This organization issues IP addresses and correlates them to a name, usually starting with *www*, called a *domain name*. If a domain name is *registered* and is correlated with an IP via DNS (domain name service), the Web server at that IP is accessible from the global Internet. Anyone around the world can view the site if the domain name is entered in a browser.

Another technology to examine is *sockets*. A socket is a simple extension of addressing or referencing. Any machine using network packets can employ sockets. We will treat sockets from a TCP/IP perspective, which means that on any network a socket can be opened at a specific port number. In this sense, a socket refers to a port number opened on the system.

Consider a Web browser pointing to a URL. The browser is accessing data located at an IP, which might be correlated to a URL, and is accessing the default port 80. Hence, if a networked machine has an IP defined, a port on the machine can be opened and used for the transfer of data over the network.

Sockets can be opened with suitable port numbers assigned to them and "channels" through which data flows. As shown previously in the query engine example, the engine might use sockets to communicate with the interface layer residing on a storage server and invoke a suitable object. As shown in Figure 6.1, the query engine communicates with the storage-side gateway interface over sockets using ports. The communication layer uses a specific port, which the query engine uses to connect to and parse the message packet. After parsing the packet, the layer would invoke the object and its method accordingly. This gateway would also be responsible for sending the data back to the query engine.

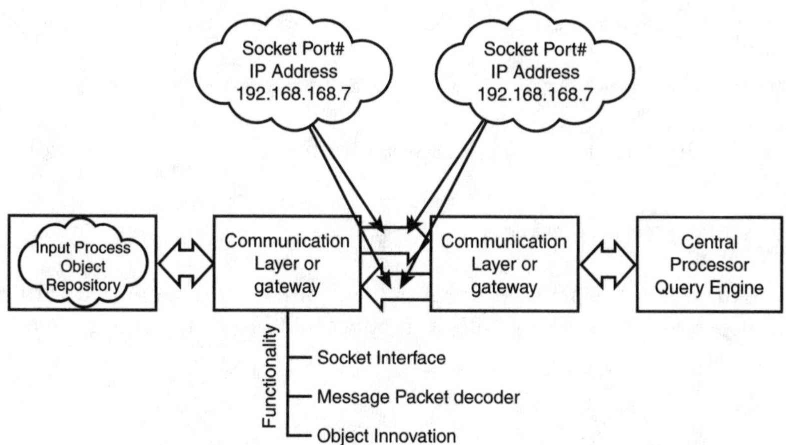

FIGURE 6.1 Socket-based implementation for Query Engine schematic.

Web services are a flexible option for extending a network: No competing resource offers the same flexibility and ease of use. Further, setting up and utilizing Web services is cost effective. Even a small business can afford to have a Web server in service and can connect to partner servers over the Internet. It's not just cost, but usage that is important. A large corporation that could set up a WAN or private network could also set up a Web server for its system interactions.

Web services have improved tremendously. They are often combined with application servers to provide services not only to view Web pages, but also to allow sophisticated applications to run. Because of their accessibility, Web servers are proven the best gateways for distributed computing. In the next section, I'll examine some examples of Web services.

Web Servers as Interfacing Gateways

How can a Web server be used to extend a system? Often, the developer uses Web services to extend a legacy system on a corporate network. To better understand this, consider the data transfer mechanism used on the Web. There are two mechanisms of data transfer on the Web:

- `POST` method—Transfers data from client to server, bundling data into the request and not the URL.
- `GET` method—Includes the data string in the URL, is less secure, and is limited by the number of characters allowed in a URL.

Any Web programmer is familiar with these methods because they define the way data would is transferred to the server. This method is found in the typical `<form>` tag, shown as follows:

```
<form name="submission" action="storedata.jsp" method="POST">

<form name="submission" action="storedata.jsp" method="GET">
```

Assume that this form has an *input* text box for the user to enter an e-mail address, as shown here:

```
<input type="text" name="email">
```

Examine the difference between these methods. If a form is submitted with `POST` as the method type, the resulting URL, as it appears in browser, would be `http://localhost/Storedata.jsp`.

Note that the URL is the one specified in the form's *action* attribute. There is no data in this URL. `POST` is secured and is capable of returning data without display.

If the form is used with the *method* type specified as `GET`, the resultant URL would be

```
http://localhost/Storedata.jsp?email=nitabarve@hotmail.com
```

The form fields appear after the `?` symbol as a name/value pair. That displays field values in the URL and is why this method is not secure.

Why use `GET` methods at all? Use depends on the purpose and application. Consider a simple search example: Assume that you have a Web site with a search feature. The user can search by keywords as shown in the following:

```
...
<form name="search" method="POST" action="searchmysite.jsp">
    <input type="text" size="10" name="keyword">
    <input type="submit" value="Go">
</form>
...
```

With the method type specified as `POST`, the user enters a keyword and views the results page (`searchmysite.jsp`). The user clicks the Favorites option in the browser interface and saves the resulting link. Because of the `POST` method type, if the user goes to the saved address, there will probably be no output or an error will be displayed. The `searchmysite.jsp` page is expecting the search keyword via `POST`, and entering `searchmysite.jsp` doesn't include this data.

If the `GET` method is used, the resulting URL is appended with the keyword. For example, `searchmysite.jsp?keyword=XML` would be a typical URL passed to the server.

The keyword entered by the user, as seen in the URL, is `XML`. Assume that the user elects to save the link as a Favorite. Later, when the user goes to the same URL as saved in Favorites, the expected result is displayed.

Distributed computing requires methods like these for transferring data from one application to another. Refer to Figure 6.2, which specifies a schematic displaying the required blocks for using the Web as a communications link for distributed computing.

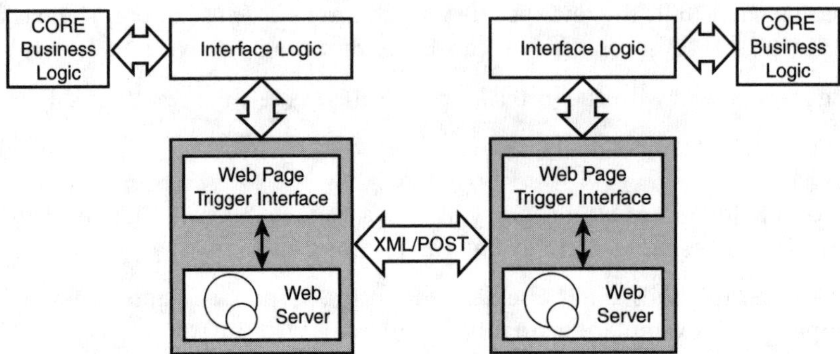

FIGURE 6.2 Schematic for using the Web as an interface for distributed computing.

Using the Web as a Transport Medium

I'll discuss the basic requirements for a system utilizing the Web for data transfer.

The core business logic includes the logic for the systems on both client and server. The interface logic is provided for making the system extensible and open-ended. The interface logic has numerous methods that expose the communication methods to third-party systems. The client interface is Web pages that handle the interaction calls from third-party systems and act as an *interface bridge* passing data between systems.

The two systems can be on different platforms and operating environments. Additionally, even Web server types can be different, with Java Web Server on one end and Internet Information Server on the other.

The `POST` mechanism allows data to be transferred between two systems and can have an embedded XML stream representing both the method calls and data. The message packet designed in a previous section might still be used here. The interface logic in the schematic might be described as similar to the interface layer in Figure 5.2. It can be functionally similar to the *gateway* block in Figure 6.1 because as the interface layer would accept the XML packet stream, decode it, invoke the appropriate method in the core business logic, and return the data.

In theory, even sockets can be used to achieve the same communication link, but a Web interface is better for these reasons:

- Sockets use a low-level mechanism and are not secure unless the data is encrypted.
- Sockets are not linked to protocols. The developer codes with an existing protocol or invents one.

- One cannot use existing applications or utilities with sockets, as sockets are at much lower level.
- Data passing through sockets can be blocked by a firewall.

The Web uses HTTP as its standard protocol. Additionally, Web services can utilize any SSL layer available and still pass through firewalls. With this protocol, it is easy to code in terms of effort required.

The only major functionality required for incorporating Web-based communication is a module, or procedure, that is capable of

- `POST`ing data to the other end, using HTTP
- Formatting and parsing an XML Packet (Message Packet / Data Packet)

The next section describes forming the communication link using a practical example.

Extending a System Using Web Services and XML

I'll show a brief example that utilizes the Web as a communications link for data exchange. The example applications are running on two different platforms and two different languages.

Consider a financial system, typically an expense management system used by a company's regional sales office. This system stores expense data for sales representatives. The regional sales office is located close to business area. The corporate headquarters is assumed to be in a different state or region. Both offices are connected via the Internet.

The sales office has an expense system developed in Java (J2EE) and uses a local database, like Oracle. Employees enter daily sales data and expenses in the system. The corporate headquarters uses a accounting system, like Peachtree, which is Windows-based software and is DDE enabled.

A weekly requirement is the transfer of expense data from sales office to headquarters and importing the data to the main accounting system. In this way, funds are allocated and checks are dispatched to the various employees.

To integrate the two systems, consider the following:

- The Sales Expense System is written in Java.
- Corporate headquarters uses the Peachtree Accounting system.
- The communication link is the public Internet.
- The sales office has a basic Web server, like Java Web Server.

A consideration on the client side, which is the corporate headquarters, is that it uses Windows-based software with which the remote system must interact. On the server side, the application is based on Sun technologies. This example uses ActiveX Documents, which was introduced with the release of Visual Basic.

It's strange that few books and articles describe the use of ActiveX Document technology. For small applications, Visual Basic might be the primary programming language, or RAD tool. ActiveX documents allow packaging to CAB files, and the controls might be downloaded to the browser. Certain limitations apply to this technology, but for our current application scope it allows coding with Visual Basic, the use of DDE to interact with third-party applications, and provides a Web browser-based interface.

An ActiveX document is created, along with a *user interface* for viewing data. What else is required? The system requires add-ons that enable this document to pull data from the sales server.

The sales server is assumed to use a Java-based application. The application has access methods, or interfaces, that might interact with the database and query the expense data. An interaction module is included for our extension to the current business logic. This module uses public interface methods of existing business-tier logic to query the data. It would essentially have a simple method like `GetExpenseData(FromDate, ToDate, SecurityKey, StatusType)`.

To accommodate future extension, the interface is defined in a flexible way by including an parameter called `StatusType`. This parameter prompts the business logic to return all expense transactions that are either unpaid (are open) or paid (are closed). `SecurityKey` would be a partial security measure to authenticate the request. It is considered partial because there would be a login authentication stage before this method, which would validate the user. This method is assumed to return an XML stream that has expense transaction data.

This module is invoked from a Web interface. This might be accomplished with a servlet or a JSP that would instantiate the module method, pass parameters, get the result, and return the data in an XML stream. In this example, this page is `QueryForExpenseData.jsp`.

Assume that this page needs parameter data to be `POST`ed on the server side. This provides some level of security, as described previously.

Now the server side is ready. The technology is decided for the client end, but communication must be added. The ActiveX document code has an additional *control* called the MSINET control (MSInet.ocx), which allows the simulation of Web references. In simulation, the control delivers the data to a URL using the `POST` or `GET` methods. The user interface accepts user login information and parameters and this control POSTs the data to the server.

The resulting schematic is as shown in Figure 6.3. The figure shows the processes involved in the communication link.

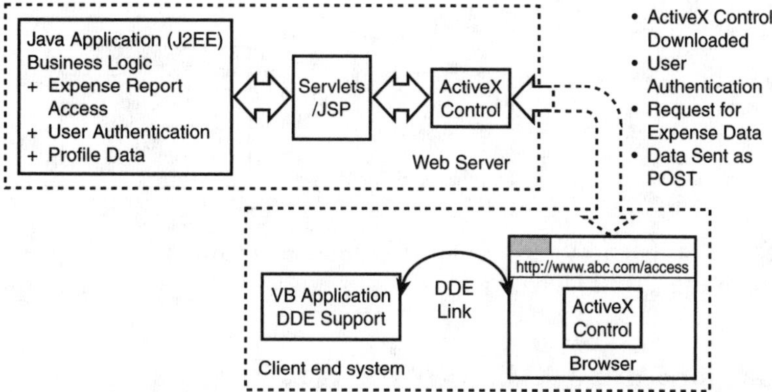

FIGURE 6.3 Using the Web as an interface for distributed computing: Approach 1 (Using ActiveX-DDE Interaction).

There can be a design variation using sockets. The resulting interface does not require a Web server at the server end (sales end) and requires a change to the way the module is triggered. Because the module needs to be triggered by a socket message, which can be a flat XML stream or ASCII string, some additional code is needed instead of the JSP. The code triggers and returns the data. This simple code is easily written using Java Sockets. The client end application can now be an installable application, like a Visual Basic application. To interact with the server using sockets, the system uses the Winsock control instead of MSInet.

DDE is now an old and rarely-used technology, but some systems still use it and it is useful to connect to those. In new systems, the corporate side accounting package might be COM enabled. This makes VB coding simpler, easier, and a bit neater. This second approach is shown in Figure 6.4.

The first approach is used to bridge online systems to corporate systems. The latter approach is also commonly used.

This simple application and extensions might prove to be powerful tools for devising and integrating large, distributed systems.

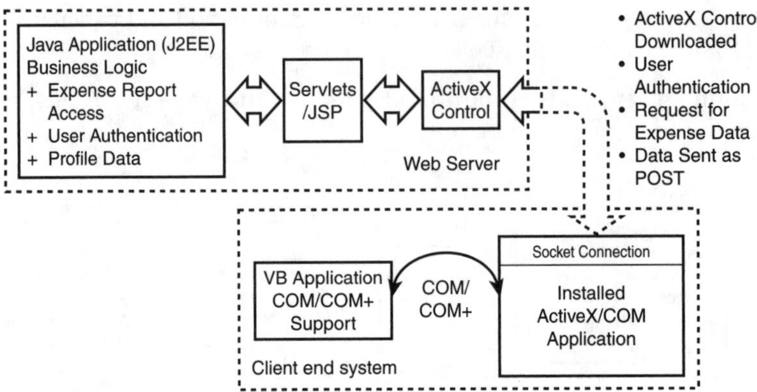

FIGURE 6.4 Using the Web as an interface for distributed computing: Approach 2 (Using Application-COM Interaction)

Transactions Using XML Over the Web

The preceding example forms many approaches for transactions using XML over the Web. Some approaches can be applied to form a realistic system. I'll explain some concepts.

The *gateway* or interface logic helps remote system interaction by receiving XML packets and invoking respective methods of the notified object. From the calling procedure's standpoint, it is invoking a method on a report object like R*emote Procedure Calls (RPC)*. RPC is a useful technique, and there is a standard XML specification for it. The current XML-RPC specification is at `http://www.xmlrpc.com/`. Again, because RPC purely uses XML over HTTP, it can pass through firewalls and is simpler than sockets or other distributed communication approaches, like COM or CORBA.

Although XML-RPC has been covered, I'll explain its importance in the current context. To perform transactions over the Web, we would often need to invoke member methods of a remote interface. The XML-RPC mechanism simplifies this to a great extent by providing a built-in mechanism to pass the method invocation call as an XML stream. A sample XML method call would look as shown in Listing 6.1.

LISTING 6.1 XML-RPC Method Call Example

```
<?xml version="1.0"?>
<methodCall>
   <methodName>InventoryFactory.UpdateInventory</methodName>
   <params>
      <param>
```

LISTING 6.1 Continued

```
        <value><i4>41</i4></value>
        <value><double>4110101</double></value>
        </param>
    </params>
  </methodCall>
```

Note that nesting suitable tags within a value tag might specify the parameter data types. In the preceding example, the `i4` data type corresponds to an integer and also corresponds to a double data type. The important point is the representation of data types in this format, which makes the data more self-describing and flexible.

This stream is similar to the mechanism we derived in previous sections. There is a slight difference, however, in the way this packet describes the method name. It specifies the destination parent name, `InventoryFactory`, which holds the member method to be called, `UpdateInventory`. This makes the representation easier and gives a bit more information about the structure of the parent type holders on the destination server. Still, with XML it's the *best practice* to support remote method invocation.

Essentially, the term *naming services*, or lookup services, is a common buzzword among remote invocation developers— CORBA uses something similar to achieve the remote method invocation, and the same with Java RMI.

SOAP is a step ahead of RPC, and you could treat it as a modified RPC specification. SOAP can be also used for creating a message-based system, and this is discussed in the section "Frameworks." Refer to Chapter 2 for a detailed discussion of these specifications.

XML for eBusiness is another concept having numerous applications for cross-bridging business systems. There are registries and repositories that hold XML governing standards in DTD and Schema formats. This generic approach helps standardize content and allows for designing and implementing free trading systems. Examples of major repositories are BizTalk.org at `http://www.bitalk.org` and OASIS at `http://www.oasis-open.org/cover`.

Oasis Open has developed a generic repository called ebXML, which facilitates trade, and it has defined the specifications for implementing the technology. The trading partners use the repository to find standard exchange formats for the business and use the formats for the exchange of data.

BizTalk holds the same promise. It has the same concept of building central repositories for different industry-wide formats. It maintains the standard DTDs and Schemas for vertical and horizontal applications, like Purchase Order and Invoice formats.

Figure 6.5 shows the generic schematic of how repositories are built and their principles of operations. These concepts apply to all standard repositories including Oasis and BizTalk. The principle of a repository is to allow various companies (members) to submit the standard schemas (XML DTDs or Schemas) to the central database, which might be referenced by another company in order to know the interchange standard. Every submission of the standard is validated, with reference to pre-defined specifications, before it can be submitted to or added to the repository. Sometimes the submitted schema might add to existing schema or document. The interfacing gateways used at the company end are then in agreement with the standards in the repository for conducting data interchange. Another advantage of having these systems in place is that software developers might use these standards to construct systems and develop products that meet a variety of business needs. This is important for companies to determine their development and integration costs and extend their businesses.

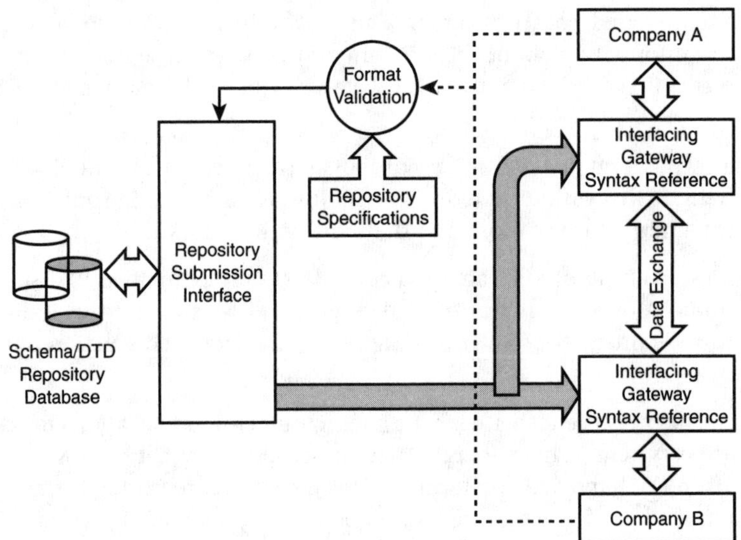

FIGURE 6.5 Principle of generic repositories.

Business To Business (B2B) e-commerce widely employs XML and relies on standard document formats for exchanging data, like entering purchase orders and supporting standard transactions. Business transactions exchange a wide variety of data: For example, in a typical procurement system, vendors require a specific format to be submitted to the central corporate system, and that is used for arriving at a price quotation.

The types of transactions occurring in business systems are quite complex and require complex interaction schemes. In all cases the actual data can be easily represented by an XML stream, which might contain all the relevant information.

The conclusion is that because of the flexibility of XML and the ease of communication over the Internet, both these technologies could provide a robust platform for distributed computing. The extensibility of systems packaging of data are the primary concerns.

Providing Flexibility and Scalability

Flexibility and scalability are major requirements to make any system open-ended and extendable. I have shown how the Web provides an easy-to-use platform to make systems scalable and how the use of XML makes them flexible.

For that matter, one could also argue that if developers were to invent a simple Flat File Protocol in ASCII, that would have done the same job. Even if that were true, the developer would have to consider the limitations and the required standardization. Many exiting mainframe systems still use flat file data structures to accommodate flexible data lengths and types.

A sample flat record would look like this:

```
STARTREC|0070|0001|040|XYZbCORPORATIONbbbbbbbbbbbbbb|NN01012001|ENDREC
```

I have used *vertical bar* (|) delimiters to make the record separation a bit clearer. The start of the record is indicated by `STARTREC` and the end of record is indicated by `ENDREC`.

The second value, `0070`, in the ASCII packet specifies the total length of the packet. After that, the value `00001` specifies the total records contained in the packet. The next value, `040`, specifies the length of one record. The data records follow this header information.

Note that the `b`, in the preceding format, indicates a blank space. As described, the simple flat file is easy to understand but requires rigorous support in what it represents. Further, it does not have any description of what record data it contains: In short, it is not self-describing. I'll show what a self-describing record would look like. Here is an example:

```
STARTREC|0103|0001|040|VENDORNAME|029|VENDORID|010|REC1|
➥XYZbCORPORATIONbbbbbbbbbbbbbb|NN01012001|ENDREC
```

I have modified the flat file to accommodate a self-describing data style. The length of each record field, `040`, is followed by the field name and field length specifications, which provide information when decoding the string. Although the refined string seems easier to decode, it still requires a flat parser and is not suitable (without a proper fixed interpretation requirement) for describing hierarchical and nested data sets.

The fact is that some legacy systems still use the preceding format. Those systems must be mapped to new systems for extensibility and portability. Ultimately, the developer needs a Data Mapper.

I'll explore this topic in detail in later sections, but the point here is that to extend a system, the developer needs to provide a suitable map interface and make it scalable.

Making the system patterns dependent can make systems very dynamic. For example, the developer could design and develop a generic XML parser class that might parse an XML file and interpret the data per a dynamic definition included in another XML file. This concept is the same as the Schema, covered in Chapter 2, "XML Overview." One important concept is dependence for parsing: Setting data values can always be done using a second set of documents used by your own parser or *styling* engine.

By providing XML as intra-communication protocol, the system can be flexible. This accommodates a high level of dynamism. Additionally, by providing supporting DTDs and Schemas, you make the parsing quite sophisticated. In a true distributed architecture, even if you locate the system modules on different machines on network, the system should still function as a single system. This is true for a system using XML as the standard protocol for intra-communication between any two modules.

Finally, the ability to provide an RPC mechanism in the system makes it extensible and scalable. The system can now support network operation and serve remote calls easily using XML and HTTP. The use of SOAP is also advisable.

Summary

The need for open-ended systems is widely recognized and important. Using an open-ended approach allows the creation of most generic approaches and models.

The next chapter introduces some basic models used to design most generic systems. This approach is essential for application modeling and techniques and serves as an important stepping stone in distributed system design.

7 Framework Based Systems

IN THIS CHAPTER

There ain't no rules around here! We're trying to accomplish something!

—Thomas A. Edison

Overview

This chapter introduces you to a generic system's formation principle. Sound complicated? Actually, it isn't that complicated. Many system architectures are in use and more are designed every day.

But I will focus on designing the most generic model for general use. This chapter walks through the evolution and arrival of such a model. It also introduces you to a useful distributed systems design concept of frameworks.

Framework Based Systems

Every system needs to have a model that describes how the architecture would be and how it can accommodate the various modules or functionalities. We, in general, need a framework.

Framework is a predefined design model that can suit diverse functional needs. In the truest sense, an ideal framework has to be generic, and it should be possible to mold it into any application quickly. The concept of framework is not new, although the word itself and the orientation are. Microprocessors can be thought of as generic frameworks because you can mold them into a desired system such as a PC using peripherals and interface chips. We also had the concept of generic microprocessors in our college days, which were used to develop the concept of the CPU.

Above all, framework will help us to better arrive at a solid system architecture that could be used to devise a full-blown application. It is important to understand the framework models as they play a central and very important role while devising a distributed system.

Frameworks—Overview

Any framework model could lead to system architecture, or rather could evolve into system architecture. But the reverse might not be true—not all systems designed and developed support a solid framework.

Consider a typical application that is used to print invoices, such as a typical accounting system. Imagine that you require the additional plug-in capability of feeding the vendor list into this system from another system, and the product codes are coming from the production system. Unless the application defines connectivity interface, you cannot include or plug in these modules. The connectivity interface might again have different needs: For example, it might require the data to be read from a third-party location that processes and fed it into the current system, or it might require data mapping to occur for a reliable data transfer. It totally depends on how the data comes out from, say, the vendor system and what is its relevance to our system. We might have to discard some data and filter it.

If the application is not designed for plugging in another interface, it is essentially not framework based. So, for a system to be framework based, it has to be easily extendable and scalable. In other words, it has to be a distributed system in a true sense. Further, a system needs to offer some predefined capabilities as a framework. This might include, but is not limited to, tracking and security, monitoring, and gateway mechanisms.

Tracking is important, and not many designers think of it while in the design phase. By incorporating tracking, you allow the system to be traced and audited. Consider a typical financial customer service system used by hundreds of CSRs for attending and performing basic activity on behalf of a calling customer. The system would have crucial capabilities such as stopping payments, ordering checks, and changing a PIN. What happens if CSR performs something illegal or wrong? There has to be a way to track what the user has done in the system, say after login. In this specific case, the CSR Call Center manager wants to know when the user logged in, what screens she went through, what data she entered, and what the results were. In a critical system, all this should be available for viewing and review. That's why we need tracking.

Another requirement of a framework would be to include generic protocol for data exchange. This would include the components built within the framework so that they can be interoperable.

Typically framework should, in general, incorporate the following:

- They should be easily extendable.
- They should have a built-in tracking and security mechanism.
- They should offer an easy way to scale.
- They should support distributed call processing.
- They should provide generic gateway type interface.
- They should offer common protocol for both intra and inter communication.
- They could offer the ability to work with third-party systems and accept plug-ins.

It is quite evident from the preceding list that framework building imposes the same requirements as a distributed system. Although the built-in capabilities in a framework could be a debatable issue, I have kept them to a minimum because tracking and security are the only required modules to be built into the system.

It would also make you, perhaps, wonder how a generic system can provide prebuilt services. You might be right, but you might not be because the whole beauty of having a framework is that you have everything predefined in terms of protocol packets flowing through the system. Every transaction, or action, taking place within the framework would have a generic skeleton (similar to interfaces in Java). It means that everything is standardized and generalized; including the data flow formats specified as skeletons. For example, if you prescribe that the length of all data packets flowing within and in/out of the system would be 75 characters and the first 20 characters would describe the header, you are standardizing and defining a communication packet skeleton for the system. That's pretty close to what a framework would have as a standard communication packet skeleton.

Usually the tracking data or log would be written into a file, but the framework should have some configuration definition stream, where you can do changes to make the data go to the database.

Framework Initialization Process

To attain a generic and dynamic level, we usually rely on dynamic loading of settings or configuration parameters in most of the systems. A framework would also have such a configuration setting file, which would define several parameters. Similar to every system, a framework would have an initialization routine that would be responsible for initializing and reading these configuration settings. Once read, the configuration setting should be used to set various behavioral characteristics or patterns that flow through the system. The initialization would essentially include basic activities to be performed before a system can be usable within the current scope. Examples of such an invocation would include something similar to the following:

- Pre-instantiate certain required engine or core objects.
- Initialize gateway for database interaction.
- Create connections (number of, as defined in settings) in connection pools and keep them ready so that they could be given out once the application demands.
- Instantiate objects and keep them alive in repositories.
- Check for proper internal functioning, such as check whether the core system initialized properly or functions by executing a small query (such as a self test routine).
- If the system is co-located with pieces sitting on other systems, communicate with other systems modules and check whether the communication link is up.
- Set default protocol and packet size.
- Set processes that can be tracked and pointers to store the tracking data.
- Set current security gateway and the level of security offered.

These are examples of initialization; in the real world, it might be involved, and many additional functionalities could exist. For example, a system module—which is supposed to serve in persistent mode—can involve reading the settings from the configuration file as they were when the system last shut down and resetting those values.

In the following sections, we will review the generic framework from systems architecture perspective. The sections describe a framework in generic terms and assume that it has to accommodate major applications—by being flexible. Also considered is the fact that the framework could be coded in any language and on any platform.

Central Processor Type Framework

Let's now look at the idea of framework, starting with the idea of the central processor, the microprocessor way. It's interesting because many embedded virtual processor frameworks have recently been introduced and used extensively. They were primarily used for achieving platform independence, such as Java. The Java engine runs on a Virtual Machine, which is a central processor. Essentially, it simulates the entire CPU architecture using software and executes the overlying byte code, which is similar to the opcode/operand approach used in CPU. It also does the job of interfacing with a third-party system, which is the OS to actually perform the actions and events.

A high-level view of such an architecture framework would consist of the following sub-blocks:

1. A Central Processor (also called a Controller) whose job is to execute the instructions (a program)
2. Program memory, which would load the sequence of instructions to be executed
3. Security and tracking system, which would allow the system to execute the instructions safely within security limits and also maintain a log of events or instructions executed
4. Interface layers, which would form the interface with external third-party systems (in this case, OS)
5. Object Repository (or pre-built functions, also called system basic functions) for performing low-level basic tasks such as initializing and setting the processor over OS

The schematic of such a system is shown in Figure 7.1. Note that the interface layer is the main interaction bridge between the machine and the OS. The system might still use some standard intra-communication protocol. Also, the instruction set space is similar to queue, which would hold various instructions to be performed in sequential form.

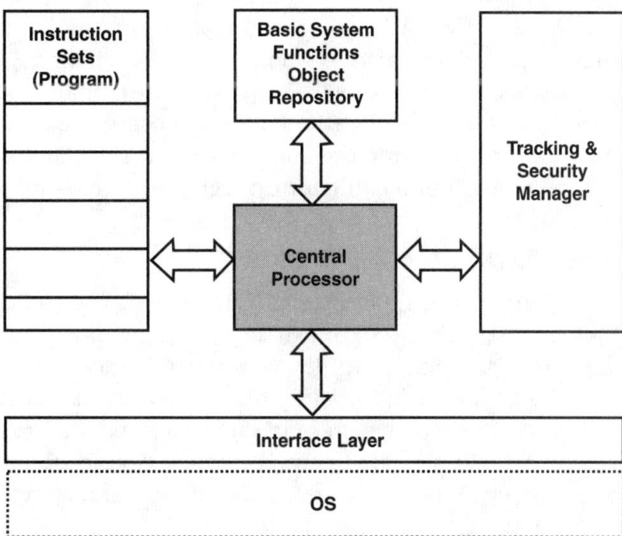

FIGURE 7.1 Central Processor or Framework Virtual Machine concept.

I will closely follow this principle in devising a framework with some additions and exceptions, as discussed next.

You could imagine that the instruction set could be viewed as a queue. This queue would hold the various tasks to be executed in sequence, and would be a sequentially *first-in-first-out (FIFO)* type of queue. Each task in the queue could be imagined to be a packet, which would describe the task parameters and the scope of execution. You can imagine this to be a simple message packet described using the XML stream.

For simplicity, assume that our model would have a queue where the tasks will be placed; in addition to it, there would be another queue where the outgoing messages or processed data packets would be placed. Again, you can assume that this is a simple XML stream.

The central processor block in the preceding schematic essentially just selects the instruction set and executes it. In our system, we would require some sort of Queue Manager block, similar to a central processor, which would select the task and execute it.

We could have a tracking and security block as-is in our model, which would be responsible for maintaining the list of tasks performed as well as the system log.

The basic system functions objects repository block could be divided into two sub-blocks—one to perform utility functions such as a math library with data transformation/mapping functionality and a second dynamic object pool. The second block would follow the factory model logic. Let's look at what it would do.

The task manager would decode the task message packet and find out which object needs to be instantiated and activated. It would pass these details to the object factory manager, which uses adapter logic to invoke or instantiate a suitable object from the repository and execute the method. In this process, the related data (parameters) is passed to the adapter from the queue manager. The adapter mechanism is covered in the section "Accommodating for Changing Patterns—Adapter Design."

Connection Pooling

Besides adding the dynamics of an adapter model, I will also add a data manager to the framework. Critical systems need some basic database connectivity. Even non-database systems, which use small text files to store temporary data, can utilize these manager services. The data manager would provide some crucial functionality—that of connecting to databases using dynamic class loaders (drivers), pooling the connections, and providing gateway services to even disk files. Connection pooling is important and can help you implement resources in a useful manner.

The schematic of a connection pool is shown in Figure 7.2. The connection pool is a program that, on initialization, creates some specified number of connections (usually such as database connection objects) and keeps them ready. Imagine that you create eight connections and keep them in an array, with each connection object referred to with the element number of the array. Now, if the application comes to the data manager and requests a connection, the data manager passes the request to connection pool. The connection pool picks up the connection object from the array elements and passes it back to the requesting application. Some additional work needs to be done here to keep accountability. What if a second application requests the connection and the connection pool returns the same element number that is in use?

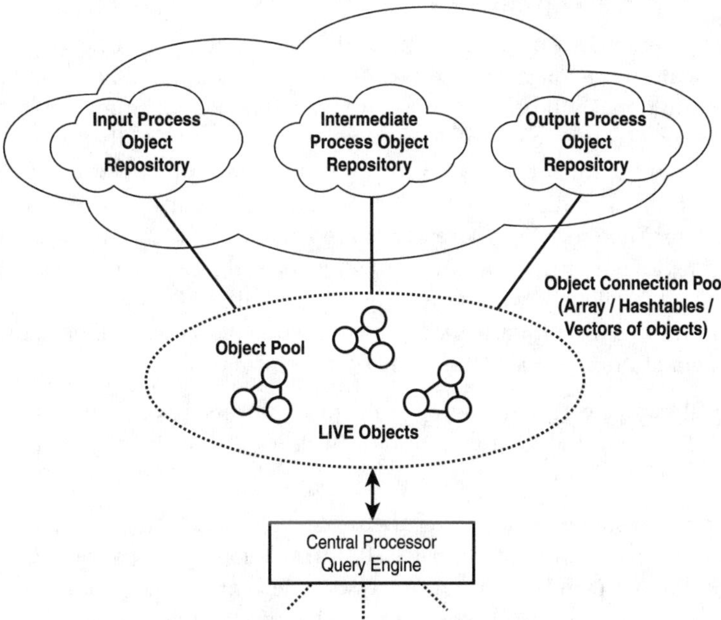

FIGURE 7.2 Connection pooling—Resource management.

We need to either come up with a connection object that has a Boolean member, which is set to either true or false depending on whether it is available or unavailable, or we could have a second array that stores Boolean true or false for the corresponding element in the connection array. The first approach is ideal for object-oriented programmers because you could quickly wrap the existing connection class and include a variable of type `Boolean`. Finally, it could provide the accessibility methods `getXXX` and `setXXX` for this member variable. The connection pool usually has a definite initialize routine, which would refer to some configuration file and decide the number of connections to be created when first started, and so on.

Another useful extension required in connection pooling is to accommodate a common scenario. What happens if the connection pool has given out all the connections and some nth application requests for a connection? The answer is that it should queue this request.

Connection pooling can be done for any objects, although the preceding example refers to database connection objects. In many systems, some objects might be used extensively, and you would require optimizing the response time by pre-instantiating the object and using connection pooling for its use.

Completing the Framework

The last requirement for our framework is that all dependent blocks within it should have a standard intra-communication protocol that should be RPC enabled. Why? Well, this would make life easier in case we have to scale our framework: for example, if the task queue grows, for a large system it could easily have around 1,000 tasks waiting in the queue at any given time and equal numbers waiting in the out queue, which has a larger size because of the data it contains. This slows down the overall system. Therefore, it is necessary to separate these blocks from the rest of the system by deploying or moving them on a separate high-end server system. If our system, as said previously, would be designed to use the RPC methodology for intra-communication using standard XML protocol, you could easily achieve this by moving them at once and achieving the best performance.

The complete framework schematic for a central processor type model is shown in Figure 7.3. There can be slight variation of this system—in the way that it processes the tasks.

Consider a complete task cycle. After the tasks are loaded into the task queue, the queue manager picks up the task, parses it, forms a command packet (again an XML packet), and passes it to the central processor. The central processor passes it to the object factory, which in turn invokes a suitable object using adapters.

After the actual method is invoked within the adapter, the return data packet is passed back to the same process and placed on an outgoing queue to be dispatched or picked up by the calling routine.

I have defined a path for message packets flowing in and out of the system. This includes the path from the queue to the queue manager and back to the queue from it. But, what about the path between the intermediate processes? Would the adapter model objects interact with the data manager and utilities modules directly? Would they be able to call the methods on these modules directly, say by using some direct interface linking? This is where the catch is.

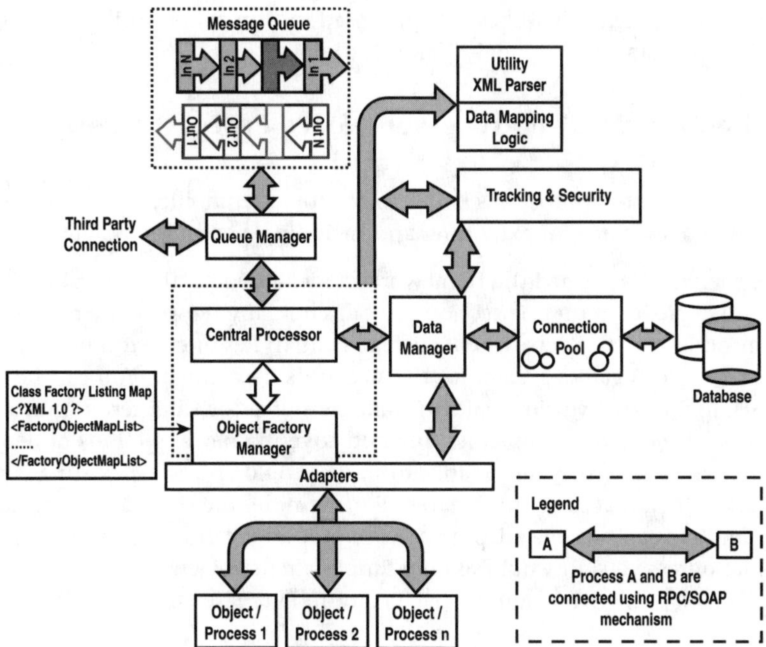

FIGURE 7.3 A generic framework schematic.

Ideally, for all internal process communication, we would prefer to use a queue and the same task cycle. So, say that an object in an adapter stream requires firing a SQL query using the data manager: It should form a suitable request task message packet and place it on the queue. The message packet will be similar to any message packet (task) placed on the queue by other processes. It would follow the same route and go to the data manager from the central processor for getting the result and again placing it on the out queue.

Although the preceding approach looks rather involved for a module within the system to communicate with the module in the system itself, it is the preferred method of communication. Why? Because it makes the system relatively more scalable by following the generic path for all processing messages. It would make the system extendable because anything within the system has to go through the queue. This would also help you attain the tracking goal because now you can monitor the in/out queues for reading (and logging) all processes and transactions occurring in the system. Besides, because of a central location, it is also easier to control the system.

Note that I have shown a class factory reference XML snap shot that would be used by the factory to reference the `object::method` relationship and accordingly pass the requirement to the adapter.

You will see examples of XML packets proposed for this framework in the section titled "Generic Framework Model—Using XML."

Extending the Central Processor—Slave Processor Design Approach

The central processor approach is better suited for extendibility, which makes it a feasible model of choice for extending and including a complex system architecture.

Imagine that you developed the framework model based on the central processor design and deployed it on one section of your company network. By *one section*, what I mean is, say, one department such as Human Resources. You need to now design and deploy again a system for the Accounts department. You can easily do this by using the same version as for Human Resources, with different protocol adapters. So, as you go on implementing and covering newer sections or departments in a third-party or your organization, you could re-use the existing code of the framework, which makes your job easier. Furthermore, the only change required is to develop and plug in suitable adapters for the new application. For example, the Human Resources version would require Employment Review, Payroll, and Overtime adapters; for Accounts you would need Taxation, Purchase Order, and Invoicing adapters.

The generalization of the architecture model in terms of framework has enabled us to achieve ease of re-usability too, which is a useful aspect.

The next step is to have a master system that would allow the top bosses in the company to use all the systems. (This is the case even for an organization that has offices over various regions or countries.) In other words, flow and integration is offered between these separate systems to introduce automation and reporting. This means that you would need to somehow control all the preceding individual systems and create a wrapper that would allow seamless integration. With the framework model, even this is easy to achieve.

Look at the schematic in Figure 7.4. Again, don't go on the complexity or on the dimensions of this schematic: It's very easy and systematic. Each of the blocks on the right side represents our central processor based framework model, which was discussed in the previous section. We have introduced some similar modules for controlling these co-located or independent frameworks.

We again have in and out queues, which are monitored and interfaced using the queue manager. We also have a central processor that accepts the task message packets from the queue manager. But, after that the schematic changes. The task packets no longer go to object factories; rather they are routed to these different subsystems. Essentially, the central processor would decode the message and find out where it belongs and accordingly place the message in the respective queue of subsystems or slaves.

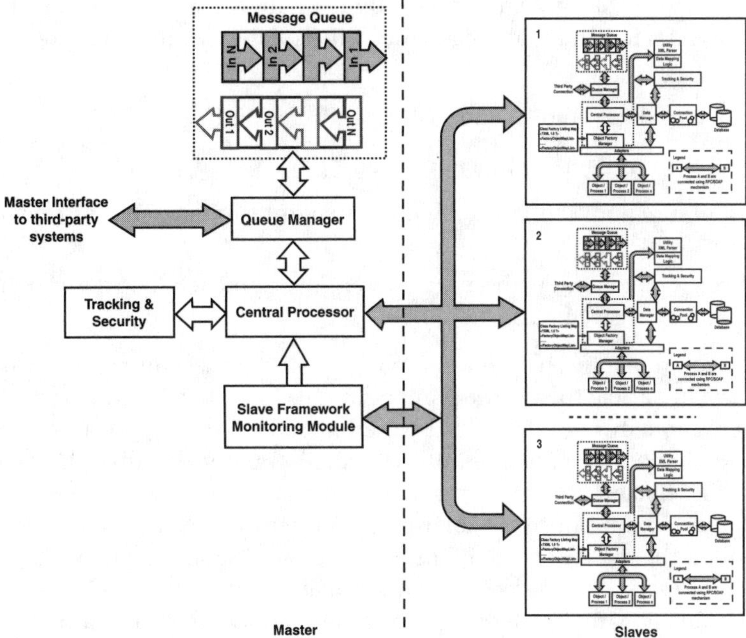

FIGURE 7.4 A generic framework—Slave processor schematic.

System Framework Monitoring Module

I introduced an additional block, which is optional, called the Slave Framework Monitoring Module. The purpose of this block is to provide feedback to the central system. The concept of feedback is not new to designers and even hardware engineers; in a closed loop system, you always take some portion of output (or processed portion of output) and feed it back to the input to make the system stabilized or intelligent. The output signal might give you some idea about the input feed logic regarding the loading effect and how much it has to wait or synchronize for reliable processing. This comparison might make the understanding much easier.

In our system, this block would feed the central processor logic with some slave management information such as the number of current jobs in the queue in each slave and related parameters. From a networked system perspective, one other thought would be that you could include some intelligence in this module to make it more useful. That would be really nice for providing a more flexible system.

Let each slave system on the network signal the master, also known as the *monitoring module*, when they wake up. This essentially means that they send a message packet to the monitoring system specifying some basic information that would allow the module to know what systems are alive on the network, and (if included in the message packet) it could also specify useful information as shown in the following list:

- System primary and secondary host addresses or IPs
- System short name or functional name
- List of functions performed by the system (or supported by the same)

I might be going too in-depth in the master-slave approach, but this should help you visualize the extensiveness of the system.

With the additional information such as the preceding second point, the monitoring system would be able to give some important feedback to where the task has to be directed in more dynamic systems. Furthermore, the last option would allow for ultimate flexibility because the monitoring module would now know what the slave system could do and even what functions it could perform. This is similar to the discovery service introduced in some systems recently, such as Jini. So the central processor on the master-end could listen for the services on the network. It would receive a broadcast from a slave that it is available and what capabilities it has, which would allow the master to re-direct inquiries looking for that service to that particular slave.

Another completely different reason why you would need to have a monitoring module is to provide a managed distribution of tasks. Consider a scenario in which you have only couple of tasks to perform—as in transaction-oriented systems such as banking or stocks—but they demand heavy resources.

You can mimic the same system on different servers or networks to achieve better processing speeds. In this case, all the systems have the same framework and adapters plugged in. Then, the job of the monitoring module would be to provide the *loading* factor feedback to the central processor. A simplistic loading factor would be to read the number of jobs in the queue of each system. This information is fed to the monitoring module at the master level, which analyzes and feeds back the current free systems to the central processor. This would allow the central processor to effectively distribute the load across the various slave systems.

A simple algorithm would be that the monitoring module passes an array of current jobs to the central processor logic as shown in the following for a master system with four slaves:

```
Array queueStats[]
queueStats [0] = 3
queueStats [1] = 2
queueStats [2] = 13
queueStats [3] = 23
```

Note that the index number corresponds to the slave on the network. The central processor, when placing the tasks in the respective slave queues, will check for the minimum number in the array and route the task to the respective slave queue accordingly. You should now be in a position to better understand the theory of frameworks and why they are required. You also saw how to build and extend them. The following sections deal with a detailed overview of individual blocks or modules of this framework.

Designing Intra-component Services

Framework is made up of several modules or blocks interconnected with a bus. The *bus* is a path through which data flows, and the protocol you propose to use over this bus is XML.

We have defined the intra-communication standard as the XML message stream, thereby making it flexible. This would allow the bus to be tapped easily while a third-party system could still receive the data.

Here are a couple of guidelines for setting up such services:

- They should support XML as a protocol with standard envelope and packet definitions.
- They should support RPC call methods (or SOAP).

By supporting RPC (or rather XML-RPC), we have to support XML. So, by promising the use of XML-RPC, we automatically use XML as a basic protocol. But, the packet definition still needs to be defined for our internal system. The schematic of the intra-component services is shown in Figure 7.5.

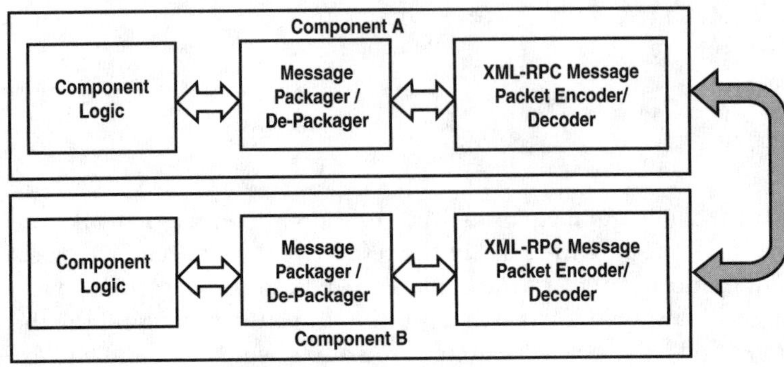

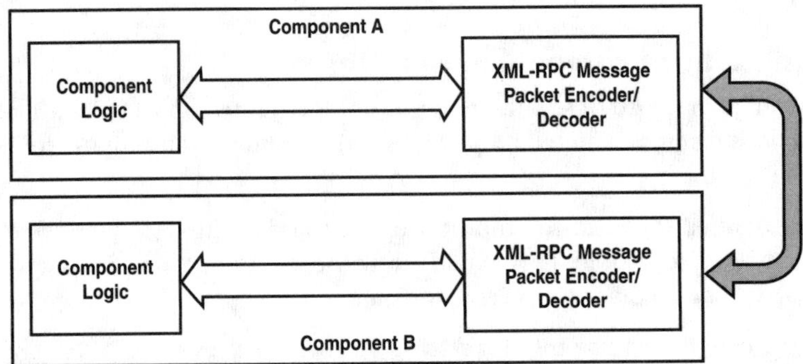

FIGURE 7.5 Intra-component Services schematic.

A typical message packet XML stream for our framework would look as shown in Listing 7.1. (This is a refined packet as compared to the previous packet because of some additional important information.)

LISTING 7.1 Message Packet Example

```
<?xml version="1.0"?>
<MessagePacket>
    <MessageHeader>
        <MessageID>98129182928</MessageID>
        <MessageDate>01012002</MessageDate>
        <MessageTime>12:02:20</MessageTime>
        <SendTo>ObjectFactoryManage</SendTo>
        <From>CentralProcessor</From>
        <Origin>
```

LISTING 7.1 Continued

```
            <OriginCaller>TransactionSystem</OriginCaller>
            <OriginCallerID>NA123</OriginCallerID>
            <OriginIPHost>192.168.168.7</OriginIPHost>
        </Origin>
        <Destination>
            <DestinationMember/>
            <DestinationID/>
            <DestinationIPHost>192.168.168.7</DestinationIPHost>
        </Destination>
        <MessageType>METHODCALL</MessageType>
    </MessageHeader>
    <MessageBody>
        <MethodReference>Accounts.GetTransactions</MethodReference>
        <Parameters>
            <Parameter>
                <Value>
                <int>
                        1111
                    </int>
                </Value>
            </Parameter>
            <Parameter>
                <Value>
                    <string>
                        NNNERT459823
                    </string>
                </Value>
            </Parameter>
        </Parameters>
    </MessageBody>
</MessagePacket>
```

The previous message would pass through the encoder layer for converting it into XML-RPC format as shown in Listing 7.2. The message header would be used to generate the RPC header, which has a pointer to the host system. The preceding message header has the source and destination, and the message de-packager has to re-assemble it and refer to some configuration file to find the actual host for the current framework. This information would be used to generate the header information required for RPC (refer to Listing 7.2 for the XML-RPC method call example).

LISTING 7.2 XML-RPC Method Call Example

```
<?xml version="1.0"?>
<methodCall>
   <methodName>Accounts.GetTransactions</methodName>
   <params>
      <param>
         <value><i4>1111</i4></value>
        <value><string>NNNERT459823</string></value>
      </param>
   </params>
   </methodCall>
```

The header generated for the example would be similar to the one shown as follows:

```
POST /RPC2 HTTP/1.0
User-Agent: Generic Framework 1.0 (WinNT)
Host: 192.168.168.7
Content-Type: text/xml
Content-length: 191
```

For arriving at an intra-component schematic, I have taken into account the following facts:

- The main interface layer is XML-RPC enabled. (Note that this can also be SOAP enabled.)
- The sub-layer, which would be a packager (or de-packager) for our internal system message packet.

The problem with this approach is that once the RPC is formed and the packet is dispatched on the other side, it could be reformed into the internal message packet. Hence, you lose the original information.

One solution to this problem is to embed the entire message string in the RPC packet and let the RPC talk to a predefined method for communication always. Whatever is passed to RPC would instantiate a fixed object method, such as `TakeCareofRPCPacket()`, which would strap the message packet out of the RPC stream and get the original message out of it.

The disadvantage of this method is you end up re-writing some RPC mechanism in your code yourselves. Consider that you receive an RPC packet with the message embedded in it as shown in Listing 7.3.

LISTING 7.3 Embedded Message Packet—Multiple Message Stream

```
<?xml version="1.0"?>
<methodCall>
   <methodName>Adapter.ExecuteTransactions</methodName>
   <params>
      <param>
        <value>c
            <string>
                &lt;?XML version="1.0" ?&gt;
                &lt;MessagePacket&gt;
                &lt;MessageHeader&gt;
                    &lt;MessageID&gt;98129182928&lt;/MessageID&gt;
                    &lt;MessageDate&gt;01012002&lt;/MessageDate&gt;
                    &lt;MessageTime&gt;12:02:20&lt;/MessageTime&gt;
                    &lt;SendTo&gt;ObjectFactoryManage&lt;/SendTo&gt;
                    &lt;From&gt;CentralProcessor&lt;/From&gt;
                    &lt;Origin&gt;
                        &lt;OriginCaller&gt;TransactionSystem&lt;/
                        ➥OriginCaller&gt;
                        &lt;OriginCallerID&gt;NA123&lt;/OriginCallerID&gt;
                        &lt;OriginIPHost&gt;192.168.168.7&lt;OriginIPHost&gt;
                    &lt;/Origin&gt;
                    &lt;Destination&gt;
                        &lt;DestinationMemeber&gt;&lt;/DestinationMember&gt;
                        &lt;DestinationID&gt;&lt;/DestinationID&gt;
                        &lt;DestinationIPHost&gt;192.168.168.7&lt;
                        ➥DestinationIPHost&gt;
                    &lt;/Destination&gt;
                    &lt;MessageType&gt;METHODCALL&lt;/MessageType&gt;
                &lt;/MessageHeader&gt;
                &lt;MessageBody&gt;
                    &lt;MethodReference&gt;Accounts.GetTransactions&lt;/
                    ➥MethodReference&gt;
                        &lt;Parameters&gt;
                            &lt;Parameter&gt;
                                &lt;Value&gt;
                                    &lt;int&gt;
                                        1111
                                    &lt;/int&gt;
                                &lt;/Value&gt;
                            &lt;/Parameter&gt;
                            &lt;Parameter&gt;
                                &lt;Value&gt;
                                    &lt;string&gt;
```

LISTING 7.3 Continued

```
                                    NNNERT459823
                                &lt;/string&gt;
                            &lt;/Value&gt;
                        &lt;/Parameter&gt;
                    &lt;/Parameters&gt;
                &lt;/MessageBody&gt;
            &lt;/MessagePacket&gt;
        </string>
      </value>
    </param>
  </params>
</methodCall>
```

Note that in this listing, the XML message stream is placed within the XML-RPC envelope and < and > has been replaced with `<` and `>`, respectively. This is to prevent any confusion created on the parsing mechanism, which would otherwise assume the internal message to be child elements.

The directive in the header then would always specify the destination host. After the preceding message is received by RPC, it is passed to a respective object member `GenericTransaction()` method of object `Adapter`. This method is assumed to be the one that would be called for all interactions for the object with the external world.

Hence, all messages sent through RPC to any module in our system would invoke this common method of the `Adapter` object. The `Adapter` object would then decode the message, get the actual message from it, and accordingly invoke the actual method within the module.

Although we have to parse the message again and get the actual message, this is useful because it would retain our message format and we do not lose our information. The secondary layer (shown as Message Packager/De-Packager on the schematic) then has to parse the XML stream, decode it, and instantiate the correct object, passing all the parameters to it. Finally, when the method finishes and returns the value, it reconstructs the original message and passes it to the RPC layer. The RPC layer, in turn, envelops it in the XML-RPC packet and delivers it to back to the caller.

Sending Messages Back to the Requester

While sending back the message packet the responder, here the Message Packer, on the Adapter, marks the `<SendTo>` tags with the address where it came `<From>` and includes suitable `<Destination>` values. The message would then be as shown in Listing 7.4.

LISTING 7.4 Packet for Sending Messages Back to the Requester

```
<?xml version="1.0"?>
<MessagePacket>
    <MessageHeader>
        <MessageID>98129182928</MessageID>
        <MessageDate>01012002</MessageDate>
        <MessageTime>12:02:20</MessageTime>
        <SendTo>ObjectFactoryManage</SendTo>
        <From>CentralProcessor</From>
        <Origin>
            <OriginCaller/>
            <OriginCallerID/>
            <OriginIPHost/>
        </Origin>
        <Destination>
            <DestinationMember> TransactionSystem </DestinationMember>
            <DestinationID>NA123</DestinationID>
            <DestinationIPHost>192.168.168.7</DestinationIPHost>
        </Destination>
        <MessageType>METHODCALLRETURN</MessageType>
    </MessageHeader>
    <MessageBody>
        <MethodReference>Accounts.GetTransactions</MethodReference>
        <Parameters>
            <Parameter>
                <Value>
                    <int>
                        1111
                    </int>
                </Value>
            </Parameter>
            <Parameter>
                <Value>
                    <string>
                        NNNERT459823
                    </string>
                </Value>
            </Parameter>
        </Parameters>
    </MessageBody>
</MessagePacket>
```

We will look into this in more detail in the section, "Generic Framework Model—Using XML."

Accommodating for Changing Patterns—Adapter Design

The Adapter type of methodology allows dynamic object invocation from the repository pool and also facilitates plugging in new objects easily into the framework. The adapter module works on the principle similar to the remote gateway interface. It gets the method details, invokes the object accordingly, and passes the relevant parameters. This might sound similar to what XML-RPC does, but this interface can be made more intelligent in terms of handling replaced objects and chaining as described before.

So for any additional functionality to be incorporated in the system, all you have to do is write the object or set of objects to perform the functionality and plug it in the system.

Usually, the type of functionality this object handles is titled as a type of adapter; for example, if your object can handle transforming XML data to an ASCII CSV string, it can be called a data transform or protocol transform adapter.

Allowing for such dynamically pluggable options in a framework is a very useful and important aspect. To come up with a generic framework—which is preprogrammed to work to offer some basic services and later extend it—is important to make it usable. Framework models could then incorporate the modules dynamically and use their services, and hence they are possible in first place.

Adapter patterns can also prove to be more important in the case of including the changing patterns in the framework. For example, if you had an adapter to calculate the current inventory value, and if for some reason you want to include an additional module that needs to use the input from the previous module, you can achieve this by using an embedding approach. Remember that this approach is especially useful when your old code is lost and you cannot find the source.

In the embedding approach, you would not have to change the code for existing modules to do it. Rather, you write two new modules: one to do the actual extended calculation and a second one that would call the first one and pass its output to the next one. This second module would be the connector module. Finally, in the adapter configuration file, you need to change the linkage of the original adapter to point to this new one.

Generic Framework Model—Using XML

I chose XML as the standard for data exchange throughout our framework. The reasons are evident because it is flexible and self describing, as well as being generic and open.

In previous sections, I also talked about using task message packets and a method to use RPC combined with our native message. In this section, we will renew the whole situation again.

In the framework schematic (central processor type), you can presume that all intra-communication between various blocks, except the Data Manager and Adapters, could reside on the same system. The Adapters model, which includes various submodules that each performs some business logic, could reside on different computers on the network. Per our convention, we could state that all the communication between the various modules, with the previously mentioned exceptions, could take place using our native packet. (This is the message packet I define later.) The other interaction needs to use the XML-RPC or SOAP mechanism because the communication needs to be done between the two modules physically residing on different systems on the network. This communication link, however, could also be established using sockets—but the issue of sockets not getting through firewall and carrying raw data makes them a bit complex to use. But, for a legacy system distributed internally on a network or WAN, they would rather prove to be useful.

Task Message Packet—Postmortem

We would start with understanding how a task message packet would look. The task packet would be the universal XML stream used to describe any task in our framework. So, it should include basic information about the task and the purpose of the task. I can summarize the requirements for the generic message packet as follows:

- It should contain the basic information such as date and time stamps for tracking purposes.
- It should specify the task type, which would be broadly defined as whether this is a method call or gateway access call (for example, data access).
- It should specify the source and destination of the message packet.
- It should specify the task packet type, which would specify whether this is task from IN queue or OUT queue.
- It should have a unique task identification number so that each task can be tracked. (Usually, you would reset a task number either after the fixed time period or after a system audit, so the task member has to be initialized accordingly from some *setting field.*)
- It should define the task contents, as would be required for the specified task type, and layout for the same.

The task message packet would then look similar the one shown in Listing 7.5.

LISTING 7.5 Task Message Packet Example

```
<?xml version="1.0"?>
<MessagePacket>
    <MessageHeader>
        <MessageID>1291829182</MessageID>
        <MessageDate>01012001</MessageDate>
        <MessageTime>12:02:45</MessageTime>
        <MessageOrigin>
            <OriginMember>Transactions.GetDailyTransactions</OriginMember>
            <OriginHost>192.168.168.10</OriginHost>
        </MessageOrigin>
        <MessageDestination>
            <DestinationMember>Adapter.GetCustomerTransactions
            ➥</DestinationMember>
            <DestinationHost>192.168.168.7</DestinationHost>
        </MessageDestination>
        <MessagePacketType>IN</MessagePacketType>
        <MessageType>PROCEDURECALL</MessageType>
    </MessageHeader>
    <MessageDetails>
        <ProcedureName>Adapter.GetCustomerTransactions</ProcedureName>
        <Parameters>
            <Param>
                <value>
                    <int>1232</int>
                </value>
            </Param>
        </Parameters>
    </MessageDetails>
</MessagePacket>
```

The listing is quite straightforward and provides an easy way to represent the message within our system in the queue. The same message packet, as you can see, could include outgoing message types. For outgoing messages the `<MessagePacketType>` value would be `OUT`, and the `<MessageDetails>` would have corresponding details, such as a resultset or return value.

Let's compare our framework by combining its approaches with say an RPC type model. This would help you in understanding some aspects of distributed computing and why we should choose specified system models. Remember, for both the approaches, we are using XML.

Consider two types of interactions:

- Synchronous interactions, similar to a method call
- Asynchronous interactions, similar to queue based approach

Before further reasoning, let me clarify that I'm not trying to prove that one method is superior to another, but I am trying to reason out when and how to use the methods.

Synchronous interactions are similar to method calls in your code. It's called synchronous because the code fragment calling that method waits for the response and then proceeds further. This is typical of all intra-code communication based on methods or procedural calls.

Asynchronous interactions, on the other hand, are always a combination of `GetXXX` and `SetXXX` methods. (The concept is the same as the one used in designing a good class, *bean,* or *activeX* control). The Set methods would call the method and would simply proceed further, and the Get method then (running as a separate thread) would try to get the actual resultset. The approach is similar to the *callback* concept. We could introduce a message *dispatcher* module. This would be responsible for dispatching all `OUT` queue messages to respective third-party modules.

Our central processor based framework follows the asynchronous approach because we use Queue as the main task container. But, we anticipate all the intra-component calls to be synchronous, using RPC. Hence, technically it could use both the asynchronous and synchronous approaches described previously. Also, note that I did not specify how the third-party system would interact with our framework. It was presumed that it would use Queue Manager as the main interface to interact. But, conditions can vary: You can have a secondary interface layer called a Synchronous Interface Layer built into the system to provide synchronous services to third-party clients.

Synchronous and Asynchronous Interactions

Finally, we would then have support for both asynchronous and synchronous third-party interactions, which is important in real-world systems.

I still propose to use XML as the protocol for both the interface types offered to a third party. So the Asynchronous or Queue Manager interface would allow the XML Message packet (shown in Listing 7.5) to be placed on or picked up from the queue, although the actual interface preceding the Queue Manager would still be something similar to the RPC type. The third-party systems—located on a separate system on the network—would use RPC to invoke the Queue Manager method and pass the Message Packet XML stream as a parameter, which would be placed on the `IN` Queue. The remote (third party) system would be returned some value to specify that everything was okay, such as OK. (Note that XML-RPC specifications specify that the returned value is 200 OK for all successful calls.) Here, I would like to specify that for a message-based interaction using queues, SOAP is ideal. SOAP was formed on the concept of messages, although a variation of SOAP called SOAP-RPC would use an RPC-type mechanism.

A real-world situation in which you need to use both approaches would be when you are defining a framework for some Web interface for an online survey mechanism. The users come online, and to register this process needs to hit the synchronous gateway because the user has to be instantly registered and given a confirmation (or issued a password). After registering, the user would fill up the survey forms. This would hit the asynchronous gateway because this process is non-confirming, and only primary data validation that could be done on the front end would serve the purpose. The data could be stored in the database whenever the queue is processed because we would require it later for analysis.

Various inter-company data transfers or inter-division information could be using asynchronous, which are done for updating corporate servers on either an EOD or EOW basis.

For all internal submodules within our framework, however, we still want to use the synchronous interface as the framework gateway. This is important because you do not want any third-party system to talk directly to an internal module (of the framework), such as the Data Manager. If such direct usage of framework components or services is allowed, the idea of framework collapses because there would be no monitoring and control of accessibility and resources. The security would suffer as well as the tracking capability. For any system to be monitored and controlled, you need a common access and exit point (old programming fundamental).

XML Map Files

Try to specify the XML file formats that would be used by Object Factories. These files would be used to determine the actual object to be called or invoked depending on the method call. I will call them map files because they define the mappings of the method calls to physical objects and would invoke them accordingly, passing the right parameters. The example of such a map file is shown in Listing 7.6.

LISTING 7.6 Map XML File Example

```
<?xml version="1.0"?>
<ObjectFactoryMapper>
    <FactoryInformation>
        <FactoryVersion>v1.2.1</FactoryVersion>
        <FactoryLocation>192.168.168.14</FactoryLocation>
```

LISTING 7.6 Map XML File Example

```
        <FactoryLastUpdated>10102000</FactoryLastUpdated>
    </FactoryInformation>
    <MapData>
        <MethodObjectReference>Adapter.GetCustomerTransactions
        ➥</MethodObjectReference>
        <MethodPrimaryLocation>192.168.168.17</MethodPrimaryLocation>
        <MethodSecondaryLocation>192.168.168.18</MethodSecondaryLocation>
        <MethodChangedName/>
        <MethodNumberofParams>1</MethodNumberofParams>
        <MethodChain/>
    </MapData>
</ObjectFactoryMapper>
```

You always want to include some guidelines in the XML stream header, which would help determine some basic information in the file. After all, I stated XML to be a self describing data stream. The basic information in the header in this listing specifies the file version number, the physical host where this file is residing, and when this file was last updated. When performing a system maintenance audit, this information could be useful. You could easily automate the audit process by writing a small code that would interpret this header information and generate a discrepancy report.

The `<MapData>` tag has considerable information to locate the actual object and some basic validation check resource, such as the number of parameters, so that the factory could verify that it is going to the correct object: Otherwise, it could raise an error accordingly. Additionally, I have included two tags—`<MethodChangeName>` and `<MethodChain>`. They would be rarely used, but might prove useful.

The `<MethodChangeName>` tag would specify whether there is an alias related to this method that should be used when invoking it on the specified server. This is rare unless some real policies changes occur within the company, such as a takeover.

`<MethodChain>` would specify whether there was an additional sub-head or processing requirement placed on the results output by the current method in scope. For example, if all current tax calculations are to be guided by some additional costs per the law and there is a component deployed on government servers that is updated to give this value, you can include that component name (or the name of the invoking object member reference) here. Now, the factory logic would use the current method to calculate the tax and it would redirect the results to the Chain method (by referring to the entry for that method in the same file under `<MapData>` tags) and get the results. Finally, it would pass this result to the calling interface.

So, in this case, XML is not only used as the format for defining the packet protocol, but also for setting configuration file.

The Tracking Record

The tracking record would be logged into the database or a file for every action executed in central processor. The tracking XML stream is shown in Listing 7.7.

LISTING 7.7 Tracking XML Document Example

```
<?xml version="1.0"?>
<TrackingPacket>
    <TrackHeader>
        <TrackDate>01012000</TrackDate>
        <TrackTime>12:30:45</TrackTime>
        <TrackOrigin>CENTRALPROCESSOR</TrackOrigin>
        <TrackInterfaceType>SYNC-GATEWAY</TrackInterfaceType>
    </TrackHeader>
    <TrackBody>
        <MessageID>1928912898</MessageID>
        <MessageType>PROCEDURECALL</MessageType>
        <MessagePacketType>IN</MessagePacketType>
        <MessageOrigin>
            <OriginMember>Transactions.GetDailyTransactions</OriginMember>
            <OriginHost>192.168.168.10</OriginHost>
        </MessageOrigin>
        <MessageDestination>
            <DestinationMember>Adapter.GetCustomerTransactions
            ➥</DestinationMember>
            <DestinationHost>192.168.168.7</DestinationHost>
        </MessageDestination>
        <MessageRedirected>
            <MessageRedirectedTo>OBJECT-FACTORY</MessageRedirectedTo>
            <MessageRedirectUDT>01012000:01:30:30</MessageRedirectUDT>
            <MessageRedirectedAt>192.168.168.13</MessageRedirectedAt>
        </MessageRedirected>
        <MessageAdditionalDetails>
            &lt; Param;&gt; &ltint;&gt;&lt1;&gt;&lt;/int&gt;&lt;/Param &gt;
        </MessageAdditionalDetails>
    </TrackBody>
</TrackingPacket>
```

The tracking XML stream could contain varying bits of information. In the preceding sample stream, I have indicated the fields that would be of normal interest. The fields of interest for a tracking record would greatly depend on the application in focus.

For a gateway service providing system, the message origin would be necessary. For a financial service company, individual access to a particular method and the parameters (such as the transaction amount) would be of interest.

To cover the cases in the usual sense, I have introduced <MessageAdditionalDetails> tag, which includes (as in the sample listing) *stringified* XML stream that could be decoded by suitable analysis or an audit program. This is another practical advantage of including a message within a message using XML. The respective systems could extract from data the pieces that interest them from the stream. For example, in this case the audit system would parse <MessageAdditionalDetails>, reform the XML stream (by replacing < and > with < and >, respectively), and parse it again to get the detail values.

Security Issues—Making the System Secure

Security issues are of prime concern in any system. I will discuss some aspects and usages from this perspective next.

Let's treat security in terms of an XML stream perspective. XML packet is a plain stream of characters and is self descriptive. One disadvantage of such packets is that if they are tapped, they could easily make sense. This could be dangerous for a mission critical system, such as trading stocks online.

Although we have many methods to secure data in the first place by encrypting it and applying security algorithms before sending, it is really complex and would make the system slow and difficult to connect with.

So, we would prefer to make the transport layer secure, which lies beneath the XML flowing through the wires. That would be easy and many pre-existing packages could be readily used to achieve it. As professionals, we all agree that specialized groups can best handle some aspects such as this.

A good security layer is readily available with almost all major Web servers—the SSL layer. SSL is widely used today and is the standard base for securely transferring the information. It is popular among Web developers who use it to transfer credit card data over the Web. We can use the same layer as well. In the previous framework model for all RPC (or SOAP) calls (or rather all third-party calls to synchronous or asynchronous system gateways), I used SSL.

XML-RPC and SOAP uses a POST mechanism that is fairly secured and reliable in the first place. If we use it over SSL, we could create a highly secured system. To use it over SSL, you would fire the RPC/SOAP POST request over the SSL layer as you fire Web pages. This is another advantage of using the Web as a gateway. Of course, the only reason why you would look at this as an advantage is that there are existing tools for the Web to make it secure, and you could just leverage those tools.

Sockets are not secure because they are the most viable to be hit by hacker attacks. But, from a programmer's perspective, using C++ or Java, sockets are raw when used in code. So it is better to limit their use. If you still want to use them, you should probably write your own protocol and apply an encryption algorithm to make it secure for transport. Again, depending on the application, I would prefer to use sockets with raw data.

SSL provides transportation layer security; besides that we would require some application level security. Application level security can come in many flavors as shown in the following:

- User level authentication
- Process level or transaction-based authentication

I have done this various times before discussing it here from the XML perspective.

The User level authentication would require embedding the username (public key) and an encrypted password (private key) in the message packet. The receiver would then parse the username and password, decrypt it, and use it for authentication. Although User level authentication cannot be thought of as completely secure, you could still use it as the first level of security in a system accepting third-party calls. The modified XML message packet, including the authentication information, is shown in Listing 7.8.

LISTING 7.8 Message Packet with User Authentication Information

```
  . . . .
<MessageHeader>
    <MessageID>1291829182</MessageID>
    <MessageDate>01012001</MessageDate>
    <MessageTime>12:02:45</MessageTime>
    <MessageOrigin>
        <OriginMember>Transactions.GetDailyTransactions</OriginMember>
        <OriginHost>192.168.168.10</OriginHost>
    </MessageOrigin>
    <MessageDestination>
        <DestinationMember>Adapter.GetCustomerTransactions
        ➥</DestinationMember>
        <DestinationHost>192.168.168.7</DestinationHost>
```

LISTING 7.8 Continued

```
        </MessageDestination>
        <MessagePacketType>IN</MessagePacketType>
        <MessageType>PROCEDURECALL</MessageType>
        <AuthenticationInfo>
            <PublicKey>NITAAJAY</PublicKey>
            <PrivateKey>DEF445EFGR4545</PrivateKey>
        </AuthenticationInfo>
    </MessageHeader>
    . . . .
```

I have included the new tag called `<AuthenticationInfo>` to envelope the public and private key values.

The process level authentication would involve authenticating each transaction initiated in the system. This level of authentication could prove useful as a basic level authentication for any processes initiated within the framework. Usually, the process would include task message packets placed on the queue and also queries hitting the synchronous gateway. All the packets would need to prove themselves as trustworthy. This can be accomplished by including a *key* with all the transactions, which the sender embeds into the packet. This can be thought of as a security key. The process level authentication could be done in a variety of ways when a remote end is involved:

- Using a Security Key string
- Trapping the IP of the requesting party
- Authenticating the user with a unique header
- Scheduling the interaction

In a security key mechanism, a fixed string (generally alphanumeric) is included in the package that can be verified against the issuer of the packet. Furthermore, the key might be encrypted, and the *access key* required to unlock the security key would be predistributed to the framework server to allow it to decode and verify the key.

Trapping IP addresses involves verifying whether the request originated from a trusted system. This is the best-known mechanism to incorporate automated security for batch gateway access or jobs processing.

Authenticating the user with a header is a simple way to differentiate the user and could be combined with another security mechanism to make them useful. In this, each user would have a specific header (such as a letterhead or digital signature) that is used to authenticate and recognize him.

The scheduling mechanism relies on a previous broadcast of accessibility. For example, a client would broadcast over a valid e-mail address that would access the gateway at a particular time from a particular location. This method could be combined with user level authentication to provide better security protection.

Additionally, a security feature can be added in terms of broadcasting the message. For example, the message packet would specify that the message is *classified* as secured and has to be processed securely by may be secured central processor.

Packaging Multiple Messages

It would be painful to decode and validate a remote user or system using the framework if it uses the framework services often. In such cases, it is better to provide a variation of message packet formats. The proposed task message packet would allow a user to issue multiple requests (tasks) in a single call or message. The results are passed back or placed in the out queue again in one single task message packet and in the same sequence as they were received.

An example of such multiple methods supporting the XML task message packet stream is shown in Listing 7.9.

LISTING 7.9 Task Message with Multiple Message Packets

```
<?xml version= "1.0" ?>
<MultipleMessagePacket>
    <MultipleMessageHeader>
        <MulitplePackageNumber>2</MulitplePackageNumber>
        <MessageOrigin>
            <OriginMember>Transactions.GetDailyTransactions</OriginMember>
            <OriginHost>192.168.168.10</OriginHost>
        </MessageOrigin>
        <MessageDestination>
            <DestinationMember>Adapter.GetCustomerTransactions
            ➥</DestinationMember>
            <DestinationHost>192.168.168.7</DestinationHost>
        </MessageDestination>
    </MultipleMessageHeader>
<MessagePacket>
    <MessageHeader>
        <MessageID>1291829182</MessageID>
        <MessageDate>01012001</MessageDate>
        <MessageTime>12:02:45</MessageTime>
        <MessageOrigin>
            <OriginMember>Transactions.GetDailyTransactions</OriginMember>
```

LISTING 7.9 Continued

```
            <OriginHost>192.168.168.10</OriginHost>
        </MessageOrigin>
        <MessageDestination>
            <DestinationMember>Adapter.GetCustomerTransactions
            ➥</DestinationMember>
            <DestinationHost>192.168.168.7</DestinationHost>
        </MessageDestination>
        <MessagePacketType>IN</MessagePacketType>
        <MessageType>PROCEDURECALL</MessageType>
    </MessageHeader>
    <MessageDetails>
        <ProcedureName>Adapter.GetCustomerTransactions</ProcedureName>
        <Parameters>
            <Param><value><int>1232</int></value></Param>
        </Parameters>
    </MessageDetails>
</MessagePacket>
<MessagePacket>
    <MessageHeader>
        <MessageID>1291829183</MessageID>
        <MessageDate>01012001</MessageDate>
        <MessageTime>12:02:45</MessageTime>
        <MessageOrigin>
            <OriginMember>Transactions.GetDailyTransactions</OriginMember>
            <OriginHost>192.168.168.10</OriginHost>
        </MessageOrigin>
        <MessageDestination>
            <DestinationMember>Adapter.GetCustomerBlanace</DestinationMember>
            <DestinationHost>192.168.168.7</DestinationHost>
        </MessageDestination>
        <MessagePacketType>IN</MessagePacketType>
        <MessageType>PROCEDURECALL</MessageType>
    </MessageHeader>
    <MessageDetails>
        <ProcedureName>Adapter.GetCustomerBalance</ProcedureName>
        <Parameters>
            <Param><value><int>1232</int></value></Param>
        </Parameters>
    </MessageDetails>
    </MessagePacket>
</MultipleMessagePacket>
```

The multiple message streams are rather simple. From the example in this listing, you can see that I have used the main message tag—`<MessagePacket>` now appears as a child to the `<MultipleMessagePacket>` tag.

I have repeated the header information because this would make it easy to parse the multiple messages on the framework end. I have also placed a header in the parent tag `<MultipleMessagePacket>`, which is consistent with the embedded message. Note that for all the messages embedded in a multiple message stream, it would not make sense if `<MessageOrigin>` and `<MessageDestination>` are different because they have to be the same for them to originate and be combined in one multiple message envelope.

Summary

The next chapter continues our venture into systems architecture. We will look into middle-tiers and see how they could be used to solve the problem of system extendibility. We will also look at various schemes and architectures for the same.

Using middle-tiers would help solve the current problem of extending old systems, which are not quite compatible with the new XML approach.

8

Designing the Middle-Tier

IN THIS CHAPTER

Should I refuse a good dinner simply because I do not understand the process of digestion?

> *—Oliver Heaviside (when criticized for using formal mathematical manipulations without understanding how they worked)*

This chapter deals with middle-tier design. It explains the concept behind middle-tier and the need to have it. It explains the functional aspects of this layer and elaborates on the design requisites for the same.

The chapter treats the layer from the XML perspective, explaining how XML could serve as a flexible protocol bundle to form an ever extensible interface engine. It also deals with using XML for object invocation and invoking an object from the interface repository. The data mapping requirements is also discussed here.

Finally, the chapter deals with other possible uses of XML in defining the system configuration settings.

Overview

The middle-tier concept is common for a systems integrator and architect. Any system requires a middleware to interact with other systems or to make itself "interact-able."

Enabling other systems to access a system is perhaps the major functional domain covered by a middleware, although the term is also occasionally used for various other intermediate systems, such as XML enabling the systems.

From a design engineer or architect point of view, any intermediate component that helps the two distinct systems to interact is a *middleware*. This is a very broad definition, and the term *distinct* means that the two systems can be proprietary in terms of the platforms and protocols they use. I will discuss middleware from this point of view because then it could be applied to a wide design requirement.

Recently, the concept of middleware was re-invented by using a term *messaging*, which means that the middleware component specializes in handling messages or transporting messages across two or more systems. This sounds logical because then the component would use messages to connect the two systems. Note that the messages can contain commands or data, which would help the receiver to act and process it accordingly.

The concept of message-oriented middleware is promising and reached quite a good level of sophistication recently. Many middlewares using the approach are available as frameworks or ready-made deployable code. We will review the design aspects of this middleware in the chapter.

Also, other popular forms of middleware are remote procedure calling and queuing. You have learned from Chapter 7, "Framework Based Systems," that a remote procedure call can be one of the aspects of middleware—to enable it to reach the source and destination. Further queuing can be the inherent capability of the middleware system to provide robust message storage and forwarding, hence processing.

What Is a Middle-Tier?

For most of us as systems designers and developers, middle-tier sounds more like an n-tier system oriented term. That's right, but that is not what we are considering here. In simple terms, a middle-tier is a middleware system that would enable two considerably distinct systems to communicate with each other and exchange data.

Typical middlewares can be one of the following major types:

- Remote Procedure Call (RPC) mechanism
- Publish/Subscribe type of Message-Oriented Middleware (MOM)
- Message Queuing (MQ)
- Transaction Processing (TP) Monitors

The Message Queuing methodology is perhaps the oldest and has been used since mainframe days. The concept of MQ has been described when discussing frameworks. Although, in the MQ based system, the various tasks are queued as messages similar to a link list. The tasks or messages are then executed either in sequential format or in accordance with the preference tokens that might be attached to the system to set the priority.

The RPC mechanism is the one in which the systems could use a remote invocation layer to instantiate objects (residing on the systems) on the other end, and hence it acts as middleware. Various protocols riding the RPC wave are in use today (such as XML-RPC and SOAP), and they are improving.

The TP systems are common in database and application server environments. Transactions support is required and necessary in many systems that need to support and manage resources and the atomicity of the sets of transactions.

Most recently, a more practical approach to the distributed processing was rediscovered and put to work—MOM. Message-Oriented Middleware is common these days, and many framework models are available to support it. Java Messaging Service (JMS) is one such MOM. Some aspects on JMS will be discussed in subsequent chapters.

How to Design a Middle-Tier Model

Middle-tiers can be any middle layer that allows different applications to interact among themselves. But this is a very broad description. Many times, the middle-tier is usually viewed as a requirement to construct a transformation database gateway. A transformation database gateway would help transform data in one format (such as ASCII) to another format (ADODB.Recordset format). Consider for example a typical data source object in Microsoft ADODB COM/COM+ that converts the ASCII file into a system required recordset object. The data source object, in this case, can be observed as a middle-tier.

Therefore, middle-tier is more of a relative term and has to be specific to the application it has been put into. Consider a typical example of adding a middle-tier for a database that would offer the various applications to query using XML and get the return dataset or action query results in XML format. Many such middle-tiers are available today. One good example is the DatabaseDom from IBM (`http://www.alphaworks.ibm.com/tech/databasedom`).

DatabaseDom is a combination of Java JDBC, IBM Data Access Bean, and DOM programming. An XML template file defines the database and XML structure. A Java Bean reads this, creates XML from the results of a database query, and also updates the database based on a new or modified XML structure. It combines the advantages of using the language structures to aid in a better searching mechanism through the XML structure (data hierarchy), such as Java hashtables.

However, designing middlewares is an application designer's choice. It can be interpreted as any layer that exists between two systems for seamless communication. It sounds like a generic definition, but it is true.

Out of the various approaches for designing middleware given in the previous section, the MOM approach is most suitable for the distributed computing paradigm. Furthermore, when combined with the TP based layer on database or the connection oriented side, this approach makes it complete to serve as a major system. Chapter 9, "Data Exchange Scenario," gives some JMS details that are MOM based. The main advantages of MOM models are as follows:

- They allow the integration of diverse systems that have completely different platforms and programming languages.
- They allow message queuing.
- They support generic message protocol.
- They allow message routing with security and guaranteed delivery.
- They allow messages to be scheduled and routed.
- They allow remote mechanisms to submit and receive messages.
- They allow publishers and subscribers to register and interact without knowing each other.

Note that not all MOM based systems support these features, but all these features are necessary for a message oriented system to act as an ideal middleware.

Let's devise a basic MOM based system. This would allow you to better understand such systems and use them as middleware. A typical MOM schematic is shown in Figure 8.1.

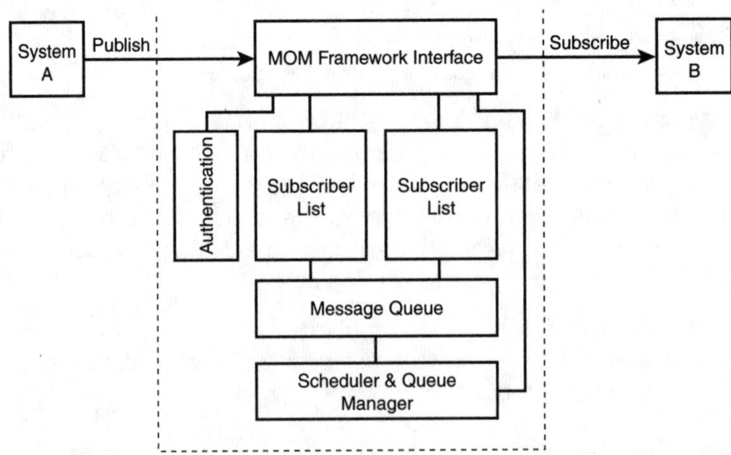

FIGURE 8.1 Message-Oriented Middleware (MOM).

The figure shows a publish/subscribe mechanism. System A submits the message to the MOM interface, which authenticates it and accordingly stores it in a message queue in a suitable format. The publisher and subscriber list allows the framework to pass and store messages so that the sender and receiver are not known to each other.

The isolation of the sender (message broadcaster or sender) and receiver (message receiver) can have many advantages in a real-world situation. Systems A and B can be of different origins and base platforms. Still, you can have a platform neutral protocol to interconnect the systems with MOM (such as XML).The System B name is listed in subscriber lists in the MOM framework because it showed availability for getting the messages. Similarly, System A has shown availability for publishing or broadcasting the message; hence it exists in a publishers list in the MOM framework.

So, when sending the message, the sender does not know the receiver and the receiver does not know the sender, although at times the sender is required to specify exactly who the receiver is—in the case of Point-to-Point (PPP) communication. With few modifications, you can use the same MOM for PPP.

The whole idea is to format the message packet such that it would tell the type of message it is as well as the destination, if any. This includes the following message broadcasting functionality in our framework:

- The message determines its type: For example, it can be PPP or Pub/Sub type.
- The message, in case of a PPP scenario, specifies the destination system.
- The message specifies the schedule for a special poling message requirement or time based broadcasting.

The last point is useful for many large systems integrated for data exchange in bulk. By including the message type and schedule parameter in the message packet, you could specify when the message is supposed to be broadcast to the receiving system (at what time) and after how long of an interval it has to be re-sent. This helps in using a simplistic message framework to perform important functions such as backing up or transferring data from one system to another depending on a schedule.

The only reason why you would merge the capability of scheduling and sending the message in a framework is that the MOM is designed to be robust. For some reason, in case the system fails to send the message or MOM fails, it has a capability of recovering all the messages and lists from persistent storage. This is another ideal application for XML. The MOM would use an XML tree dump to store the queue (persistent queue file) and list details at any point of time. This way, on point of failure of the MOM framework, the entire data can be stored on disk, and hence it can be persisted. Many modern languages give the capability to flatten or serialize the object data and dump it to a file, which would make this functionality easier to implement.

You will see the typical message packet examples for our MOM framework in the next section.

Using a Framework Approach for Middle-Tier Design

I have previously discussed frameworks in detail. I will use the same approach to arrive at a middle-tier design.

Although designing middleware has several approaches, the MOM based middleware with a combination of some dynamic processing capability will create a useful middleware for most purposes.

The MOM based system discussed in the previous section is simplistic and robust. It is capable of isolating senders and receivers, and it also allows PPP. Furthermore, the model has a scheduler, which makes the use of such an extensive framework in terms of message types that it could support. However, it should be clear that MOM is not exactly the middleware: It is merely a messaging middleware and not robust enough to be generic.

To devise a middleware from the MOM model, we need to include some additional capabilities in the system. This would allow it to not only act as message passer, but also allow it to do limited transformation and processing as and when needed. I will try to design or arrive at such a mode in the following section.

Framework Reviewed from the Middle-Tier Perspective

If you look closely at the generic framework mode, you would find that is closely resembles the schematic in Figure 8.1.

The principle of robust system design is to allow for the accumulation of tasks so that if the system cannot attend it ASAP, it can do it later. Hence, all major systems exhibit some form of queuing capabilities.

When queuing becomes evident, another factor that needs to be addressed is the message formats or tasks formats. This calls for the generalization of all the tasks in packet format so that you can replicate any task using it. This calls for using a generic protocol, such as XML. Although it has slight variations, the ORB (and RMI from Sun) has the same design architecture. ORB, similar to XML, is also a generic protocol, which allows CORBA objects to communicate over the network. But because of the complexity of a CORBA system, its use is still limited.

We intend to design a similar model, which could be used by average developers for building a robust system.

Figure 8.2 shows the schematic from Figure 8.1 in a more elaborate format. It shows the connection protocol used for connecting to the framework and to the database.

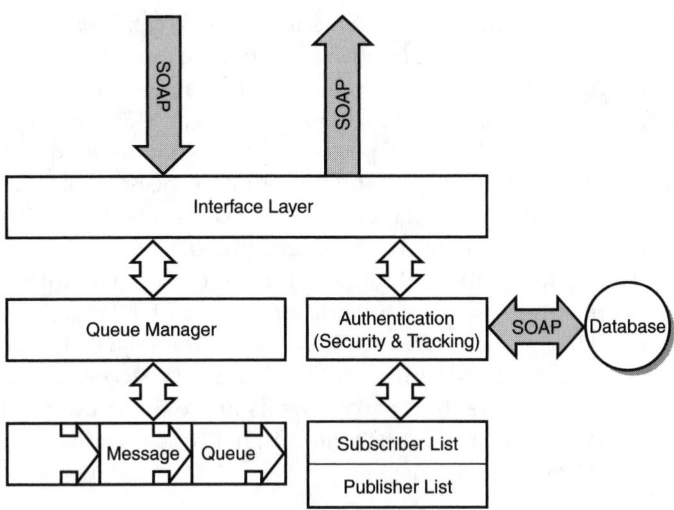

FIGURE 8.2 Message-Oriented Middleware—framework approach.

The following list gives a brief description of each system block.

- Interface layer—Allows third-party systems to interact with the middleware. The communication channel between the framework and the systems are of SOAP type to support remote message reception and transfer.
- Queue Manager—Manages the messages written into and read from the queue. It also addresses message-scheduling depending on the message types. The queue manager might also include the capability to dump system messages for persisting so that the system could restart in the same mode.
- Message queue—Stacks holding messages. Each message has a unique message ID and preference class.
- Authentication (Security & Tracking)—Generates a track log for all system actions and stores them in a track database. The database interface layer supports SOAP to allow for remote tracking database interaction.
- Subscriber & Publisher list—Stores the list of third-party systems and the location information for communicating with them. I will discuss the importance of this list from the isolation and routing perspective.

SOAP is used as the protocol in the schematic for the obvious reason of its capacity to use generic XML for message formatting and remote procedure call capacities. SOAP has emerged as the standard for remote system accessibility middleware design. Many systems in existence today use proprietary XML format to simulate task messages, but recently W3C has placed a specification under development for standardizing these messages. SOAP, which is result of this standardization, has many advantages. Because it is a standard, you could assume that the middleware would be useful to major systems. It has offered product companies an opportunity to develop middlewares that would support a majority of system interactions. Besides, such standards allow the standardization of a task message packet, which proves useful in B2B and distributed applications. It would be easier, in the near future, to maintain generic repositories of SOAP message packets as used by each system. This would allow the third-party systems to use the same message formats to develop an internal task message scheme and hence standardize and interact with the systems in a more open manner.

I have adopted the concept of publish/subscribe messaging for the preceding framework. In the real world, the middleware should be capable of interacting and isolating the systems between which it sits. This makes it secure and safer. Furthermore, such a middleware would prove useful in terms of testing the system without the second system in place. From a systems design and development perspective, this ability to develop both the systems in parallel could prove to be a faster system development and better integrated testing. To test the systems, the other end system could be simulated as a message receiver and sender, which emulates the behavior required. Hence, emulators could be easily designed to be in place and run test plans or schemes for the system.

The authentication module in the schematic bears the same functionality as in our generic framework model. To devise a useful middleware, it is desirable to allow a configuration setting that would allow the setting of such a layer. The main features or settings in the configuration file would include

- Setting the message pattern or template for a log (track) message.
- Setting the remote database accessibility patterns for transferring the track message packet. This would also include a *drill* level setting, which would specify what level of details would be captured from a tracked message packet.
- Dynamic setting for selecting the message types to be tracked (selective tracking).

In our system, either you could track all the messages or a few of them, depending on the audit requirements for the system.

The dynamic setting of a remote database would allow the middleware system to be configurable to store track records in the database suitable for a deployed environment.

The major assumption I made here is that as the XML system would grow in the future, every database would support an extended form of an interaction layer, which would allow the SQL to be passed in XML formats. This is more likely in SOAP, which would be the standard exchange protocol. This assumption, although futuristic, is wise because many already available middlewares are using it. These layers could be deployed on the database end quite easily and are as efficient.

The Queue Manager

The queue manager would be the control manager for the queue. Ideally, it would control the messages to maneuver and flow through the systems. It would also provide the system components with accessibility to the queue and get the messages in and out of the queue. The queue manager, hence, provides an interface for the inter-system or third-party systems to interact with the queue in all possible ways.

The queue manager has the following functionality:

- To set and get messages from the queue
- To poll the queue and watch out for major message types (for example, scheduled message types)
- To garbage collect old messages
- To provide tracking details of current messages and messages in process

Queue manager functionality is simple. It provides a complete interface to queue overall. Any system block or module interacting with the queue has to go through the queue manager. The queue manager can also have the additional responsibility of authenticating messages (depending on types), and the authentication module would be the Authorization block. This is specific with what overall functionality you want to design your middleware.

The middleware messaging system would have a configuration setting of defining a message to be of an old type. This would depend on the timestamp appearing on the message packet and the current system timestamp. All old messages are to be deleted or refreshed, which would again depend on the setting.

The subscriber and publisher list are simple memory stores, which have references of where each of those are located. The list maintains current subscribers and publishers registered with the middleware. Again, the registration stream is pure XML so that we do not have any dependency on platform or language. Furthermore, various settings can be offered within the middleware to make the subscription and publishing more specific. For example, the middleware can provide the following functionalities:

- Subscribe for a definite message type; would require proper authorization
- Publish and limit the message passing to stated list of subscribers
- Time dependency tag for subscription

Let's see what all the capabilities mean and why they are required.

The first functionality would give the subscriber an ability to set some sort of message filter. This is similar to filter settings in your messenger or e-mail software. This would be useful for a public board-based middleware system. In some special cases, it would prove useful to let a subscriber provide a suitable authorization key so that it does not read all messages of the stated types.

The second listing would allow the publisher to specifically direct the message to limited subscribers. This is similar to the PPP messaging type, except that there might be multiple receivers. As soon as such a message is received, the queue manager would manage the routing of the message to a particular subscriber per the given list.

The time dependency tag can be for both the parties. The publisher would specify that it would not publish any message that is old, and all such messages should be rejected by the system. The subscriber system would specify that it is not interested in any message that is *X* seconds, minutes, hours, or days old. The message would contain the numeric and unit settings for these types. Hence, the subscriber and publisher lists are a set of XML stream with all these settings.

In the real world, the system maintaining these lists would be composed of a DOM representation of an XML stream, which would add or edit the tree nodes depending on the client settings (by subscriber and publisher). This is also an example of a DOM tree application (as databases) in some systems. However, after suitable time intervals, the tree should be traced and saved in some form of file for persistence.

Before I go further into defining the message streams for the middleware to complete the architecture and outlining it, I would like to include few more things in it. On many occasions, the middleware framework you are designing would need to offer some transformation services of the data contained in the message body. This could mean transforming a flat-file (or ASCII) data into EDI or any other format. For this purpose, I will provide a ready to use transformation engine, which is extendable.

For transformation services, I will include a simple XSLT engine, which uses an XSL document as a transformation guide. Also, I will invent a new message type to specify that the message body needs a transformation service before it can be broadcasted or routed further. The new schematic is shown in Figure 8.3, with such a transformation service.

The addition to our original model is the XSLT processor. The message would contain a pointer to the XSL document to be used for transformation. The XSL document could either be maintained on the internal store or referred to using an URI reference in the message packet.

Let's arrive at some basic message types or formats for our middleware framework. This will help you visualize how you need to use the model. Listing 8.1 shows the message packet, which a publisher would post into the MOM model.

LISTING 8.1 Generic Message Packet—Publisher

```
<?xml version="1.0"?>
<!-- XML Message packet for Publishing the message -->
<PublisherMessage>
    <Header>
        <PublishedBy>192.168.168.12</PublishedBy>
        <PublisherID>N1234</PublisherID>
        <PublishedOn>01012001-01:10:03</PublishedOn>
        <MessageType>TRANSQUERY</MessageType>
        <ScheduledDeliveryOn></ScheduledDeliveryOn>
        <PollScheduleInterval></PollScheduleInterval>
        <ReceiversList>
            <Receiver>
                <ReceiverHost>192.168.168.22</ReceiverHost>
            </Receiver>
        </ReceiversList>
    </Header>
    <Body>
        <QueryMethodName>getTransactionforAccount</QueryMethodName>
        <Parameters>
            <Parameter>
                <Name>AccountID</Name>
                <Value><String>NN12334455</String></Value>
            </Parameter>
        </Parameters>
    </Body>
</PublisherMessage>
```

Let's see what the various tags represent in the message shown in Listing 8.1. The message is divided into header and body sections. The header contains a definition of the message origin and specifies the message type. The message type can be of many types in a middleware. Here, the message type `TRANSQUERY` specifies that the message is a type of query method. The preceding message packet shows the message format because it would be internal to the MOM framework. The message would be authenticated for the subscriber and then stored (pushed) on the message queue. The interface layer constructs this message packet after receiving the information from the external world. The message received from the external world or other systems is in SOAP format, with the preceding information embedded in it.

The SOAP message would invoke the SOAP layer located on the interface layer so that it triggers the subscribe message method in the framework. The complete flow is specified in Figure 8.3.

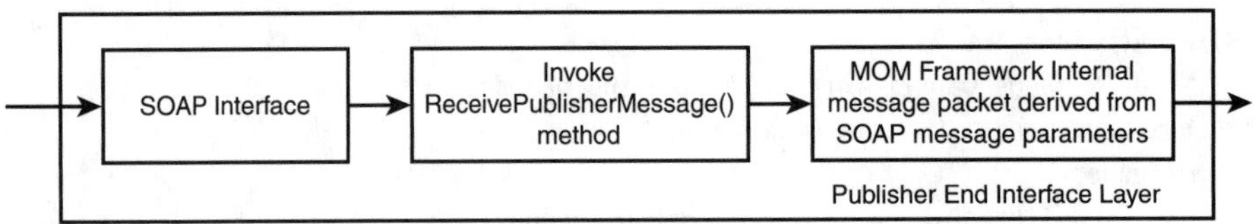

FIGURE 8.3 A detailed schematic of a layer to receive a publisher message.

The message, as shown in the figure, is actually generated by the interface layer logic. The layer is a standard SOAP interface, which receives the message packet from the publisher in SOAP format. The sample message received from the publisher client is shown in Listing 8.2.

LISTING 8.2 SOAP Message Sample Received from the Publisher

```
POST /publisher HTTP/1.1
Host: 192.168.168.56
Content-Type: text/xml; charset="utf-8"
Content-Length: xxx
SOAPAction: "http://mymomframework.com/publisher"

<env:Envelope xmlns:env="http://www.w3.org/2001/06/soap-envelope">
<env:Header xmlns:env="http://www.w3.org/2001/06/soap-envelope" >
  <s:Securitylevel xmlns:t="http://mysample.com/sec" env:mustUnderstand="1" >
    2
  </s:Securitylevel>
</env:Header>
 <env:Body>
  <m:PublishtheMessage
        env:encodingStyle="http://www.w3.org/2001/06/soap-encoding"
        xmlns:m="http://mymomframework.com/publisher">
         <MainHeader xsi:type="xsd:string">
        &lt;PublishedBy xsi:type="xsd:string"
        ➥&gt;192.168.168.12&lt;/PublishedBy&gt;
```

LISTING 8.2 Continued

```
        &lt;PublisherID xsi:type="xsd:string"&gt;N1234&lt;/PublisherID&gt;
        &lt;PublishedOn xsi:type="xsd:string"&gt;01012001-01:10:03
        ➥&lt;/PublishedOn&gt;
        &lt;MessageType xsi:type="xsd:string"&gt;TRANSQUERY&lt;/MessageType&gt;
        &lt;ScheduledDeliveryOn xsi:type="xsd:string"&gt;
        ➥&lt;/ScheduledDeliveryOn&gt;
        &lt;PollScheduleInterval xsi:type="xsd:string"&gt;
        ➥&lt;/PollScheduleInterval&gt;
     </MainHeader>
       <ReceiverList xsi:type="xsd:string">
        &lt;ReceiversList&gt;
            &lt;Receiver&gt;
                &lt;ReceiverHost&gt;192.168.168.22&lt;/ReceiverHost&gt;
            &lt;/Receiver&gt;
        &lt;/ReceiversList&gt;
     </ReceiverList>
     <MethodDetails xsi:type="xsd:string">
        &lt;QueryMethodName>getTransactionforAccount&lt;/QueryMethodName>
        &lt;Parameters&gt;
            &lt;Parameter&gt;
                &lt;Name&gt;AccountID&lt;/Name&gt;
                &lt;Value&gt;&lt;String&gt;NN12334455&lt;/String&gt;
                ➥&lt;/Value&gt;
            &lt;/Parameter&gt;
        &lt;/Parameters&gt;
     </MethodDetails>
  </m: PublishtheMessage>
 </env:Body>
</env:Envelope>
```

The SOAP message format shown in Listing 8.2 is almost the same as the one in Listing 8.1, except that I have included a header and a method call to the framework SOAP layer. The method takes three main parameters, which is realistically an XML stream in string format. Alternatively, I could have represented the whole message stream as a string parameter and passed only one parameter. The message can be further simplified, but for the current scope and to show how to arrive at SOAP message, this example is sufficient.

The SOAP message specified that the publisher would trigger the method called `PublishtheMessage` on the interface layer. This is a standard method that accepts the preceding parameters. Hence, all publishers would use the same format as shown previously to publish the message. The preceding exercise would allow you to arrive at a SOAP envelope for any application purpose. The interface layer would then decode the actual message (see Listing 8.1) from it and pass it to the internal blocks for attaching the same in a message queue.

Accommodating Interfaces in a Framework

The framework approach for the middleware model would need to accommodate more functionality. For example, the model needs to handle the customized functionality required for deploying in different environments.

The deployment specifications impose additional requirements on our model in terms of the support required from the middleware. To reason out the requirements, consider a few real-world examples.

Consider the middleware for forming a bridge between a legacy data store and other systems on the network. This would require the system to provide the following functionality:

- Provide PPP and Pub/Sub messaging services
- Provide data transformation functionality
- Provide application specific data packets for pre-existing systems

The most recent model (shown in Figure 8.3) covers the first two requirements listed. The first one is provided in the form of offering MOM functionality and the second one by an XSLT processor. The third option is application specific. In the current example, such application specific service would be similar to providing a processed bank statement data from the database to an online transaction module, as shown in Figure 8.4.

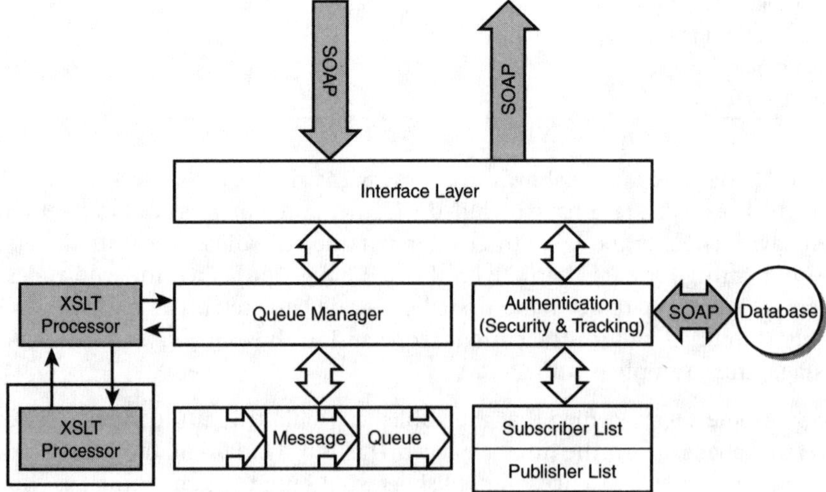

FIGURE 8.4 Message-Oriented Middleware with a transformation engine.

To go one step ahead, imagine that the online system for users to access their account information exists. Also, it has to be extended to provide the transaction information to the user through the Web interface. This could be done by providing a middleware model similar to the one presented before with the additional requirement of providing the data to this pre-exiting online system in a transaction packet format. Note that the word *transaction* is used in a banking perspective and would mean a typical bank statement like listing.

Again, the transaction data existing on the back-end system would not be in the required format or would not be a simple query made on the system. This scenario is typical of the diverse legacy systems existing today. Of course, redesigning the entire system is one way, but not a practical approach. So, the middleware needs to have some intelligence in terms of processing the request from the online system and forwarding it in a desired format to the back-end database gateway. It could also divide the information requirement into subqueries and query for the data independently. Finally, after receiving the resultset, it has to reassemble the data and provide it to the online system.

Consider this scenario in terms of XML messaging and using our middleware. The schematic of the entire system is shown in Figure 8.5.

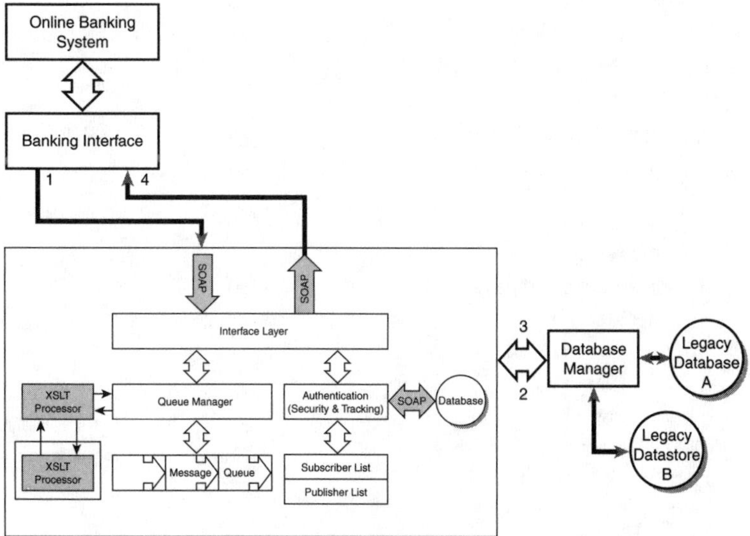

FIGURE 8.5 Middleware Framework Application schematic.

The figure shows the various steps involved in the workflow. Consider the type of message format you would receive at point 1 in the figure. Note that I are showing only the major message file format for better understanding the issue. Listing 8.3 shows the message or request format, which would flow from the banking interface to the middleware (point 1).

LISTING 8.3 XML Packet Flowing from the Banking Interface to the Middleware—Reference Point 1


```
<?xml version="1.0"?>
<!-- XML Message packet from banking interface to middleware -->
<BankQueryPacket>
    <QueryHeader>
        <QueryTimeStamp>01012001:11:21:02</QueryTimeStamp>
        <FromHost>192.168.168.22</FormHost>
        <ToHost>192.168.168.12</ToHost>
        <QueryType>TRANSACTIONHISTORY</QueryType>
    </QueryHeader>
    <QueryBody>
        <QueryName>getTransactionHistory</QueryName>
        <QueryParameters>
            <Param name="AccountID">
                <String>
                    NN12345
                </String>
            </Param>
            <Param name="FromDate>
                <Date>
                    01012000
                </Date>
            </Param>
            <Param name="ToDate>
                <Date>
                    03012000
                </Date>
            </Param>
        </QueryParameters>
        <QueryResultSetContainer>
            <Set number="1">
                <Type>
                    HEADER
                </Type>
                <MetaDataSet>
```

LISTING 8.3 Continued

```
                <DataElement>
                    <String>
                        Title
                    </String>
            </DataElement>
                </MetaData>
            </Set>
            <Set number="2">
                <Type>
                    DETAILS
                </Type>
                <MetaDataSet>
                    <DataElement>
                        <Number>
                            Serial
                        </Number>
                    </DataElement>
                    <DataElement>
                        <Date>
                             Date
                        </Date>
                    </DataElement>
                    <DataElement>
                        <String>
                            Title
                        </String>
                    </DataElement>
                    <DataElement>
                        <Float>
                            Amount
                        </Float>
                    </DataElement>
                    <DataElement>
                        <String>
                            Type
                        </String>
                    </DataElement>
            </Set>
        </QueryResultSetContainer>
    </QueryBody>
<BankQueryPacket>
```

Listing 8.3 shows the XML packet to be sent to the middleware from the bank system. It also includes the usual query name and specifies the message type. Additionally, it also specifies the resultset format desired. This is a novel approach for querying a system.

XML has major advantages hidden in representing the data, as seen before. But the ability to query with a *container* mechanism would allow the responding system to be more useful. The query packet specifies the groups of data and their levels of relativity because they would be defined in a resultset XML stream.

The `<Type>` element specifies the occurrence of the metadata element. The resultset would contain various sets and eventually many `<DataElement>`s. This makes the container more robust to represent the return format desired. This is a new scheme for querying a system, which allows the ability to specify the format for the resulting data.

There can be alternative ways to pass the metadata requirement: The request could have an URI pointer to a schema or DTD definition. The middleware system can then pick up the schema and use it to format the dataset. *XSL (eXtensible Stylesheet Language)* is also another option to use. XSL is a language for expressing stylesheets. It consists of XSL Transformations (XSLT), which is a language for transforming XML documents; the XML Path Language (XPath), an expression language used by XSLT to access or refer to parts of an XML document; and the third part is XSL Formatting Objects, which is an XML vocabulary for specifying formatting semantics. Refer to `http://www.w3.org/Style/XSL/` for more details.

The preceding example should provide you with insight for possible designs, which can evolve by using XML although the ability for the middleware to be able to process special custom functions is required. This calls for an additional modification in our current middleware. Figure 8.6 shows the possible modification to the middleware in the form of a schematic extension.

The extension layer using interfaces and adapter logic has been directly adopted from the discussion of frameworks in Chapter 7. The figure shows additional layers that are described as follows:

- Object Factory Manager—This layer is responsible for keeping into account the various interfaces available in the system. It interfaces the underlying adapters to the queue manager. Any new interfaces or business object included in the adapter pool has to be notified or identified to this module. The module could also provide invocation rules and triggers for adapters to instantiate the business objects. The object factory behaves more like a name server.
- Adapters—The adapters provide interfacing and trigger conversion from the object factory to the actual real object. They instantiate the object based on their location characteristics. For example, the object can be located locally or has to be called using remote invocation mechanisms (XML-RPC or SOAP).

Whereas the object factory accounts for various objects and their parametric readout, the adapter maintains the actual trigger mechanisms for the same. Therefore, an adapter is, by definition, an object that embeds the business logic, which can be dynamically invoked (instantiated).

- Business Object—The business object is customized code modules that are dependent on an application. The adapter provides the flexibility to allow multiple business objects' availability to the queue manager.

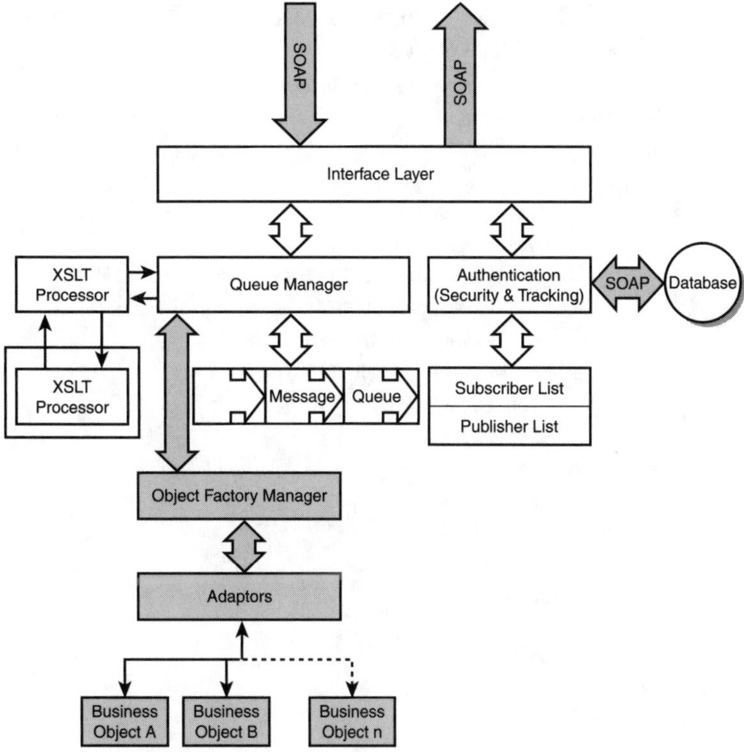

FIGURE 8.6 Message-Oriented Middleware schematic—with adapters.

Hence, the object factory provides a simple service of noting the various services available to the queue manager. The functionality of queue manager would be extended with respect to the previous design because it has to now call the task message in the queue and verify whether it requires any business object services. The task message can have a simple tag that could specify the requirement for the business object and the name as shown here:

```
<?xml version="1.0"?>
<QueueMessagePacket>
    <QueueHeader>
        . . . .
        <DependentProcessing>
            <Required>YES</Required>
            <ObjectName>objAccountInquiry</ObjectName>
            <ObjectKeywords>
                <Keyword>BALANCE</Keyword>
                <Keyword>ACCOUNT BALANCE</Keyword>
                <Keyword>AMOUNT</Keyword>
                <Keyword>TOTAL AMOUNT</Keyword>
            </ObjectKeywords>
            <Parameters>
                <Param>
                    <Identification>
                        <ObjectKeywords>
                            <Keyword>ACCOUNT</Keyword>
                            <Keyword>ACCOUNT#</Keyword>
                            <Keyword>ID</Keyword>
                            <Keyword>ACCOUNTID</Keyword>
                        </ObjectKeywords>
                    </Identification>
                    <Value>
                        <String>
                            NN12345
                        <String>
                    </Value>
                </Param>
            </Parameters>
        </DependentProcessing>
    </QueueHeader>
    <QueueMessageBody>
        . . . .
    </QueueMessageBody>
</QueueMessagePacket>
```

I have added a tag called `<DependentProcessing>` that defines the object to be called and also specifies any parameters and values required for the same. I have extended the intelligence contained in the message packet by further including the `<ObjectKeywords>` tag. This tag holds various possible keywords, which could be used to hunt for a suitable object in case the object name mentioned in the `<ObjectName>` fails. This provides for the queue manager to be more interactive from the task message perspective.

The security concerns of various objects being called can be handled by embedding an authentication string pair, namely a username (public key) and password (private key). The password would be in a predefined encrypted format.

I have also associated the parameters with the keyword tags so that if the method check fails and the system hunts for the similar object, based on a hunting rule, it could accordingly pass the right parameter. The preceding simple example consists of only one parameter, so there would be little use of these keywords. However, in a real-world application, the object constructor method would have multiple parameters.

As mentioned, the queue manager would have some rule depending on what it would choose as the right object. Although this approach sounds somewhat strange for a simple legacy (middleware) system, it will make sense when taking the diversity of a system into consideration. The approach is, however, ideal for a public query gateway type of middleware requirement. Typically, the public system would be the public person profile inquiry service.

The object factory could have the requirement of listing a packet pattern defined for the adapter to register the objects available, which is shown in Listing 8.4.

LISTING 8.4 XML Stream for Registering an Adapter with the Object Factory

```
<?xml version="1.0"?>
<!-- XML packet for registering the objects available in the system-->
<!--Fired by Adapter to Object Factory to register a object-->
<RegisterObject>
    <RegisterHeader>
        <TimeStamp>01012001:08:20:13</TimeStamp>
    </RegisterHeader>
    <RegisterDetails>
        <ObjectName>objAccountBalance</ObjectName>
        <ObjectKeywords>
            <Keyword>BALANCE</Keyword>
            <Keyword>ACCOUNT BALANCE</Keyword>
        </ObjectKeywords>
        <Parameters>
            <Param name="Account" Type="String">
                <Identification>
                    <ObjectKeywords>
                        <Keyword>ACCOUNT</Keyword>
                        <Keyword>ACCOUNT#</Keyword>
                        <Keyword>ACCOUNTID</Keyword>
                    </ObjectKeywords>
                </Identification>
            </Param>
```

LISTING 8.4 Continued

```
        </Parameters>
    </RegisterDetails>
</RegisterObject>
```

If you compare the Listing 8.4 XML stream with the previous one, it would be easy to reason out why I chose the hunting mechanism. Listing 8.4 specifies the object name, which is different from the queue message packet. So the queue manager, under normal conditions, would reject the request because no matching object is found in the registry with the object factory. But, in an enhanced scenario, the queue manager would request a keyword list from the object factory for all objects and match it with the queue message requirement. If the keyword matches, the queue manager requests the object factory to place a call on that object and pass the parameters (again based on keywords).

This mechanism is involved, but would provide a useful fail-safe mechanism in a large system design. Figure 8.7 describes the entire sequence and flow of operations (with interactions) for the hunting mechanism based system.

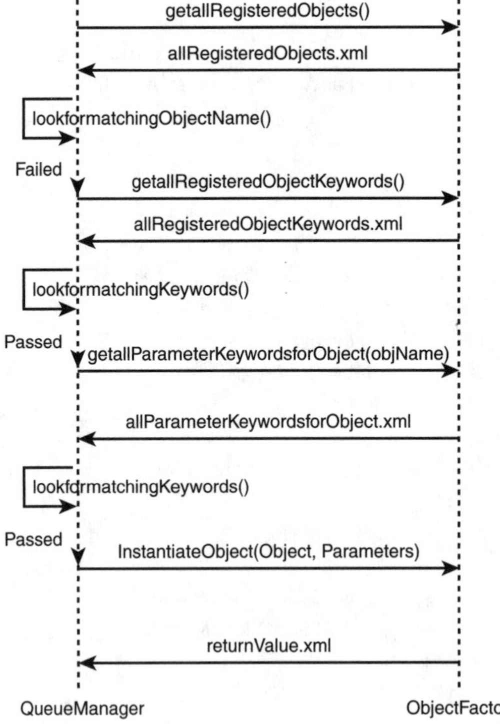

FIGURE 8.7 Interaction Sequence diagram—Hunt Rule design.

Such hunting (or discovery) mechanisms could be seen in Jini, for example. Jini network technology provides simple mechanisms that enable devices to connect to form an impromptu community—a community put together without any planning, installation, or human intervention. Each device provides services that other devices in the community can use. These devices provide their own interfaces, which ensure reliability and compatibility. The Java programming language is the key to making Jini technology work. For more information on Jini, refer to `http://www.jini.org`.

Adapters as Objective Repositories

Adapters in our model would serve more like repositories. They would account for the various available objects and their use of syntaxes. Although, in many models a separate object such as the Adapter Binding interface would share the functionality of managing a custom object repository.

In a simplistic sense, a repository can also be viewed as an object bank and can be extended (as it is usually is) to form a resource pool as discussed in a previous chapter. You will see how XML could be used as a base protocol for such models.

The objects that are available would have to submit their availability, which would include the following details:

- Object name, with keywords
- Default action constructor and parameters, with data types and keywords
- Availability in terms of location, which would specify whether it is located locally or on the remote end
- Invocation details for a local and remote invocation, which would include hostname and security keys (if any)

Hence, the objects provide these details to the adapter, which filters and passes them to the factory. Technically, the objects interact with the adapter listener, `objAdapterListenerInterface()`, interface, and the adapter interacts with the object factory listener, `objFactoryListenerInterface()`. We could quickly arrive at a sample XML stream for the object to adapter interface using the preceding list, as shown in Listing 8.5.

LISTING 8.5 XML Stream for Registering an Object with the Adapter

```
<?xml version="1.0"?>
<!-- XML packet for registering the objects available in the system-->
<!--Fired by Object to Adapter to register itself-->
<RegisterObject>
    <RegisterHeader>
        <TimeStamp>01012001:08:20:13</TimeStamp>
```

LISTING 8.5 Continued

```
        <LocationData>
            <Location>REMOTE</Location>
            <RemoteAccess>
                <Host>192.168.168.3</Host>
                <Port>443</Port>
                <SecurityInfo>
                    <PublicKey>NA1234</PublicKey>
                    <PrivateKey>
                        <Value>Y345FT343J65</Value>
                        <Reference>128-RSA</Reference>
                    </PrivateKey>
                </SecurityInfo>
            </RemoteAccess>
    </RegisterHeader>
    <RegisterDetails>
        <ObjectName>objAccountBalance</ObjectName>
        <ObjectKeywords>
            <Keyword>BALANCE</Keyword>
            <Keyword>ACCOUNT BALANCE</Keyword>
        </ObjectKeywords>
        <Parameters>
            <Param name="Account" Type="String">
                <Identification>
                    <ObjectKeywords>
                        <Keyword>ACCOUNT</Keyword>
                        <Keyword>ACCOUNT#</Keyword>
                        <Keyword>ACCOUNTID</Keyword>
                    </ObjectKeywords>
                </Identification>
            </Param>
        </Parameters>
    </RegisterDetails>
</RegisterObject>
```

Listing 8.5 appears to be the same as Listing 8.4 except that it has an additional `<RemoteAccess>` tag in the header. Our simple adapter would save this tag for its reference in an XML map file and forward all other streams to the main object factory.

The remote access details would be used to connect to the object; in case it is locally residing, it would be invoked by dynamic class loading—`Class.forName()` in Java or `CreateObject()` in Visual Basic. If the object is, however, located remotely, any RPC mechanism could be used, such as XML-RPC or SOAP. XML-RPC would be simple, light, and sufficient in most cases.

As mentioned earlier, the private and public keys allow the authorization of the remote method calls for the object layer. The example shows a username such as public key and encrypted public key—assuming that the remote end would have a decryption algorithm to get the actual password and verify the call.

We should all realize and agree that the ability of calling and loading an object dynamically has made the adapter mechanism possible. This can be used efficiently in the distributed computing environment when used jointly with the remote procedure call methodology.

The adapter could do more than act as a dynamic instantiation handler. As mentioned before, it can provide resource management for at least some of the local classes. By resource management, I mean something similar to the concept of connection pooling, which is common in the database world. The approach is simple—create enough number of objects and keep them ready so that they could be used quickly. This eliminates the time required to instantiate them, and also by limiting the number of objects created in the system, you could provide resource management. For example, you could create only five instances of a specific object and keep them ready. To use the objects in this environment, a slight modification is required, such as adding a Boolean flag that would tell whether this object instance is already in use or is free. Now, at any point of time, all the applications demanding the object would be handed over to the instance and the corresponding flag would be turned to true (specify that the object is *in use*). After five requests use all five of them, you could either create a new one or refuse the request. Another alternative would be to queue the requests and serve it when the object is available.

Many resource management models use a more extended approach. They allow the additional requests to be queued and served on some priority or on a first come first served basis. This method offers many advantages—it saves resources, it limits the number of object instantiated at any given point of time, and it speeds up the process of using objects. It also adds a requirement to wrap the objects so that it can be determined whether they are in use at any given point of time. You could also have a monitoring console coupled to this connection pool that displays a graph of the number of connections used at any given point of time and would have a configuration setting that allows the administrator to direct the pool manager to increase the number of objects instantiated depending on resource usage.

A Common Middle-Tier Engine Design Model

There can be many possible models used to architect a middleware. As seen previously, we have applied our framework guideline to arrive at a specific high-level architecture for it.

By adding the XSLT processor and object factory layers with the functionality of middleware having processing capabilities, we have the concept of an engine.

In this section, I will refine and reason out the middleware model from the engine functionality perspective.

Design Architecture

Before designing a middleware, we have to analyze various options as shown in the following list:

- What types of interface systems are on both sides?
- What are the various processing capabilities required for the middleware to perform?
- Does middleware need to provide remote accessibility?
- Does middleware require interacting with a remote system for processing capabilities?

As the systems grow in isolation, diversity in the basic system architectures is the major reason why the middleware would be required. The middleware would require providing system interface capabilities with remote accessibility.

On the other hand, the middleware would be required to open up the legacy system to third-party systems.

Simple middlewares we have been dealing with are transformation engines, which are dumb algorithms that convert one data packet format to another—for example, converting a CSV (Comma Separated Values; a delimited ASCII) file to XML format and vice versa.

We can now identify the major features for a middleware engine from the previous discussion, which would appear as follows:

- Provide remote invocation capabilities
- Provide transform services
- Provide processing capabilities, which might be application specific
- Provide messaging services for better accessibility and use

Figure 8.6 provides a schematic, which includes all the components for a good middleware. It goes a step ahead by providing database interaction capabilities.

Let's review the mode and make some re-adjustments. For our middleware to be more accessible as gateways, it would be useful to incorporate some recent libraries such as ebXML. This would make it easier for the systems to use the middleware engine for integrating different systems and even third-party systems.

JAXM (similar to JMS from Sun, at `http://java.sun.com/xml/jaxm/index.html`), along with ebXML (electronic business XML, at `http://www.ebxml.org/specs/ebMS.pdf`), could be used productively in such an architecture. JAXM can have a sender and receiver. A receiver can act as both a sender and a receiver per the requirement. JAXM supports SOAP specifications and a message-describing layer (such as ebXML) could be easily added or used with it.

JAXM is formed around two main API packages: `javax.xml.messaging` and `javax.xml.soap`.

The ebXML initiative by UN/CEFACT (United Nations Center for Trade Facilitation and Electronic Business) and OASIS (Organization for the Advancement of Structured Information Standards) aims to create and conduct business over the Internet. ebXML comprises message formatting, business processes, and registry services specifications, among others. In ebXML, an entire message is called a *message package*. A message package has one header container and zero or more payload containers. Most of the ebXML-specific elements exist in the header container, which includes the elements that describe how the message will route, what type of operations it will perform, the unique identifier for the message, and so on.

To make the discussion on ebXML complete, Listing 8.6 shows a sample ebXML packet transferred by a mail client to the messaging system (JAXM).

LISTING 8.6 Sample ebXML Message Packet—Header and Payload (Body)

```
--121212.6343437126.JavaMail.Administrator.u8222
Content-Type: text/xml

<SOAP-ENV:Envelope
xmlns:SOAP-ENV="http://schemas.xmlsoap.org/soap/envelope/"
xmlns:eb="http://www.ebxml.org/namespaces/messageHeader"
xmlns:xlink="http://www.w3.org/1999/xlink">
<SOAP-ENV:Header>
<eb:MessageHeader SOAP-ENV:actor="1" version="1.0">
  <eb:From>
  <eb:PartyId>mailto:response@bankserver.com</eb:PartyId>
  </eb:From>
  <eb:To>
```

LISTING 8.6 Sample ebXML Message Packet—Header and Payload (Body)

```
    <eb:PartyId>mailto:partner@bankserver.com</eb:PartyId>
    </eb:To>
    <eb:CPAId>123</eb:CPAId>
    <eb:ConversationId>1717182</eb:ConversationId>
    <eb:Service>urn:services:QueryTransfers</eb:Service>
    <eb:Action>QueryAllTransfers</eb:Action>
    <eb:MessageData>
    <eb:MessageId>7478474574576</eb:MessageId>
    <eb:Timestamp>2001-07-20T9:31:12Z</eb:Timestamp>
    </eb:MessageData>
  </eb:MessageHeader>
  </SOAP-ENV:Header>
  <SOAP-ENV:Body>
  <eb:Manifest>
    <eb:Reference xlink:href="amttransfer@bankserver.com" xlink:type="simple">
    <eb:Description>Money Transfer</eb:Description>
    </eb:Reference>
  </eb:Manifest>
  </SOAP-ENV:Body>
  </SOAP-ENV:Envelope>
  --121212.666177126.JavaMail.Administrator.u3499
  Content-Type: text/xml
  Content-Id: amttransfer@bankserver.com

  <?xml version="1.0" encoding="UTF-8"?>
  <trans:interaccountTransfer xmlns:trans="http://bankserver.com/interaccounttx">
  <trans:accountFrom>12346</trans:accountFrom>
  <trans:accountTo>12345</trans:accountTo>
  <trans:amount>$2,000.00</trans:amount>
  </trans: interaccountTransfer>

  --121212.666177126.JavaMail.Administrator.u8222--
```

In Listing 8.6, the message header shows the linkage information and defines the sender receiver path. The lines beginning with markers `--` specify the MIME inset, and they separate the message header with the body or payload. Note the XLink reference in the `<eb:Maifest>` tag, which points to the payload container ID (MIME type) specified by `amttransfer@bankserver.com`.

Let's get back to our model from Figure 8.6. We will try to divide the system composition to make it a bit easier from a designing perspective. The system can be grouped as shown in the following list:

- Messaging Middleware—This includes the Interface layer, Queue Manager, Queue, Subscriber list, and Publisher list.
- In-built processing services—XSLT Processor.
- Custom Adapter Object Factory—Object Factory, Adapters, Objects.
- Database interconnection services.
- System synchronizer.

This simplifies the approach to choose the available models for designing the system. In the In-built processing services, you would add the ebXML processing capability as discussed before. The synchronizer would provide services to communicate in between modules internal to systems and hence controls the system bus.

Figure 8.8 illustrates a modified schematic, which shows a high-level division of the services we would require in the middleware component. Of course, you could filter the services per the requirement.

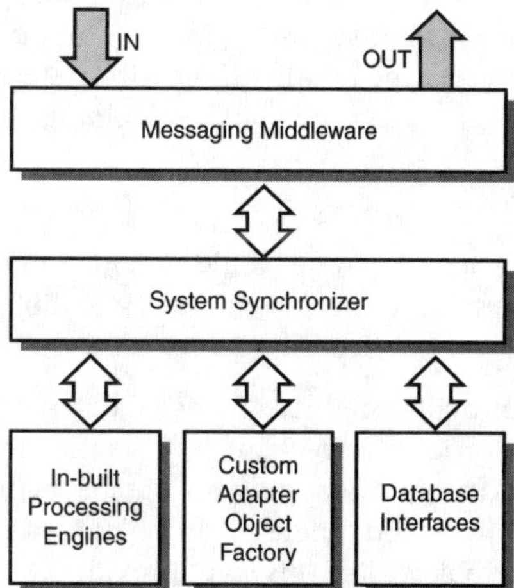

FIGURE 8.8 Simplified view of a middleware system.

The main reason for reviewing the original model was to make probable design suggestions. Note that for each block in the figure, you could find a corresponding ready to use package or development environment available today. Some such packages or development environments are shown in the following list:

- Messaging Middleware—JMS, JAXM, BizTalk
- In-built processing services—Apache
- Custom Adapter Object Factory—Custom built
- Database interconnection Services—BizTalk, Oracle, Allora
- System synchronizer—Custom built

Available freeware and open source XML products have made it easier for you to quickly assemble components and create a good system.

Now you should understand that the model view is also important when you arrive at a design. A single architecture can be presented in various formats or forms depending on how you group the modules or blocks. The most promising way to group should be such that you can find an equivalent package for all the modules readily available.

We still need to code the synchronizer and the custom adapters, but that business logic needs to be part of the middleware engine. My intention in this section is to show how you could leverage the existing tools with respect to system modeling because time is of essence in designing and developing large-scale systems.

An XML Wrapper for Objects

Fundamentally speaking, a middleware would provide interfacing services or “interface-ability” to a system so that it could be extendible. Many times, though, it is not necessary to have a full-fledged middleware as in previous sections.

A simple example is to provide a resultset from a database to an application using XML, or rather the application that reckons XML as the input/output protocol. This simple application would require wrapping the database connection object so that it has a `getRestsetAsXML()` method. There might be numerous occasions to use the concept of wrapping the objects like this so to provide XML capabilities.

The savvy reason to provide wrapping is to XML-enable your application or service. A simple application, such as an accounting package, can boost its capabilities to interact with the external world by simply providing a wrapper service that interacts with the internal database or business logic and provides an XML gateway. This is simple, but could be a powerful way to share data. The idea of wrapping could open up many possibilities to the basic application because then you could couple to the RPC library and remote enable or SOAP enable your application.

Often in distributed systems design, XML has started to become a driving force to integrate systems. Many times you need XML to be used for simplistic mechanisms such as coupling the systems, and the only purpose it might serve is to provide data in a language and platform independent format. CSV and various other flat-file formats serve the same purpose, but their use is limited in a way because they tie up to standards or specifications. And this specification usually grows proprietary. XML meets this need by providing a described instance of data. XML is often viewed as the protocol that requires and consumes bandwidth, but given the networking arena we have lots of bandwidth. Limitation of bandwidth might be a consideration in consumer based XML applications and in wireless worlds, but does not forbid its use. It is important to point out that the bandwidth requirement, although technical, is a major constraint in some cases. For example, the raw ASCII text takes up and consumes more bandwidth than the same text transferred using a carrier or modem protocols such as ZModem. Conceptually, because XML comprises of readable characters that require a full 8 bits to describe each data character, it requires more bandwidth as compared to other protocols.

How to Know There Is Enough Dynamism—Data Mapping

Representation of data and using linked parameters call for dynamism. Perhaps the oldest form of dynamism we had in the system is by using initialization files, which provide a way to dynamically assign default values or function calls in a system or module. This allows for the system to be customizable and configurable depending on the type of use.

A definite limit and level of dynamism must be included in the design of a system. The level definition is dependent on the system use. For example, if we were developing a product such as an ERP system to be deployed on diverse customer locations involved in different businesses, we would prefer the highest level of dynamism available. If it is a typical in-house system and we know it has to be used for, say, an on-site contracting business, dynamism would be limited.

The rule of thumb is the more the system is dynamic, the more flexible it is and the more time it takes to design it. Dynamic system deployment can be extremely complex because the deployment personnel or integrator has to account for various settings. The customization level provided in the system can cross most complex boundaries such as those of all ERP systems existing today. This results in creating a whole simplified programming platform to make the deployment easier, similar to how SAP uses ABAP.

Our effort in incorporating dynamism in the system is relative to the possible settings in the system. Consider a typical example of a dealer system. The dealer provides parts from certain company to all the companies, both domestic and international. Let's concentrate on the issue of the requirement of such a system to be integrated to existing system. The data fields in the existing system can be different, including the data types used. Furthermore, the system data schemas would be completely different, including the internal table design. If both the systems were relational databases, it would involve mapping the fields and tables between the two. However, if the two systems have different back ends, such as one is a relational database and the second one has a CSV format, the mapping requirement would change again in terms of the final outcome required. This mapping would define or specify what fields from the CSV formatted file would be used, formatted, and finally mapped to the respective database table fields. Notice that this mapping requires the specification of some sort of filter routine for getting rid of the extra fields and then reformatting the data set for mapping.

First, consider the issue of providing a mapping to the relational system in terms of database schemas. This involves two things—one to derive metadata from the two systems and two to set the required map information. Figure 8.9 shows the schematic layout for a typical data mapping application.

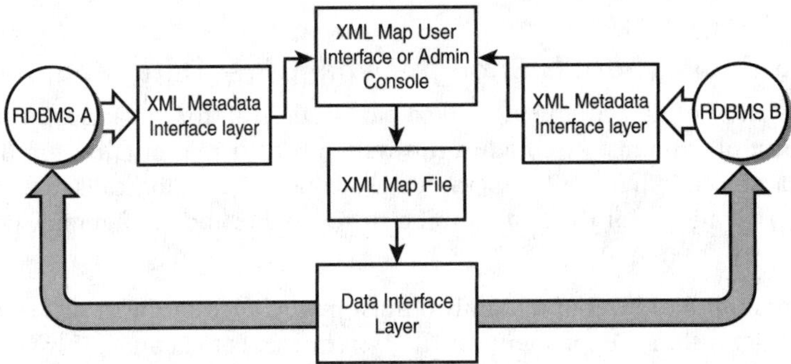

FIGURE 8.9 Schematic layout for data mapping.

The user interface or admin console for configuring the map file and generating it would be a screen with metadata from RDBMS A appearing as the dynamic selection in the first column vis-à-vis metadata from RDBMS B as second column. Figure 8.10 shows the proposed simple GUI.

Note that the GUI is enough to catch the complex mapping requirement. Once the metadata from both ends is available to the GUI module, it would create the respective metadata DOM tree in memory using a simple DOM parser for XML. Then the user would undergo the following sequence of actions to map the data:

- Select a table from RDBMS A.
- The previous action would fill in all the select boxes in RDBMS A Fields row with the field names from A.
- User selects a table name from RDBMS B.

- The previous action would fill in all the select boxes in RDBMS B Fields row with the field names from B.
- The user then selects a field from the second column and one from the third column, which would map to each other.

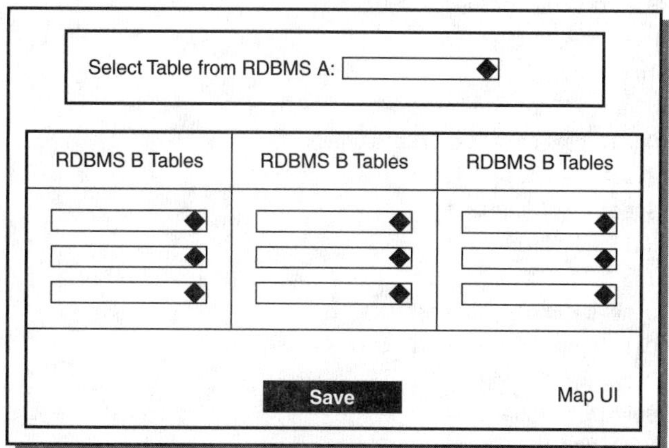

FIGURE 8.10 GUI layout for data mapping.

The preceding GUI is flexible enough, but would require some work in terms of validation so that the same field cannot be mapped to two fields. Also, the field data types can form the basis of validation, again per the requirement.

After the user selects the entries from the respective select boxes, he can click the Save button to generate the map file.

The metadata format arriving from the metadata interface layer could be in a simple table fields tag format as shown in Listing 8.7. Listing 8.8 shows a sample map file generated. These listings will make the purpose clearer.

LISTING 8.7 Metadata Document as Received from the RDBMS Metadata Interface Layer

```
<?xml version="1.0"?>
<!-- XML document representing RDBM system meta-data-->
<RDBMSAMetaData>
    <Table name="EmployeeMaster">
        <Field name="EmployeeID">
            <DataType>Numeric</DataType>
            <Size>8</Size>
            <Special>PKEY</Special>
            <Null>NO</Null>
```

LISTING 8.7 Continued

```
        </Field>
        <Field name="EmployeeProfileID">
            <DataType>Numeric</DataType>
            <Size>8</Size>
            <Special>FKEY</Special>
            <Null>NO</Null>
        </Field>
        <Field name="EmployeeLastName">
            <DataType>Character</DataType>
            <Size>12</Size>
            <Special></Special>
            <Null>NO</Null>
        </Field>
        <Field name="EmployeeFirstID">
            <DataType>Character</DataType>
            <Size>10</Size>
            <Special></Special>
            <Null>NO</Null>
        </Field>
        <Field name="EmployeeSalutation">
            <DataType>Character</DataType>
            <Size>4</Size>
            <Special></Special>
            <Null>YES</Null>
        </Field>
        <Field name="EmployeeTel">
            <DataType>Numeric</DataType>
            <Size>10</Size>
            <Special></Special>
            <Null></Null>
        </Field>
    <Table>
</RDBMSAMetaData>
```

Listing 8.7 can be used to define any RDBMS schema. Note the use of the `<Special>` tag, which specifies whether the field is a primary or foreign key. Furthermore, the `<Null>` tag specifies the extra condition indicating whether the field can be empty. You can have an additional tag such as `<Default>` to specify the default field value, which can be important in data transformation. For representing complex data types—as in Oracle, which supports a nested tables concept—we could use the `<Complex>` tag with the `<Table>` inset child tag.

LISTING 8.8 Data Map File Example

```
<?xml version="1.0"?>
<!-- Sample data map file-->
<DataMapScheme>
    <MapEntry number="1">
        <Database name="RDBMSA">
            <Table>EmployeeMaster</Table>
            <Field>EmployeeID</Field>
        </Database>
        <Database name="RDBMSB">
            <Table>EmployeeRecord</Table>
            <Field>EmployeeCode</Field>
        </Database>
    </MapEntry>
    <MapEntry number="2">
        <Database name="RDBMSA">
            <Table>EmployeeMaster</Table>
            <Field>EmployeeTel</Field>
        </Database>
        <Database name="RDBMSB">
            <Table>EmployeeRecord</Table>
            <Field>EmployeePhone</Field>
        </Database>
    </MapEntry>
</DataMapScheme>
```

I have shown only one field map entry in Listing 8.8. The file representation can have various formats. The listing shows each independent entry from the database to the table with a field perspective. At times, especially when you want to reference fields from one database set to another, it would be easier to represent the preceding XML as shown in Listing 8.9.

LISTING 8.9 Data Map File Example—Database as a Base Element

```
<?xml version="1.0"?>
<!-- Sample data map file-->
<DataMapScheme>
    <Database name="RDBMSA">
        <Table>EmployeeMaster</Table>
        <MapDetails number="1">
            <Field>EmployeeID</Field>
            <MapDatabase>RDBMSB</MapDatabase>
```

LISTING 8.9 Continued

```
            <MapTable>EmployeeRecord</MapTable>
            <MapField>EmployeeCode</MapField>
        </MapDetails>
        <MapDetails number="2">
            <Field>EmployeeTel</Field>
            <MapDatabase>RDBMSB</MapDatabase>
            <MapTable>EmployeeRecord</MapTable>
            <MapField>EmployeePhone</MapField>
        </MapDetails>
    </Database>
</DataMapScheme>
```

With reference to tables, if you were to find out how many corresponding fields are associated with the other database fields, it would be easier to do that from Listing 8.9, rather than Listing 8.8. The listing arranges each table under a respective database (here RDBMSA) and has dynamic nesting to specify the corresponding field mapping. Hence, formulating the XML document is equally important, and you have to closely analyze the situation in which it is to be used.

If for some applications Listing 8.8 suits and for other applications Listing 8.9 suits, it is suggested to provide anyone as the output from the map file and then have suitable XML transformation to convert into another desired format. You could use either custom code or XML style sheets, which are more flexible and easily manageable.

The other information you could include in the preceding map file is that of the data types. It might occur at times that the data mapping is among the dissimilar data types—for example, `EmployeeID` can be numeric in one system and can be alphanumeric in another. At such times, it is possible to transform numeric into alphanumeric, but not the other way around. This has to be indicated and not allowed in the file. We could account for such special cases using a `<Direction>` tag, which would be similar to a vector indication, specifying which way the transformation is specified in the file. For example, specifying the following tag in Listing 8.8 could tell the parsing logic that this map file applies only from RDMSA to RDMSB and not the other way around.

```
<Direction>
    <Unidirectional>YES</Unidirectional>
    <From>RDBMSA</From>
   <To>RDBMSB</To>
</Direction>
```

Mapping can be a useful technique to connect or join two XML systems based on dissimilar data schemas.

Mapping of Formats

Data mapping is not limited to XML-to-XML map representations. It can be used to map formats too. For example, you could use a data-mapping file to map XML data to a flat-file format. Although this topic is more related to data transforming, it still uses a data map file for referencing the required information. Consider that you have an XML system to be interfaced to a flat-file system, such as a mainframe. Note that throughout this book, I refer to mainframe files as flat files. This is not exactly how they are arranged in mainframe databases or files. But major interfaces available to exchange data with these back ends are more in flat-file format—that is, at least the information is passed to such systems as flat files.

The flat-file record format is specific to a data position and has to follow the layout very closely. In the simple example here, consider the following definition of flat-file format required by the back-end system, which stores the employee contact information.

```
Record format for Employee contact information database:
Record size: 112 [size 6]
Error code: 00 - OK, XX - error number [any number other then 00] [size 2]
Field name: Employee Name
Field Length: 35
Field Name: Employee ID
Field Length: 15
Field Name: Telephone
Field Length: 10
Field Name: Email
Field Length: 50
```

The preceding format is relatively simple. On first thought, this format can be represented in XML format as shown in Listing 8.10.

LISTING 8.10 A Data Map File for Flat-File Representation

```
<?xml version="1.0"?>
<!--XML map file for flat file format-->
<FlatFileRecordMap>
    <Element>
        <Name>Record Size</Name>
        <Type>FIXEDVALUE</Type>
        <Size>6</Size>
        <DefaultValue>112</DefaultValue>
    </Element>
```

LISTING 8.10 Continued

```
    <Element>
        <Name>Error Code</Name>
        <Type>VALUE</Type>
        <Size>2</Size>
        <DefaultValue></DefaultValue>
    </Element>
    <Element>
        <Name>Employee Name</Name>
        <Type>VALUE</Type>
        <Size>35</Size>
        <DefaultValue></DefaultValue>
    </Element>
    <Element>
        <Name>Employee ID</Name>
        <Type>VALUE</Type>
        <Size>15</Size>
        <DefaultValue></DefaultValue>
    </Element>
    <Element>
        <Name>Telephone</Name>
        <Type>VALUE</Type>
        <Size>10</Size>
        <DefaultValue></DefaultValue>
    </Element>
    <Element>
        <Name>Email</Name>
        <Type>VALUE</Type>
        <Size>50</Size>
        <DefaultValue></DefaultValue>
    </Element>
</FlatFileRecordMap>
```

The XML stream in Listing 8.10 could be used by a simple code routine that would reference each element and arrive at the exact characters required in the main stream by padding spaces. The `<Type>` tag allows the application to arrive at the stream effectively because the preceding representation allows default values to be specified. Technically for the type specified as `FIXEDVALUE` and some default value, it would be the same as having a fixed or static declaration in code. We could enhance the XML stream further by including different types such as `ENUMVALUE` for specifying the enumerated values. In our example, if error code could be either 00 (no error) or 01 (some error), we could have specified them as an enumeration.

```
<Element>
    <Name>Error Code</Name>
    <Type>ENUMVALUE</Type>
    <Size>2</Size>
    <DefaultValue></DefaultValue>
    <Enum>
        <Value name="No Error">00</Value>
        <Value name="Some Error">01</Value>
    </Enum>
</Element>
```

The XML stream shown in Listing 8.10 can be used in conjunction with another map file, which would specify which XML tags map to the occurrence number in the flat file. So the transform module would refer to the map file for mapping XML elements to the flat file and then refer to the file in Listing 8.10 to convert the same into a Flat stream.

Hence, the initial argument that the XML stream in Listing 8.10 is not the map file is correct. Rather, it is the transform map file.

XML Based Configuration Definitions

Just as you need to make the data transformation dynamic, you need to have some settings that the application could use for initialization. These settings could reflect various startup configuration details and can also be invoked by a soft trigger.

Configuration settings are oldies in applications. Perhaps the most recent ones you have used were the Windows INI files. This INI or initialization files allow an application to define the startup behavior. It is also possible for the applications to dump the close down information in these files and use it for persistent behavior.

XML for configuration files is already an applied field and is in use today. It is similar to INI files and can be used by an XML enabled application for defining the startup parameters. Consider a simple example. A typical EAI (Enterprise application interface) system would deal with the following requirements:

- To dynamically invoke a suitable adapter as part of settings to interface with the client end ERP system
- To specify the default user and department information
- To specify the default parameters for interfacing with the ERP system

To get a clearer idea, the sample system schematic is shown in Figure 8.11. The schematic is simple and shows that the EAI system interacts with the actual client ERP system. Also, the system uses a suitable adapter invoked by the binding interface layer.

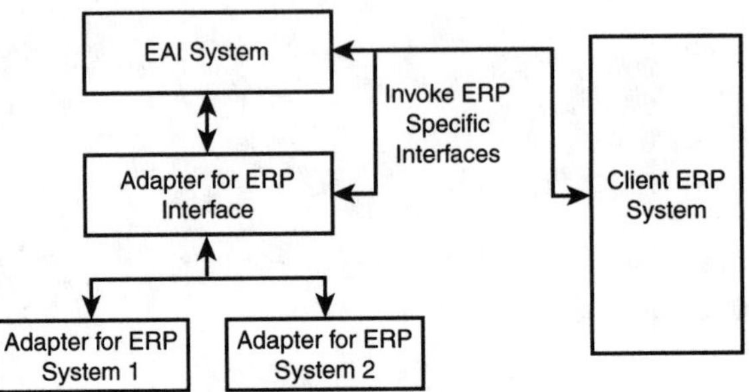

FIGURE 8.11 The EAI system schematic interfacing with the ERP system.

For the EAI system to interact with the ERP system, it needs basic authentication information and also some settings that would specify the ERP system type. We could use an XML configuration file to define these settings easily as shown in Listing 8.11.

LISTING 8.11 XML Configuration File Example

```
<?xml version="1.0"?>
<!-- XML config file sample -->
<EAIConfiguration>
    <ERPAuthentication>
        <UserID>NitaAR</UserID>
        <PrivateKey>AS123DFEDNN</PrivateKey>
        <AuthenticationCode>ASDFR45454</AuthnticationCode>
    </ERPAuthentication>
    <ERPUserCostCenter>
        <UserID>NitaAR</UserID>
        <DepartmentName>GARMENTS</DepartmentName>
        <DepartmentCode>N-GAR-94087</DepartmentCode>
    </ERPUserCostCenter>
    <AdapterConfigSetting>
        <ERPSystem>LAWSON</ERPSystem>
        <DefaultParameters>
            <Param number="1">
                <Name>FTPServer</Name>
                <Value>192.168.168.17</Value>
            </Param>
            <Param number="2">
                <Name>FTPUsername</Name>
                <Value>EVOLVEWARE</Value>
```

LISTING 8.11 Continued

```
            </Param>
            <Param number="3">
                <Name>FTPPassword</Name>
                <Value>EW00001</Value>
            </Param>
            <Param number="4">
                <Name>VendorID</Name>
                <Value>EAIV019201</Value>
            </Param>
    </AdapterConfigSetting>
</EAIConfiguration>
```

The configuration file shown in Listing 8.11 is simple and easier to modify manually. Furthermore, the advantage of having the file in XML format is ease of administration because it is possible to modify the file on-the-fly using a standard parsing mechanism.

Often because of the basic system architecture that uses XML as its native protocol, it is better to have the same format for configuration files.

A futuristic advantage of having such configuration files defined is to make it possible for the system administrator to access the files using a simple XML based editor and edit them. The same argument and format could be used for defining system settings options such as in connection pools wherein we need to specify the number of active connections to be created at startup. The advantage of having the configuration files defined for pooling is that they could be reconfigured on-the-fly by unattended scripts, such as some sort of rule based system, instead of the administrator.

In theory, we think of configuration files only for system startup definitions. But, they can be used even in an intermediate layer as dynamic configuration definitions. In an n-tier system having the capability to interact with an application on a remote server, for example, you could have a configuration setting that specifies the IP address of the server. In case of a system changeover or maintenance, you could change the configuration IP setting to a secondary server for the time being. For many reasons, it is always a good idea to provide a dynamic refresh method in a configurable component. In this example, if we were to change the configuration, which would have been read at startup, when the application is running we need to change the tag value in the XML configuration file and manually trigger a refresh method on the startup process (soft-trigger mechanism). This will dynamically affect the settings by re-reading the configuration file.

XML also offers a possibility of inventing new tags that could be used to dynamically create settings tags in the configuration files. The system could be made roughly dynamic to interact with the newfound tags and accordingly do some settings internally.

Consider that you are dealing with a communications system that interfaces with some hardware through a serial port. Currently because of serious communication speed limitations, we need to introduce some amount of delay (a typical `sleep()` mechanism) to synchronize with the data packets. The system fine-tuning sets this sleep timing, which is set by sensing the clock speed of the CPU. Now, in the future some faster systems will come into existence and your code will need a new fine-tuning requirement. A simple occasion such as this could provide a better insight into the architecture. If you made your system robust enough to look out for help in some place, like a configuration file, it would look there to see some new information tags. Add some additional tags to this configuration file, such as `<CPUType>` specifying the type of CPU and `<CPUSpeed>` for the speed, and then the system could sense for such tags using the `<Keywords>` technique. The system would look out for tags matching `CPU` and `Speed`, and any new tag that has one or both of these would match the search criteria. After the match occurs, the tag is read and accordingly interpreted and included dynamically in the operation. Although this example is more on the knowledge based systems side, it will help you understand the importance of XML configuration files and keywords in files.

Summary

The next chapter gives an important introduction and lists the various techniques for exchanging data between two systems. Various data exchange formats and scenarios are discussed, including EDI and hierarchical data sets.

The chapter also gives a design approach path and an overview to model database warehouses. It also discusses the possibility of applying XML for drawing inferences (data mining) from huge data sets distributed over the corporate arena.

9 Data Exchange Scenario

IN THIS CHAPTER

- Overview
- EDI Overview
- Hierarchy Data Models
- XML Wrappers to Represent and Wrap Data Packets

It is a very sad thing that nowadays there is so little useless information.

—*Oscar Wilde*

This chapter discusses the existing data packaging protocols and their overview. The data exchange forms popular in electronic data interfacing worlds are also discussed.

The generic form of the hierarchical data representation model is considered to give a definitive idea on information presentation as it exists in packaging large-scale databases.

It shows the way XML can be used to bundle and represent these popular packaging and interchange methods.

The topic of data warehousing is treated to mark the chapter as complete from the data interface and exchange viewpoint. The query model for large database intensive operations is considered and XML is shown to make a generic open-ended approach when devising such systems.

XML based transaction systems are introduced. The database concept and SQL lingo are overviewed and the XML query mechanism is discussed to indicate the technologies existing in the market for database interaction. Finally, the XML oriented query engine is discussed. The chapter closes with a detailed discussion on message packet based systems. The system design for the same is specified and handled from a XML centric architecture design approach.

Overview

Data exchange is the primary motto of all systems. For an enterprisewide system, it is crucial that data can be exchanged at any pace.

Data exchange might involve adapting to various different sets of terminology, packet definitions, or protocols. Hence, we need to deal with high-level definitions of data, called the metadata. *Metadata* is data about data and usually describes the schema's forms.

The importance of standardizing the data transfer formats was realized long ago. Various standards were formulated and used to make the data universal and recognizable by a majority of systems by using standard extensions. The global electronic marketplace was soon realized because inter-system communication relied on universal standards. So, the trend of using electronic forms of data grew, and we ended up in an electronic age.

Over the past few decades, various forms of packaging methods were invented and used. The most popular one is *EDI (Electronic Data Interchange)*. I will discuss what EDI is and how people use it. Later you will see what an EDI packet is actually composed of. You will see the actual representation of an EDI packet and how to create one from reference documents. Also, you will see how you could relate it to XML.

Hierarchical data representation is another popular buzzword in use. We use such representation to represent nested data formats, such as categorized reports. These data representation formats are also used in representing some filesystems such as *HFS (Hierarchical File System)*. We will look into such data representation formats and how you can use XML to represent such formats and put it to use.

Because of the high availability of dispersed data among distributed corporate databases, the newborn concept—which is widely used today—is that of data warehousing and data mining. Data mining is the state of art application that helps you analyze raw data collected in huge databases and draw inferences. Hence, they are also called *inference engines*.

We will look into data representation and drawing inferences from it using XML terminology. We will use XML wrappers to wrap the old channel protocols, such as EDI and hierarchical data formats, and make them available to a new breed of systems. XML would be used to wrap things by using some sort of transformation. And the transformation would involve some sort of guidance file or a map file. The map file would provide how the packet fields are to be mapped to the corresponding entities in between two reference systems. For example, the map file would provide the field-based map details between two database systems.

XML can be used to represent complex data formats or patterns, and it allows such data packets to be transmitted through available channels for better data transfers.

One recently introduced concept of using XML is to represent the query format. This is a relatively new use of XML and is quite interesting. You have seen XML used for defining configuration settings. Some standards such as XQuery are still in their draft versions and will be finalized soon. You could refer to `http://www.w3.org/TR/xquery/`

for official XQuery specifications. But, it is still worth taking a look at what it is and how it would be used for querying Web documents or a collection of documents. The same concept was recently enhanced to include some databases in the fold, where various databases were introduced that allowed querying via XML.

Finally, we will review the framework model again from a message perspective. The message-based approach is very flexible and allows the enormous possibility of extension and universal system construct.

EDI Overview

EDI stands for Electronic Data Interchange and has been around for many decades now. It was and still is widely used for transferring the data related to inventory and hence allows for a flexible way to update systems separated by huge distances.

A typical EDI usage scenario could be that of the auto industry. The auto manufacturer uses parts shipped into the manufacturing facility from various locations. At any given point of time, the production facility would use EDI to locate and hence forecast a strategy for scheduling the jobs.

From an information engineering perspective, EDI is a packet of data (similar to XML) flowing through a network. The communication medium used can vary depending on availability. The EDI packet can be transferred using a network (LAN/WAN) or through e-mail. The receiving end system would use suitable decoding logic to extract this standard EDI packet packed in wrappers depending on the communication medium.

This EDI packet, which consists of data arranged in some sort of format, is standardized. This is true for any system to be globally acceptable and programmable. For example, if the auto manufacturer is dealing with part suppliers from diverse locations, the data must be represented in a format recognized by all. Because a single vendor could deal with different manufacturers, this requirement becomes more important.

Just as we have a *Document Type Definition (DTD)* document for specifying data embedded in an XML stream, we have something called SEF for EDI. SEF stands for *Standard Exchange Format* and is a file that describes the data layout in an EDI file. So, an EDI packet consists of data, and the corresponding SEF file would contain the instructions to interpret it. Any EDI processing engine could then use these two files to derive the actual data.

EDI is a flat (like ASCII) packet of data stream, wherein the data is represented in a sequential manner. Note that this is similar to the flat-file records discussed in Chapter 3, "Parsing an XML Document." SEF is also a flat description file.

Over the years, EDI was standardized, and even the Federal government has defined some usage guidelines for governing the electronic transactions. Because EDI is a widely used standard and much in place, we will look at the various aspects of EDI message packet and how it is formatted in greater detail.

We can further use XML to represent EDI data and hence make our modern system available for use by a wide range of systems.

EDI as an Information Transfer Protocol

As mentioned in the previous section, EDI is a flat stream of data. Let's look at what the message format or data packet are like.

Figure 9.1 shows the structure of a generic EDI packet. Note that it is similar to most flat records used in many data systems. The packet example shown in the figure refers to a simple invoice example.

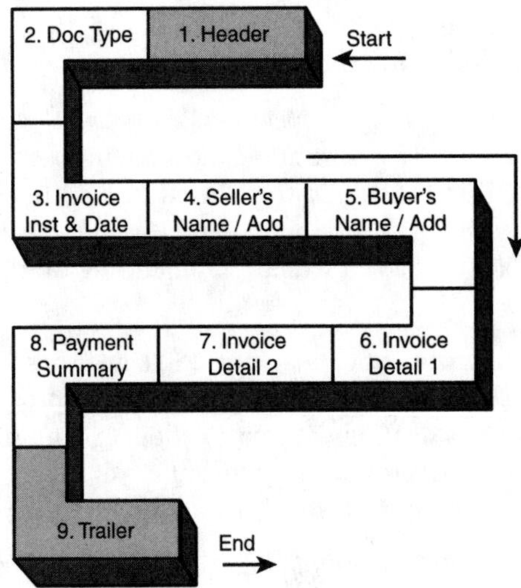

FIGURE 9.1 A sample EDI message showing the main elements of the package.

The packet has a header and trailer to mark the start and end of an EDI record. The header is followed by a document type descriptor, which would specify what type of EDI packet this is. Here it would be something such as an invoice. The invoice date and code number follows this. Then comes the buyer and seller details followed by the invoice details and summary.

As seen the entire paper based invoice is converted in a stream of characters divided in terms of records. Essentially, items 2, 3, 4, and 5 constitute the invoice header. Items 6, 7, and 8 form the details portion of the same invoice. The header (1) and trailer (9) are EDI packet related items.

The sample packet shows the layout of an invoice in EDI terms. Different business tasks would require different packet descriptions. Consider Figure 9.2, which shows the typical interactions involved in the actual business world. These entire interactions are governed by defining specific EDI packets for the purpose. As seen from the figure, the interactions involve actual data packets and acknowledgements as in the real world. The last portion is of electronic payment, similar to our payment gateway services today. This electronic payment packet would essentially flow from the buyer end to its banker, who finally deposits the amount to the seller's account through the seller's banker.

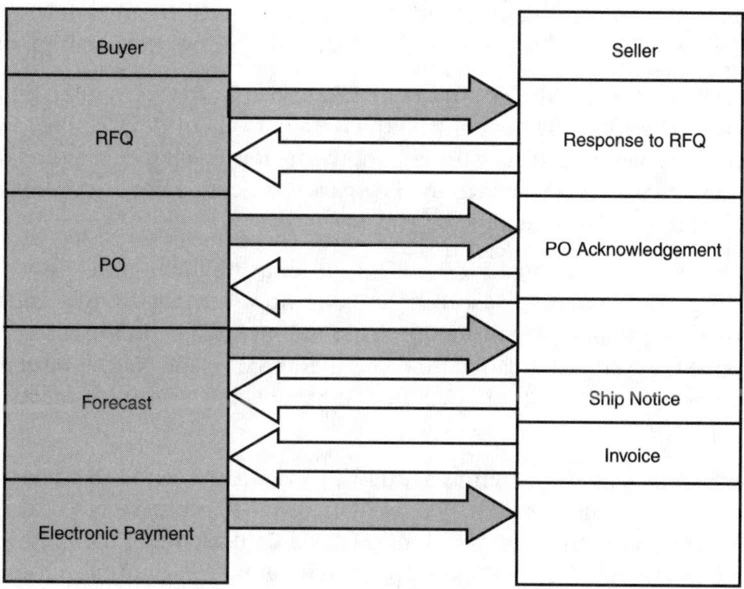

FIGURE 9.2 Example of an EDI business partnership.

The EDI packet, hence, is a flat-file representation of hierarchical data. You could imagine that the invoice consists of a hierarchy by interpreting the invoice title as parent and header and details at the same level with the invoice details having further children as each item detail list.

The packet can be sent and received using a variety of protocols or communication mediums. Perhaps the most used ones are SMTP and FTP. It's interesting how the systems using such protocols could be used to support the distributed computing and information exchange scenario.

The system sending the data would form the EDI packet (by forming the flat file and then transforming into EDI) and send it over the FTP link. At a particular time, the system on the other end would sense this data. By sensing, I mean that the system would be polling: It would sleep for a specific time and try to access the folder (predefined) to see if anything is in it. If it finds the message packet, it reads and converts the EDI packet into a flat-file format, using an application interface, and then passes it to the actual application. It would then finally move the packet from this folder to an archive folder. When these packets are collectively processed, this action is usually called *batch processing*. This might be a crude way to operate because the system would be responsive with the tolerance limit specified by the sleep timing event. But, the important point is the system behaves as distributed. It is also interesting to see how the folder can be used as a queue for storing the incoming message.

With SMTP, the system would bundle the EDI packet in the form of an e-mail and send it over. The receiving system would have a mail client programmed to listen to incoming messages, which is again polling the mail gateway per the time definitions. After a message packet is received, the EDI packet is derived (say from the attachment) and flows through the same process as before.

Specific standards are defined for the EDI transfer using these protocols, especially SMTP. The X.400 standard is just that. X.400 is, however, not a single standard but a number ranging from X.400 to X.440. X.400 is a message handling system standard similar to SMTP. Many standard gateways support SMTP and X.400 to some extent. More information on X.400 can be found at `http://www.itu.int/itudoc/teltopic/x400/`.

The flow of a typical EDI system is as shown in Figure 9.3. The EDI packet is received through a channel and passed to the receiving gateway. Once received, the gateway passes it to the X12 formatter. X12 is an EDI standards defining committee that looks into developing and maintaining EDI standards. You can find out more about X12 at `http://www.x12.org/x12org/about/index.html?whatis.html`.

The application programming interface would then interpret the EDI packet, decode it, and pass it to a flat-file formatter. The flat-file formatter assembles the packet in the flat format, which is finally passed to the application. For outgoing messages, the same sequence applies in reverse order.

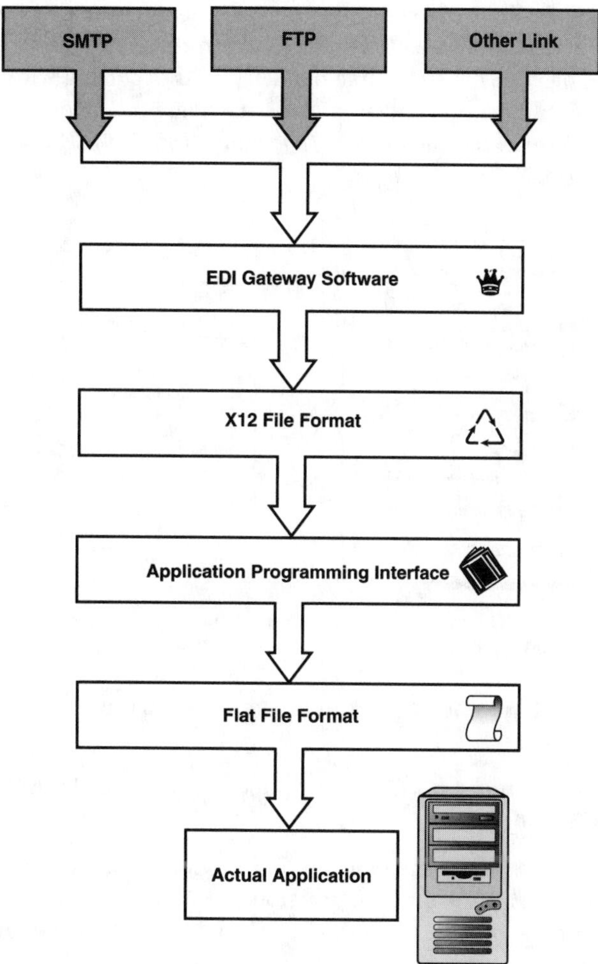

FIGURE 9.3 EDI software application integration.

EDI Packet Example

Let's see what the EDI packet actually looks like. The EDI packet is structured in the form of envelopes. This is similar to the e-mailing system, for example. The message you type in is wrapped within specific envelopes and then broadcast through the gateway to the receiver's mailbox.

The composition of EDI is shown in Figure 9.4. The figure marks various envelopes that cover the actual data to be transmitted. From this figure, you can see that a single EDI message can have multiple data elements occurring within data segments. Each data packet is enveloped by a unique data element. Various data elements are enveloped into distinct transaction sets. The figure also shows the various transaction sets supported in EDI.

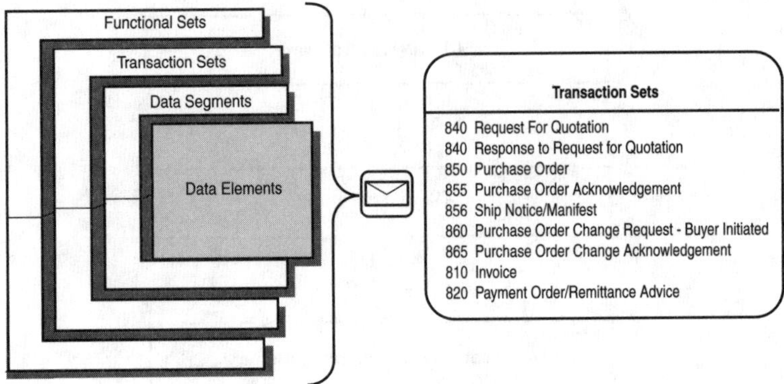

FIGURE 9.4 EDI envelopes.

Note that in EDI all transactions are numbered and each number corresponds to a specific transaction.

Furthermore, all the transactions are enveloped in functional sets. So, the outermost envelope is a functional set.

If you have multiple messages to embed in a single EDI packet, you would collect all the data segments with the same transaction number and bundle them together to form a transaction envelope. After that, you would collect all the transaction sets and form a functional set. That's it! Your packet is ready.

It's true that EDI is not simple and that people really require some hands on practice to get the feel. The material in these sections will still give you a definite idea of what EDI is and allow you to interpret the systems using it in a better way.

Let's review Figure 9.2 in light of the transaction numbers in Figure 9.4. We could label each flow with the respective transaction and arrive at Figure 9.5.

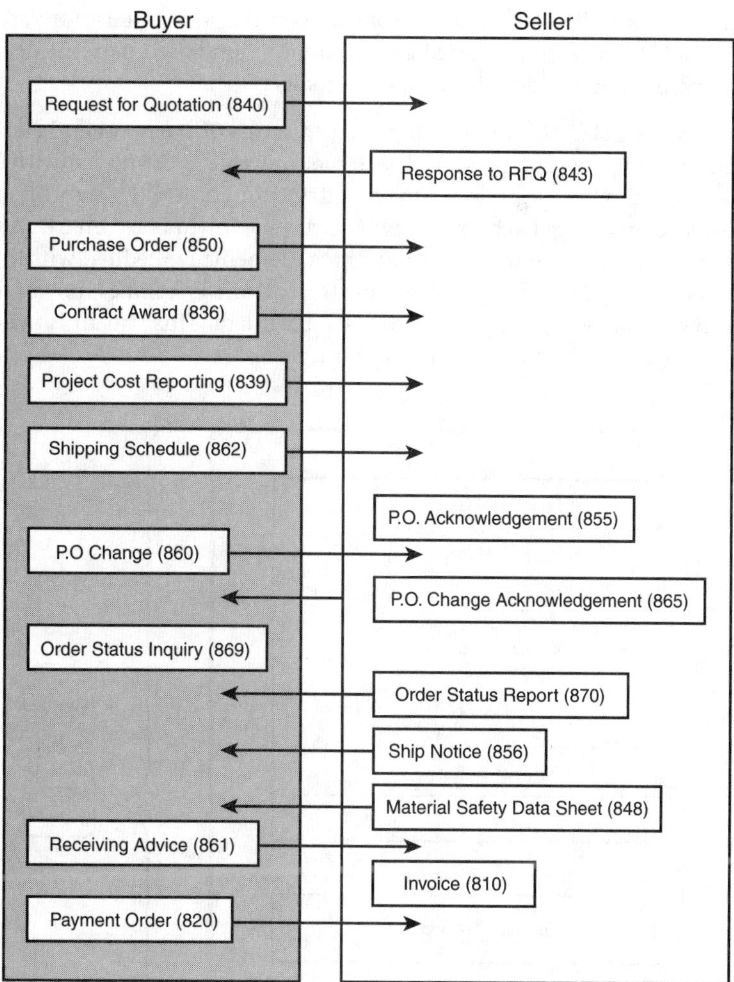

FIGURE 9.5 The EDI business partnership from a transaction perspective.

Now, you should have a clear picture of what EDI is and how it is used in real-world systems. In the real world, the existing systems would do the entire process using automated process logic and hence create an electronic marketplace. As seen the EDI transactions largely evolved to solve the material requirement and supply problem. This would reduce the time to produce a commodity and automate the system. You could further imagine an EDI transaction to update the inventory depending on materials ordered and received. Hence, you would recognize the message in the EDI world in a transaction number, which would then define the entire layout of the data pattern.

The standards committee and bodies work on defining the pattern for various transactions. EDI has various standards and transaction based patterns defined per the industry and has a wide following even today.

Figure 9.6 shows a skeleton of an EDI packet in terms of start and end elements as it is defined in the real world. As seen, the actual message is contained within ISA and IEA ends. Each functional group is enveloped within GS and GE tags. I'll call them tags for easy referencing. Each transaction set is enveloped between ST and SE. Each of these transaction elements would have data elements embedded within it as described before. The receiving end would strap off the envelopes, one at a time, and flatten the data elements as a stream of string data. This stream is parsed to get suitable data by using some programming interface.

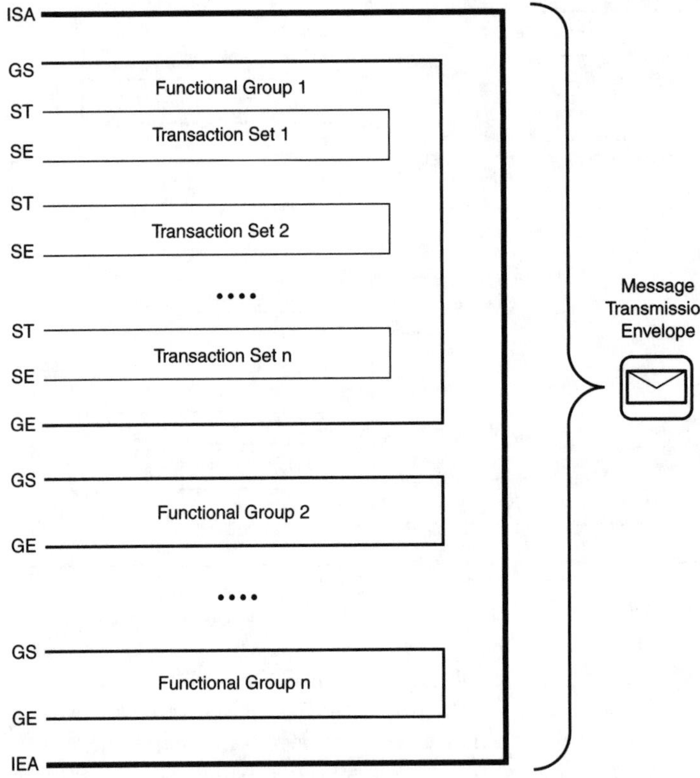

FIGURE 9.6 EDI envelope—a transmission envelope schematic layout.

Let's see what the EDI message stream looks like. Consider the views of data element segments. A suitable delimiter separates each entity in the segment. The concept of delimiter is not new, and we are conversant with ASCII comma-delimited files (called CSV, Comma Separated Values) in which the field entities and values are separated by a , used as a delimiter. Similarly, in tab separated value types of data files, the data elements are separated by a tab.

You can use any delimiter for this purpose, and usually the choice is dependent on the sending or receiving systems. In the example shown in Figure 9.7, the delimiter used is `*`, which is common in major EDI systems today. As shown, each element or entity is separated by a `*`, and the entire element is marked with some sort of begin marker (`BEG`) and end marker—here it is `NL` or a new line character for the end marker. Two examples are shown in this figure: The first example has all the data elements within it, and the second one has one element missing. The important point to note is that the empty element is marked by two `*`. This is important because the receiving system should be able to decode the segment. As you can imagine, the receiving system logic would be quite straightforward. The system would arrive at this data segment and start parsing the record and its data values depending on the occurrence of `*` and until it reaches the `NL` character.

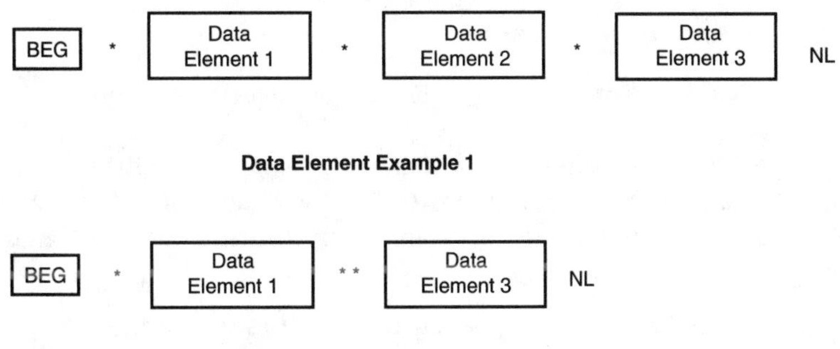

FIGURE 9.7 Segment examples.

EDI records are always constructed from some sort of standard (instruction manual) document. You have to interpret and use the definitions of each record and its element positions with attributes to construct the EDI record. Figure 9.8 shows the EDI descriptor entry from a standard EDI manual.

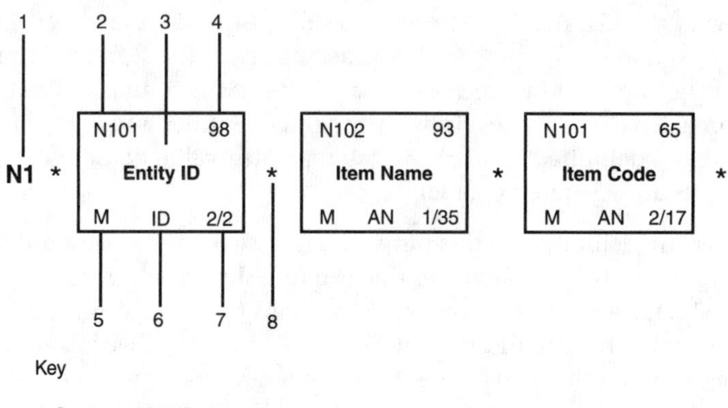

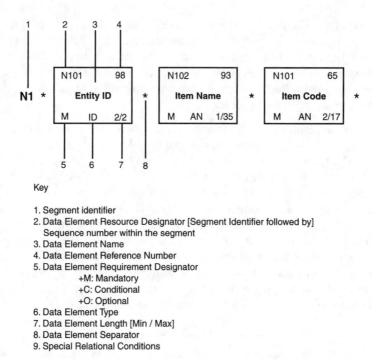

Key

1. Segment identifier
2. Data Element Resource Designator [Segment Identifier followed by] Sequence number within the segment
3. Data Element Name
4. Data Element Reference Number
5. Data Element Requirement Designator
   +M: Mandatory
   +C: Conditional
   +O: Optional
6. Data Element Type
7. Data Element Length [Min / Max]
8. Data Element Separator
9. Special Relational Conditions

FIGURE 9.8 Data element description—EDI element reference example.

A segment begins with a segment identifier, which is some specified character(s) (such as BEG). Each element or entity is described with a set of different attributes. The various attributes, which are important when constructing an EDI message from the manual syntax, are as follows:

- Data Element Resource Designator—This specifies the location of this data element in this segment preceded with the segment reference element.
- Data Element Name—The name of this data entity.
- Data Element Reference Number—This is how it would be referenced in the application and in the manual.
- Data Element Requirement Designator—This specifies whether this element is required or optional; similar to DTD or schema definitions for an XML document.
- Data Element Type—Broadly, this is a data type such as numeric, alphanumeric, or key-id.

- Data Element Length—This specifies the length this data element would occupy. It has both minimum and maximum length specifiers, which is typical for a flat record description based validation engine requirement.
- Data Element Separator—This specifies the delimiter to be used.

As seen here, the reference manual definition specifies the entire description of the element and its placement. This entire standard has to be referenced on the receiving end to be able to decode the data elements. But there is lot of hard-coding to be done and it's not flexible because we would end up creating an element position dependent engine for parsing. This is the shortcoming of using flat record types. Also, there is no way you could specify a hierarchy cleanly in this type of record format.

I could summarize the key terms in an EDI record or packet as follows:

- Segment Identifier serves as a label for data within the segment.
- Data Element Reference Designator is made up of the Segment Identifier followed by a two-digit number that defines the position of the data within the segment.
- Data Element Reference Number is the identifying number for each element's corresponding definition in the ASC X12 Data Dictionary.
- Data Element Name is the name associated with the Data Element.
- X12 Requirement.

  M—Mandatory

  O—Optional

  C—Conditional

- Data Element—Type Definitions are as follows:

  ID—Identifier per ASC X12 Data Dictionary

  AN—Alphanumeric

  DT—Date

  Nn—Numeric with implied decimal (no decimal appears)

  R—Numeric with explicit decimal (decimal appears)

  TM—Time

- Data Element Size

All data elements are assigned a minimum and maximum character length. For example, a 4/6 entry means a minimum of 4 characters and maximum of 6 characters.

A working example of an EDI message using 850 type transaction number for a purchase order is shown in Listing 9.1.

LISTING 9.1 Sample 850 Purchase Order Transaction EDI Message with Comments in Italic

```
ST*850*000000561
Transaction Set Header*Transaction Set ID(850=Purchase Order)
➥*Transaction Set Control Number

BEG*00*BE*N1A12345***010101
Beginning Segment for PO*Transaction Set Purpose(00=Original)
➥*PO Type(BE=Blanket Order)*PO Number***PO Date(YYMMDD)

N1*SE*PERISOL INCORPORATION*92*12345
Name*Entity ID Code(SE=Selling Party)
➥*Name*ID Code Qualifier(92=Assigned by Buyer)*ID Code

PER*CW*NITA
Administrative Communications Contact*Contact Function Code(CW=Confirm with)
➥*Name

N1*BY*EVOLVEWARE INCORPORATION*92*B2
N3*St 772692000
Address Information*Street Address

N4*CALIFORNIA*CA*94087
Geographic Location*City Name*State Code*Postal Code

PO1*000110*8000000*EA*12.000*CT*BP*130918-001*VP*330918-021
Baseline Item Data*PO Line Number*Quantity*Unit of Measure Code(EA=Each)
➥*Unit Price*Basis of Unit Price Code(CT=Contract Price)
➥*Product ID         Qualifier(BP=Buyer's part Number)
➥*Product ID*Product ID Qualifier(VP=Vendor's Part Number)
➥*Product ID(Vendor Part Number)

CTT*1
Transaction Totals*Number of Line Items

SE*11*000000345
Transaction Set Trailer*Number of Included Segments*Transaction Control Number
```

EDI in Use Today

EDI is still used as a main data packaging protocol across businesses around the world. Hence, for a new arena of the distributed computing world, we need to provide support for such an interchange.

Across businesses, EDI usage would include even access to the legacy gateway system. This makes it necessary to consider the EDI as a major transfer protocol and include it in XML constructs. I will discuss the use of EDI from the perspective of utilizing it for business integration. So for truly distributed systems, it is important that we provide suitable capability for systems to compute the data format and the capability to decode the same.

For a typical scenario of a supply chain and ERP based applications, we want to have this interface in place. Many supplier based systems integration would require interfacing with pre-existing ERP applications such as SAP, Oracle Financials, Lawson, and many more. We will look more into legacy based middle-tier design in the next section of this book.

Businesses have utilized EDI gateways in existing systems, and we will use the same for inter-communication layer in our design.

In our framework model described in Chapter 3, we could consider such a scenario of communicating with an existing EDI system. The interface could be imagined to have a client-side middle-tier, which interacts with the EDI system. This middle-tier would then pass the data packets to the framework at the other end, which would use some sort of adapter for decoding the same.

Hierarchical Data Models

Another common format of data representation is hierarchy based. Hierarchical representation is perhaps the oldest methodology to represent complex data. After all, the concept of XML and its widespread use is because of the easiest way it could represent such data.

Because of its capability to represent data in hierarchy format, XML has found a relatively wide and new field of application—of data presentation. We will look into these aspects next.

Hierarchy Data Representation

In simplistic terms, a hierarchy is any model in which each element is either a parent or child. Usually hierarchy starts from the base element called root, which is the parent of all the elements existing in the model. Each element in this representation could essentially be the child of the root and parent of other children. The importance of hierarchical data representation is so much that we could represent any present day system models based on it.

Consider your file structure in the hard drive, for example. It is a hierarchy of drive letter, which is root, and each folder in the drive as a child under root. Furthermore, each folder can have subfolders or files that would be children of the parent folder. Some practical filesystems are based on this simplistic hierarchical representation concept—such as a Unix or Macintosh filesystem called *Hierarchical File System (HFS)*.

Figure 9.9 shows a simplistic hierarchy of an organizational chart. This is also called a tree structure in theory. The root element here is CEO and the members of the company fall under her. For the figure shown, you can see that it has root as CEO and three child *nodes* under it, which in turn have sub-nodes. Yes, even the *DOM (Document Object Model)* model is hierarchical. DOM can describe an HTML document and the same model flows for XML. DOM based XML parsers are discussed in Chapter 2, "XML Overview," which follow from the hierarchy model.

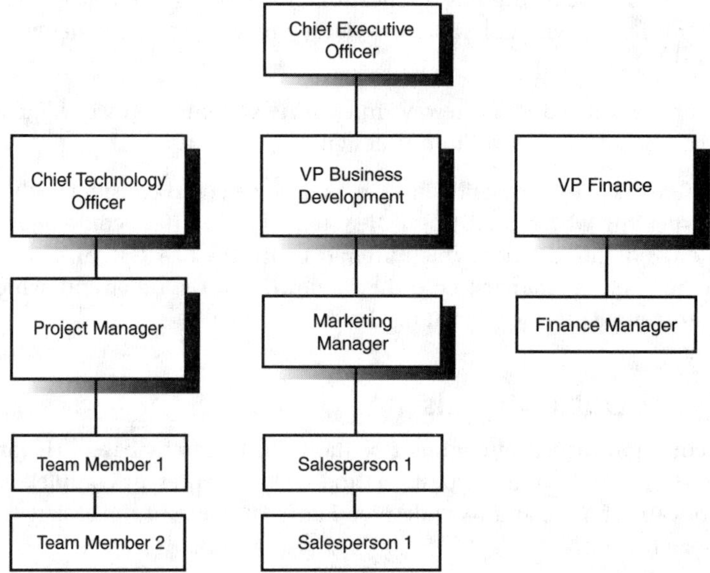

FIGURE 9.9 Hierarchical data schematic—organizational chart example.

Even the object model could be easily represented using hierarchy. Each object container is a root element, and objects within it are child elements. Member variables or methods of these objects could be further viewed as children of parent objects.

Representing Complex Data as Hierarchy

One major reason for us to study hierarchy is its ability to represent complex data.

To reason this out, let's see how a typical categorized company report would look. Figure 9.10 shows the report and its hierarchy view. The report title is at its root, and the various nodes are zones.

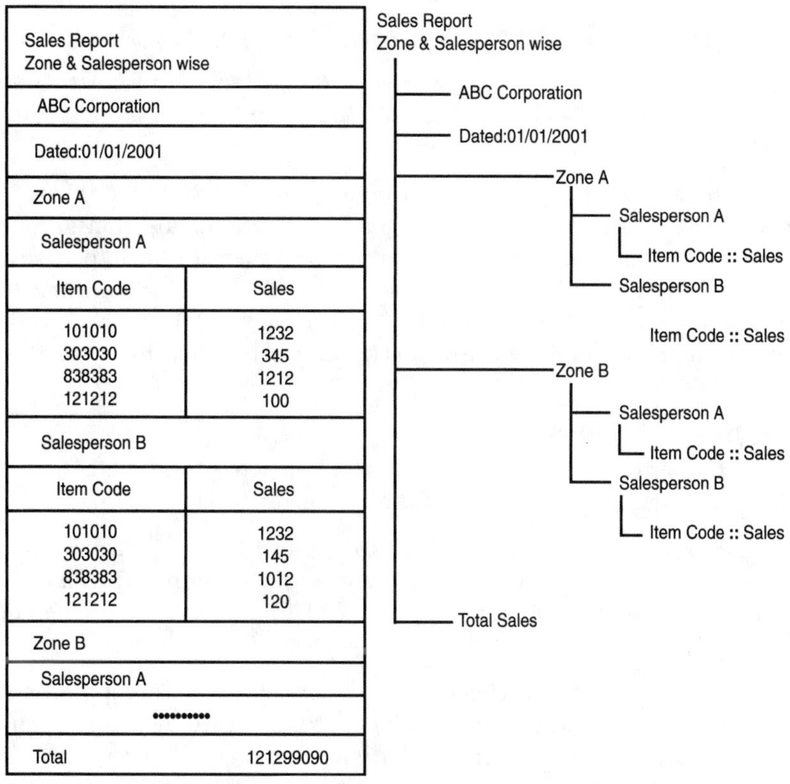

FIGURE 9.10 Report example and its hierarchical representation.

It is easy to arrive at what such a report is meant to represent. The report has Zone as nodes below root and Salesperson below it, which is parent to sales figures. Hence, the report represents a Zonewise Sales report categorized by Salesperson. As the level of report nodes increase, the report description would increase. Don't worry: This has nothing to do with our text, but is just an example of how automatic report generating tools would use a report title to arrive at report data. In other words, it is an example of using the report title as a query.

But, still it should be clear how such engines work. So, I am presenting this theory. A typical inference engine would try to analyze the data definitions, especially the metadata, in accordance with the report title (for example). Metadata representation in the hierarchy could tell a lot about the data itself. For example, it could describe the whole schema of a database, which could be easily used to arrive at the required fields upon analysis of the query statement.

XML Wrappers to Represent and Wrap Data Packets

The preceding theory was to explain the various representation formats and their use in the current industry. Now let's consider their use in terms of our modern system using XML.

You will now learn how you could construct systems that would be able to utilize our XML based model. The only easy option is to create suitable transform wrappers so that the same data could be routed to different systems in the respective formats. Hence, we arrive at the concept of wrappers. Wrappers might be a misnomer because actually we are interested in formatting the packets into XML and back to the native format, depending on whether the data is flowing in or out of the system.

XML and EDI Formats

EDI is a flat string of data delimited by suitable characters to separate the indicating and data elements. On the other hand, XML is hierarchical.

To design a converter for converting XML data to EDI and vice versa, we would need to design a mapping mechanism. This module would parse the EDI message and generate the XML packet corresponding to the EDI message. Also, on the other hand, it would take the XML packet and generate an EDI message.

For this, consider a simplistic reference document approach. This approach suggests having a reference document in XML, which would be used by the program to encode and decode an EDI packet. Let us try to construct such a reference document for 850 EDI PO transactions as shown in Listing 9.1 in the previous sections. The listing for such a reference XML document—for the first two line definitions of an EDI packet—is as shown in Listing 9.2.

LISTING 9.2 XML EDI Reference Document

```
<?xml version="1.0"?>
<!-- XML EDI reference schema document -->
<XMLEDI>
    <EDITransPacket>
        <EDITransNumber>850</EDITransNumber>
        <EDITransDescription>Purchase Order</EDITransDescription>
```

LISTING 9.2 Continued

```
        <EDITransShortName>PO</EDITransShortName>
        <EDIDelimiter>*</EDIDelimter>
        <EDITransSchema>
            <Line number="1">
                <Element number="1">
                    <ElementName>Transaction Set Header</ElementName>
                    <DefaultValue>ST</DefaultValue>
                </Element>

                <Element number="2">
                    <ElementName>Transaction Set ID</ElementName>
                    <DefaultValue>850</DefaultValue>
                </Element>
                <Element number="3">
                    <ElementName>Transaction Set Control Number</ElementName>
                    <DefaultValue></DefaultValue>
                </Element>
            </Line>
            <Line number="2">
                <Element number="1">
                    <ElementName>Beginning Segment for PO</ElementName>
                    <DefaultValue>BEG</DefaultValue>
                </Element>

                <Element number="2">
                    <ElementName>Transaction Set Purpose</ElementName>
                    <DefaultValue>00</DefaultValue>
                    <Enum>
                        <Pair>
                            <Type>Original</Type>
                            <Value>00</Value>
                        </Pair>
                        <Pair>
                            <Type>Copy</Type>
                            <Value>01</Value>
                        </Pair>
                    </Enum>
                </Element>
                <Element number="3">
                    <ElementName>PO Type</ElementName>
                    <DefaultValue>BO</DefaultValue>
```

LISTING 9.2 Continued

```
                    <Enum>
                        <Pair>
                            <Type>Blanket Order</Type>
                            <Value>BO</Value>
                        </Pair>
                        <Pair>
                            <Type>TP Order</Type>
                            <Value>B1</Value>
                        </Pair>
                    </Enum>
                </Element>
                <Element number="4">
                    <ElementName>PO Number</ElementName>
                    <DefaultValue></DefaultValue>
                </Element>
                <Element number="5">
                </Element>
                <Element number="6">
                </Element>
                <Element number="7">
                    <ElementName>PO Date</ElementName>
                    <DefaultValue>TODAY</DefaultValue>
                    <Format>MMDDYY</Format>
                </Element>
            </Line>
        </EDITransSchema>
    <EDITransPacket>
</XMLEDI>
```

This shows only the first two lines for simplicity because the remaining line definitions could be easily constructed based on the layout given.

Let's study this listing closely. Various EDI transactions would have individual `<EDITransPacket>` entries in the listing. Each transaction packet would have some header definition to make the application display suitable messages when in parsing mode or to allow other applications to determine the EDI scheme included. Some critical packet construction information is also included in the scheme such as the delimiter used, which would make the transforming application generate a suitable compatible EDI packet or parse an EDI message.

Each `<EDITransPacket>` has `<EDITransSchema>`, which has various `<Line>` tags. In previous discussions, you have seen that a single EDI packet has various elements distributed over several lines. Hence, the scheme document describes each element occurring line by line. This makes the scheme XML stream big, but it is easier to visualize and use.

It is interesting to note some tags used internally to define each element within the line. Each `<Line>` has `<Element>` tags, which in turn have element level descriptions. Each element has a name and default value associated with it. Note that for some elements such as PO number, no default value is specified and hence the tag is left empty. You see the use of `<Enum>` tag, which would act as a reference scheme for validating an EDI stream through an application. All allowable values for the element could be specified in these tags in the form of type/value pairs as shown.

Finally, for some special field types such as Date, format specifications are included. This is crucial when designing interfaces to upgrade old systems. Many systems still use eight positions for date definitions, and we should provide the format specifications wherever possible to avoid possible data errors.

After you form the reference schema as shown in the listing, it could be easily used in an application to encode and decode EDI packets. In terms of coding, you would include an initialization routine, which would be called when your XML Encoder/Decoder engine is instantiated. You would read the preceding XML scheme and parse it for referencing.

To be specific, you would use a DOM based XML parser to retrieve the elements and store them in memory for referencing when encoding or decoding the packets. DOM is useful here because by using a DOM representation, you would be able to relate various child elements quickly and hence formulate the EDI or XML packet quickly. This is in contrast with SAX parser, which is usually good for parsing data embedded in XML document because then you would not require a copy of the document to be available for reference later. So, you would usually parse the data within the XML document construct suitable SQL stream and pass it to the data manager.

Use of a parser type depends on your choice, but the preceding discussion would guide you to use the respective parsers per the applications. Because we are treating the previous XML stream as a reference stream, we will refer to it every time the application encodes or decodes the packet: Hence, it is efficient to use DOM and create a memory mapping for the document. This would make the parsing and interpreting elements easy and faster.

Other than the simplistic view of using a plain XML document to represent an EDI mapping capability, the standard schema references for EDI could be found in many repositories such as BizTalk.

XML and Hierarchical Data Formats

Hierarchy data formats exist at many places in an enterprise. A simple enterprise MIS report involves hierarchy as discussed before.

Another matured technology used for accessing directories is *LDAP (Lightweight Directory Access Protocol)*. LDAP is used in enterprises around the world to quickly locate a business or a person. Public LDAP directories open a wealth of information for trading houses to locate partners and clients.

As mentioned earlier, a directory structure is a hierarchy, and hence XML representation is a natural fit for LDAP. Some work on making directories accessible from XML interfaces is already done. Organizations such as DSML (Directory Service Markup Language)(`http://www.dsml.org`) are providing XML extensions for directory access and LDAP.

Listing 9.3, adopted from the DSML, shows a directory entry.

LISTING 9.3 Sample DSML Directory Entry

```
<dsml:entry dn="uid=prabbit,ou=development,o=bowstreet,c=us">
  <dsml:objectclass>
    <dsml:oc-value>top</dsml:oc-value>
    <dsml:oc-value>person</dsml:oc-value>
    <dsml:oc-value>organizationalPerson</dsml:oc-value>
    <dsml:oc-value>inetOrgPerson</dsml:oc-value>
  </dsml:objectclass>
  <dsml:attr name="sn"><dsml:value>Rabbit</dsml:value></dsml:attr>
  <dsml:attr name="uid"><dsml:value>prabbit</dsml:value></dsml:attr>
  <dsml:attr name="mail"><dsml:value>prabbit@dsml.org</dsml:value></dsml:attr>
  <dsml:attr name="givenname"><dsml:value>Peter</dsml:value></dsml:attr>
  <dsml:attr name="cn"><dsml:value>Peter Rabbit</dsml:value></dsml:attr>
</dsml:entry>
```

As you can see, each entry in the DSML document is defined by an element type entry. In this listing, the prefix `dsml` is used on XML elements to indicate that they belong to the DSML Namespace (`http://www.dsml.org/DSML`).

The entry element contains elements representing the entry's directory attributes. The distinguished name of the entry is indicated by the XML attribute `dn`. The distinguished name is represented as an XML attribute rather than a child element because of its identifying characteristic. The object classes of an entry are represented by `oc-value` child elements of an `objectclass` element. The content of each `oc-value` element indicates an object class to which the entry belongs.

Directory attributes (with the exception of `objectclass`) are represented by an `attr` element. This element has a mandatory XML attribute name, which indicates a name of the directory attribute. (A directory attribute might have more than one name, but only one needs to be expressed in the name attribute.)

The value or values of a directory attribute are expressed in child elements of the type value.

The attributes listed in a previous single directory entry example are as follows:

- `sn`—surname
- `uid`—user ID
- `mail`—e-mail address
- `givenname`—alternate name or also known as
- `cn`—contact/complete name

Other than representing directories, XML could be used as the standard protocol for packaging the reports generated by various systems.

The report data of complex hierarchical reports could be represented as XML and provided as the input source to an XML Graph engine, which would generate user customized graphs. A more practical explanation would be that the user defines inference rules; the inference engine generates the report data in XML format and forwards it to the user browser. The applet or ActiveX control sitting in the user's browser refers to this XML stream and uses it as a data source to show the data graphically or in any user specified format. The important thing to be noted is that the entire processing is done on the client end.

Another variation of using XML to represent hierarchical data is in navigational tool kits. Consider Web site navigation. A company offering catalog services to its clients would have hundreds of categories and thousands of products under each category. The user could select the useful categories, and the user end tool could pull the XML format of this data. Once the data resides on the user end, he could use the client end scripting to analyze, search, and view it in a variety of formats. This and previous methods highlight the use of XML to improve user experience in terms of interface.

The same principle can be extended to distributed computing. You can consider that the third-party application acts as the user from the previous discussion. Instead of the user clicking and demanding data, the application passes the query to the server and the server responds giving data in XML format or returns the URL referencing the XML document. The remote application can now use the URL and get the required data and process it per its requirement to formulate and process the data.

Combining the query mechanisms given later in this chapter, you could create powerful user end data scrapping applications.

The data in the typical hierarchical report shown in Figure 9.10 could be easily represented using XML as shown in Listing 9.4.

LISTING 9.4 XML Representation for a Multi-Level Hierarchical Report

```
<?xml version="1.0"?>
<!-- XML representation of hierarchical report in fig 5.10 -->
<SalesReport>
    <ReportHeader>
        <Title>Sales Report</Title>
        <SubTitle>Zone & Sales Person wise</SubTitle>
        <Keywords>
            <Key>Zones</Key>
            <Key>SalesPerson</Key>
            <Key>ItemSales</Key>
            <Key>Sales</Key>
        </Keywords>
        <Company>ABC Corporation</Company>
        <ReportDate>01012001</ReportDate>
    </ReportHeader>
    <ReportBody>
        <Zones>
            <Zonewise>
                <ZoneName>Zone A</ZoneName>
                <SalesPerson>
                    <SalesPersonName>Sales Person A</SalesPersonName>
                    <Items>
                        <ItemSales>
                            <ItemCode>010101</ItemCode>
                            <Sales>2300</Sales>
                        </ItemSales>
                    </Items>
                <SalesPerson>
            </Zonewise>
            <Zonewise>
                <ZoneName>Zone B</ZoneName>
                <SalesPerson>
                    <SalesPersonName>Sales Person B</SalesPersonName>
                    <Items>
                        <ItemSales>
```

LISTING 9.4 Continued

```
                        <ItemCode>010101</ItemCode>
                        <Sales>2300</Sales>
                    </ItemSales>
                    <ItemSales>
                        <ItemCode>010231</ItemCode>
                        <Sales>200</Sales>
                    </ItemSales>
                </Items>
            <SalesPerson>
        </Zonewise>
    <Zones>
</ReportBody>
<ReportTrailer>
    <TotalSales>2500</TotalSales>
</ReportTrailer>
</SalesReport>
```

The listing shows how easily the hierarchical data can be represented using XML. I have added a section of `<Keywords>` in the report to facilitate the formatting engine to reformat the report and represent it per the user requirement.

The `<Keys>` specifies the logical nodes, which would make sense if combined. For example, the formatting engine would give the following options to the user after studying the keys in the keywords tag:

- Zonewise or aggregate report
- Salesperson wise report or aggregate report
- Item Sales aggregate report
- Saleswise aggregate report

The list specifies each type of report that could be generated by the reporting engine. To respond back with the type of report the user selects from this list, the engine would simply parse the respective nodes mentioned as keys. The parsed nodes would appear as the report body, and the total of numeric entries would be displayed below as the total.

Summary

In practice, data collections or stores are more in use today than ever before. Huge data centers are the result of archiving and gathering numerous amount of information all over the corporation.

The challenge is to utilize this diverse and distributed information in the right way. This usage would involve deriving the sales trend, forecasting the future profits, or just about anything. Chapter 10, "Databases and Warehousing," looks into aspects of data center usage,applying XML to those scenarios, and using inference engines.

10

Databases and Warehousing

IN THIS CHAPTER

- Data Warehousing And Representation
- Open-Ended System Data Exchange—XML Transactions
- XML Engine for Database Interfacing
- Generic Message Packets Based Systems—a Design Approach

An undefined problem has an infinite number of solutions.

—*Robert A. Humphrey*

Data Warehousing and Representation

Databases are common and everywhere today. Why is it important for us here? Well, it's important when dealing with different systems, hence databases, and applying our design for interconnecting these two systems. The distributed systems then need to deal with the distributed databases.

Furthermore, there are many possibilities of designing a distributed application for deriving inferences from present data collections.

This chapter deals with using our modeling theory with data centers and warehouses. It discusses using XML as a standard inter-system protocol even for these data center type applications.

Data Warehouse—An Introduction

Data warehouse deals with a collection of data in sensible (logically combined in data sets, depending on the business need) formats, and the inference engine is used to draw inference reports from them.

I want to mention that inference engines are primarily used for collectively analyzing data that is dispersed among various databases. The data is usually among the databases that are different in all ways, including schema design and even data formats.

Let's look at how a typical data warehouse would be derived and set up. Figure 10.1 shows a typical arrangement for deriving and forming a data warehouse in a typical legacy system. The source of data for a typical data warehouse today would be a corporate database.

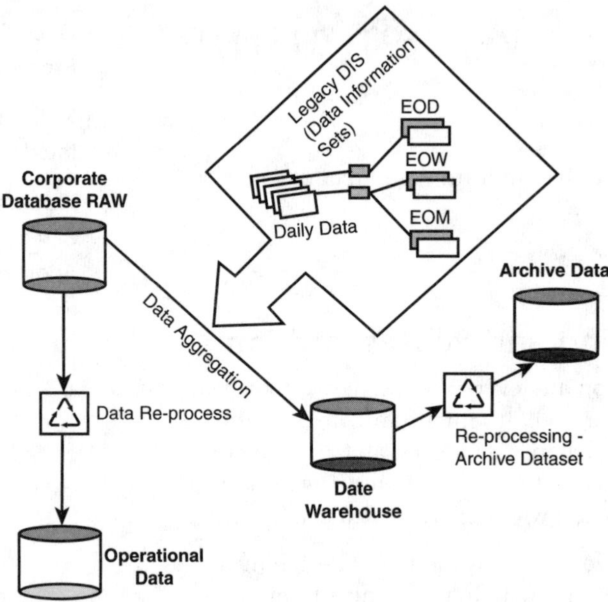

FIGURE 10.1 Data warehouse derivation in a corporate environment.

A corporate database can have a number of aggregated databases, but we would still be able to view these enumerated database occurrences as one single huge database. The type of data in this database is termed *raw*; the reason is that it would be collected by various applications, which would be (in most cases) not closely or tightly coupled with each other.

Even if an individual application sees the data as organized, from an aggregate view perspective it will be raw.

To arrive at some sensible data divisions, the raw database is usually divided into operational data and "warehouse-able" data. To mark the differences between these, consider operational data that is derived from raw data. The data collected through diverse application needs to be organized so that some different applications would be able to use it in the future. Usually, operational dataset is the raw dataset that would be required for the applications (currently serving) to operate eventually. These datasets can be arrived at by forming a set of required data schema and then rearranging the data.

The data warehouse end dataset would be various flavors:

- Dataset resulting from daily job processing
- Dataset resulting from weekly job processing
- Dataset resulting from monthly job processing

The list could go on, but the important thing is that we somehow aggregate daily collected data to form a dataset suitable for a warehouse.

This fundamental aspect of data collection and division is important in huge systems and is very effective in the long run. Behind the data warehouse sits an archive database. Archive is a generic term used in connection with storing histories. But, here I refer to it in light of a data warehousing archive. A data warehouse database could be viewed as consisting of both the main warehouse database and the archive database.

If one inquires on the importance of creating a data warehouse, we have to take a look at why it is done in the first place. The most general reasons for creating a data warehouse could be for several business and technical reasons. For example, businesses might use historical data to interpret and forecast futuristic trends; vendors might use it to arrive at inventory or stock requirements, for strategic planning, and for daily performance figure comparison. Technical reasons would include predicting the required data storage for a growing business. The actual reason is, as would be evident on quick thought, to draw inferences.

Is drawing inferences the same as generating reports? It isn't in this perspective. Report generation usually involves deriving data from some table schema with a known relation model. It might include one or more complex queries to the database, which are fired in sequence in the form of stored procedures.

But the inference engine would do more than that. The capability of inference engines can include, but is not limited to, the following:

- Derive data definitions—metadata
- Apply schema modeling to pre-existing schemas
- Track schemas and metadata to reformulate the inferences
- Drill data to hunt for specific data definitions
- Derive correlation between different schemas based on rules
- Map the data, based on context, irrespective of their data types

Data Warehousing in Large-Scale Systems

The previous section gives a generic overview of how a data warehouse is formed. Essentially in very large-scale database systems, data warehouse would itself appear to be distributed.

The inference engine needs to derive inferences from these distributed databases and hence would require a singular gateway to interact with them. The concept of database gateways is not new, and they have existed for several years now. I will deal with a few designs in the following sections, which would allow you to visualize how a gateway should function and how it is formed.

Another reference to an inference engine is the concept of data mining. Both have the same goal and both try to hunt for intelligence in a data jungle.

As you could visualize metadata, which is data about data, it plays an important role in inference engines. For example, in a typical corporate database, there could be a single field occurring with two names—for example, *Cost* would appear as *Rate* in some schema definitions. In this scenario, for the inference engine to gauge and arrive at a logical inference report, you would have to provide this correlation of fields as aliases. *Aliases* are commonly used in system design for referring to the same term by different names. In diverse business applications—typically integrating different databases—the term aliases would be used to refer to fields used for storing the same type of data. For example, database D1 in System A would use a field name called TotalAmount and the database D2 in System B would have a field name called GrandTotal to represent the total amount as it appears on the invoice. The system would need to deal with both the databases to process the results, and hence might refer to both the fields with one name or the other per the requirement. Internally, the formulation would be the same for TotalAmount and GrandTotal. Hence, they could be called aliases of each other.

Another useful aspect is that of viewing the data in various dimensions. When you correlate different data fields, you end up assigning dimensions. The concept is simple, but useful, for generating useful reports. Consider that you are analyzing the total monthly sales for one year. This is two-dimensional data and involves essentially two fields. If you look at a report that specifies not only the monthly sales over one year, but also a further breakdown on sales to represent items sold by each salesman, it is a three-dimensional report. Hence, three fields are represented in a report. We arrive at the concept of multidimensional data, often referred to as a *cube* in data mining. Technically, the cube is a method to view the data. Database designers would be conversant with the concept of *views* used for fetching the data as collections of different data schemas—the same concept, when extended to relate a wide range of schemas to derive intelligence, can be termed as a multidimensional view or cube.

OLAP (Online Analytical Processing) is a technique used to address the requirement of querying large amounts of data after organizing it in a logical combination of datasets. OLAP is a direct alternative to a conventional database (RDBMS, relational database management systems) that performs multidimensional analysis of enterprise data including complex calculations, trend analysis, and modeling. Under OLAP theory, data cubes are precomputed multidimensional views of the data. The cube is usually three-dimensional data represented as a set of attributes, which can be field names or aliases. For example, a cube might be defined on the attributes as `<part, customer, date>`. Note that the cube defines a data view covering three attributes and can be used to create more aggregate cubes, such as `<part, year>`, which can be easily derived from the preceding dataset.

Finally, to conclude the discussion of inference engines, you could visualize the various dimensions of data as a hierarchy. And, as you saw in the previous sections, they could be easily represented using the XML format.

Querying Data Warehouse—Data Mining

To support distributed applications over distributed databases, we need to have a gateway access. The gateway access would allow applications to view the distributed database as a single schema to a query.

Data mining involves a lot more than querying the distributed databases. But you would still look into how the aspect of distributed databases viewed as single database could be constructed in a useful manner. I discuss this topic in this book so that you can understand how distributed applications can talk to distributed databases.

It is worthwhile to mention here that I am considering a scenario in which the application in the distributed framework wants to view the distributed database as a single database.

Figure 10.2 shows the simplistic approach of serving an application in the distributed database arena. It actually provides a centralized gateway database. Various databases distributed across the network are dumped (with schema and data) into this central database. The application would then query this single database and get the required data.

Although the approach is simple, it would require that the database be bridged by suitable applications to maintain synchronization with the data stores. This would be a costly affair and can generate heavy network traffic. Hence, we would require that a scheduler be in place, which would schedule the synchronization routines accordingly to maintain minimal network traffic. Also, this would require a big storage space at the central database location.

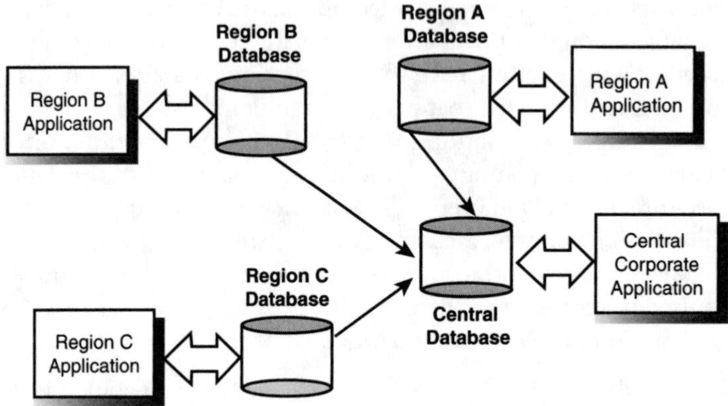

FIGURE 10.2 A central corporate database connected to regional data stores.

A more practical approach is shown in Figure 10.3. As shown, the central database is replaced by a central query engine. The applications would pass the query to the central engine. The engine would then deal with resolving the query parameters and locations and accordingly fire it at the various locations.

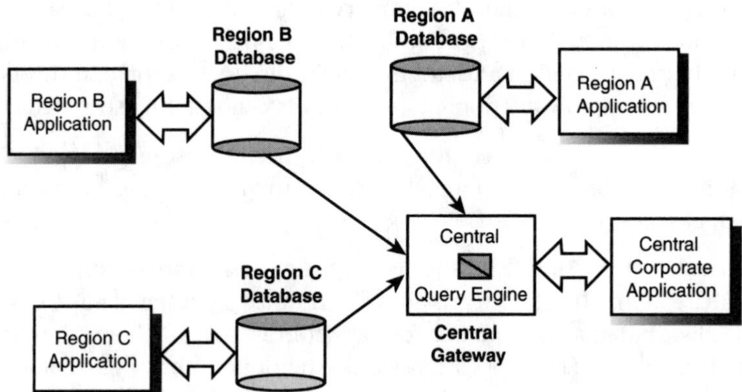

FIGURE 10.3 A central corporate gateway connected to regional data stores.

Consider two databases located at two different locations, with domains as `192.168.168.34` and `192.168.168.35`. You could use suitable resolution software to make the following query work from a central query engine:

```
Select a.AccountID, b.TransAmount from AccountsMaster@192.168.168.34 a,
TransactionMater@192.168.168.35 b where a.AccountID = b.AccountID
```

This is a sample query and is presented only for visualizing the possible representation, which would be issued by the application to the query engine.

Usually in distributed computing, the important thing to consider is the description of the source itself. In other words we want the data source or object source to be willing to provide a description of its own. This is true for all successfully designed systems. Consider CORBA: The true power is realized by the central naming service resolving the request calls and accordingly invoking an object. Even for the distributed framework architecture in Chapter 3, "Parsing an XML Document," I insist on having a centralized processor for interacting with adapters to dynamically resolve a message packet and process the request.

To make our database gateway more interactive and extensive, we would like to provide a way in which the application would be able to get an idea of what is inside it. All schemas are represented using metadata. Metadata is, in the simplistic sense, a description of various tables and fields (with data types) of an entire database. Providing such a node would make our life easier as the application developer or gateway interface layer developer.

Figure 10.4 shows how can you make the database gateway more informative by providing an additional stage. As shown, I broke the interface into two parts—one is the query interface and another is the metadata manager interface. The query interface is to provide query-oriented services to the application. The metadata interface would provide metadata when queried by the application.

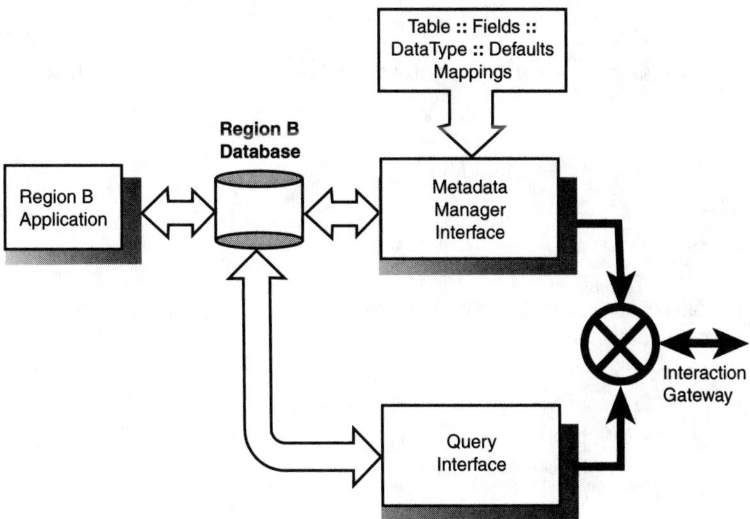

FIGURE 10.4 Making the database interface gateway informative.

The importance of providing a metadata node would be clear if you consider the approach to design either the central query engine or an interface engine itself because both these applications would require the database details for issuing the application query and accordingly breaking it up into respective database level queries. The case of the interface engine is more complex. It requires interacting with the metadata layer, determining the data definitions, and searching in the knowledge base or rule mappings for similar fields occurring in another database to arrive at a result report.

I propose the preceding concept because I can imagine that the next generation of databases support such metadata interface layers, which would be capable of providing metadata descriptions in an XML way.

A typical example of representing metadata using XML can be as follows. Consider an `EmployeeMaster` table with the following fields:

- EmployeeID [Numeric] [8]
- EmployeeName [Char] [35]
- DepartmentID [Numeric] [8]
- CreateDate [Date] [8]
- ContactTel [Numeric] [11]

The schema has three parts in one entry—field name, field type, and field length. Usually this information is sufficient to construct a table in a database.

You could easily represent the previous metadata schema using XML as shown in Listing 10.1.

LISTING 10.1 XML Based Metadata Representation

```
<?xml version="1.0"?>
<!-- XML based meta-data or schema representation -->
<TableSchema>
    <TableName>EmployeeMaster</TableName>
    <TableFields>
        <Field>
            <FieldName>EmployeeID</FieldName>
            <FieldType>NUMERIC</FieldType>
            <FieldLength>8</FieldLength>
        </Field>
        <Field>
            <FieldName>EmployeeName</FieldName>
```

LISTING 10.1 Continued

```
            <FieldType>CHAR</FieldType>
            <FieldLength>35</FieldLength>
        </Field>
        <Field>
            <FieldName>DepartmentID</FieldName>
            <FieldType>NUMERIC</FieldType>
            <FieldLength>8</FieldLength>
        </Field>
        <Field>
            <FieldName>CreateDate</FieldName>
            <FieldType>DATE</FieldType>
            <FieldLength>8</FieldLength>
        </Field>
        <Field>
            <FieldName>ContactTel</FieldName>
            <FieldType>NUMERIC</FieldType>
            <FieldLength>11</FieldLength>
        </Field>
    </TableFields>
</TableSchema>
```

This listing is self-descriptive and simple. Of course, a real-world listing would be more complex, and it would include various additional parameters such as Table Allocated Disk Space, Database Name, Physical Disk Path for Table Creation, and so on.

Essentially, you would have a database creation script in XML format. The advantage of representing a database creation script in the form of XML is that the same script could then be used by the metadata interface layer for referencing when answering metadata related queries.

If you now think about including some intelligence and knowledge in the preceding schema, you could add a tag called `<Aliases>` as shown in Listing 10.2.

LISTING 10.2 XML Based Metadata and Inference Engine Representation

```
<?xml version="1.0"?>
<!-- XML based meta-data or schema representation for Inference Engine-->
<TableSchema>
    <TableName>EmployeeMaster</TableName>
    <TableAliases>
        <AliasName>EmployeeDetails</AliasName>
        <AliasKeyword>Employee</AliasKeyword>
```

LISTING 10.2 Continued

```
        <AliasScope>BRIEF</AliasScope>
        <AliasExtend>Employees of Region A</AliasExtend>
    </TableAliases>
    <TableFields>
        <Field>
            <FieldName>EmployeeID</FieldName>
            <FieldType>NUMERIC</FieldType>
            <FieldLength>8</FieldLength>
            <FieldWeight>PRIMARYKEY</FieldWeight>
            <FieldAliases>
                <AliasName>EmployeeCode</AliasName>
                <AliasKeyword>ID</AliasKeyword>
                <AliasScope>REGIONAL</AliasScope>
                <AliasExtend>Employee Reference for Region A</AliasExtend>
            </FieldAliases>
        </Field>
        <Field>
            <FieldName>EmployeeName</FieldName>
            <FieldType>CHAR</FieldType>
            <FieldLength>35</FieldLength>
            <FieldWeight>NORMAL</FieldWeight>
            <FieldAliases>
                <AliasName>Employee</AliasName>
                <AliasKeyword>Employee Name</AliasKeyword>
                <AliasScope>REGIONAL</AliasScope>
                <AliasExtend>Employee Names for Region A</AliasExtend>
            </FieldAliases>
        </Field>
        <Field>
            <FieldName>DepartmentID</FieldName>
            <FieldType>NUMERIC</FieldType>
            <FieldLength>8</FieldLength>
            <FieldWeight>FOREIGNKEY</FieldWeight>
            <FieldAliases>
                <AliasName>DepartmentCode</AliasName>
                <AliasKeyword>ID</AliasKeyword>
                <AliasScope>REGIONAL</AliasScope>
                <AliasExtend>Employee Department Reference for Region A
                ➥</AliasExtend>
            </FieldAliases>
        </Field>
```

LISTING 10.2 Continued

```
        <Field>
            <FieldName>CreateDate</FieldName>
            <FieldType>DATE</FieldType>
            <FieldLength>8</FieldLength>
            <FieldWeight>SYSTEM</FieldWeight>
            <FieldAliases>
                <AliasName>Creation</AliasName>
                <AliasKeyword>DATE</AliasKeyword>
                <AliasScope>REGIONAL</AliasScope>
                <AliasExtend>Creation Date for Region A</AliasExtend>
            </FieldAliases>
        </Field>
        <Field>
            <FieldName>ContactTel</FieldName>
            <FieldType>NUMERIC</FieldType>
            <FieldLength>11</FieldLength>
            <FieldWeight>NORMAL</FieldWeight>
            <FieldAliases>
                <AliasName>Telephone</AliasName>
                <AliasKeyword>PHONE</AliasKeyword>
                <AliasScope>REGIONAL</AliasScope>
                <AliasExtend>Employee Phone for Region A</AliasExtend>
            </FieldAliases>
        </Field>
    </TableFields>
</TableSchema>
```

Although this listing appears to be lengthy, it is self-descriptive. Various new aspects are included in this listing.

A `<FieldWeight>` tag is included to make the field level description of the schema complete.

Both table levels and field levels have an `<Aliases>` tag, which includes a description of the alias. You could imagine these tags to be updated depending on the DBA or administrator settings for defining rules for the interface engine. The previous example shows only 4 tags associated with describing an alias, but in the real-world there can be 40 of those.

Let's talk about the data mapping aspect. Data mapping is similar to a filter for input data, which is realigned or reassigned depending on the requirement of the system connected at the output.

Figure 10.5 shows an extended system using the data mapping approach to construct a data-transformation bridge. Again, this would be important for transforming the data from a corporate raw database into a data warehouse.

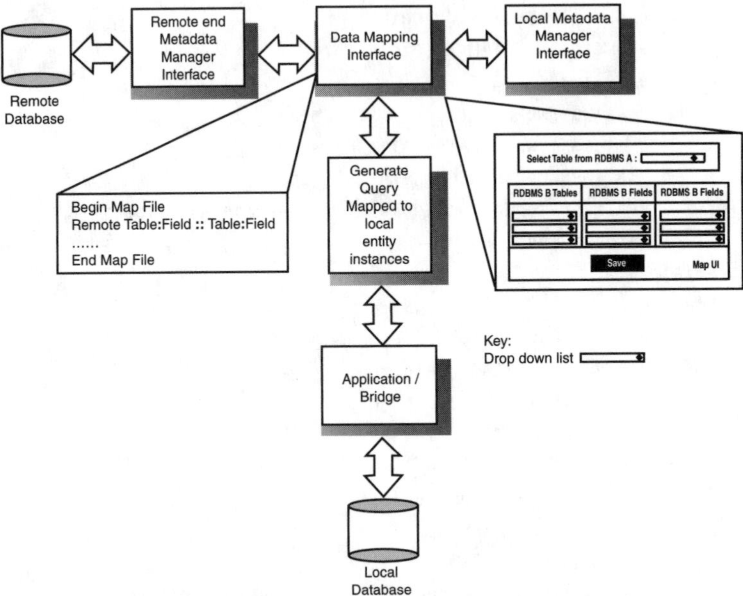

FIGURE 10.5 A detailed schematic for data exchange.

The only addition to this scheme is that of the data mapping stage, which interacts with the remote and local metadata layer. The data-mapping interface would refer to a map file to transform the remote data stream in terms of local database requirements. This would involve renaming the field names in resultsets and even discarding some fields.

The system administrator would use a mapping interface from the admin control panel. This could be a simple Web page that would query both remote and local metadata interfaces and allow the administrator to map the local tables and fields to remote schema. It might also allow the administrator to associate some validation rules when converting the data from one form of schema to another.

A simple map user interface would be as shown in Figure 10.5. The admin would select the main table from the remote end and use the row level select boxes to map it to the local schema. The interface could easily be developed using simple Web based tools and could use simple client end scripting tools such as JavaScript to parse and display the XML data.

The Save button would store the screen mappings in the form of an XML map file (see Listing 10.3).

LISTING 10.3 XML Map File Example

```
<?xml version="1.0"?>
<!-- XML map file -->
<MapSchema>
    <MapData>
        <MapTableRemote>EmployeeMaster</MapTable>
<MapTableLocal>EmployeeProfile</MapTableLocal>
<FieldNameRemote>EmployeeID</FieldNameRemote>
<FieldNameLocal>EmployeeCode</FieldNameLocal>
<FieldTypeRemote>NUMERIC</FieldTypeRemote>
<FieldTypeLocal>CHAR</FieldTypeLocal>
<FieldConvertRules>
    <MapBy>LENGTH</MapBy>
    <Discard>DECIMALS</Discard>
    <MaxSize>8</MaxSize>
</FieldConvertRules>
    </MapData>
    <MapData>
        <MapTableRemote>EmployeeMaster</MapTable>
<MapTableLocal>EmployeeProfile</MapTableLocal>
<FieldNameRemote>EmployeeName</FieldNameRemote>
<FieldNameLocal>PersonnelName</FieldNameLocal>
<FieldTypeRemote>CHAR</FieldTypeRemote>
<FieldTypeLocal>CHAR</FieldTypeLocal>
<FieldConvertRules>
    <MapBy>LENGTH</MapBy>
    <Discard></Discard>
    <MaxSize>35</MaxSize>
</FieldConvertRules>
    </MapData>
```

The preceding map file shows some rules embedded to help the mapping interface to better map the data. The rules are again formulated and input by the admin using a suitable interface.

It is worth mentioning that the preceding map file considers the possibility of two fields from the same local table being mapped to two fields from different tables at the remote end. Hence, I have repeated the table reference tag `<MapTableRemote>` and `<MapTableLocal>` with all field mapping entries.

The mapping logic would then get the data packet from the remote database and use the suitable custom parser to parse it and generate a corresponding resultset XML file suitable for local database.

For a typical RDBMS database, the preceding logic would read the resultset file, construct SQL queries, and fire them on the database.

If we consider the inference engine or data mining scenario, we would arrive the schematic in Figure 10.6. This includes a new module titled Data Extractor, which is coupled to a business rules block. The data mapping would still serve the same functionality, but now the resultset would be reformulated using predefined business rules, which is then displayed as a report. Furthermore, many inference engines have a graphic engine capability, which allows them to display the result in graphical formats.

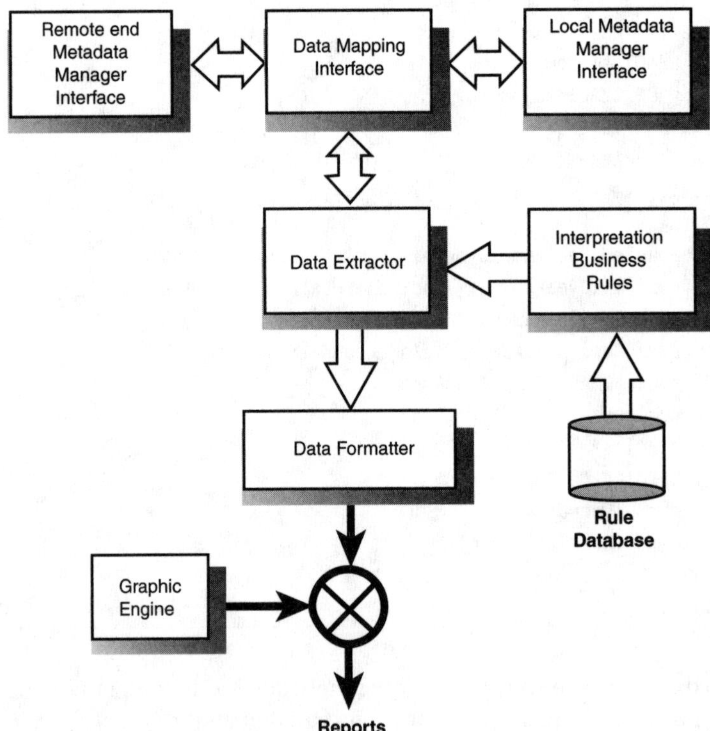

FIGURE 10.6 Schematic of a data interface and reporting engine.

The inference engine would use the metadata interface of the remote and local ends extensively. It would refer to predefined aliases and business rules and try to draw a relationship between diverse data descriptions from the tables that are not related at all. You could imagine various patterns of workings in this scenario, which would be useful for devising a complex and complete system.

Putting it All Together—XML as Query and Resultset Language

So, I have used XML to specify the map data and metadata in the previous section. For a system to support XML as the native protocol, it would be necessary that all the interfaces support XML packaging.

From a database perspective, this means that both the query end and the resultset end should represent data in the form of XML. You have seen how a resultset could be represented using XML before, but I will discuss it again just to review and make this treatment complete.

XML based query interfaces are a relatively new discovery. This means embedding a query in XML. A quick look at Listing 10.4 reveals a very preliminary view of such a query.

LISTING 10.4 An XML Packet with an Embedded SQL Query

```
<?xml version="1.0"?>
<!-- XML based SQL query -->
<SQL>
    <Statement>Select * from EmployeeMaster where EmployeeID = ?</Statement>
    <StatementType>STDSQL</StatementType>
    <Parameters>
        <ParamValue>123212</ParamValue>
    </Parameters>
</SQL>
```

The SQL is represented in the `<Statement>` tag, which also has an additional description to specify what type of query is embedded. This is necessary for the packet to be "migrate-able." Here the `<StatementType>` tag specifies that the query is a standard SQL type. The query parameter values positions are indicated with a `?`. This is common in many standard query representations. The values are specified in the `<Parameters>` tag.

The parsing mechanism or tier at the database end would be pretty simple too. The parser would parse each SQL tag and extract the query. Then it would extract the values and replace them sequentially in the query string at various `?` positions.

You can even embed a stored procedure in the previous format: The `<StatementType>` would specify `STORPROC`.

The resultset can be easily represented using XML. I have presented some examples before. But certain databases today, such as Oracle, provide the nested tables capability, which could make the resultset represented with XML useful. Nested table is more like a product specific approach and is not usually easily transformable. Because it is a product specific approach, it is usually optimized for the particular database product.

For example, a table storing purchase orders could have nested tables embedded in some of its columns called *table objects* or *embedded schemas*. This ability allows RDBMS to represent complex hierarchical data formats and schemas. Hence, using nested capabilities, a single table could embed the header and details table schemas. The resultset generated from the query on such a table would result in hierarchical data, which can be represented in XML format quite conveniently.

Open-Ended System Data Exchange—XML Transactions

Every data exchange in an open-ended system using XML must have a specific data exchange agreement.

Of course, there is no way to guess what type of system would be interfaced in the future with your application. But the main concern is to XML enable your system.

Transaction support systems would need to support varied third-party calls and the posting of events, which can be achieved using XML as a support protocol. One other important issue is that of setting an XML standard in the system. Many bodies are working on standardizing the XML packet formats today, but still there is no global body imposing those on XML based transaction systems.

Therefore, it is advisable to use simplistic exchange formats for XML packets in the system. By simplistic format, I mean that the XML packet should have tags as element names with limited links. We have good standards, such as XLink, to base links in our documents, but I would still insist on keeping the packet format simple. The most simple XML stream, for example, would be the one that can be parsed by the simplest parser without needing to use special linkages. The system should be able to derive data (but might not validate it) from it without referring to the corresponding DTD.

This might sound strange, but increasing reliability on special formatting tools and parsers could create certain impositions on the technology, and the impositions would be global.

Consider a schematic for a simple system as shown in Figure 10.7. The client end or third-party application would interact with the system over the Web through a specified port number.

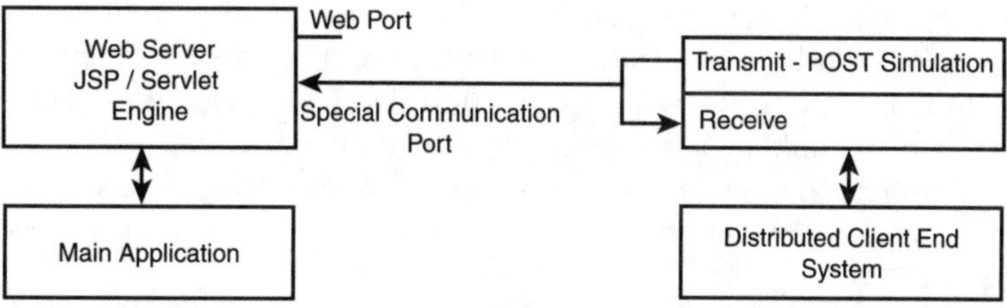

FIGURE 10.7 A schematic of a transaction supporting open system.

For doing a transaction in such a system, the client-end application would format the query and pass it to the `POST` simulator. This simulator layer is simple code that `POST`s this parameter on the other end. I prefer the `POST` method because of the reasons mentioned in Chapter 3.

The main application would catch the `POST` request in XML format and decode it. Now, there can be two scenarios for completing the transaction initiated by the client-end system. Either the main application would cause the transaction to occur as soon as it gets it and reports back to the client end by returning the response (same as in XML-RPC), or after waiting for the transaction to be processed from the input queue of its internal process, the main application simulates a `POST` on the client and acknowledges the transaction.

Huge transaction based systems would use the second mechanism because usually the transactions posted would be pushed in some sort of internal system queue. The main application could be a banking system and the third party would be an affiliate merchant location posting customer charges for ATM purchases.

It should be worth mentioning that TCP/IP is stateless protocol, and we have to define some session to make it stateful.

For a Web site designer, often the statelessness causes issues. Let's see why a stateless approach would cause problems in a normal workflow design pattern.

In a typical Web site oriented requirement, which requires member login, the user can log in the site using the username and password. After the user logs in, it is often a requirement that all the site pages should be available to the user. Now the login welcome page would have more than one link to go to the limited access pages. Under these circumstances, it is often necessary—at each user-selected option—to know whether the user has logged in. Usually, if TCP/IP had been a stateful protocol, it is easy to check whether the user is still in the same workflow pattern as he was after he had logged in. The stateful aspect could be viewed as a stack that saves all the stepping options or all user clicks and actions. Then, with any user click, you could easily parse the stack and check if the user was logged in at any point of time and accordingly redirect to a suitable page!

But, because TCP/IP is stateless, you need to manage the state explicitly on the Web server end. You could use a session to do this. Every time the user comes to the Web site, the hit is associated with a unique session ID. The developer has access to this unique ID, which could be used to refer to a session. A session, in turn, covers all the user's actions once the session is allocated until the user either shuts down the browser or moves to another site.

Web servers often allow the session ID to be used in code. It provides an ability to define session scope variables, which are useable and limited to the session duration, hence proving the statefulness required for the workflow patterns to be implemented.

XML Engine for Database Interfacing

All existing databases or back ends today are mostly relational or hierarchical. To "XML-enable" them, you need to extend or rather add an XML-tier.

Adding an XML-tier is similar to, in theory, adding a middle-tier for processing requests. This middle-tier would essentially convert the data packet into XML format and act as a bridge between an XML based application and the database.

Database and SQL

A database could be extended to support XML by wrapping the incoming and outgoing packet. Perhaps converting is a better word for this layer.

Figure 10.8 shows a schematic of such a layer. The database gateway and the application have an XML middle-tier, which consists of an XML query interface and XML formatter. This design is similar to designing a data source class for an unknown database. For example, using ADODB from Microsoft, you can write a simple data source class to wrap and present a text file as a database to the front end.

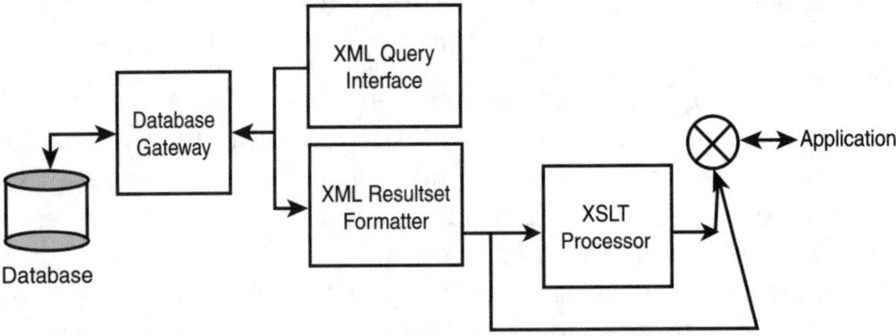

FIGURE 10.8 A schematic of a data interface layer for supporting XML.

The XML query interface would interpret the incoming XML query packets. As you have seen before, a SQL query can be embedded within an XML packet and passed to this module, which would parse the SQL statement and format it per the back-end requirement. You could imagine that depending on the database activity supported, each of the database vendors would provide you this interface layer in the form of an API package.

The XML resultset formatter would format the resultset in XML format and pass it directly to the application or add some style to it using an XSLT processor.

The resultset would be a simplistic XML representation of two-dimensional tables and field data for most of the databases. There are exceptions such as Oracle, which support complex table schema definitions as described in the next sections.

Unfortunately, the technology is new and we do not have any standards defined to design this interface layer or middle-tier. Neither do we have a specific global standard to represent a SQL query using XML and the resultset. This means that either you have to design your own middle-tier or use the database vendor provided API.

My main intention for the preceding discussion is to give you an idea of how such interfaces work and were designed.

XML for Specifying Query

There are many specific query languages, and most of them are vendor specific. Let's review a standard query interface: XQL. XQL has major participation resulting in XML Query definitions.

XQL represents a query language to query any XML document. It can be said to be an XML modeled query language similar to XSL.

XQL is simple to interpret and represent. A single string is taken to be an element name. For example, the following string would return all `<stock>` elements:

```
stock
```

The / indicates a child operator in a hierarchy. The following query returns all `<quotes>` elements that are children of `<stock>` elements:

```
stock/quotes
```

The root of the document is represented by the / operator:

```
/market/stock/quotes
```

In XML, the root of the document is the document itself, and the parent of all roots in the preceding example is `<market>`.

The content or value is specified with the = operator, as in the next example. The following query returns all the quotes with 30.34:

```
stock/quotes='30.34'
```

Attribute names begin with @, and they are treated as children of the elements to which they belong:

```
stock/quotes/company/address/@type='URL'
```

The descendant operator represented by // indicates any number of intervening levels. The following example query would show all the company under stock:

```
stock//company
```

You can apply a filter by using []. The following sample query would return all companies having an attribute of type URL:

```
stock/quotes/company[@type='URL']
```

This would return company names.

You could specify multiple conditions and combine those using Boolean operators as in the following example:

```
stock/quotes='30.34'[@companytype='XYZ' and @areacode='408']
```

Also, you could query for specific sections of an XML document by using the syntax shown in the following example:

```
stock/quotes/company/section[0,2 To 4,6]
```

This query refers to sections 0, 2, 3, 4, and 6 under company.

Consider the sample document shown in Listing 10.5.

LISTING 10.5 Sample XML Purchase Order

```
<?xml version="1.0"?>
<POcollection>
<PO>
  <customer>
       XYZ, CA
  </customer>
  <entries n=2>
     <entry quantity=1  total_price="780.00">
        <product maker="EW" prod_name="Test Suite" price="780.00"/>
```

LISTING 10.5 Continued

```
     </entry>
     <entry quantity=1  total_price="220.00">
        <product maker="PERISOL" prod_name="XML-EDI Engine" price="220.00"/>
     </entry>
  </entries>
</PO>
<PO>
  <customer>
      ABC, CA
  </customer>
  <entries n=1>
     <entry quantity=1  total_price="320.00">
        <product maker="PERISOL" prod_name="Memory Tracer" price="320.00"/>
     </entry>
  </entries>
</PO>
</POcollection>
```

Now you will see a few examples that show how XQL would work on the preceding documents. Refer to Listings 10.6 and 10.7 to see the sample queries and the resulting XML stream.

LISTING 10.6 XQL Example—1

```
Query:
   //customer

Result:
<xql:result>
<customer>
         XYZ, CA
     </customer>
     <customer>
         ABC
     </customer>
</xql:result>
```

LISTING 10.7 XQL Example—2

```
Query:
   //product[@maker='PERISOL']

Result:
<xql:result>
<product maker="PERISOL" prod_name="XML-EDI Engine" price="220.00"/>
       <product maker="PERISOL" prod_name="Memory Tracer" price="320.00"/>
</xql:result>
```

After XQL, the recent query standard now being formulated at W3C is XQuery. XQuery is similar to XQL, but has a bit of different representations and some good additions.

Consider the following sample query, which would return all the employees with last name `Barve`:

```
document("employeelist.xml")//section[2]//profile[lastname = "Barve"]
```

The query starts with a specification of which document to consider for a query, followed by which section of a document to refer to (as in XQL). Under that section, there would be a profile element with the attribute value as `Barve`.

The following query would return all employees present in sections 1 to 5 of a document:

```
document("employeelist.xml")//section[1 To 5]//profile/name
```

The following example shows how to find title of purchases that are referenced by `<titref>` elements in the ledger of "*purchaseledger.xml*" with title "*abc*":

```
document("purchaseledger.xml")//ledger[title =
"abc"]//titref/@refid=>purchases/title
```

You can also include expressions in XQuery. The following example returns the annual cost from a monthly loan installment:

```
//account[name="Nita"]/monthlyinstal * 12
```

A variable name is specified in XQuery by a $ sign.

Another last important clause in XQuery is the `FLWR` (Flower) expression. It is a For-Let-Where-Return clause. It makes the XQuery behave as a function, which is useful. Consider the following example:

```
FOR $b IN document("invoices.xml")//invoice
WHERE $b/billto = "Nita Ajay"
AND $b/year = "2001"
RETURN $b/invtitle
```

This returns invoice titles of the invoices that are billed to `Nita Ajay` for the year `2001`.

Consider the following example query, which would make the usage more clear. I have adopted it from the XQuery documentation at `http://www.w3c.com`.

The following example returns each book whose price is greater than the average price, returns the title of the book, and returns the amount by which the book's price exceeds the average price.

```
<result>
   {
    LET $a := avg(document("bib.xml")//book/price)
    FOR $b IN document("bib.xml")//book
    WHERE $b/price > $a
    RETURN
       <expensive_book>
          {$b/title}
          <price_difference>
             {$b/price - $a}
          </price_difference>
       </expensive_book>
   }
</result>
```

XML-Tier for Databases

Recently, many vendors have introduced various types of XML-tiers to accept and provide XML formats.

Oracle translates the chain of object references from the database into the hierarchical structure of XML elements. In an object-relational database, the field Employment in the table `EmploymentProfile` is modeled as an object reference of type `EmploymentType` (see Listing 10.8).

LISTING 10.8 Schema Scripts in Oracle

```
CREATE TABLE EMPLOYMENTPROFILE
{
     EmployeeID     NUMERIC (8),
     EmployeeName CHAR (35),
     Employment     EmploymentType // object reference
```

LISTING 10.8 Continued

```
}

CREATE TYPE EmploymentType as OBJECT
{
     EmploymentCode VARCHAR (50),
     EmploymentDesc VARCHAR (50)
}
```

An XML document generated from the simple query (`Select * from EmploymentProfile`) would resemble the one shown in Listing 10.9.

LISTING 10.9 XML Resultset Document

```
<?xml version="1.0"?>
<!-- XML result-set document -->
<ROWSET>
    <ROW num="1">
        <EmployeeID>1212323</EmployeeID>
        <EmployeeName>Nita Barve</EmployeeName>
        <Employment>
            <EmploymentCode>FT918291</EmploymentCode>
            <EmploymentDesc>Full Time Level A</EmploymentDesc>
        </Employment>
    </ROW>
</ROWSET>
```

Listing 10.10 shows the code for extracting XML from the database using Oracle thin drivers. Note that usually the term *thin* refers to the native drivers provided by the database manufacturer in the JDBC world. Because the example uses the drivers provided by the Oracle database manufacturer, which are optimized for accessing the database, they are efficient and provide access to proprietary abilities of the database aspects.

LISTING 10.10 Extracting XML from the Database

```
import oracle.jdbc.driver.*;
import oracle.xml.sql.query.OracleXMLQuery;
import java.lang.*;
import java.sql.*;

// class to test XML document generation as String
class testXMLSQL {
```

LISTING 10.10 Continued

```
  public static void main(String[] args)
  {
    try {
     // Create the connection
     Connection conn  = getConnection("scott","tiger");

     // Create the query class
     OracleXMLQuery qry = new OracleXMLQuery(conn,
        "SELECT  * FROM EmploymentProfile");

     // Get the XML string
     String str = qry.getXMLString();

     // Print the XML output
     System.out.println("The XML output is:\n"+str);

     // Always close the query to get rid of any resources..
     qry.close();
    } catch(SQLException e) {
     System.out.println(e.toString());
    }
  }

  // Get the connection given the user name and password.!
  private static Connection getConnection(String username,
       String password)
       throws SQLException
  {
     // register the JDBC driver..
      DriverManager.registerDriver(new
         oracle.jdbc.driver.OracleDriver());

     // Create the connection using the OCI8 driver
      Connection conn =
       DriverManager.getConnection(
          "jdbc:oracle:thin:@dlsun489:1521:ORCL",
          username,password);

     return conn;
  }
}
```

As seen from the listing, an instance of `OracleXMLQuery` is created and used to execute the query. The `getXMLString()` gets the XML string as shown in Listing 10.1. To retrieve the XMLDOM type of object, use `getXMLDOM()`.

XML representation and methods are as many as there are database vendors in the market. The preceding example would serve as a good example of how database constructs and their vendors are trying to provide for and accept XML.

Generic Message Packets Based Systems—a Design Approach

Although I covered message packet based systems in a previous chapter, it is worth taking a second look on the design issues in such systems.

Various frameworks exist for offering the core system with messaging services. *JMS (Java Messaging Service)* is one such approach. Another initiative is ebXML and the SOAP initiative for messaging.

The message-based systems either provide a framework to exchange messages or rather listen to messages. We will take a close second look at what they mean to us from the distributed computing perspective.

All message based systems or frameworks provide excitation routines to broadcast and catch messages. But not all systems bind to a particular messaging packet types. This is a useful consideration because ideally a messaging system should deal with broadcasting or delivering messages and no core processing logic should be embedded in them. This helps us to achieve maximum flexibility in terms of using message packets we require.

Moreover, it becomes important to provide a packet structure independent system to an existing client who already has a message packet structure in place. This is true because many systems in the last decade or two followed the concept of packaging jobs in the form of record layout. These jobs were then routed to a suitable scheduler that executes them in sequence or depending on the priority assigned.

These job records could be imagined as messages or message packets. To upgrade such a system and provide support for new enterprise applications, you need to utilize some architecture that would extend it and not involve much re-design.

A generic message framework would just do that. It would allow you to broadcast the same message packet to an existing system and some wrapping services to make it suitable for advanced applications designed over the framework. This would provide a seamless integration of old and new systems.

Modeling a Message Based System

Let's look at the model of a typical message based system or messaging service framework.

Such systems are termed *MOM (Message-Oriented Middleware)*. Using middleware, application developers can reliably move data between applications via a programming interface. Translation, security, message delivery, communication protocols, and other similar issues are all handled transparently by the middleware.

The messaging systems are divided into two forms as listed and defined in the following:

- Point-to-Point is the one in which data from point P1 is transferred to a message queue at point P2 and picked up by the application at P2. This system is also called message queuing.
- Publish/Subscribe is the one in which multiple senders or receivers are involved—such as feeding stock quotes to trading floor brokers' desks.

As you can see from this list, Publish/Subscribe is more of a real-time messaging system as compared to Point-to-Point.

As industry experts began to realize the need to incorporate messaging middleware in their systems, they designed them. Many vendor centric systems came into existence. But, the problem was cross compatibility between the two systems. Hence, there was need for standard specifications.

One such specification released in 1999 was the *JMS (Java Messaging Service)* specifications from Sun Microsystems.

The simplest and the closest example of a message-based system is our post office. The sender sends the message to the post office and it is delivered to the receiver. There can be many types of message sending configurations as shown in the following:

- One-to-one
- One-to-many
- Many-to-many

For one-to-many and many-to-many, the Publish/Subscribe type of messaging system is used. In such systems, the subscriber does not have to know who the publisher is and vice versa.

The process for publishing a message to a topic is simple and consists of the following steps:

1. Look up the topic
2. Create and start a topic connection
3. Create a topic session
4. Create a publisher
5. Create a message

The process for subscribing to a message in JMS is as follows:

1. Look up the topic
2. Create and start a topic connection
3. Create a topic session
4. Create a subscriber
5. Install an asynchronous listener/callback on the subscriber object.

Jut as in our e-mail system, JMS has message selectors that allow receivers to filter and select messages. Furthermore, when the sender marks the message as *durable,* the message has to be delivered under any circumstances. This means that even if the network is down, the messaging system has to cache (or persist) the message and relay it whenever the network is available.

A JMS message consists of three parts as listed here:

- The Header consists of various fields required for routing and identification of the message.
- The Property consists of application specific fields in name/value pair and is optional.
- The Body contains the actual message.

The following message types are supported by JMS:

- `BytesMessage` is a stream of un-interpreted bytes.
- `MapMessage` is a set of name/value pairs where names are strings and values are Java primitive types. The entries can be accessed sequentially or randomly by name, and the order of the entries is undefined.
- `TextMessage` is a message instance using the `java.util.string` class. You can assume that the messages from this class will be used for XML messages.

- `StreamMessage` is a stream of Java primitive values that is filled and read sequentially.
- `ObjectMessage` is a message containing a Java object that can be serialized.

Because this is a Java-based framework, the message types provided are a wide range of data packets.

To summarize, a middleware must have the following features for it to be applicable in the commercial world:

- Administration and monitoring
- Load balancing
- Fault tolerance
- Error notification
- Topology support
- Routing methodologies
- Diverse protocols support
- Security and tracking

Figure 10.9 shows the major messaging system framework components and the interaction between them. Note that the message broker is responsible for receiving and broadcasting the messages to respective receivers through the point-to-point channel or subscribers through the queue channel.

Because I am talking about the messaging services, take a look at some broadcast and link services that would allow you to construct a distributed framework using existing components.

Achieving Maximum Scalability Through Message Packets

Using message packets in a messaging system would solve the problem of message flow in a distributed system, provided there is a robust mechanism to link to other systems over the network.

Consider that you are the best loan providing agency, and you are developing an application to pick up loan rates and schemes from various financial systems depending on user requirement. You need some mechanism to link to the enterprise systems to query them and get the results. The scope of such a design covers the *Enterprise Application Integration (EAI)* model.

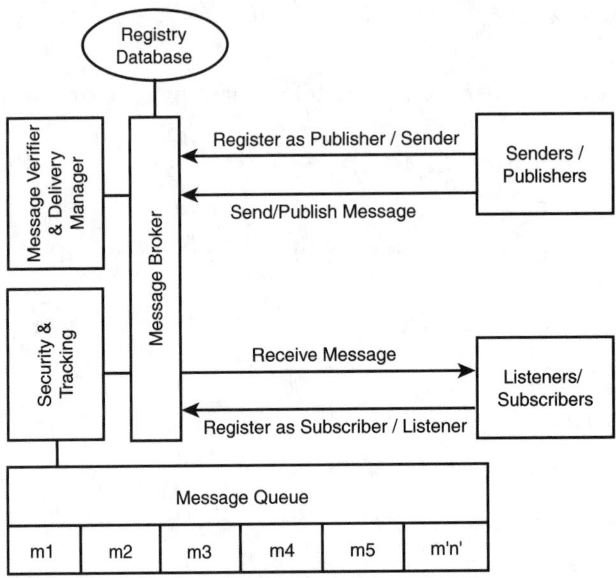

FIGURE 10.9 A Message Service framework.

Moreover, if you were maintaining several accounts, you would require dynamically querying the various systems for finding a product over them. Hence, you would require discovering them and then using them.

A technology that provides you with the ability to hunt for systems and discover them is Jini. Jini has been around for quite a few years, but until recently no practical use was found. Jini is powerful and has a strong distributed conceptuality in terms of architecture.

The following list shows the features of the Jini Technology Services:

- `httpd`—A client needs the `httpd` to be able to download the Java classes offered by the service provider. The class files can be packaged into Java archive (jar) files. This provides an efficient way of transmitting Java program code over networks.
- `rmid`—It is used by the LS and offers the ability to activate programs. Jini uses RMI to invoke methods on remote Java objects.
- `LS`—Here, a service provider registers its service. Note that a service is any application or code that provides some data processing function or business logic required for the application in scope. Once a service is registered, a client can use it.

The working of a typical Jini system is shown in Figure 10.10. The main aspect of a Jini system is Lookup Service (LS). The LS allows the service providers to register their interfaces with it. The service providers use a discovery process to find the LS location.

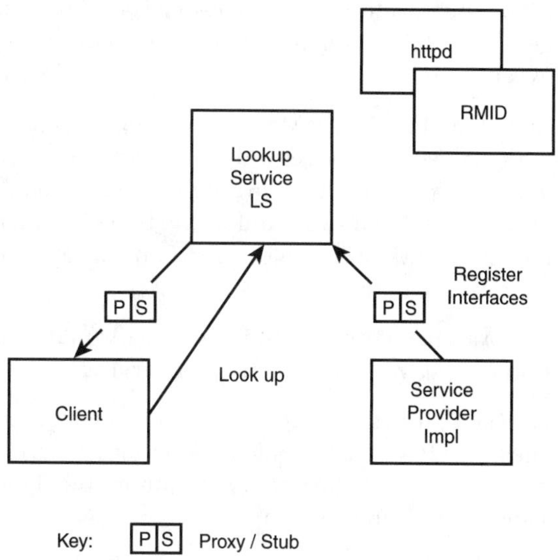

FIGURE 10.10 A schematic of a Jini Service-based system.

Discovery protocol is based on IP Multicast protocol. Once the service provider discovers the LS, it *joins* with it. Finally it uploads the *proxy* object to the LS service, which marks the completion of the registration process.

The client now *looks up* and uses the discovery mechanism to locate LS. It passes the requirement query to the LS, and the LS finds the closest match and returns the proxy to the client. Now the client downloads the object code and uses it.

As seen from the discussions, use of Jini like services would allow you to develop robust systems in the B2B marketplace. Collaboration over the Web to construct distributed systems would be easy.

There are some important concepts of Jini as a framework. For example, Jini uses *RMI (Remote Method Invocation)*, and the compiler generates a proxy and stubs. Note that the proxy and stubs are the same as for normal RMI requirements. RMI uses a standard mechanism, which is employed in major RPC systems, for communicating with remote objects: stubs and skeletons. A stub for a remote object acts as a client's local representative or a proxy for the remote object. The caller invokes a method on the local stub, which is responsible for carrying out the method call on the remote object. In RMI, a stub for a remote object implements the same set of remote interfaces that a remote object implements. The stub residing on the client end marshals (writes and transmits) the parameters to a remote skeleton sitting on a remote *Java Virtual Machine (JVM)*. The skeleton unmarshals (reads) the parameters and invokes the method on the actual object. Finally, it returns the value to the stub, which unmarshals and uses it.

Jini LS has a concept of leasing. This is similar to giving an apartment on lease. All service providers need to register services only for a particular lease period. The service providers have to worry about renewing the leases when they expire. The LS service would get rid of all expired leases unless the providers themselves renew them. This functionality allows the LS to be robust and always updated with the latest list of providers on the network.

To consider a simple example of how to code Jini, that would require setting up a Jini lookup server on the network and creating the service.

After the service is created, it has to be registered with the lookup server. Listing 10.11 shows the client service, which would look up for the service located on Jini Lookup Server. Note that this code fragment is common usually for obtaining a reference to a service with the lookup server.

LISTING 10.11 Jini—Obtaining a Reference for Lookup Service and Obtaining the Reference at the Client Side

```
//java imports.
import java.util.*;
import java.io.*;

//RMI imports.
import java.rmi.RemoteException;
import java.rmi.RMISecurityManager;

//JINI Package imports.
import net.jini.discovery.DiscoveryListener;
import net.jini.discovery.DiscoveryEvent;
import net.jini.discovery.LookupDiscovery;
import net.jini.core.lookup.ServiceRegistrar;
import net.jini.core.lookup.ServiceTemplate;

/**
 * Class that act's as Client for invoking
 * getMessage method remotely on HelloWorldService
```

LISTING 10.11 Continued

```
 * using JINI.
 *
 * @author : Ajay M R
 * @version : $1.0$
 */

public class JINIClient implements Runnable {

    // to facilitate search.
    protected ServiceTemplate template;

    //discover services.
    protected LookupDiscovery disco;

    /**
     * Inner class that will facilitate & take part in
     * the discovery protocol.
     */
    class Listener implements DiscoveryListener {

        /**
         * Invoked when new lookup service is available.
         * @param DisoveryEvent discovery event object which encapsulates
         *                      service registrars.
         */
        public void discovered( DiscoveryEvent event ) {

            ServiceRegistrar[] newregs = event.getRegistrars();

            for ( int i=0; i<newregs.length; i++) {

                lookForService( newregs[i] );

            }//for loop ends here.
        }//discovered method ends here.

        /**
         * called when we find a new lookup service.
         * @param DisoveryEvent discovery event object which encapsulates
         *                      service registrars.
         */
```

LISTING 10.11 Continued

```
        public void discarded( DiscoveryEvent event) {
            //do nothing here.. since its the client.
        }//discard method ends here.

    }//Listner class ends here.


    /**
     * public constructor.
     */
    public JINIClient() throws IOException {

        //Initialization for query string.
        Class[] types = {HelloWorldServiceInterface.class};

        //Initialize template to perform lookup search.
        template = new ServiceTemplate(null, types, null);

        //set the Security manager.
        if ( System.getSecurityManager() == null )
        System.setSecurityManager( new RMISecurityManager() );

        //search the group for available services.. in our case we'll search
        //for public groups only.
        disco = new LookupDiscovery( new String[] {""} );

        //Install a listener.
        disco.addDiscoveryListener( new Listener() );

    }//public constructor ends here.

    /**
     * Once we've found the lookup service, search for the proxy's
     * that implement HelloWorldServiceInterface.
     *
     * @param ServiceRegistrar service registrar object.
     * @return Object object received by marshalling after lookup.
     */
    protected Object lookForService(ServiceRegistrar registrar) {

        Object o = null;
```

LISTING 10.11 Continued

```
        try {

            //the actual searching is done here by calling lookup.
            o = registrar.lookup( template );

        }catch (RemoteException ex){
            System.out.println("HelloWorldClient: Error in Lookup "+
            ex.getMessage() );
            return null;
        }

        if ( o == null ) {
            System.err.println("HelloWorldClient: No Matching Services");
            return null;
        }

        System.out.println("HelloWorldService: Got a matching Service "+
        "& invoking method on it");

        String output = ( (HelloWorldServiceInterface)o).getMessage();

        System.out.println("HelloWorldService: output after method "+
        "invocation - "+output);

        //exit the application since we do not need the object anymore.l
        //Note: this is true only in current scenario i.e. HelloWorld.
        System.exit(1);

        return o;

    }//lookForService method ends here.

    /**
     * this thread does nothing but keeps the VM from exiting
     * while we do discovery.
     */
    public void run(){

        while ( true ) {
```

LISTING 10.11 Continued

```
            try {
                Thread.sleep(1000000);
        }catch(InterruptedException ex) {}

        }//while ends here.

    }//run ends here.


    /**
     * main entry point for this program.
     * <b> Steps :
     * - Instantiate our HelloWorldClient. <br>
     * - Start the background thread which will keep the VM running. <br>
     */
    public static void main(String[] args){

        try {

            JINIClient client = new JINIClient();
            new Thread( client).start();

        }catch( IOException ioex ){
            System.out.println("HelloWorldClient: Error - "+ioex.getMessage() );
        }//catch ends here.

    }//main method ends here.

}//JiniClient class ends here.
```

The implementation of the client is quite straightforward. Let's identify the major operation of the preceding client to better understand the implementation.

1. The client initializes what kind of service it requires to look for in the lookup.
2. It needs to discover the lookup server.
3. Once it finds the lookup server, it has to pass the required service reference, initialized in the first step.
4. The lookup service returns the reference to the service and the client executes the method on the referenced object to get the result.

The code in which the client sets the type of service it would require to look up is as shown here:

```
//Initialization for query string.
Class[] types = {SomeServiceInterface.class};

//Initialize template to perform lookup search.
template = new ServiceTemplate(null, types, null);
```

This code is included in the client class constructor. The type of service we are looking for matches the `SomeServiceInterface` definition. The client code then sets the security manager and launches the discovery mechanism.

```
//search the group for available services.. in our case we'll search
//for public groups only.
disco = new LookupDiscovery( new String[] {""} );

//Install a listener.
disco.addDiscoveryListener( new Listener() );
```

Note that the `LookupDiscovery()` method takes a group, which allows the client to search for the particular service group in which it is interested. This could be a good idea for the lookup type of mechanism using framework. The group adds an additional level of filter because imagine that a practical Jini service has 1,000 or 10,000 services, belonging to various groups, registered. The group based categorical classification allows a client to get the required bunch of services (and not all) easily. In my simple example, however, I have passed a empty string as group, which means that I am interested in getting the entire listing.

The lookup for the service is performed by the `lookForService()` method in the listing.

The code that registers the service with the lookup server is as shown in Listing 10.12.

LISTING 10.12 Code to Register a Class with the Lookup Server as a Service

```
//java imports.
import java.util.*;
import java.io.*;

//RMI imports.
import java.rmi.RemoteException;
import java.rmi.RMISecurityManager;
```

LISTING 10.12 Continued

```
//JINI imports.
import net.jini.discovery.DiscoveryListener;
import net.jini.discovery.DiscoveryEvent;
import net.jini.discovery.LookupDiscovery;
import net.jini.core.lookup.ServiceItem;
import net.jini.core.lookup.ServiceRegistrar;
import net.jini.core.lookup.ServiceRegistration;

/**
 * This class will find the lookup services and
 * publish the proxy.<br><i>
 * NOTE: This class isn't involved in helping the proxy
 *       but it only helps it manage its JINI responsibilities. </i>
 *
 * @author : Sandesh Salunke, Ravinder Khokhar
 * @version : $Revision 1.0$
 */

public class SomeService implements Runnable {

    //Leased time.
    protected final int LEASE_TIME = 10*60*1000;

    //HashMap to track new/current registrations.
    protected HashMap registrations = new HashMap();

    protected ServiceItem item;
    protected LookupDiscovery disco;

    /**
     * Inner class to listen for discovery events.
     */
    class Listener implements DiscoveryListener {

        /**
         * Invoked when we find a new lookup service.
         * @param DiscoveryEvent discovery event object which encapsulates
         *                       registrars.
         */
        public void discovered( DiscoveryEvent event ) {
```

LISTING 10.12 Continued

```
            System.out.println("HelloWorldService -> Listener : Discovered "+
            "a lookup service");

            ServiceRegistrar[] newregs = event.getRegistrars();

            for ( int i=0; i<newregs.length; i++) {

                if ( !registrations.containsKey( newregs[i] ) )
                registerWithLookup( newregs[i] );

            }//for loop ends here.

        }//discovered method ends here.


        /**
         * Invoked only when we explicitly discard a lookup
         * service, not "automatically" when a lookup
         * service goes down. Once Discovered, there is NO
         * ongoing communication with a lookup service.
         * @param DiscoveryEvent discovery event object which encapsulates
         *                      registrars.
         */
        public void discarded( DiscoveryEvent event ){

            ServiceRegistrar[] deadregs = event.getRegistrars();

            for ( int i=0; i<deadregs.length; i++ )
            registrations.remove( deadregs[i] );

        }//discarded method ends here.

    }//inner class Listener ends here.


    /**
     * public Constructor.
     */
    public SomeService() throws IOException {
```

LISTING 10.12 Continued

```
    // parameter description :
    // 1. null - this is the ServiceID, if you pass null
    //           a globally unique ID is allocated.
    //
    // 2. instance of the service proxy object.
    //
    // 3. null - a list of attributes that we wish to
    //           associate with the service proxy. these
    //           attributes can be specific to any purpose
    //           like proxy for printer or scanner will have some
    //           unique attributes.
    item = new ServiceItem( null, createProxy(), null );

    //set the security manager
    if ( System.getSecurityManager() == null ) {
        System.setSecurityManager( new RMISecurityManager() );
    }

    //Search the public group, which by convention
    //is named by an empty string
disco = new LookupDiscovery( new String[] { "" } );

    //Install a listener.
    disco.addDiscoveryListener( new Listener() );

}//SomeService constructor ends here.

//to create a proxy service.
protected SomeServiceInterface createProxy() {

    return new SomeServiceProxy();

}//SomeServiceInterface ends here.


/**
 * This will involves remote calls, and may take while to complete.
 * Thus since it's called form discovered(). it will prevent us
 * from responding in a timely fashion to new discovery events.
 * So in future this functionality will be accomplished by spinning
 * off a new thread to do this work.
```

LISTING 10.12 Continued

```
     * @param ServiceRegistrar service registrars object to register
     *                          our services.
     */
    synchronized void registerWithLookup( ServiceRegistrar registrar ) {

        ServiceRegistration registration = null;

        try {

            registration = registrar.register( item, LEASE_TIME );

        }catch( RemoteException ex) {
            System.out.println("SomeService - Couldn't register :"+
            ex.getMessage() );
            return;
        }//catch ends here.

        // if this is our first registration, use the service
        // ID returned to us.
        if ( item.serviceID == null ) {
            item.serviceID = registration.getServiceID();
            System.out.println("HelloWorldService: set service ID to "+
            item.serviceID);
        }//if ends here.

    }//registerWithLookup method ends here.

    /**
     *this thread does nothing but sleeps, but it
     * makes sure the VM does not exit's.
     */
    public void run(){

        while ( true ) {

            try {
                Thread.sleep(1000000);
        }catch(InterruptedException ex) {}

        }//while ends here.
```

LISTING 10.12 Continued

```
    }//run ends here.


    /**
     * <i>Main entry point.</i>
     * Creates a new SomeService and start
     * background thread which will prevent VM from exiting.
     */
    public static void main(String[] args){

        try {

            // start service.
            SomeService SomeService = new SomeService();

            // assign it to a thread which will prevent
            // it from kicked out by VM
            new Thread( SomeService ).start();

        }catch(IOException ioex ){

            System.out.println("SomeService - Couldn't create service: "+
            ioex.getMessage() );

        }//catch ends here.

    }// main method ends here.

}//SomeService class ends here.
```

As seen, the code in the listing for registering the `SomeService()` proxy with the lookup server is pretty straightforward.

The `SomeServiceProxy` would be as shown in Listing 10.13.

LISTING 10.13 The `SomeServiceProxy` Class

```
//java imports.
import java.util.*;
import java.io.*;
//RMI imports.
import java.rmi.RemoteException;
import java.rmi.RMISecurityManager;
```

LISTING 10.13 Continued

```
//JINI imports.
import net.jini.discovery.DiscoveryListener;
import net.jini.discovery.DiscoveryEvent;
import net.jini.discovery.LookupDiscovery;
import net.jini.core.lookup.ServiceItem;
import net.jini.core.lookup.ServiceRegistrar;
import net.jini.core.lookup.ServiceRegistration;

/**
 * Light weight proxy object for Hello World Service
 * which will be downloaded by the client using JINI protocol.
 * It implements Serializable to support run time serialization over the
 * network to client side. The behavior of proxy is specified by
 * HelloWorldInterface interface thus restricting the proxy to provide
 * implementation for getMessage() method which is defined under
 * HelloWorldServiceInterface interface.
 *
 * @author : Ravinder Khokhar
 * @version : $Revision 1.0$
 */
class SomeServiceProxy implements Serializable,
                                            SomeServiceInterface {
    /**
     * public constructor needed.
     */
    public SomeServiceProxy() {

    }//public constructor ends here.

    /**
     * returns a 'hello world' message.
     * @return String 'Hello World' String.
     */
    public String getMessage(){

        return "Hello World from SomeServiceProxy";

    }//getMessage method ends here.

}//SomeServiceProxy ends here.
```

The only reason the preceding Jini code appears in this chapter is to make you conversant with how the recent service oriented frameworks could make your life easier in terms of implementing distributed systems.

Message Packet Based System Extendibility

A practical message based system or systems could be interconnected using the lookup logic described previously.

Its hard for a open-ended system designer to rely on a specific implementation, but still Jini and JMS (Java Messaging Service) provide a pretty much open architecture for you to devise a highly distributed open-ended system.

Furthermore, by adding an XML-RPC and SOAP mechanism, you could extend the interactivity to a much larger extent. Let's try to devise a message-based system based on the principles learned in the preceding sections. To make it interesting, consider a simple case of designing a financial query system offered by an agency, which would allow or include the following:

- Allow corporate users to query the central loan services offered by the agency from their end using their system
- Include a mechanism to interact with other legacy financial systems and banking systems to arrive at the best results
- Allow the user to procure a loan instantly and file an application with the resulting financial or banking system

You essentially have to design a multitier system that would be distributed at both the client and the subscribing bank or financial corporations.

The important aspect to note here is that when a client is searching for loan rates or offerings, the system would have to traverse all the existing or available financial systems and produce the results accordingly.

This could be easily set up using a central lookup architecture located at the agency end. For the systems located on the financial organization's end, you have dual possibilities:

- To provide suitable deployable components that would broadcast the availability and service details to the agency servers
- For existing systems located on the financial organizations end, which offer such interaction that they could be used and sensed per their deployed capabilities

Usually, if you are dealing with hundreds of diverse clients, you could imagine that consistency serves a better purpose.

Hence, you could insist in such scenarios that instead of providing services to both the types listed previously, you provide a service that would include only one approach.

The first scenario requires that an agency supplied component be installed on the client-end system. Although it involves delivery and installation to be deployed at the client end, it is still a good approach because the agency could offer a more flexible and workable approach and the design can be faster and gradual. Because you go on developing and deploying for each client, the interaction could be slow with the second approach.

From a broader perspective, you could consider some standard systems to exist at client locations. This would then simplify the design on your side because then your deployable component could sense the system and accordingly deploy only the required adaptors for interacting with the client-end system.

You would then have a central message based system located at an agency. The system would also have a lookup server such as mechanism, which would be pinged by the client-end deployed modules to broadcast the availability.

A schematic of such a system is shown in Figure 10.11. The setup shows only one financial system and one user-end system. In real-life, there would be many financial systems and many user systems.

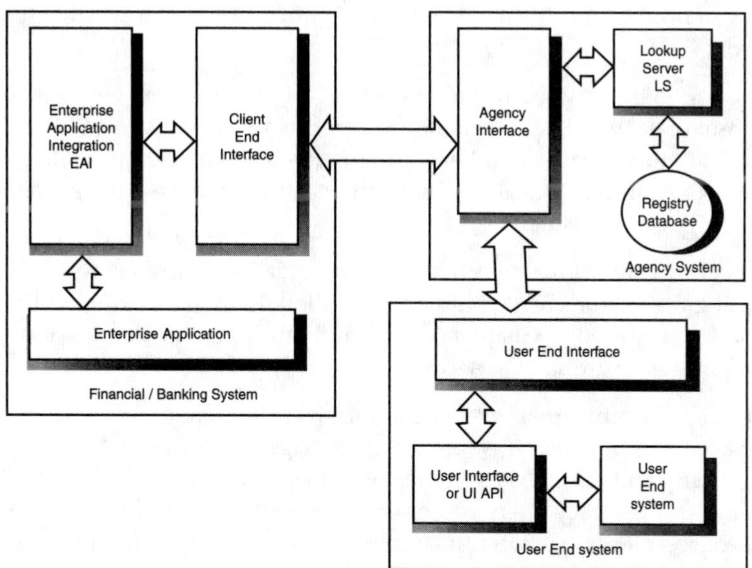

FIGURE 10.11 A schematic of a typical lookup service-based messaging system.

I have mimicked lookup services similar to the one Jini offers. The lookup service uses a system registry to store the currently available service providers.

The financial system would supply the availability and method interactivity details using a SOAP message. The SOAP message would be supplied to the Lookup server once the enterprise system starts or becomes available. I would also include a sort of leasing mechanism in the financial end system. By this, I mean that the SOAP message broadcast by the system and registered in the lookup registry would have a specific time stamp. And some sort of pooling routine at the agency end would scan the registry for all old messages and garbage collect them. A similar time controlled mechanism would be running on the client end financial system, which would retransmit the register message after the lease has expired.

It is worth pointing out what amount of data a financial system needs to provide to register itself. Let's consider that the information required would include the client end system location, method names, and parameter requirements. Think about standardizing your approach by providing a standard choice of service names. Consider, for example, that you provide services of type `LOAN_TYPES_INQUIRY`, `LOAN_INTEREST_RATES_INQUIRY`, and `OTHER_FINANCIAL_AIDS`. You need to provide the ability in the client end application to dynamically compute and broadcast the supported services. The service means queries in a real sense, and by broadcasting the supported services, your client end module merely enters into an agreement that it would be able to provide the resultset to queries with the preceding keywords. Of course, you need to also fit the parameters required for these services within this framework.

You could store the services at the agency end and the requirement to invoke them in the form of an XML file. The reason for storing the services in an XML file is that you can add more services to it later, and the remote end client module could refer to this file dynamically and accordingly broadcast the service types in case you decide to change the names.

Additionally, to allow for extensibility, you provide a working API for your framework; using which, the client could code additional services. If you use the framework models discussed in Chapter 3, this would mean essentially developing an adaptor for each or group of services.

The user's end system would place an inquiry with the agency interface giving specific keywords in which it is interested. The agency LS would then go through the system registry and place a query to all available providers. The client end EAI would interface with the legacy offers and return back the query results to the agency. The agency collects all the query results from various financial organizations and presents or sends an aggregate resultset to the user end.

You would even provide a set of APIs for the user end. The user would use this API to integrate the agency tools in his application.

Consider a few sample SOAP calls, which you could use in your model.

The SOAP envelope shown in Listing 10.14 is simple. It calls an interface called `RegisterClientEAI`, which has a method called `RegisterServices()`. As you see in the simple message envelope, we are passing the services to be registered as a plain string with * as the delimiter. The interface code would resemble that shown in Listing 10.15 using Java.

LISTING 10.14 SOAP Message to Register a Service with LS

```
<SOAP-ENV:Envelope xmlns:SOAP-ENV="http://schemas.xmlsoap.org/soap/envelope/"
xmlns:xsi="http://www.w3.org/1999/XMLSchema-instance"
xmlns:xsd="http://www.w3.org/1999/XMLSchema">
     <SOAP-ENV:Header>
     </SOAP-ENV:Header>
     <SOAP-ENV:Body>
         <ns1:RegisterServices xmlns:ns1="RegisterClientEAI" SOAP-
ENV:encodingStyle="http://schemas.xmlsoap.org/soap/encoding/">
                 <services xsi:type="xsd:string">
LOAN_TYPES_INQUIRY*LOAN_INTEREST_RATES_INQUIRY</services>
        <regtime xsi:type="xsd:string">11:20:00:01012001</regtime>
         </ns1:RegisterServices>
    </SOAP-ENV:Body>
</SOAP-ENV:Envelope>
```

LISTING 10.15 Interface Code for `RegisterClientEAI` Class

```
public interface RegisterClientEAI
{
    public String RegisterServices(String services, String regtime);
}
```

The pooling mechanism on the client EAI and agency side could be easily achieved by extending threads in Java.

The registry database on the agency side can be a simple memory stored XML document, with persistence so that the same could be retrieved and used in a fallback situation. The persistence could be achieved easily by including a write method, which would write the XML stream to a disk file every time a node is added or updated. This approach is also useful in practical situations where you need to create a memory image of a database for a faster query.

Because I am already discussing the XML and databases, I want to mention that many attempts were recently made to improve back-end performance. Fine-tuning and performance monitoring of a database is crucial in many legacy networks. You have seen various methods such as clustering, solid state disk drives, and other mechanisms used to achieve the speed. There is also a possibility of using a simple memory space (RAM)—such as an XML document constructed from the database using a DOM parser and applying XQuery/XQL queries to retrieve data. This would probably make your understanding of XQuery and its importance clearer. One such schematic is shown in Figure 10.12.

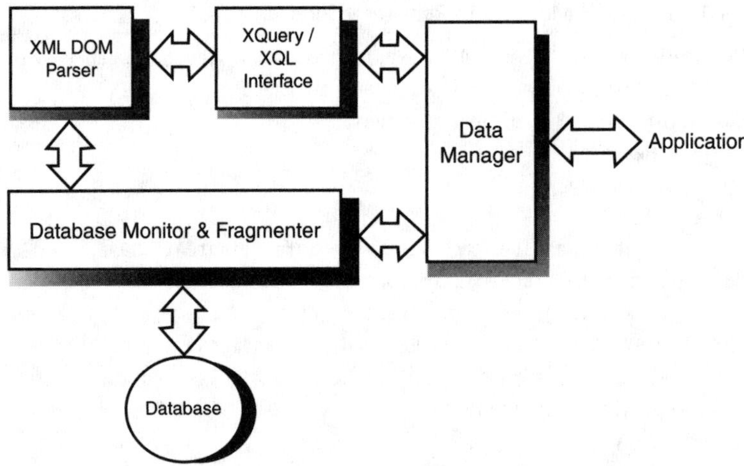

FIGURE 10.12 A schematic of a database performance improvement using an XML layer.

As shown, the database has a monitoring layer that decides the portions of the database to be transferred on the XML end. The database portion would be stored as a DOM tree and could be queried using the XQuery interface. The data manager has accountability in terms of what data resides on the XML side and accordingly redirects the incoming queries from application to respective stage.

By making the database-monitoring layer controlled, the data stored on the XML end can be changed dynamically to get optimum performance.

Summary

The next chapter of this book is the first chapter of Part II, "Case Studies." In the series of chapters included in this part, I will try to practically design and develop some real-world systems. They are referred to as case studies because they present some problem cases and their design solutions. I have collected a few cases of how XML could be used to solve and can be included in practical systems for making the system open-ended and extensible.

I will consider some real-world system problems, which probably all system designers and architects face many times. I will try to point to specific technologies that exist for solving the current problem and mention them in the course of designing and implementing the design.

I have tried to explain major architecture blocks and given code samples wherever necessary. It is worth mentioning that the case studies give a design and architectural solution to the problems rather than concentrating on coding.

PART II
Case Studies

This description will provide a brief insight into how this section is arranged and what is the purpose of this section.

Throughout the book, I talk about system models and architectures. I have also placed many application highlights wherever possible to give you a better idea of what the application would be. This section consists of four distinct case studies.

The purpose of the case studies is to give you a better handle on applying what you have learned. It serves the purpose of looking at some real-world systems and how you can apply these models to make them more flexible and scalable. XML is used and applied throughout the case study literature.

Each of the case studies is arranged or divided in five sub-sections. "Problem Statement" identifies what the case deals with, which includes the usual client requirement statement. It specifies what the requirement is, in terms of the existing system and desired extension.

The second sub-section, "Working on Architecture and Design," includes the reasoning for applying a design. It gives the general architecture proposed for the problem statement and defines (at a much higher level) what the modules would do in terms of functionality. This section is core to your knowledge attained so far and opens up possible options for the design and architecture.

The third section specifies the actual design. This is a detailed overview of what the previous section has shown. I have included class (or interface) representations and workflow diagrams, wherever necessary, to make the design clear. The important aspect is the reason for each of the interfaces and why they exist.

The fourth section lists the UML notes for the objects to be included in the design. Each object method is listed as adopted from the design model. This section, especially for the third and fourth case study, includes some sample code to give you a better idea of what we are trying to do and how.

Finally, each case study ends with a conclusion, which would specify the possible extensions and refinement in the design.

Case studies 1, Chapter 11, "Extending Existing Close-Ended Systems," and 2, Chapter 12, "Designing Extensive and Scalable Systems," show the approach to design and list the detailed class interfaces and methods. This provides an opportunity for you to see how I arrived at the specific design and methods in a model.

Case studies 3, Chapter 13, "Cross-Platform and Diverse System Integration," and 4, Chapter 14, "Implementing an ERP System," show the approach for integration aspects and concentrate more on the interface models rather than actual systems. They propose a core model that would be useful for many generic models. Furthermore, they also show the importance of XML usage by using it for cross platform/language integration.

I have provided a basic skeleton code for all possible case studies. Remember, the code routines are solely to support the model proposed and not a complete system in itself.

I have tried to avoid basic coding—my main focus is on applying design models. There are many books with actual coding with respect to Java or Visual Basic.

11

Extending Existing Close-Ended Systems

IN THIS CHAPTER

Problem Statement

An existing ERP system deals with various inter-company operations and support. The departments covered include Purchase, Inventory, and Accounts (customers' account information). Although the business has many internal divisions, and therefore operations, we need to consider only a broad view of the system.

The system uses a command stack and a result dump stack. The concept of the stack is a file dump to a specific folder. The internals of the system can be understood by following the typical scenario explained next.

The Inventory module generates a materials requirement request and places the requirement document in a specific folder. The Purchase module polls this folder and receives the document, verifies it, and generates a purchase order in the system. The module also generates the order document, which, again, is placed in a specific folder. The Accounts module polls the folder and receives this document, verifies it as the purchase order released, and enters the payment schedule in the accounting database.

As seen in this simplistic workflow, the system uses the folders as stack "banks" to dump the information that must be passed between modules. The respective modules poll specific folders, and as soon as they find a document in them, it is picked and validated for further processing.

The interpretation of a database-coupled system discussed under the topic of open systems can be applied here. Figure 11.1 shows the high-level schematic of such a system. As shown, the internal system transactions occur using folders as temporary storage places.

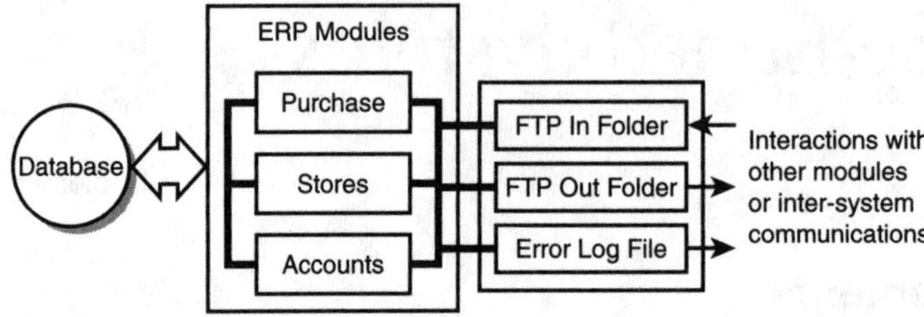

FIGURE 11.1 Schematic of a typical ERP system.

Often, making these various folders accessible by *File Transfer Protocol* (*FTP*) easily extends such systems. The schematic shows that the existing ERP system has this in place, and hence these folders can be accessed using FTP. Also, there is an Error dump folder that is accessed for collecting all errors. Because the error dumps are "taps" at various places in the existing system, no direct FTP access is available to these places.

It would be worth noting that FTP is a fairly primitive protocol used for many years. It was invented merely to solve the purpose of transferring data, in ASCII or binary formats, via TCP/IP. It does not have the robust error correcting capabilities of other transfer protocols available today.

We need to extend this system and make it open so that the system can be accessible by using application logic through Web and remote call mechanisms.

This allows company branches or subsidiaries to use the existing system to reflect the invoices on the main system. In this way the main company Accounts section accounts for all the invoices and hence allocates suitable funds.

The requirement imposed is that the branch locations are using a Windows-based accounting system, which supports DDE as the inter-operating mechanism. A complicating matter is that some branches favor the use of Web interfaces.

In short, we need to design an interaction layer or other middleware for the closed ERP system so that we can access its Purchase folder via FTP and create invoices from remote systems.

Working on Architecture and Design

Looking at the problem statement and the schematic of Figure 11.1, we conclude that the following are major requirements for the Interface system:

- To support FTP accessibility
- To provide Remote Access Service including Web services
- To provide FTP service, so that the error dump can be uploaded to, and referred to, at the middleware level

On the branch or subsidiary end, the secondary interface takes care of interacting with the Windows package using DDE. It interfaces with the preceding interface layer using a remote mechanism that integrates the third-party system with the main system.

Effectively, we would arrive at the scenario in Figure 11.2. The schematic shown is still a high-level reference to our model, but displays the major functional blocks in our proposed system. It shows a special FTP module, collocated with respect to the Interface system so that it properly uploads the error packets.

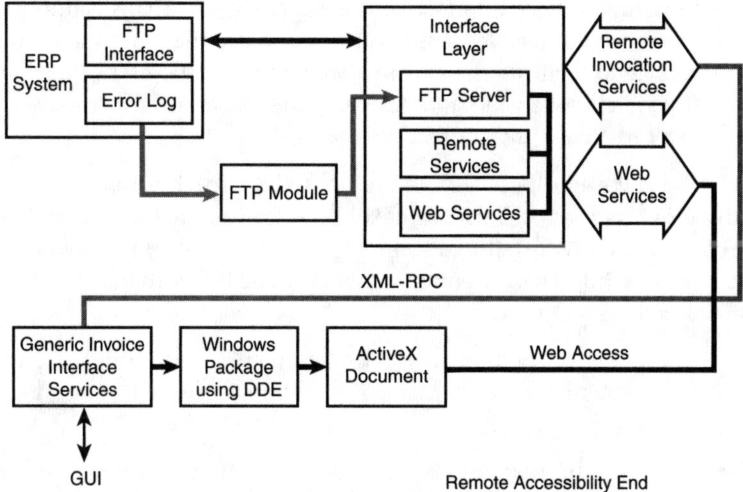

FIGURE 11.2 Schematic of the ERP system with user extensions.

The Web Services layer and Remote Services layer provide Web accessibility and RPC services for distributed access.

On the branch or subsidiary end, we have more than one solution. Let's review this part of the schematic, which can very well be a separate "animal" to deal with! The subsidiary end system has the following requirements:

- Allows the transfer of existing invoices into the main system
- Allows entering the new invoices into the main and local accounting systems, which are Windows-based

The first option is more like a utility service tool. It allows the newly-installed locations to upload existing invoices into the main system as a job or batch process.

The second option is usable after the utility tool has been used. All newer invoices are entered using this new interface, which automatically updates both systems. Hence, it makes the user's life easier so that he does not have to update the main system daily with the utility.

We propose the utility tool to be a ActiveX document-based Web interface that would talk with the Windows-based system using DDE. It would gather all invoices and upload them to the main system through our Interface.

The generic interface shown in the schematic could be a Visual Basic program that mimics the existing invoice interface of the current system. This is important because the user would need less time to learn and use the new system. By designing the user interface to replicate the existing, we will make the user's life easier! This is typical of any system extension and design in the real world because users typically hate to transfer to a new user interface.

Let us reason why we proposed an ActiveX-based approach for utility tool. Because it is a utility tool for occasional use, it makes sense to use the tool only when needed instead of permanently installing it on a user's system. Given the chance that we would change the interface and options, it would be better to control the tool from the Interface side.

For the second piece, it would be used daily by the user and would be customized to suit the current system front end; hence it would make sense to have it as installable item.

The preceding suggestions should be viewed as system maintenance and deployment issues for the designer or system architect.

The Actual Design

Let us agree and accept that our interface be considered middleware. Let's see a more detailed view of the interface or middleware.

Figure 11.3 shows the schematic of the actual middleware. It shows the architecture of the proposed system. We have again used the open-end framework model from our discussions in previous section of this book.

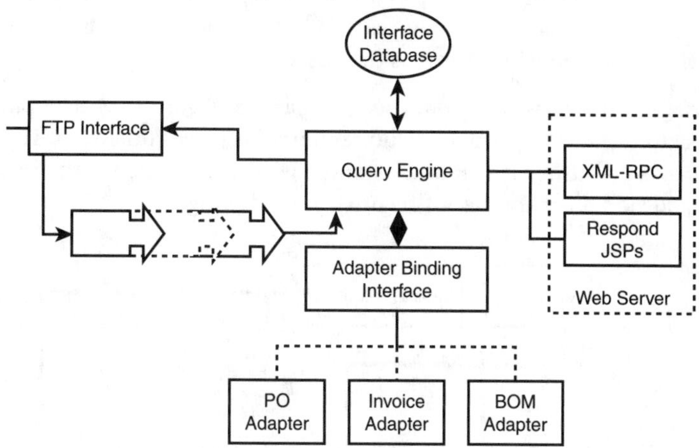

FIGURE 11.3 Schematic of a proposed interface/middleware.

The query engine is the core part, which executes all queries in the middleware. The queries are assumed to be generic message XML packets that represent all possible query options. The adapter binding logic is used by the query engine to work on the request and invokes an adapter that performs any required business function.

The adapters shown in the schematic refer to specific modules in the ERP system. The specific adapters are responsible for generating the required FTP format load document for the target business function. If, for example, we create an Open Purchase Order in the system, the query engine asks the adapter binder to invoke the PO Adapter. The PO Adapter provides business logic for converting the request into the format required by the ERP system and also incorporates validation services. Hence, the adapters in our current system provide the services of formatting the incoming data packets into a suitable system-required flat-file format.

These adapters are dynamically invoked, at runtime, using a typical XML map file, which is often called the binding map file or the binder.

This approach of providing adapters corresponding to the business process provides a flexible way to extend the system to other modules or provide more functionality in the future. For example, to add a specific module adapter, we need to create the adapter, deploy it, and set its configuration information in the binding map file.

The FTP Interface object would deal with FTP interactions with the ERP end. This is more like a helper class that would take care of the interface requirements, such as uploading and downloading.

To conclude, the core engine services are provided by the query engine, which uses the Web server to provide Web services and RPC services. The RPC layer is an XML-RPC installed over the Web server, as discussed previously.

The Interface database is shown in the schematic of Figure 11.3. The purpose of this database is to provide any storage requirements for the middleware. The exact usage of the database is clearer if you understand Figure 11.4, which is the same schematic with the additional capabilities of security and tracking.

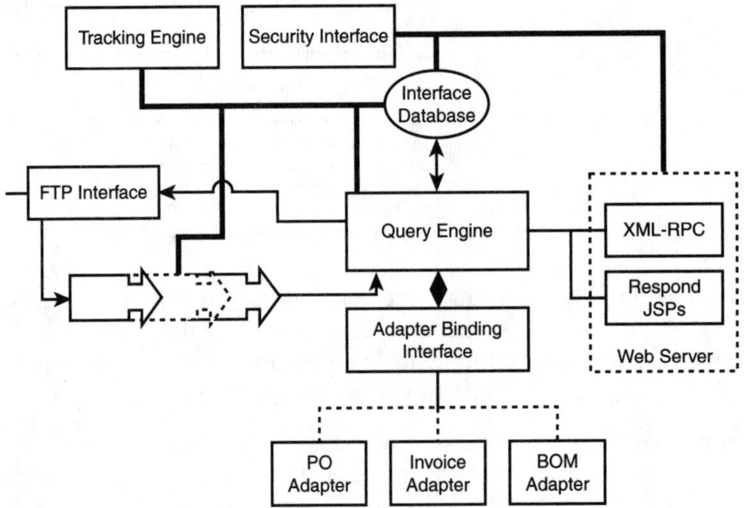

FIGURE 11.4 Middleware with tracking and security.

The security object would provide process accessibility and authentication services. The tracking would provide the ability to track and log all the events and transactions. The tracking module would typically have a level setting that would define at what detail level the processes would be tracked. Typical track levels would be Code, Debug, Events, Warnings, and Errors. Each level would cover all levels subordinate to it. The entire tracking log and the authentication information would be stored in the database to provide better concurrent access capabilities. The interface database could be a small footprint database like mySQL.

Implementing the Design

The implementation of the schematic would be identifying major classes. Usually it would be convenient to arrive at the require classes correlated to each block in the schematic and then add helper classes or objects. Then these classes could be assigned to suitable packages, in a Java-based scenario. There would be conventions used for the package hierarchy and naming the classes.

For naming, we follow the typical upper- and lowercase nomenclature. It is a good idea to have the classes ending with the keyword `interface`, if they are abstract interfaces, and to specify the implementation by the keyword `impl`. These keywords are usually appended at the end of the class or object name.

The interface definitions, with additional information on the method parameters, are found in intfc_definitions.txt, which is downloadable from this book's page at `samspublishing.com`. This helps you to have a clearer view of what I mean by a correlation with the schematic.

Table 11.1 gives the correlation between the schematic in Figure 11.4 and intfc_definitions.txt.

TABLE 11.1 Relationship Between Schematic Blocks and Interfaces

Schematic Block Reference	Interfaces
Query Engine	`QueryEngineInterface`
Adapter Binding Interface	`AdapterBinderInterface`
Adapters (PO, Invoice, Accounts)	`AdapterInterface`
FTP Interface	`FTPInterface`
Error Queue	`ErrorQueueInterface`
Tracking Interface	`TrackingInterface`
Security Interface	`SecurityInterface`
XML-RPC	`RPCCommunicationInterface`, `SOAPCommunicationInterface`
Web Services (JSP/Servlet)	`Web Server`
Interface Database	`DatabaseInterface`

The helper classes in the design are as follows.

- `LogInterface`: Provides logging services.
- `GenericXMLMessageInterface`: Provides generic XML message services: This is the message packet we would use to represent any message packet in our system.
- `XMLDocumentInstance`: Represents any XML document format held as an XML document object.

Although I provide the explanation for each of the interface classes and their methods, I explain the basic flow in my system involving all the classes. This helps you to "reason out" major classes and concepts of inventing class methods.

Figure 11.5 shows the flow of a complete request cycle in the system. It shows the various interfaces involved and their methods called in sequence of operation. The steps are numbered from 1 through 4. The steps that are numbered with H*x* are more like helper steps, specifying the internal method code flow.

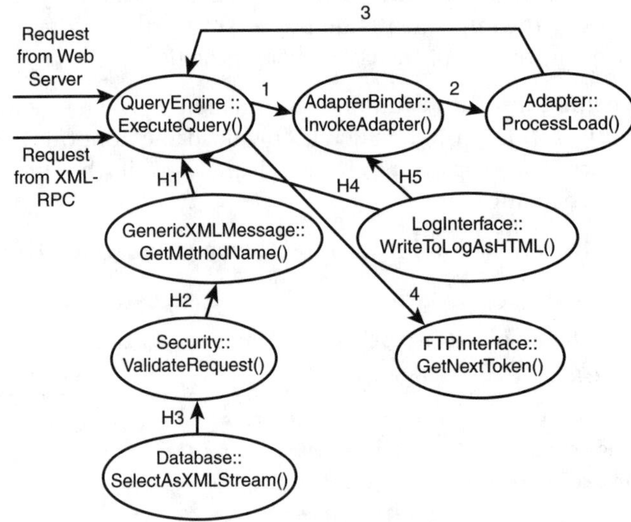

FIGURE 11.5 Process flow for a typical request.

Let's rationalize this design! As the previous section suggests, I am utilizing the generic message packet type of architecture. The query engine is the component central to the entire system. It executes a query message task packet that follows the generic XML message packet. A sample packet is shown in Listing 11.1.

LISTING 11.1 Example of a Generic Message Packet

```
<?xml version="1.0"?>
<TaskMessagePacket>
    <Header>
        <TimeStamp>01/01/2001:01:01:12</TimeStamp>
        <MessageFrom>192.168.168.1</MessageFrom>
        <SecurityKey>Askjas7878ask</SecurityKey>
        <UserID>NitaAjay</UserID>
```

LISTING 11.1 Continued

```
        <MessageType>WEBREQUEST</MessageType>
        <MessageRequestTitle>VALIDATE USER</MessageRequestTitle>
    </Header>
    <Details>
        <Parameters>
            <Param number="1">
                <Name>UserID</Name>
                <Value>NITA</Value>
            </Param>
            <Param number="2">
                <Name>Password</Name>
                <Value>SAKHI</Value>
            </Param>
            <Param number="3">
                <Name>ClientIP</Name>
                <Value>201.121.344.12</Value>
            </Param>
        </Parameters>
    </Details>
</TaskMessagePacket>
```

The request shown in Listing 11.1 appears to be simple. The query engine uses the `<UserID>` and `<SecurityKey>` to authenticate the message and passes it to the adapter binder. The adapter binder uses the `<MessageType>` and `<MessageRequestTitle>` to arrive at a specific adapter suitable for the request. The adapter binder refers to a binding file, which is a simple XML file mapping the request with the adapter object name. The adapter binder then invokes the object (by name or late binding) and passes the request to it for processing.

If late binding or instantiating class by name is slow, the model needs to provide a form of `BindingHelper` mechanism. This mechanism creates the DOM representation of the XML binding file in memory, hence improving performance, and could also act as a connection reservoir by pre-instantiating the various objects beforehand. This allows the helper to hand over the pre-existing instance to the adapter binder and hence could be very fast. The concept of such in-memory requirements collectively forms *services* or rather startup services. These startup services initiate as part of starting the system and hence provide the mechanism to build system required memory DOM trees and setting default parameters.

The importance of the `<MessageType>` tag would be evident if you imagine that it would be used as the primary level of authentication and to determine what suitable way the request needs to be processed. Because the specified value states WEBREQUEST, it could mean that the authentication is not trivial and that the request assumes a synchronous execution.

The message request title typical to our system would be INVOICE REQUEST. This would mean that the incoming message packet has a set of invoice definition tags in the details section. The respective adapter would consume the message and produce the required FTP load. Once the adapter is ready with the results, it could either package it in standard message format with a suitable request title, like FTP INVOICE LOAD, and forward it to a query engine for processing, or it could directly invoke the method on FTPInterface to process it.

For some message request titles, like INVOICE LOAD, the query engine could have an internal mechanism or logic flow to deliver it to the FTP interface directly because it would not require the adapter to process it. This would also be viewed, alternatively because a separate map file for message processing requirements. The file would map the message request title with suitable processing requirements. For example, it would specify that the message request title INVOICE LOAD would not require the use of adapters and hence would not have to go through binder interfaces.

Let's examine the interface design patterns proposed in this case. In QueryEngineInterface you see that there is a method called SetErrorQueueReference(). And if you observe the MainSystemInterface there is a method called GetErrorQueueReference(), which actually creates a single instance of ErrorQueueInterface and passes its pointer or reference to the various objects that need to use it.

This method of instantiating an object once and passing references to users would prove useful for the framework to use limited resources. In the model we could have included even the Security and Tracking interface GetXXX and SetXXX methods in MainSystemInterface and provided their reference to the entire system. All objects in the system having Services type of behavior could be made to follow this pattern. This also allows us to include a controlled instantiation behavior. This means that in the MainSystemInterface we could decide beforehand, depending on the configuration settings or monitoring of the usage, how many instances need to be created and used.

Further, all interfaces having Initialize type methods are assumed to use a configuration settings file, which would be an XML settings file referred to at the startup for defining initial values.

Also note that all the bulk information flow in the system is in the form of an XML document. For example, the TrackingInterface has a method called AppendTrackRecord(), which would be called by the query engine for all message type tracking. This method accepts the value as an XML document. This idea of assuming parameters in XML stream format is another powerful feature: It allows us to pass the information as a plain character stream or an XML object format that can have multiple parameter settings in it. Perhaps you have a method that requires parameters, and after final system design, you find that the integration with the client system needs more than the assigned or defined parameters. Under these circumstances, it would make sense to let the client system pass multiple parameters as XML strings. On the later end where the actual component needs to use them, you could parse the required parameters for use.

All the methods follow the same message packet format as shown in Listing 11.1, except that the detailed section layout would depend on the message type and request title value.

Let's consider the subsidiary-located component. The ActiveX document to be designed must interact with the Windows-based system using DDE. ActiveX is a technology found in the Visual Basic IDE. We find many things in it interesting for our case. Because we need to interact with the client Windows-based system, using DDE, the ActiveX document is ideal. Besides this, the technology allows you to use VB code as-is in developing the logic and use the ActiveX controls in VB.

The Inet (MSINET.ocx, Microsoft Internet Transfer Control) control provided with Visual Basic 5.0 and 6.0 is a simple-to-use component that allows us to simulate the `POST` event. The following shows a code fragment that uses this control to access a servlet by the `POST` method.

```
' set the protocol for the transfer
InetLogin.Protocol = icHTTP
' prepare the data stream
dta = "password=" & Trim(LoginPassword) & "&" & "username=" & Trim(LoginUName)
' set pointer to the middleware system, here it points to a servlet
mydoc = "myservlet"
uri = http://192.168.168/
' set the POST header
hdr = "User-Agent:Mozilla/4.0" & vbCrLf & "Accept-Language:en-us" & vbCrLf & "Con-
tent-Type:application/x-www-form-urlencoded"
'Logging in, hit the servlet on middleware end
 InetLogin.Execute uri & mydoc, "POST", dta, hdr
```

The preceding example shows the control renamed to `InetLogin`, which has a method named `Execute`. The real values are name/value pairs of data sent to the web server. The return request can be read in the `InetLogin_StateChanged()` event. This event is triggered whenever the controls state changes. To check for the returned action after the preceding request, you would have the following code in the `StateChanged` event:

```
If State = icResponseCompleted Then
    'Get first chunk
    vtData = InetLogin.GetChunk(1024)
    ' read all the data, end of data chunk is arrived when length
    ' of data returned is 0.
    Do While Not bdone
        ' form data packet
            strData1 = strData1 & vtData
            DoEvents
            ' Get next chunk.
            vtData = InetLogin.GetChunk(1024, icString)
            If Len(vtData) = 0 Then
               bdone = True
            End If
    Loop
End If
```

The preceding routine can fetch all the data in chunks until the returned chunk is zero. The DDE can be easily implemented using the following sample code:

```
TextBoxLink.LinkItem = "file=purchasejournal,field=description"
TextBoxLink.Text = ReportDescription
TextBoxLink.LinkPoke

TextBoxLink.LinkItem = "file=purchasejournal,field=ACCOUNT"
TextBoxLink.Text = ULiab
TextBoxLink.LinkPoke

TextBoxLink.LinkItem = "file=purchasejournal,field=firstdistribution,save"
TextBoxLink.Text = last_distribution
TextBoxLink.LinkPoke
```

This example is typical for working with the Peachtree Accounting system.

Finally, the front end, used to input the invoice, would provide the functionality to broadcast the data to the Windows-based system, using DDE, and could send the data back to the main system, simultaneously, through our proposed interface using an RPC call.

Review of Interfaces

Let us review some interfaces from the proposed design, which will allow us to understand the methods provided in them.

The `QueryEngineInterface` is a core class that handles all the requests. The class interface looks like that shown in Listing 11.2.

LISTING 11.2 The `QueryEngineInterface`

```
package sams;

import sams.ErrorQueueInterface;
import sams.XMLDocumentInstance;

/* Query engine is the core for executing all the message
➥tasks. It processes the query messages and allocates
➥a token for each for inter-system QoS. */
public interface QueryEngineInterface
{
    /* Initializes the engine. Would basically set the
➥various internal defaults after reading the associated
➥configuration file. */
    public abstract boolean InitializeEngine();

/* Main method of the interface, which would execute the
➥generic message packet task and return the results
➥in XML format to the calling method. If some error
➥occurs in the process the resultant XML stream would
➥contain the reference error token for picking that
➥error from error queue. */
    public abstract XMLDocumentInstance ExecuteQuery
➥ (XMLDocumentInstance QueryPacket);

/* Allows users to inquire about query status. The query is
➥referred by the Token#. */
    public abstract int InquireAboutQueryStatus
➥ (double QueryToken, char MthodName);
    /* This sets the reference object for using the
➥Error Queue in the system. */
    public abstract boolean SetErrorQueueReference
➥ (ErrorQueueInterface ErrorQueueReference);

}
/* END CLASS DEFINITION QueryEngineInterface */
```

The QueryEngine class implements the QueryEngineInterface and it has three main methods.

- InitializeEngine()
- ExecuteQuery()
- SetErrorQueueReference()

The InitializeEngine() method would be called to preset the configuration settings, which would (usually) be picked from an XML configuration file. The settings would include possible security options or setting the security level (mode) and starting token number. This starting token number would be incremented and assigned to incoming messages.

The main method in the engine is ExecuteQuery(), which takes the query message packet, generic format, and processes it. The method returns the XML result set packet, which follows the XMLDocumentInstance interface. The XMLDocumentInstance interface is provided to simplify the interface coupling views and could be imagined as an XML object from parsers, with XML stream represented as DOM. One of the tags in the result XML set would be the <TokenNumber>. This number can be used for inquiring about the status of a query, InquireAboutQueryStatus(), for an asynchronous message handling mechanism.

It would be an option (and a good idea) to make the ExecuteQuery() method threadable rather than making the query engine component threadable. This would mean that for handling each new query, the engine would spawn a new thread to execute the query. Under these circumstances, the configuration file would contain more settings information, like the maximum number of threads to be allowed.

The SetErrorQueueReference() method, which appears in most of the objects, provides the instantiated reference pointer to the current error queue created for the entire system. This error queue would be created when the entire system is started or initialized, in the MainSystemInterface class's InitializeService() method.

Another example to consider in light of using QueryEngine and singular referencing is the RPCCommunicationInterface, shown in Listing 11.3.

LISTING 11.3 RPCCommunicationInterface

```
package sams;

import sams.XMLDocumentInstance;

/* RPC Communication interface allows XML-RPC to be used
➥to interact with the query engine. */
```

LISTING 11.3 Continued

```
public interface RPCCommunicationInterface
{
/* Initialize RPC services, reads the security and configuration
➥parameters and also acts as wrapper on current RPC
➥services over web services. */
    public abstract boolean InitializeRPCServices();

    /* Set central processor reference. */
    public abstract void SetCentralProcessorReferences();

    /* Process RPC Request passed as parameter, returns
➥the results in XML format. */
    public abstract XMLDocumentInstance ProcessRPCRequest
➥ (XMLDocumentInstance RPCRequest);

    /* Validate RPC Request XML stream. */
    public abstract boolean ValidateRPCRequest
➥ (XMLDocumentInstance RPCRequestXML);

}
/* END CLASS DEFINITION RPCCommunicationInterface */
```

In the `RPCCommunicationInterface` class, we have a method to set reference to a Central Processor, which is an alias for the Query Engine. Again, `MainSystemInterface` would provide this. This reference would be used by RPC to call the `ExecuteQuery()` method on the existing instance of the `QueryEngine`, once it receives the request from a remote port. Of course, the `ProcessRPCRequest()` method would process and reformat the incoming request in the system-required message packet format. `GenericXMLMessageInterface` would provide this facility to all systemwide interfaces.

This interface provides various methods to form the system-required message packet, which makes the developer's life easier: just use the class to generate the required message packet. The interface provides `GenerateMessagePacket()` for returning the system specific message packet.

Summary

The interfaces and the code samples provide a quick glance at the system contents. The code can be repacked in sub-level packages and divided further.

One such widely used package convention is that of STORM. The package division would be like this:

```
sams.core.api.queryengine
sams.core.api.adapter
sams.core.api.utility.helper
sams.core.api.utility.logger
sams.core.api.audit.tracker
sams.core.api.audit.security
```

The corresponding implementations code would go in these:

```
sams.core.impl.queryengine
sams.core.impl.adapter
sams.core.impl.utility.helper
sams.core.impl.utility.logger
sams.core.impl.audit.tracker
sams.core.impl.audit.security
```

The model classes are generic and can be refined in many ways. The rule-of-thumb in specifying the role of classes or interfaces in the model is to decide its behavior beforehand. Though this is typical for all object design, in distributed computing terms it would mean whether you want to set up the class (or combination of classes) as a service or just a usable utility.

We broadly identify the class as a service if it has a proper initialization method. This method is required for *service behavior* because it would involve reading preset parameters and setting behaviors. Often this configuration file would specify the preset values from a System Administration interface. In the model design, if we have to remove an adapter or include a new one, we could copy the new source to its respective folder on the remote end and use a Web-based utility tool to either add the new adapter or delete the old one. The adapter binding map file would be effectively modified by this set of Web interfaces and would reflect the changes. Alternatively, this could be done manually by modifying the XML settings file.

The effective use of XML in defining map files is perhaps the best use in a world of static definitions. Combinations of such files to configure the workflow can result in creating an extremely dynamic behavior. Consider, for example, the structure of a binding map file as in our present system, which is shown in Listing 11.3.

LISTING 11.3 Binding Map File Example

```
<?xml version="1.0"?>
<BindingMapFile>
    <MapEntry number="1">
        <MessageRequestTitle>VALIDATE USER</MessageRequestTitle>
```

LISTING 11.3 Continued

```
        <PreferenceRespondTo>
            <MessageType>WEBREQUEST</MessageType>
            <Mandatory>NO</Mandatory>
        </PreferenceRespondTo>
        <ObjectName>objValidateUser</ObjectName>
    </MapEntry>
</BindingMapFile>
```

The Binding map file is extensive. It specifies which object is invoked or used for the specified method request title. The use of message type in binding map file in the listing shows how various rules can be imposed on object types depending on what they are designed for. Here the `<PreferenceRespondTo>` tag uses message type to set the characteristics for the object usage. The `<Mandatory>` tag specifies whether the rule is to be enforced. The binding file mapping from Listing 11.3 would tell the binding logic that even if the request originated from a different system (other than the Web), it could still use the method. If the `<Mandatory>` level was set to "yes," the binding logic would know that this object need not be used, and it could browse the file further to get another object name.

Because we have assumed that all our adapter patterns would follow the adapter interface, we have not specified any default method to be invoked on it. But, the binding map file entry could specify not only the object name but also the method name to be invoked for this particular request title type.

Many additional extensions are possible for the previous model. Typical for fault tolerance, the system could provide a request-caching mechanism. This could be a queue object that handles the forwarding of requests throughout the systems. The advantage of this approach is that the intermediate queues or caches would dump the request they process into an XML file. So, in case the system fails or there is a sudden power failure, a suitable recovery mechanism can be easily built to read these dump files and re-create and re-route the requests.

12 Designing Extensive and Scalable Systems: Banking

IN THIS CHAPTER

Problem Statement

A complete banking system has to be implemented. Typically, the banking system would include a master database for accounts and transactions, interaction with ATMs and merchant gateways, and providing account accessibility to counter representatives (and online users). The system needs to support normal back office users who attend customers at counters as well as remote accessibility for merchants.

The system has to also provide interface services to the various ATM locations. In addition to these mechanisms would be the Web merchant services gateway option, which would allow authentication services for charging the debit and credit cards on a customer account.

The bank would also like to provide online banking services to its customers, who could use the online interface to access their accounts and alter their profiles. As a part of their account access, for example, they could view balances and transactions online.

The system would interact with the bank database for storing the transactional and other form of data.

Working On Architecture and Design

The problem statement sounds simple; rather, it is a very high-level requirement. This case study represents the design from a ground zero level: We do not have to worry about any existing system, but we will be concerned about how other systems will interact with us.

Devising banking and other financial systems in terms of architecture is always challenging because they involve wide coverage and complex business logic. As I have mentioned before, we will concentrate on achieving the framework for implementing such a flexible and open-ended banking system.

The requirements schematic for the problem statement can be represented as shown in Figure 12.1. The central block in this schematic is the banking system, and actors are users using the system on counters. Other partial actors are the requests coming from ATM, Merchant, and Web merchant gateways. The gateways for these services would be coupled to the bank system over remote connectivity, and we would safely communicate through SSL.

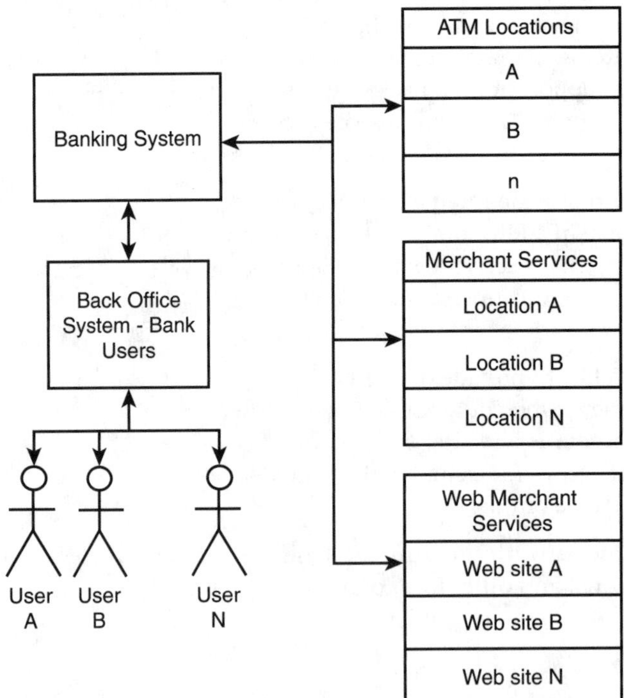

FIGURE 12.1 System requirements—Objective schematic.

We will use the scalable open-ended model developed in a previous section of the book. This would also allow you to visualize how generic models could be effectively used for specific applications. The architecture of the system and the core components remain intact, whereas only the business components (the adapters) change. Figure 12.2 shows the open-ended model, slightly re-arranged for our application.

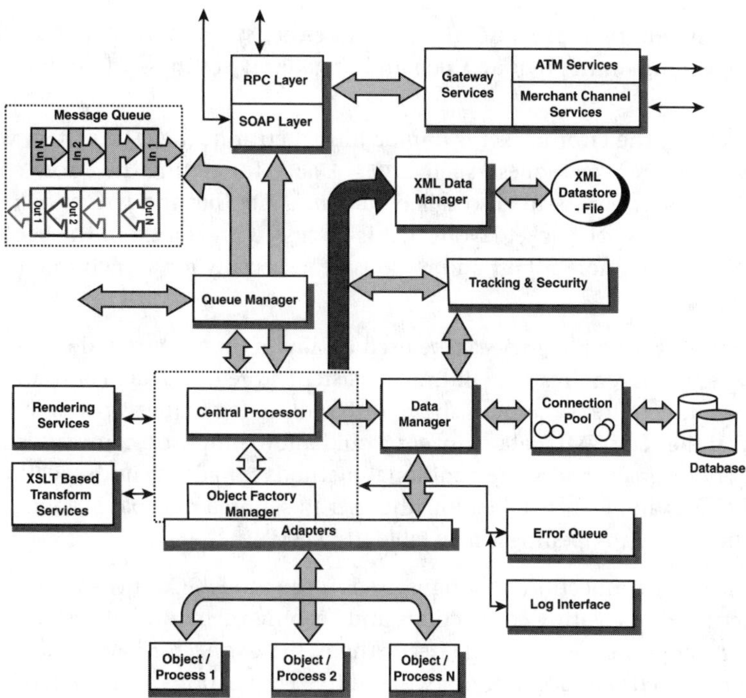

FIGURE 12.2 Banking System schematic.

Again, the system uses a generic message packet that represents all system tasks. The message type would specify the different type of tasks as discussed before.

Only extensions to our previous system are those of the remote communication end to form the gateway services, and I have introduced an XML based database construct.

The remote access end is a simple XML-RPC or SOAP layer communicating over the Internet. All the gateway calls are directed to this layer, which reformats the packet as required internally by the system. For example, a typical merchant gateway action request would involve the following:

- Validating the PIN and card details.
- The request is broadcast by the remote end and hits the gateway, which is an extension of the remote layer.
- The request is picked up and the data is re-assembled in to the system-required generic message task packet.
- The system then processes the request, either synchronous or asynchronous, depending on the request's demand or gateway settings, and returns the result.

For any errors, the error packet is dumped in an error queue. The system would offer a special message type request, such as `GET ERROR`, for getting the error generated for a specific request or task-id (also called a *token*). Note that the system follows the same generic message packet layout that is discussed previously in the book. This makes the system more robust and responsive, especially for asynchronous requests handling.

The XML Data store ideology can be used ideally in many system designs, especially for a system that requires a small time persistent store or queue. For example, the logger would require some swap space for handling log requests before it writes to the actual file. The XML data manager would allow simplistic commands in the form of XQuery language and some additional methods for adding and updating the dataset. For example, it would allow the user to set up a new parent node, which would be similar to opening a new table in RDBMS.

The concept of connection pooling is used in the model. Connection pooling refers to presetting and creating connections and keeping them alive at system startup. When any application or module needs them, the connector hands them over and maintains the current account of used and free connections. This method helps to limit the resources required for processing the given number of requests at any given point of time. The number of connections to be created at a minimum and to accumulate (or recreate when the minimum connections are used) and increase them to the maximum setting are usually specified in the configuration file. It would allow the fixed number of connections to be always available, allowing the data manager to interact with the database.

The Actual Design

The actual design is fairly straightforward, and much of it is explained in Chapter 5, "Open-Ended Systems."

A special inset on the Web based interaction as used in the system is shown in Figure 12.3. The figure shows how the middle-tier would manage the client end Web connectivity. This schematic would give a rough idea for the systems designer to include components specific to rendering needs, the Render Interfaces. These interfaces provide a facility to generate a stream in HTML, text, or any other format so that they could be rendered on the container. For example, to render the XML documents on the browser, we could have a method such as `RenderAsHTML()` in `RenderingInterface`, which would take an XML stream as input and create a suitable HTML representation. The representation created would be more related to the message type tag value because different message types would mean different rendering requirements. Also, the rendering engine could take default template references and could generate an HTML stream that can be completely displayed by combining the rendered output and the template.

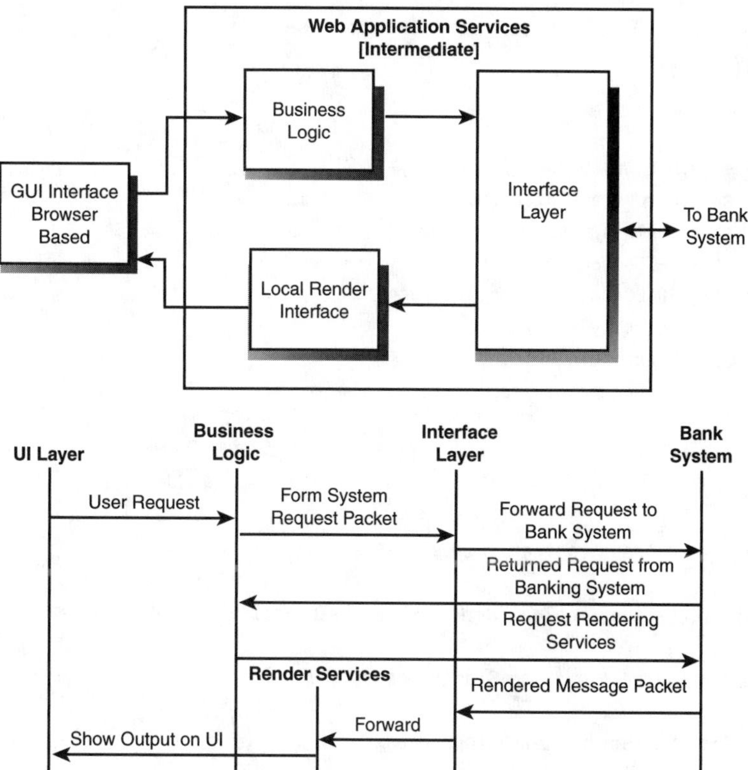

FIGURE 12.3 Interfacing with a Banking System schematic.

Figure 12.3 also shows the sequence diagram to show how the events occur in the middle-tier when it is in process or responding to a client request. Note that we are keeping the request type, again, as a generic message packet.

Implementing the Design

Implementing the design is now pretty straightforward. As you must have observed, that many interface types can be adopted from the previous case study.

The detailed interface definitions for the entire system can be downloaded from the book's page on the `www.samspublishing.com` site.

I will review some interfaces included in the design to clarify the system workings. Consider the system CORE component, the `CentralProcessorInterface`, shown in Listing 12.1.

LISTING 12.1 The `CentralProcessorInterface`

```
package sams;


import sams.DatabaseManagerInterface;
import sams.ErrorQueueInterface;
import sams.LogInterface;
import sams.RPCCommunicationInterface;
import sams.SOAPCommunicationInterface;
import sams.SecurityInterface;
import sams.TrackingInterface;
import sams.XMLDocumentInstance;

public interface CentralProcessorInterface
{

    public abstract boolean InitializeProcessor();

    public abstract boolean SetMaxProcessesInParallel(int MaxProcesses);

    public abstract boolean StartProcessor();

    public abstract boolean StopProcessor();

    public abstract boolean SetIntermediateDelay(double DelayTime);

    public abstract XMLDocumentInstance ProcessRequestDirect
    ➥(XMLDocumentInstance Request);

    public abstract XMLDocumentInstance InquireOnRequestStatus
    ➥(double TokenNumber);
```

LISTING 12.1 Continued

```
    public abstract XMLDocumentInstance ProcessRequest
    ➥(XMLDocumentInstance RequestPacket);

    public abstract boolean PersistProcesses(char FilePath, char FileName);

    public abstract boolean ResumeFromPersist();

    public abstract LogInterface GetLogInterfaceReference();

    public abstract RPCCommunicationInterface GetRPCComReference();

    public abstract SOAPCommunicationInterface GetSOAPComReference();

    public abstract DatabaseManagerInterface GetDataManagerReference();

    public abstract SecurityInterface GetSecurityReference();

    public abstract TrackingInterface GetTrackingReference();

    public abstract ErrorQueueInterface GetErrorQueueReference();

}
/* END CLASS DEFINITION CentralProcessorInterface */
```

Besides the usual methods, of particular interest to us in the preceding interface is the method called `SetMaxProcessesInParallel()`. This method allows the central processor to behave flexibly. For example, setting a value of `50` using this method would mean that the core central processor would spawn as much as 50 threads to process the incoming query requests. Hence, we are effectively asking the processes to handle 50 requests at any given point of time.

Depending on the current processes in the queue, and maybe from the system performance module feedback, the system monitoring module could set this value as being suitable for optimum performance. Again, if this method is not called, at start up this value could be provided as one of the configuration values in the configuration XML file for the system.

Note that the `SetErrorQueueReference()` method appears in most of the interfaces. Again, the principle use of getting the same reference (or rather setting the same reference for the error queue) throughout the system is so that only one object is created systemwide. These intricacies in development do not usually come up during the design phase. But, it is better to consider such low levels when putting an architecture together. This method would be used by all system interfaces to get the reference to the error queue—a single instance created in the `CentralProcessorInterface` at the system startup.

The methods `GetRPCComReference()` and `GetSOAPComReference()` have the same purpose as for the error queue reference. Note that even in `RPCCommunicationsInterface` and `SOAPCommunicationsInterface`, we have a `SetCentralProcessorReference()` method. This sounds strange doesn't it? Why do both have to set a reference to themselves, something similar to circular referencing, which can be dangerous?

Actually, the reason I have provided these methods in the Central processor and also in the other two communications interfaces is that the implementer could decide what to use. Note that if the implementer uses the `GetXXX` methods in the central processor, he cannot essentially use the `SetCentralProcessorReference()` method in those communication interfaces. Using the central processor end methods would allow and make sure that the communication classes are instantiated only once and used by the entire system. Whereas if you choose to use the `SetXXX` methods in the communication interfaces (RPC and SOAP), each time the communication layer is required, a new instance will be created.

As seen in the interface code, the central processor instantiates all the objects in the system and makes them accessible to the entire system by a set of `GetXXX` methods. This method of creating a single instance and providing the reference to multiple objects, when required, is often a resource friendly technique. Besides, for some system aspects such as tracking and security, such an approach would provide an easier way to manage and account for its accessibility—although it is not suggested to have all objects as singular; but some that are responsible for providing security and audit or those used scarcely might have this design approach.

From a functional view, the processor offers a couple of interesting methods. `ProcessRequestDirect()` allows the request to transfer directly to the resulting adapter through a binder. This would be typically for bank gateway interface, especially for interfacing an ATM box. The `ProcessRequest()` would dump the request in a queue and return the token number for the request to the caller. The caller then has to inquire on request status with the token number.

Other important methods are Persist methods, which allow a smooth shutdown and restart of the processor framework. On a persist trigger, the central processor could complete direct requests (or current requests under processing) and then dump (or save) the current indirect queue processes, the token number, in an XML Persist file. This would be necessary if the system has to be stopped, in terms of processing, for security reasons.

Summary

The evolution of a data feed methodology using XML stream has made the design presentation quite simple.

To stress more on systems modeling, I have presented this case study using the open-ended model proposed in a previous section of this book.

The central processor method could have a complex working. For example, there can be a rule specified in XML format. The rule file would dictate some system performance based information such as how many maximum processes could be executed in parallel and what subsystem to use in case the current number is exceeded. This brings us to the scalability views you studied in the open-ended systems section. Modeling complex systems is easier if we could have clear specifics for the behavior in the XML format. This simplifies the future changes and use.

Perhaps the preceding system would always use the `ProcessRequestDirect()` method internally until the total request reaches a certain point. Again, this can be specified in the preceding rule file, which would suggest that the `ProcessRequest()` method use the queue instead of a direct method because the load has increased. It is this flexibility in the architecture that would allow us to model futuristic systems today.

13

Cross Platform and Diverse System Integration: A CSR Application

IN THIS CHAPTER

- Problem Statement
- Working on Architecture and Design
- The Actual Design
- Implementing the Design

Problem Statement

The problem statement consists of a *CSR (Customer Service Representative)* application. The CSRs would use the system to attend to service calls from various organizations; hence they need access to diverse systems. This can be true for even a single organization that has different locations and multiple platforms used for development.

It is required that the application in focus should offer a dynamic addition of the service location and allow you to quickly configure the new location. Say, for example, that some company, Silicon Electronics, joins the service of this CSR crew. Then, the system would need to access the Silicon system that might be at different locations to answer the Silicon client calls.

Furthermore, the CSR system itself is hooked to a main server, which has authentication and CSR security and tracking databases. This main server would authenticate the CSR login in the system and also provide the various roles for each of the representatives. The *role* is common in most organization systems because it provides the ability for the managers, supervisors, and representatives to have access to various options. Typically, in a CSR based system the roles would be manager, supervisor, and CSR. The manager would have access to all user details and would be able to view call attending reports and critical billing information. The supervisor would be able to see each CSR's details, which would specify how each CSR has used the system and audit it using track records. In a role-based system, the user login would determine the role assumed by her in the system, which is set in the user profile setting by the administrator. This role-based access makes sure that—depending on the level, which can be a normal user, representative, supervisor, and manager—the options of the CSR front end change.

The objective schematic of such a system is shown in Figure 13.1. Note that the main server is the CORE legacy system and that each client location is the location where the CSR service clients reside, for whom the CSR performs the representation function.

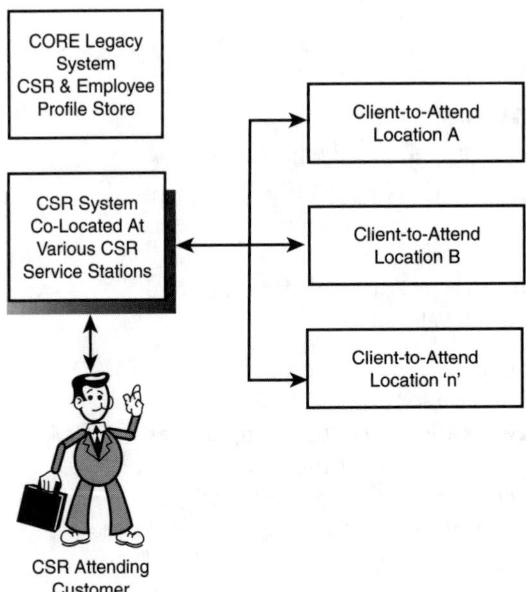

FIGURE 13.1 System requirements—Objective schematic.

Working on Architecture and Design

I want to present a novel approach for the current system. Let's go through some system requirements. The following list specifies some major requirements:

- Access remote legacy system for login authentication and tracking
- Ability to identify and search the client-end system dynamically
- Distributed CSR application offering UI services

The capability for the system to dynamically identify and hook up with a client-end system suggests using some sort of lookup mechanism. Jini architecture is a good example of such a mechanism. I would use the same principle here, but I won't use Jini for reasons I mention later in this section.

A lookup server is basically a program that listens to a certain port and waits for some client. When the client hooks up with it, it offers the capability to store the client past service details. The client service details would include where the client is located (IP address) and what services it offers (service templates or keywords). This service provided by the lookup server would allow clients to register the service with it.

The second service provided by the lookup server is to allow the clients to inquire. The clients might come to the server port and inquire, which specifies what type of service they are interested in. The lookup server performs the search and returns the matching service details, which the client could use to interact directly using an RPC mechanism. In our system, the client host system would be the system in which we need to hook up; hence the client company name or ID could be used as a matching key.

Finally, for all the services registered with it, the lookup server provides a leasing mechanism. By this mechanism, the server allocates some lease timeframe to each service that registers with it. This lease time parameter comes from the service itself, which would specify the timeframe for which it is interested for the lookup to store service details in its database. The timeframe could be specified in seconds or minutes. (Let's assume.) Furthermore, at the lookup end, there would be an independent thread scanning through the service storage (XML DOM tree), say, every five seconds, to see whether any lease is expired. In case any lease has expired or is due to expire in the next five seconds, it would trigger an event at the service location end. This would allow the service location code to know that the lease is about to expire and that they need to re-register it for using lookup services. If the resultant server is down, its lease has expired anyway. This mechanism is robust and makes the architecture fail-safe.

To offer the abilities described previously, we propose a lookup server in our architecture. Figure 13.2 shows the schematic of our proposed architecture.

The main server is assumed to be a typical mainframe that uses screen scrapping to read and dump the information into the mainframe. Screen scrapping is a relatively old mechanism used often to access old character terminals or screens. In character-based screens, typically 80 columns by 32 rows, the position of data entered and the result provided is fixed because the programs present the data depending on specific predefined formats. COBOL users would be familiar with the presentation concept used in it (Copybooks). Because the data entry and result formats, as they appear on the screen, are fixed, you could use a program to read and write the screen. This technique of reading and writing from the character screen is termed *screen scraping*.

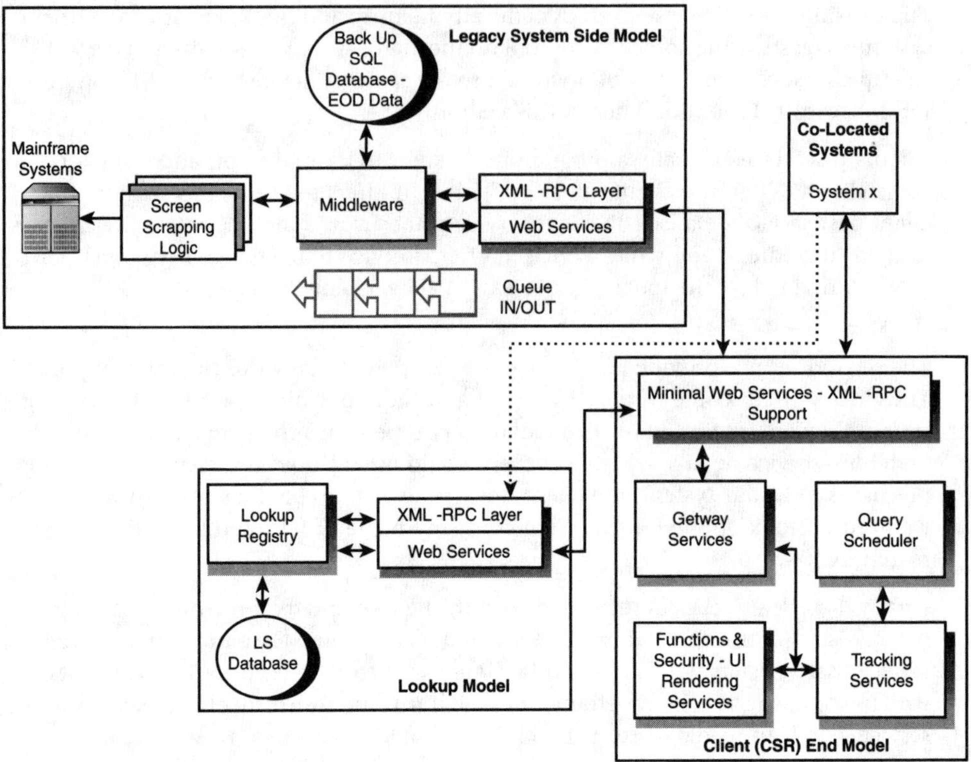

FIGURE 13.2 A proposed CSR system schematic.

The middleware in this system would be responsible for transferring the data from the screens to the main Web based RPC interface.

The CSR system is composed of minimal gateway services and a user interface to represent the available options. The CSR system would be co-located on the CSR end. It would use RPC to go to the main system and authenticate with the system and get the list of allowed functions.

The co-located system is the client end system that needs to be queried for attending customers. It has an RPC interaction layer, which acts as middleware for our XML query packet.

The lookup server could reside anywhere on the network. It would again use an RPC layer or Web interface to interact with various co-located and CSR systems. Note that this architecture would allow even multiple co-located CSR systems to be used. Because the lookup server is available on the Web, you could quickly set up the CSR station at a different location and still use the system as-is. The *lookup server (LS)* would use a simple registry, such as an XML DOM object, to store the current services registered. It might persist the data in an XML file and also generate usage logs, as required.

For any functions initiated on the CSR end, the CSR system would inquire with the lookup server and go to the final co-located system to get the results. The details of the lookup workflow are explained next.

The Actual Design

The actual design would involve implementing the CSR end system and the LS. It is assumed that the main server system and co-located client systems exists.

The lookup server could be easily implemented using IIS and a few lines of Visual Basic code, which uses XML DOM or Collection objects for storing the registry entries.

The client-end systems could use either a Web interface or RPC mechanism to register the services. Similarly, the LS end might use Web or RPC services to post the lease renewal event.

The flow diagram for the LS mechanism is shown in Figure 13.3. Each co-located client end system would have a `StartUp()` method that would actually initiate the registering. It would trigger the `RegisterAsService()` method internally, which would actually use the POST or RPC mechanism to hit the LS end. The LS end has a generic method `RegisterService()` for all the incoming requests. This method would accept the XML packet for registration, validate it, and trigger the internal (friend) `Register()` method. The flow shows that suitable `RegistrationCode` is passed back to the co-located system, which could be viewed as token for registration. The lease expiry is triggered by the `LeaseExpiredEvent()` method, which triggers `LeaseRenewalCycle()` at the co-located system end. Furthermore, this method would trigger the `RenewLease()` method, which would use the `RegistrationCode` to re-register the service. Note that passing the registration code can either do renewal or the service might simply re-register, depending on the implementation.

Note that if only specific IPs are allowed to be registered with the lookup or the registration packet is designed to have some username and password flowing into the system, the authentication has to be done in the `RegisterService()` method.

Finally, at the LS end, the `ExpiredServiceGarbageCollector()` would keep checking the expired leases and firing lease renewal events to suitable systems.

The CSR system could be a simple VB application that would (at startup) query the main system with the XML message packet with the CSR login information. The main system middleware interface would return a resultant XML packet after authenticating the login information, which would contain the usable functions list. The CSR end system would use the list to display the navigation bar in the system.

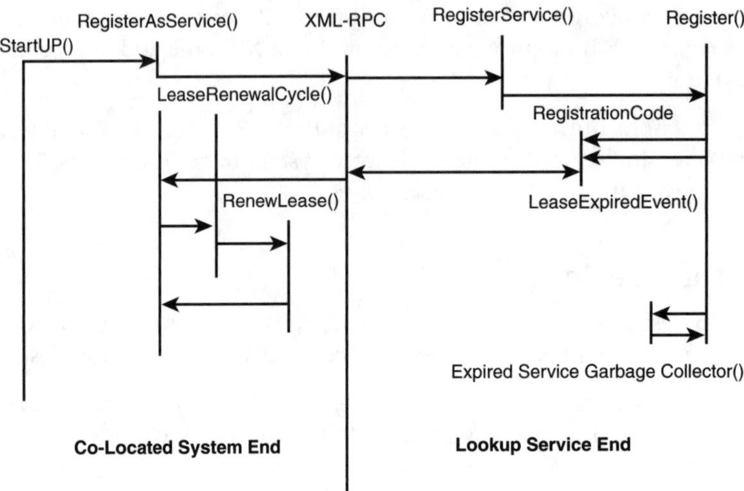

FIGURE 13.3 Service registration and lease renewal mechanisms.

There are many ways in which one could possibly design the front end for the CSR system. A neat approach would be to design a "standalone ActiveX EXE " program. The advantage of this type of project under VB is that the project can act because source or third-party programs could use public objects within this code. The CSR user interface could then have a left hand navigation bar, which would show the available functions listed as command buttons; the titles and number of these command buttons depend on the functions returned from the main server.

The CSR central workspace or form space would be a browser embedded in the application. A single click on any functional navigation bars would trigger a request that might be routed to the main system or lookup and co-located system by the internal gateway services. The response could be rendered on the browser or some custom control. While we are designing the application in VB, it would be easier to embed the Web browser control supplied with it as an ActiveX control.

Because the CSR end system would require RPC support (XML-RPC), it would have a small Web server (such as PWS, Microsoft Personal Web Server) embedded in it. Hence, all the CSR click actions on the navigation bars could cause creating a message packet and posting it on the local Web server, which would pass it to the internal gateway services. The gateway services would parse the XML message packet, generate a suitable RPC request, and interact with the other systems. Finally, it would return the results on a CSR front-end browser.

This sounds a bit complex, but it can be easily done using VB. Alternatively, the Web server and the logic on the CSR end could be located on one single machine at the CSR end, and all the CSRs would hit this internal Web sever for processing the request. The second approach has an advantage in terms of manageability, but it is evident that the combination of XML and the Web can create really scalable systems. Figure 13.4 shows the schematic and flow at the CSR end. The XML generic packet is a generic request, and the sample code showing the use is available online for download.

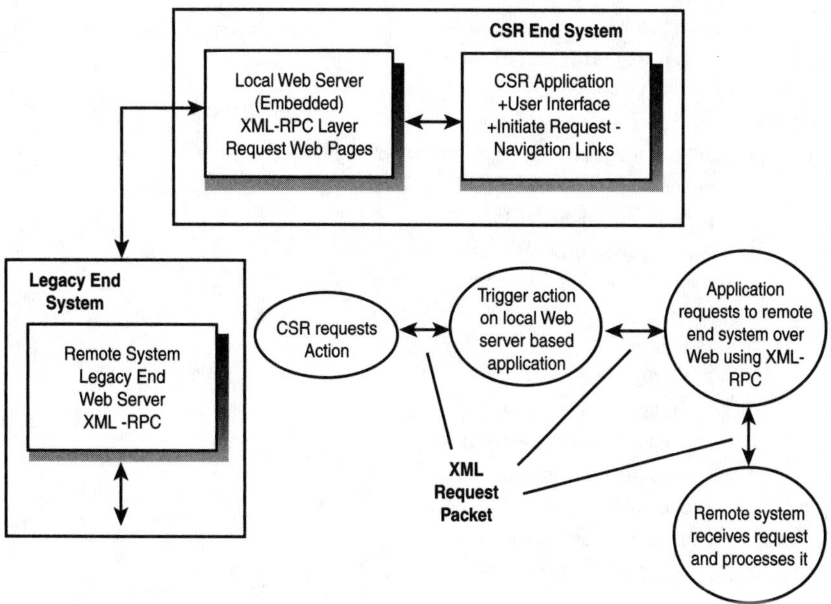

FIGURE 13.4 System Interaction schematic—CSR end.

Implementing the Design

I won't provide interface level definitions and code for this case because it is straightforward. However, let's review how you can achieve this by viewing some aspects of the approach, especially the LS mechanism.

Listing 13.1 shows the XML packet that can be used by the co-located system to register with LS.

LISTING 13.1 XML Packet for Registering with LS

```
<?xml version="1"?>
<GenericMessageBOD>
    <BODHeader>
        <SentBy>192.168.168.12</SentBy>
        <SentDateTime>01012002:12:32:10</SendDateTime>
        <Authentication>
            <PublicKey>Silicon</PublicKey>
            <PrivateKey>ASSD23343DF34</PrivateKey>
        </Authentication>
        <BODType>LSRegister</BODType>
    </BODHeader>
    <BODDetails>
        <MethodName>RegisterService</MethodName>
        <Parameters>
            <Parameter number="1">
                <Type>Simple</Type>
                <Name>RegisterIP</Name>
                <Value>192.168.168.12</Value>
            </Parameter>
            <Parameter number="2">
                <Type>Simple</Type>
                <Name>LeaseTime</Name>
                <Value>60</Value>
            </Parameter>
            <Parameter number="3">
                <Type>Simple</Type>
                <Name>MatchBy</Name>
                <Value>Silicon</Value>
            </Parameter>
            <Parameter number="4">
                <Type>Complex</Type>
                <Name>RegisteredServices</Name>
                <Value>
                    <ComplexType>
                        <ServiceParameter>
                            <CName>Service</CName>
                            <CValue>STOPPAY</CValue>
                        </ServiceParameter>
                        <ServiceParameter>
                            <CName>Service</CName>
                            <CValue>EDITPIN</CValue>
```

LISTING 13.1 Continued

```
                    </ServiceParameter>
                </ComplexType>
</Value>
            </Parameter>
        </Parameters>
    </BODDetails>
</GenericMessageBOD>
```

Note that Listing 13.1 still follows the generic message packet layout. The only difference is the `<BODDetails>` tag that holds the service registration values. This listing suggests that the `RegisterService()` method, which is called at the LS end, would have a layout such as the following:

```
Public XMLDOMobj RegisterService(String IP, Integer Lease, String TemplateName,
➥ String ServiceListAsXML)
```

The last parameter, specifying the list of services supported by the co-located system, is assumed to be a string for simplicity. The code within this method could parse the string and accordingly move the registered services offered names out.

Here are a couple of variations: Either the XML-RPC layer at the LS end would kick the `RegisterService()` method and pass these parameters, or the second approach would simply kick the `RegisterService()` method and pass the entire message packet. This could be useful if the method needs to be used for direct Web based interaction. The method definition would then resemble the following:

```
Public XMLDOMobj RegisterService(String IP, Integer Lease, String TemplateName,
➥ String ServiceListAsXML, Optional XMLDOMobj GenericMessageBOD)
```

I just added the last parameter, which could be the entire packet shown in the listing as optional. So, I need to pass some dummy values to all other parameters so that the method call is successful. The code would check whether the `GenericMessageBOD` object has anything (not equal to anything) and accordingly use it and ignore the other parameters passed.

Another important thing to note is the way that parameters are defined in the XML packet. The `<Type>` tag would specify how the parameters are to be parsed or interpreted. A complex type would mean that there is a sub-XML packet as a parameter.

Let's take a look at the XML packet for an inquiry with the LS, which would be used by the CSR end system to search for a co-located system.

Before showing the listing, note that the CSR end system would post the inquiry on LS with a possible client company name (referred to as `<MatchBy>` tag in Listing 13.1) and the service type interested. Assume that the customer calls the CSR and specifies that he is a member of the Silicon group and needs to change his PIN in that system. Then the CSR end system would inquire with the message packet shown in Listing 13.2.

LISTING 13.2 XML Packet for Inquiring with LS

```
<?xml version="1"?>
<GenericMessageBOD>
    <BODHeader>
        <SentBy>192.168.168.1</SentBy>
        <SentDateTime>01012002:02:32:10</SendDateTime>
        <Authentication>
            <PublicKey>SystemEW</PublicKey>
            <PrivateKey>ASSD23343DF34</PrivateKey>
        </Authentication>
        <BODType>LSInquire</BODType>
    </BODHeader>
    <BODDetails>
        <MethodName>InquireForService</MethodName>
        <Parameters>
            <Parameter number="1">
                <Type>Simple</Type>
                <Name>MatchBy</Name>
                <Value>Silicon</Value>
            </Parameter>
            <Parameter number="2">
                <Type>Complex</Type>
                <Name>ServiceKey</Name>
                <Value>
                    <ComplexType>
                        <ServiceParameter>
                            <CName>Service</CName>
                            <CValue>EDITPIN</CValue>
                        </ServiceParameter>
                    </ComplexType>
                </Value>
            </Parameter>
        </Parameters>
    </BODDetails>
</GenericMessageBOD>
```

As shown in Listing 13.2, I am using the same message packet definition with a different details section. The message type now specifies that this is an inquiry type of request, and the details section specifies the resultant method name and the match keyword. The LS, on receiving this request, would query the XML DOM tree (the registry) and match the `MatchBy` value. Once it finds the match, it would try to match the *services requested* criteria. If both the matches are successful and the service occurs in the registry, it would return the co-located system details to the CSR end system. If the match fails, a suitable message packet would be posted back to the system specifying that the error occurred. The CSR end system could use an error map XML file to render the suitable message back to the user.

The CSR system would finally go to the co-located system and request for the action. Listing 13.3 shows the XML message packet for the same.

LISTING 13.3 XML Packet for Requesting an Action on a Co-Located System, Originating from the CSR System

```
<?xml version="1"?>
<GenericMessageBOD>
    <BODHeader>
        <SentBy>192.168.168.1</SentBy>
        <SentDateTime>01012002:02:33:09</SendDateTime>
        <Authentication>
            <PublicKey>SystemEW</PublicKey>
            <PrivateKey>ASSD23343DF34</PrivateKey>
        </Authentication>
        <BODType>COLocatedReq</BODType>
    </BODHeader>
    <BODDetails>
        <MethodName>processRequest</MethodName>
        <Parameters>
            <Parameter number="1">
                <Type>Simple</Type>
                <Name>AccountID</Name>
                <Value>1212-3333-4444-6767</Value>
            </Parameter>
            <Parameter number="2">
                <Type>Simple</Type>
                <Name>MothersMaiden</Name>
                <Value>SHAH</Value>
            </Parameter>
            <Parameter number="3">
                <Type>Simple</Type>
```

LISTING 13.3 Continued

```
                <Name>OldPIN</Name>
                <Value>ERFS</Value>
            </Parameter>
            <Parameter number="4">
                <Type>Simple</Type>
                <Name>NewPIN</Name>
                <Value>NITA</Value>
            </Parameter>
            <Parameter number="5">
                <Type>Simple</Type>
                <Name>ProcessType</Name>
                <Value>ChangePin</Value>
            </Parameter>
        </Parameters>
    </BODDetails>
</GenericMessageBOD>
```

The additional parameter, number `5`, would allow the co-located system to accordingly invoke a suitable business adapter and pass the request. Note that it has a value of `ChangePin` in this example, and the co-located system would have a suitable binding map file representing this `ProcessType` mapped to a suitable object.

Listing 13.3 shows how a simplistic message packet design could make a system consistent and extendable.

Summary

Using XML packets common for the entire system, in terms of layout and design, could simplify the system tremendously.

The system discussed in this case study uses the same concept of a generic task message packet design. It also introduced the concept of LS, which is a central naming server. As distributed processing needs increase, the ability to have such a central server available for reference to various systems would be useful. CORBA and Java RMI/Jini architectures have used the design and concept of lookups for a long time.

To add a further level of robustness in the system, multiple LS could exist on networks, or the same LS can exist on another system as standby. The resulting co-located and CSR end systems can then have primary and secondary LS IPs defined in their configuration so that they could use the other if the first one fails.

Because all the interaction is over the Web, you could utilize the SSL mechanism to make them secure and viable for industrywide use. Furthermore, the LS relies on the XML-RPC/Web Services to work; hence it doesn't matter what the co-located or CSR systems are coded in.

LS can be made even more extensive and intelligent by including the concept of keywords in specifying services. This means that the `<ServiceParameter>` in Listing 13.1 could have an additional tag called `<Keywords>`, which would have multiple keys to enhance the matching capabilities. The resultant `<ServiceParameter>` stream would resemble the following:

```
<ServiceParameter>
    <CName>Service</CName>
    <CValue>STOPPAY</CValue>
    <Keywords>
        <Key number="1">Stop payment</Key>
        <Key number="2">Cancel payment</Key>
        <Key number="3">Hold payments</Key>
        <Key number="4">Stop check</Key>
</ServiceParameter>
```

It would be useful for every organization to have its own LS service providers, where the collaboration partners could find the resources for system bridging and interactions. This ideology would further bring into existence the collaborative systems concept in the B2B world.

14

Implementing an ERP System: Vendor Purchases

IN THIS CHAPTER

Problem Statement

The problem statement is to integrate our legacy system with a vendor system to create a purchase order in the vendor system. The vendor system could need diverse data feeds, ranging from XML to CSV (Comma Separated Values)/ASCII format.

The legacy system needs to interface with the vendor system component and be able to configure the interface to suit the vendor specific system. Typically, a vendor would have a custom system or ERP system such as Oracle Financials, SAP, Lawson, or JD Edwards.

Furthermore, the vendor system might or might not take part in the interaction. This depends on the system availability. Consider, for example, that three vendors are supplying the material to the company. These three vendors might have their own systems, S1, S2, and S3. At times it is possible that one of the systems, S1, S2, or S3, or even more than one, might be unavailable for some reason. Under these circumstances, the legacy system would need some accountability so that it knows the availability of the vendor system. Hence, the vendor system might or might not take part in the interaction.

It can be assumed that the legacy side has a Web interface, which is used by the purchase officer to view the quotes submitted by various vendors. The view would provide the comparison statements for all the quotes, which would depend on the rates, terms, conditions, and other factors.

Depending on the most feasible quote, the officer would place the order with the vendor system. The system should then file the order, a purchase order (PO), on the resultant vendor system by directly interacting with it.

Working on Architecture and Design

Before stepping into architecture and design, let's construct the objective schematic diagram. Such a schematic for the system is shown in Figure 14.1.

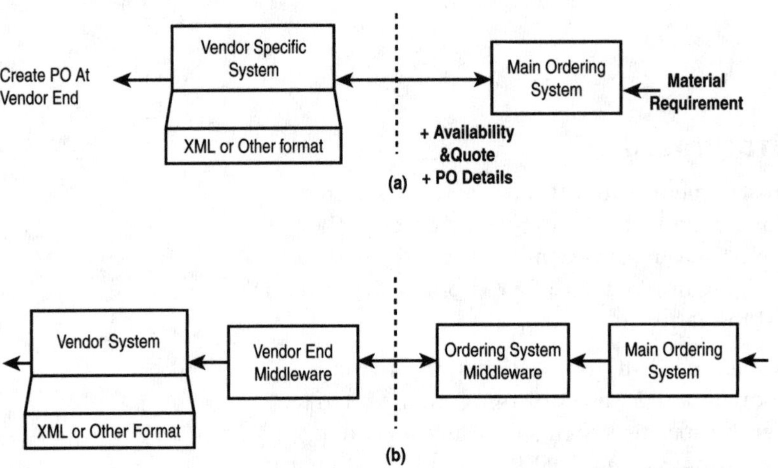

FIGURE 14.1 Schematics of (a) System Requirement objective and (b) Elaborated solution.

The material requirement request triggers from the legacy end by the system or purchase officer through business logic or Web interface (as described earlier).

The vendor specific system could require that the data be in any format. Hence, it would involve reforming, repackaging, or reformatting the data packet suitably. This is shown as (a) in Figure 14.1. Part (b) of the figure shows how you would view the solution. The schematic shows a very simplistic approach of adding the middleware to do the job.

We need to design a legacy end middleware and vendor end deployable package. Let's consider some conditions for the current system:

- The vendor end system might or might not be available, which means that when the legacy system needs to send the request for creating a PO in the vendor system, it might or might not be available.
- The system needs to provide a variety of options in terms of interactivity at the vendor end because the vendor end might have different systems (ERP systems), which also need to be configured easily.

- The vendor end deployed component has to be configured over the Web from a remote location (possibly from the legacy end).

Considering the business process, you could gauge that the purchase business logic or the officer sitting at legacy end, who does the purchasing of item, needs to verify that the vendor offers the required item and that the vendor system is available.

The Actual Design

Putting it all together, we would arrive at the following requirements list, which my model should fulfill:

- Ability to interact with the vendor end middleware over distributed a network (Internet)
- Ability to gauge the vendor system availability
- Ability to offer remote configuration mechanism for the vendor end middleware system
- Ability to configure the binding between the middleware and vendor end system to make sure that you use the vendor system specific defaults to initiate the PO

Offering XML-RPC interactivity could cover the first option. The second option could be achieved by implementing the lookup server (LS) strategy (see Chapter 13, "Cross-Platform and Diverse System Integration: A CSR Application"). The third option requires a Web-based interface that would allow the legacy side administrator to configure the vendor end system after it deployed. The final point requires an adapter type of design pattern, which means that the mapping file would specify which adapter needs to be invoked for the specific vendor system.

It is important to realize some specific intricacies to the system. For example, the vendor end system, especially if it is one of the large ERP systems, needs to have a specific definition of PO format. To make this point clear, consider Table 14.1.

TABLE 14.1 PO Format Requirements for Some Popular ERP Systems

ERP System	PO Format and Interaction Notes
JD Edwards	Offers direct C/Java API for firing the PO
Lawson	Requires the PO to be in specific CSV format, which needs to be FTPed to a specific folder
Oracle	Requires a PO in OAG (Open Application Group) or any other standard format, such as Rosettanet, `http://www.rosettanet.org/` and iFX, `http://www.ifxforum.org`) format, which is an XML format

Table 14.1 gives you the practical overview of why you need to worry about the interaction with different vendor systems. Also, note that each of these ERP systems would require more specific information, related to the ERP settings. These settings involve some values that are needed for the remote system to interact with the host system. Typically, the minimum setting parameter values are the valid user ID and security code for any of these systems. But, there are many default or required parameters in real life because the ERP system would require some vendor end specific information such as location and department codes.

We are not looking at how to design a system to interact with specific ERP systems, but this theory suggests that we would require a more flexible methodology at the vendor end of the system that would allow setting these parameters.

Implementing the Design

Figure 14.2 shows the schematic of the proposed model. Note that, as mentioned before, it uses the lookup server (LS) mechanism to allow vendor systems to dynamically interact and register, specifying their availability.

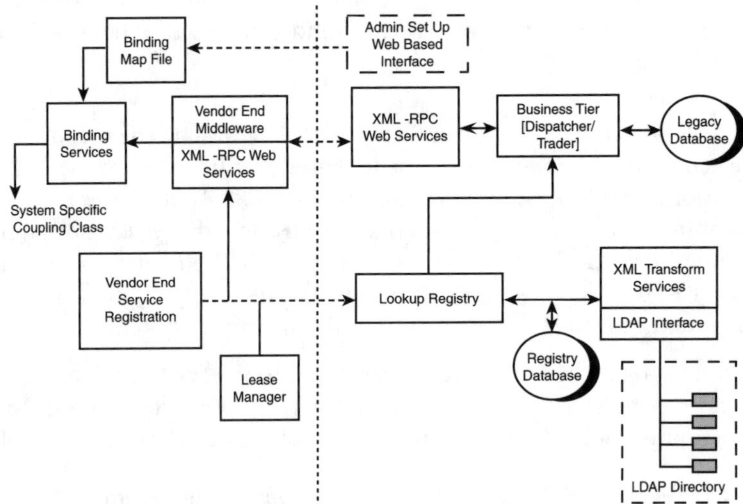

FIGURE 14.2 A schematic of a proposed system architecture.

The actual design of the LS portion would be similar to previous case study. Again, I propose using the generic message packet used in that case study to make it easier.

Figure 14.2 shows a variation for the LS registry. The schematic shows that the registry is tapping the LDAP server through XML transform services. The LDAP server is a more secured and organized way to store the entries. This is particularly useful for a large-scale system because once in the LDAP directory, the entry could be accessed by any application legacy wide, and hence becomes traceable. This is an alternative way to store the registry entries, or it could be added for robust support.

Of specific interest to us are the binding interfaces on the vendor end. This binding interface logic would dynamically invoke the adapter depending on the setting. Listing 14.1 shows a sample binding map file.

LISTING 14.1 Sample XML Stream for a Binding Map File

```
<?xml version="1"?>
<BindingMapSpecification>
    <BindingMap>
        <RequestType>PO_CREATION</RequestType>
        <AdapterMapName>JDEdwards</AdapterMapName>
        <AdapterObjectName>objJDEdwardsAdapter</AdapterObjectName>
        <RequestMethod>processRequest</RequestMethod>
    </BindingMap>
</BindingMapSpecification>
```

Listing 14.1 maps the request type to a specific adapter class on the vendor end. The example shows that the vendor system is set to JD Edwards's adapter.

Listing 14.2 shows the adapter specific default parameter file, which stores the name/value pair. This is more similar to a metadata as required for that ERP system.

LISTING 14.2 Sample XML Stream for Adapter Specific Metadata Name/Value Definitions

```
<?xml version="1"?>
<AdapterMetaData>
    <AdapterMapName>JDEdwards</AdapterMapName>
    <MetaDataValues>
        <MetaData number="1">
            <DataName>COMPID</DataName>
            <DataValue>NNNAA1212</DataValue>
        </MetaData>
        <MetaData number="2">
            <DataName>LOCATIONCODE</DataName>
            <DataValue>1010</DataValue>
        </MetaData>
```

LISTING 14.2 Continued

```
            <DataName>USERID</DataName>
            <DataValue>RAJU</DataValue>
        </MetaData>
        <MetaData number="4">
            <DataName>SECURTIYCODE</DataName>
            <DataValue>SIMRAN</DataValue>
        </MetaData>
    </MetaDataValues>
</AdapterMetaData>
```

The interpretation of this metadata file is also simple because each `<AdapterMetaData>` tag contains the adapter name and multiple name/value pairs of the metadata. This metadata could be set by the remote end admin through a servlet or JSPs running on the vendor end, which would accordingly modify the XML file.

The legacy side of the system needs to store the listing of vendor IP addresses so that the system admin could go to the admin URLs and configure the systems. This URL would be entered in the legacy end system when setting up the vendor and hence would be part of the deployment configuration.

Furthermore, we could include a concept of second-level authentication for the business logic on the legacy end so that it interacts with only genuine vendor end systems. The LS, assumed to be residing on the legacy end, can ask for the additional authentication key when the service is registering. The business logic would then use this key to be compared with the key stored locally, which is again set as part of the process of configuring the vendor (part of the deployment configuration).

The high-level flow diagram for the system is shown in Figure 14.3 for major processes. Note that each flow is traceable from top to bottom and is independent of the other. The four flows in the figure explain the various workflows associated with the system.

The first flow indicates the flow of setting up and starting the service on the vendor end. Once the vendor end application is deployed, the remote interface, which would be a Web based interface, would be used to set the name of the respective adapter in the binding map file. The interfaces would again be used to set the lookup server details by the system admin. The lease renewal time periods and renew lease scheduler are all set using these interfaces.

In the second flow, the administrator would start the services, which again can be through a remote Web interface. Once the services are started, the service would be registered with the lookup after referring to the lookup server IPs set in the previous step.

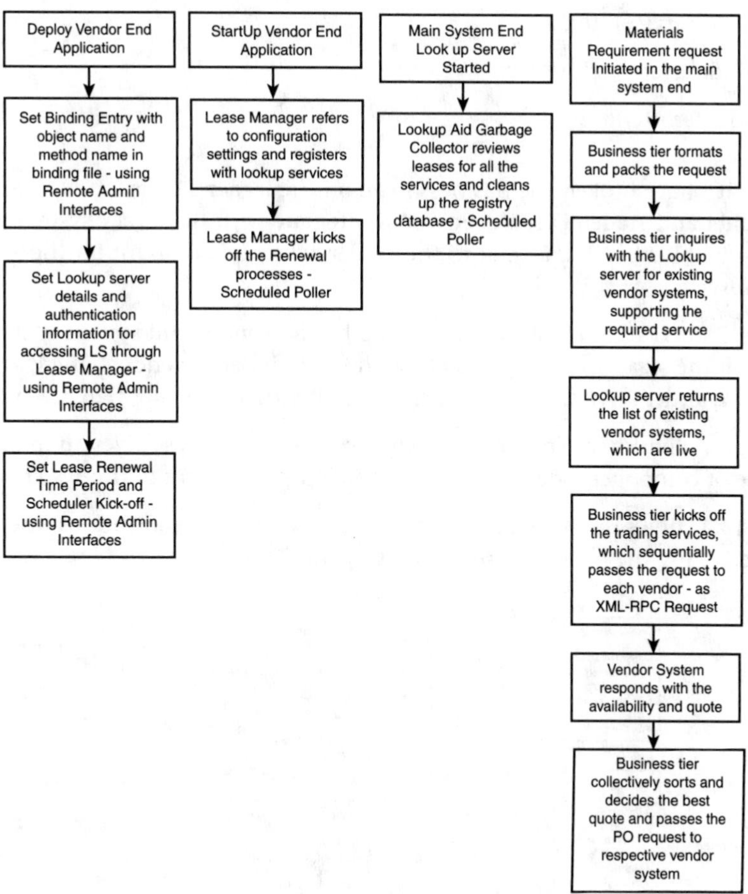

FIGURE 14.3 Flow diagrams showing the various system processes.

Note that in the third flow, which is for the legacy end system, the startup process is specified. This flow should precede all the flows in the figure because it starts the lookup server.

The final flow shows the various steps involved in sending the PO from the legacy end to the vendor end. It shows the end-to-end workflow for the actual process after the system is set.

The major interfaces, which are new for this design, are listed as follows:

- DispatcherInterface
- TraderInterface

- OrderServiceInterface
- BindingServicesInterface
- AdapterInterface

Note that I have broken the business logic on the legacy side into two interfaces: Dispatcher and Trader. Dispatcher would integrate with the legacy system and pass the required PO in XML format to the Trader, which would hunt for the vendor end Order services.

The Order services availability is registered by the vendor end system at startup, with the LS on the legacy side. So depending on the number of vendors, the LS would have that many order services registered with it, rather than the ones that are available.

This logical division of components with the specific names solves an important purpose of component identification and documentation for future system extension.

Figure 14.4 shows the schematic that has the system flow and various interfaces involved. Only the major interfaces are shown.

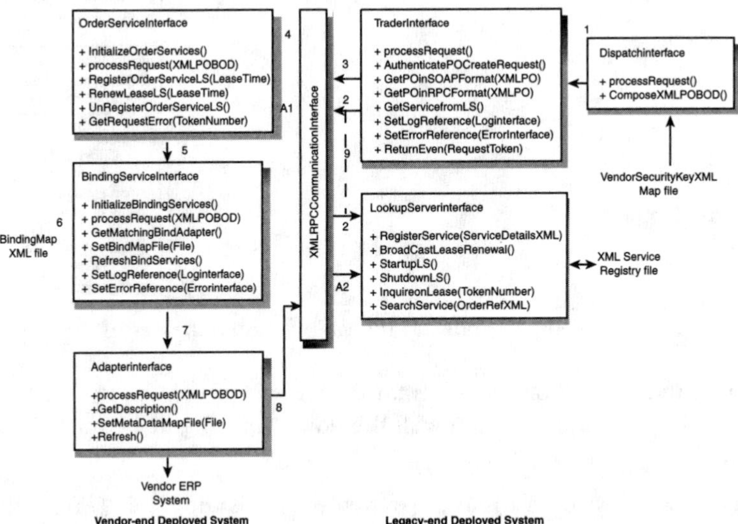

FIGURE 14.4 Schematic and flow with reference to interfaces in the system.

The flow is marked with numbers (1 through 9). The startup process is indicated by labels A1 and A2, which trigger the service registration process. The Dispatcher integrates the legacy end system and packages the PO in XML format. The XML-PO is passed to the Trader `processRequest()` method (step 1). The Trader looks up the order service in LS (step 2). Although we assume that the LS resides on the same server as Trader, it is suggested to perform the lookup as an RPC request; this would allow us to place the LS on the network in later stages.

After getting the service details, the Trader hits the Order service through the RPC mechanism (step 3) and passes the XML-PO (step 4). The Order service `processRequest()` method passes the PO to Binding Services by calling the `processRequest()` method (step 5). The Binding service performs the search in the local binding map file (step 6) and then invokes the suitable adapter (step 7). The `processRequest()` method of the adapter executes the ERP specific workflow, which includes repackaging the XML-PO format into ERP required format. Finally, the return success or error message is routed back to the Trader end (step 8 and 9).

Note that I have included a method called `SetMetaDataMapFile()` to set the metadata mapping. On the vendor side, the ERP specific adapter would pick up the PO in the XML format received from the legacy end and re-arrange it to suit the format. At this point in time, there can be specific metadata required to fill in the default values, and also the actual PO metadata would require distinct mapping at the vendor end. The metadata map file approach makes the system entirely flexible so that any element in the incoming PO from the legacy side could be dynamically mapped to the vendor system specific requirement. The `GetDescription()` returns the implementation specific message description for the adapter version that would be useful to generate the log message.

The LS interface offers some basic methods required for the services to register, which would invoke the `RegisterService()` method. The `BroadCastLeaseRenewal()` method communicates the lease expiry to a suitable Order service by invoking the respective `RenewLeaseLS()` method on the vendor end. The method is used mostly internally in the LS and is shown as available to external for elaborating how the LS would work internally. The trader would use `SearchService()` to look up a vendor end order service.

Summary

The use of central LS simplifies the accountability of the various services running and available on a network. The accountability would be in terms of logging the various clients inquiring with the lookup services and hence creating a tracking log. Not until recently has this methodology been adapted to production architectures.

Furthermore, maintaining a simplified method naming and input remains a major highlight in the design. For example, all the interfaces in the system use a common method `processRequest()` that acts as a main processing method. This is possible because of the use of the XML stream.

A typical variation to the way that input parameters are accepted in the system could be the use of XML in the form of a DOM object or as a string. The `processRequest()` methods could have overloading in terms of the type of parameters accepted. The two variations of these method definitions are shown here:

```
processRequest(XMLDOMObject objXML)

processRequest(String strXML)
```

As I mentioned before, Jini uses the same principle, except that it allows multicast discovery hunting. This means that the Order services could use a multicast request to look for an LS existing anywhere on the network. Although this approach would not require the IPs for the LS to be preset on the vendor end, it is not feasible because if you launch the LS on the public Internet, it is not practical: The request would usually timeout or would never reach the LS.

Hence, as compared to readily available functionality, my model accomplishes some most desirable aspects. For a distributed system to work securely and safely, it is necessary that we are able to utilize the available mechanism. This includes SSL over Web and XML-RPC mechanisms.

Even without XML-RPC, we could easily use the Web POST mechanism to accomplish the communication for registering and using the Order services. The only difference would be the code triggering of the Web pages, such as servlet or ASP page, which then triggers the page on the other end and POSTs the XML stream. Then the page on the other end instantiates the interfaces or business logic components to the process and returns the requests.

A

Popular XML Editors

IN THIS CHAPTER

- XML Spy
- XMetal
- EditML Pro from NetBryx Technologies

Many XML editors have been introduced to the market, and some developers have at least one editor installed. Even if many editors are available, few are suitable regarding ease of use and functionality.

The basic requirements of an XML editor are the capability of composing an XML document, DTD, or schema, association, and validation. The following sections present editors that fulfill these requirements and have sophisticated features.

XML Spy

XML Spy, from Altova, Inc., offers many features supporting typical XML application design and adds a form editor and XSLT designer. XML Spy is a complete suite of products within an integrated development environment, or IDE. Refer to `http://www.xmlspy.com` for more information and a downloadable evaluation version.

We will go through the major scenarios to use the software. XML Spy provides several windows that show various aspects of your XML document (see Figure A.1):

- The left area consists of the Project and Info windows.
- The central area is the Main window where documents are edited and viewed.
- The right area contains three Entry helper windows to insert, or append, elements, attributes, and entities.

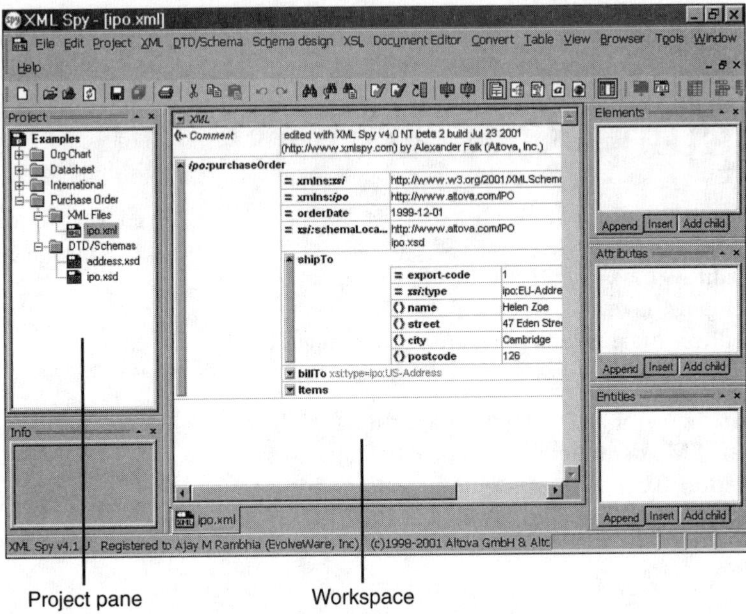

FIGURE A.1 Initial view of the XMLSpy editor.

Different views can be displayed: Schema view, Text view, Document Editor view, Browser view, Custom view, or Enhanced Grid view. The latter incorporates a special view, called the Database/Table view, which collapses recurring XML data into a table form.

When the software is loaded, the left panel displays an Explorer-like view and makes a few ready-to-use examples available. Clicking the Examples folder expands it into two subfolders. Double-click the Purchase Order folder to open its XML files and DTD/Schemas. In the XML files folder, a `ipo.xml` is a suitable example file to use.

Double-click the filename, and the workspace displays the file in XML Spy's Custom view. Note that the view shows up and down arrows as command buttons. Figure A.2 shows the arrows highlighted.

Alternatively, from the View menu select Text View to display the XML as text in the window. This view is suitable for most expert users. Figure A.3 shows a Text view of an XML document.

Another important feature of the editor is the Validation option. After creating an XML document, press F8 or use the XML menu's Validate option to validate the current document.

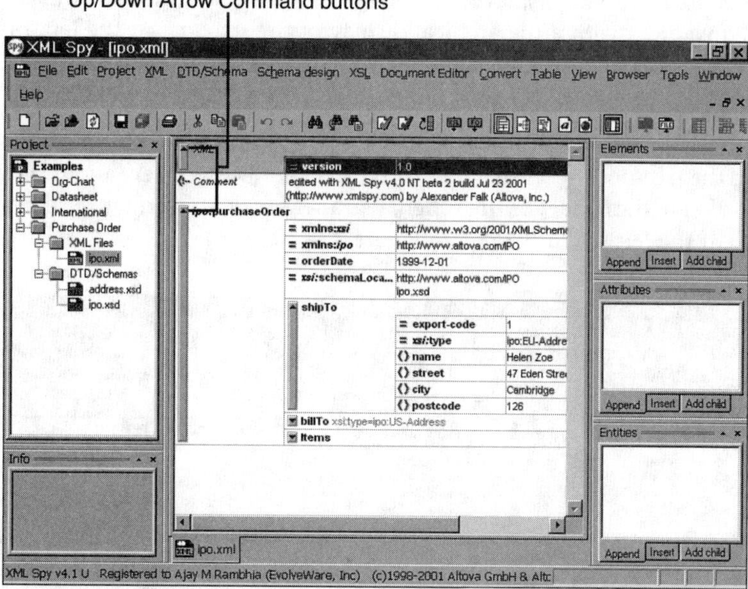

FIGURE A.2 The editor Custom view.

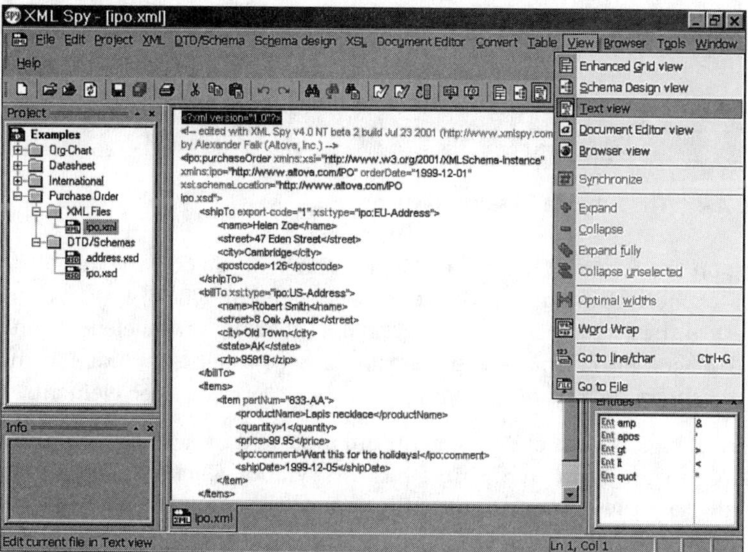

FIGURE A.3 Text view of an XML document.

XML documents can be displayed in the Browser view, and XML Spy makes schema design convenient with a hierarchical display of the schema. At the left, open the DTD/Schemas folder and double-click `ipo.xsd` to open it in the workspace. The schema, as displayed by XML Spy, might look a bit strange, but it is logical once the developer is familiar with it.

Clicking the tree-node icon switches to the Schema Design view and displays an editable, hierarchical view of the schema as a whole or an element. Each element has this icon at the left side as shown in Figure A.4.

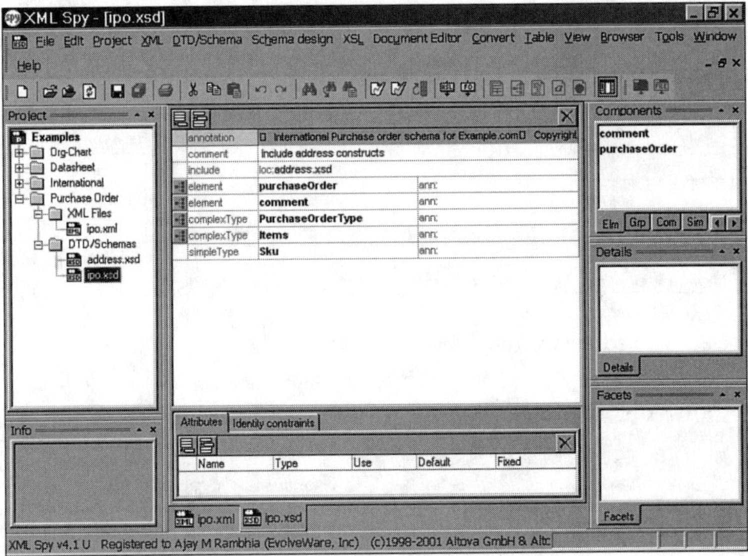

FIGURE A.4 The Schema Design view icon.

Clicking on the Schema Design View icon, which appears on the default toolbar, displays a Schema Design view of the selected element. Clicking the Schema View icon next to the `PurchaseOrder` element enables viewing of the element and its child nodes. The view also displays and identifies any comments included in the element. Figure A.5 shows the default schema view for the `PurchaseOrder` element.

Note that elements with child elements are indicated by a plus (+) symbol to the right. As shown in Figure A.5, `shipTo` has this symbol. Clicking the plus symbol to the left displays the elements under this parent.

In Figure A.5, note the expanded tree designated by an elliptical symbol. The node name appears under a broken-line rectangle: In this way, XML Spy indicates an optional element. This makes the Visual Schema view of great value.

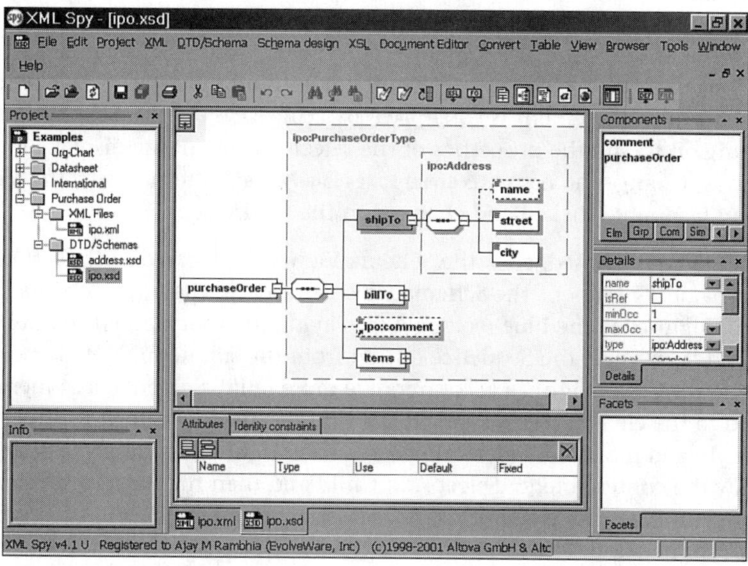

FIGURE A.5 Default schema view for the `PurchaseOrder` element.

XML Spy offers many options for attaching a schema or DTD to an XML document and validating it after attachment.

I'll create a simple schema for `GenericMessagePacket`. Assume that the packet has the following code:

```
<?xml version="1.0"?>
<GenericMessagePacket>
    <Header>
        <SentFrom></SentFrom>
        <SentTo></SentTo>
        <MessageDate></MessageDate>
        <MessageType></MessageType>
    </Header>
    <Details>
        <MethodName></MethodName>
        <Parameters>
            <Params>
                <ParamName></ParamName>
                <ParamValue></ParamValue>
            </Params>
        </Parameters>
    </Details>
```

To design the schema for the message packet, select File, New. This displays a dialog box showing the types of files to define. Select the .xsd—W3C Schema option and click OK. The workspace shows the document with a single starting element. The default name of the element is `ENTER_NAME_OF_ROOT_ELEMENT_HERE`. Select the element by clicking on it, and the properties of the selected element are displayed in the Details box. Change the name to **`GenericMessagePacket`**. Alternatively, the element name can be double-clicked and changed in the workspace.

After the name is defined, click the Schema View icon, located to the left of the element name. This opens the Schema view workspace where the schema can be designed. Right-click the blue rectangle displaying the root element name, select Add Child, and then select the Sequence option from the submenu. Note that to add a node (one with the + sign) to accommodate more child elements, a sequence must be added to the element. This displays the drum-shaped icon next to the root element. To add more child elements to the root, right-click the drum-shaped icon to display the context menu. Select Add Child and then the Element option from the submenu. Enter the element name as **`Header`** and press Return. Add one more sequence to the Header to accommodate the header's child elements. Again, from the second drum-shaped icon, right-click to display the Context menu to add a new child element as before. Rename the new element **`SentFrom`**. Move to the Details window and set the type to **`xsd:string`**. This assigns the data type to the element. Note that all element properties can be set from this window. Figure A.6 shows the workspace after adding the `SentFrom` element.

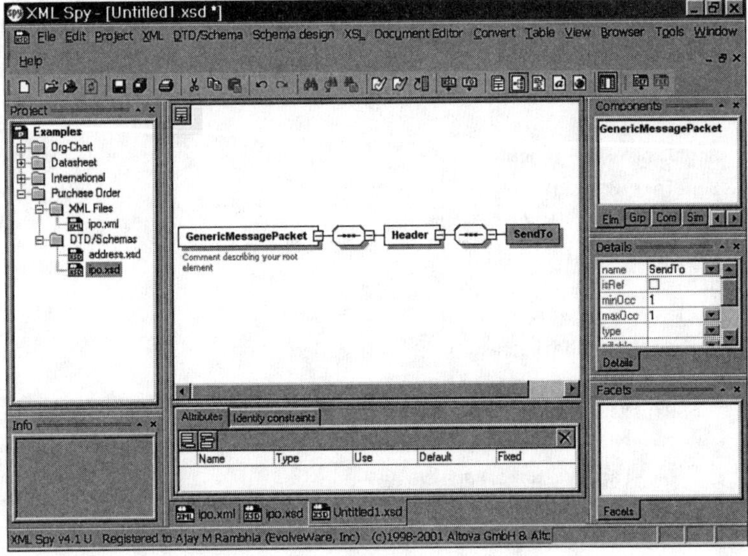

FIGURE A.6 Workspace after adding an element.

Similarly, add other elements to complete the schema. Special attention is required for the `Params` tags because these tags are optional. To make the tags optional, right-click the element name and select Optional from the menu. This changes the rectangle icon to a dotted surface indicating the optional characteristics. The `Params` could occur multiple times and, if so, set the `maxOcc` property to unbounded from Details. Go to the View As Text option and view the completed schema.

Although many editors are available in the marketplace today, I find that XML Spy offers the best features for dealing with XML documents, schemas, and DTDs. Moreover, the product is updated frequently.

XMetal

XMetal, from SoftQuad, is another good XML editor. SoftQuad has experience in creating HTML editors with its popular range of HotMetal products.

You can download an evaluation version of the product from the SoftQuad site at `http://www.softquad.com`.

The editor allows creating and editing XML files via an easy user interface. When opening a file, the Select window displays the various options. Options provided include Blank XML document, SGML document, and others. When selecting Blank XML document, the editor prompts the user to select a DTD file or schema for editing.

When opening an existing XML file, XMetal prompts the user to choose a DTD or schema for the file or open it without a DTD or schema association. With the latter option, there is no validation in the document while editing it.

XMetal allows viewing the document in many of the supported view modes. A single document might be viewed as plain text, normal, tags on, or preview. Expert XML users might use the plain text option to edit the XML file directly. The Normal view would show the file contents as-is with no tags. The Tags On view is a special view that shows the element tags embedded within the text and values within the document. This is convenient for users because it displays the free text layout with tags in a pictorial format as shown in Figure A.7.

In an open XML document, adding an element is as easy as right-clicking on the right pane, which has two tabs: Used and All. In the Plain Text view, the All tab shows the various elements defined, and the Used tab shows elements actually used. The menu displays an Add Element option that displays a dialog box for adding a new element. The dialog box also allows the user to specify whether the element contains data or is an empty element. Alternatively, you could also use the Insert menu to insert an element.

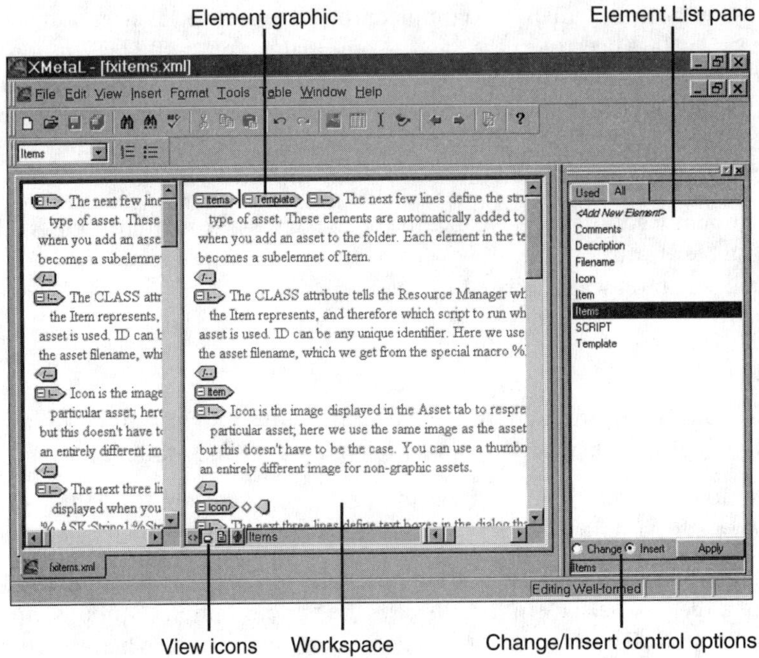

FIGURE A.7 XMetal Document views and panes.

The editor comes with a macro-building capability the same as most text editors have. It can also record and save a macro. This makes it handy to save a task and reuse it to create a new file or edit a file.

While in any view, elements can be changed to any other available element. Place the insertion point inside the element. Select the Change Element option from the Edit menu or, if the Element List window is visible, click the Change radio button at the bottom of the Element List window. Click the All tab and select the desired element. Click the Apply button.

Another important feature provided by the editor is Database import. The feature allows querying a data source, such as an RDBMS or spreadsheet, and writing the results as an XML document. This feature is useful for creating data manager map files and quickly creating XML markups for the schema set.

EditML Pro from NetBryx Technologies

EditML Pro, from NetBryx Technologies, is another easy-to-use tool for XML editing and for creating DTDs and Schemas from scratch. The important aspects of this tool are simplicity and ease of use. The current evaluation version of the product can be downloaded from the company Web site at `http://www.editml.com/`.

Once it is installed and running, EditML opens with two panes. The left pane shows the current drives and files (shared) on the system. The right pane has four tabs—TreeView, SourceView, PreView, and DTDView. The TreeView is the simplest for beginners to use. It shows the default Root element defined and has the attribute listing in tabular format on the right side.

To create an XML file, right-click on root and select the Insert Child Element option as shown in Figure A.8. This creates a child node that you can name in-place. You can rename any node, including root, at any point in the development process. To add an element at the same level, the relevant menu option is Insert Element. Note that you cannot insert a second root element.

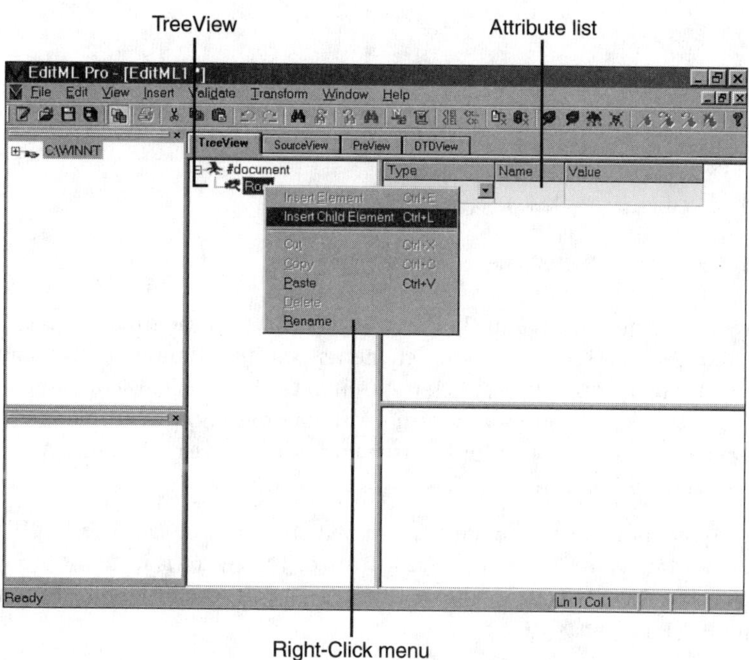

FIGURE A.8 Creating an XML document.

SourceView shows a simple XML text view for the composition in TreeView. The editor's two-way inception ensures that the manual addition of an attribute causes it to appear in the TreeView. This makes editing easier using the views you find suitable. Figure A.9 shows the TreeView for a typical XML document and the DTD View tab.

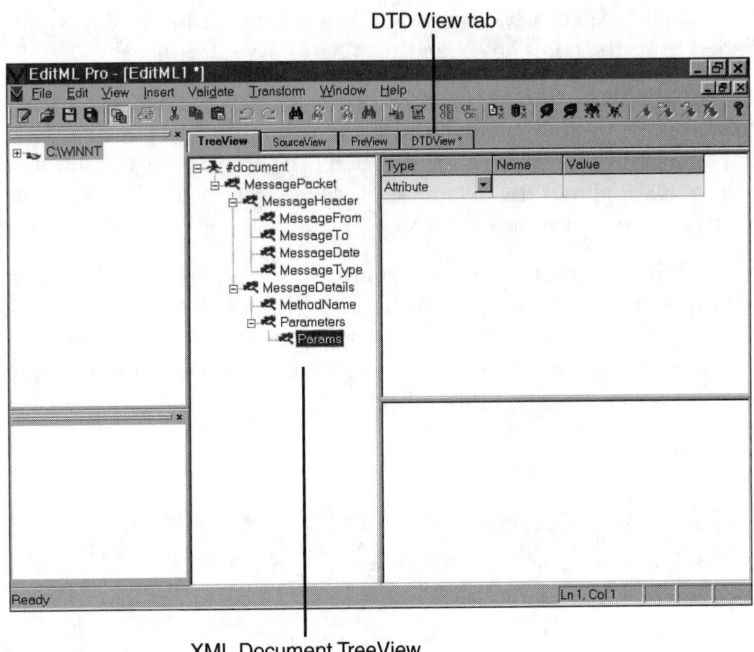

FIGURE A.9 The XML document TreeView.

PreView shows the XML file in the browser. DTDView is the final tab and is usually empty. To create a DTD for the XML elements you have defined in previous views, either TreeView or SourceView, click the Generate DTD toolbar icon. You can also find the Generate DTD option under the Validate menu on the top menu bar. This allows generation of the DTD for the current XML file created. Figure A.10 shows the Generate DTD option and the DTDView.

Similarly, you could also generate schema, which would replace the TreeView with the generated schema. Another useful feature of the editor is its ability to generate HTML files for the XML file in the workspace. The editor automatically generates the associated XSL for the XML.

The editor also offers the ability to import database tables as XML files and generate the schema files for the same.

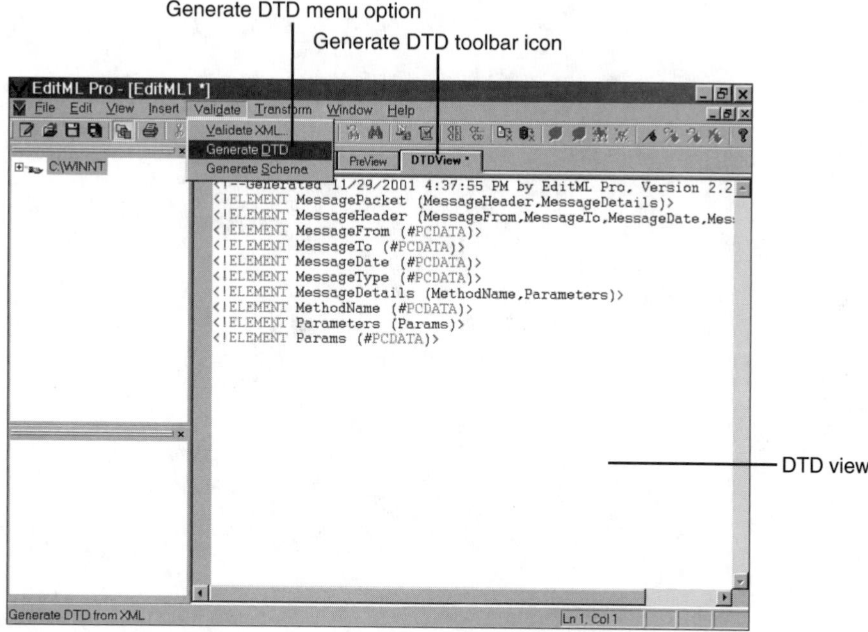

FIGURE A.10 Generate the DTD option and DTDView.

Summary

XML editors offer the developer a more productive design and coding environment than typical "programmer's editors" do. Extra features related to DTDs, Schemas, and data importing add up to a useful tool for both novices and professionals.

B

Popular XML-Enabled Servers

IN THIS CHAPTER

- GoXML Products from XML Global Technologies
- Native XML and XML-Enabled Databases
- dbXML
- Ipedo XML Database

XML-enabled products are abundant in the market today. Even for older programs, which never opened any options for third-party systems interaction, XML-enabling is a necessity. This is not to make programs more exposed, but rather to make them able to integrate with other programs.

As I explained in Chapter 13, "Cross-Platform and Diverse System Integration," it's good to have a native XML or XML-enabled database for an XML application. This makes it easier to interact with the database and use it in the application workflow with XML as the native protocol.

GoXML Products From XML Global Technologies

XML Global provides perhaps the best range of products for XML-oriented services. This includes the Transform and DB products. The company produces other products, but I will concentrate on these two because they fall within the scope of this book.

The GoXML DB product is a native XML database capable of storing and querying XML documents. GoXML allows the use of the W3C XPath/XQuery query language with Quilt extensions. It indexes on XML documents—not only on the values of the elements, but also on the attributes!

Other great features are the use of multiple AND and OR predicate processing, support for SQL-like expressions, and unique transaction support with Read, Write, and Update locks. It also has good transactional support with robust crash recovery.

To start the DB product, released or v2.0 beta, run the GoXML application that opens with the login dialog box. If using a fresh installation, leave the username and password fields empty and click Ok. The default administrator view is displayed and is similar to most enterprise database manager or administrator views. Figure B.1 shows the view.

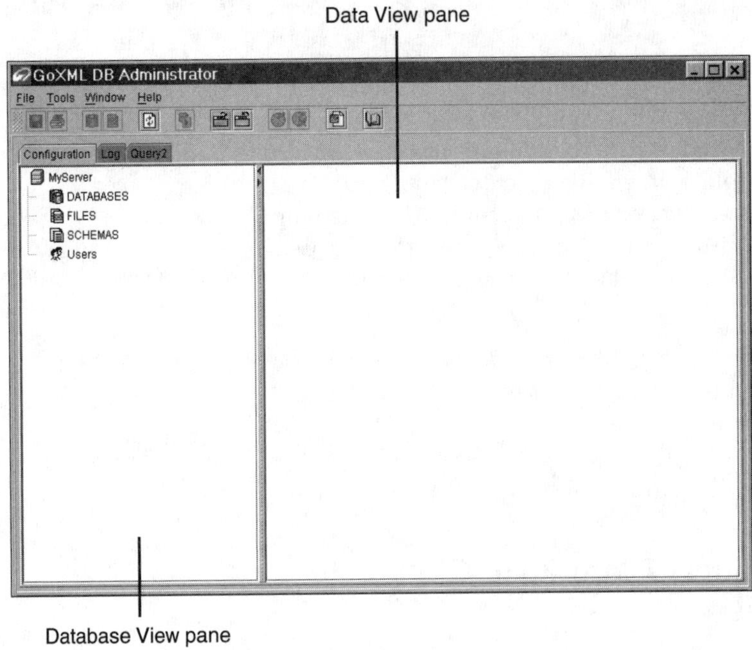

FIGURE B.1 GoXML DB Administrator view.

All queries in GoXML DB are written in XQuery. Enter a new query by clicking the New Query Pane button in the toolbar. This opens the Query1 tab. In the Enter Query pane, enter the following query:

```
for $var in root("Books", "Root1")

return $var
```

Note that GoXML DB comes with a sample database named Books and the preceding query uses this database. After entering the query, click the Execute Query button to execute the query. The resultset is displayed in the Resultset pane as shown in Figure B.2.

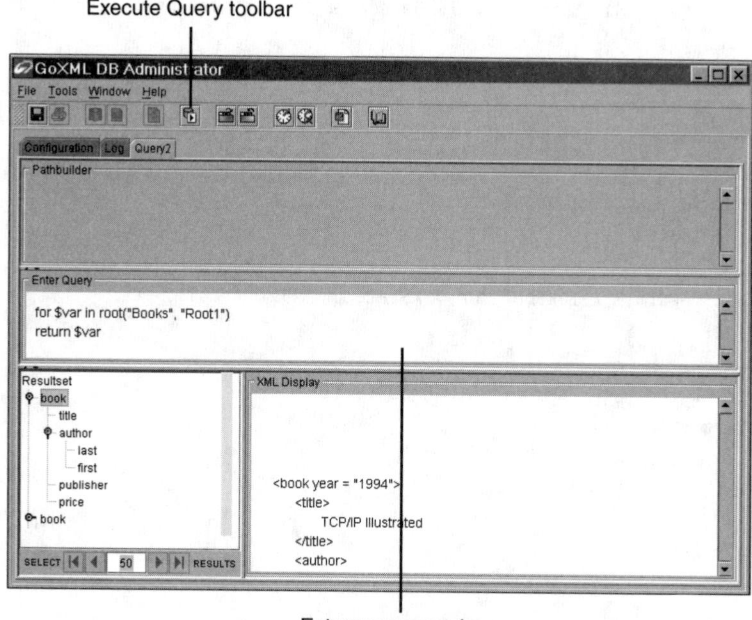

FIGURE B.2 Running the query from the Administrator window.

I'll begin with the Java APIs supplied with the DB product. These enable querying the database from within the code. This feature makes the product ideal for XML applications because it offers the capability of sequence. These query sequences are similar to the SQL RDBMS counterpart, except for the query language statements. Consider the following code fragment for querying the database to return all Persons.

```
// Please note that the following code fragment
// creates the connection and gets the result set
SystemManager.setInstallType(SystemManager.IT_MONOLITHIC);
String url = "http//www.MyServer.com";
println (url.toString());

Server srv = SystemManager.getServer(url);
XConnection xc = srv.getXConnection(sm.getAuthenticationInfo
➥("administrator","goxmldb"));
println (xc.toString());
```

```
String qry = "FOR $a IN root(\"File=PersonsDB.xd\",\"Persons\")/* RETURN $a";
println (qry);

xc.beginTransaction();
println("Transaction Started");

XStatement xs = xc.createStatement();
println(xs.toString());

XResultSet result = xs.execute(qry, XStatement.SF_DEFAULT);
println(result.toString());

FlexStringBuffer fsb = new FlexStringBuffer();
result.beforeFirst();

while (result.nextValue())
{
println("Result: " + fsb);
result.fsbGet(fsb, false);
}
xs.close();
xc.commitTransaction();
xc.close();
```

Note the following steps in the code:

- Get the server reference from the system manager.
- Create the connection `XConnection`.
- Begin transaction on the connection.
- Create the statement `XStatement`.
- Execute the query and return the resultset.
- Scroll through the resultset.
- Commit the transaction over the connection.
- Close the connection.

From the preceding list, it is evident that the object sequencing is similar to the JDBC approach.

Native XML and XML-Enabled Databases

There is a difference between databases that can be used here. Native XML databases differ from XML-Enabled databases in three main ways:

- Native XML databases can preserve physical structure, like CDATA sections, as well as comments, DTDs, and related attributes.
- Native XML databases can store XML documents without understanding their schemas (DTD).
- The only interface to the data in a native XML databases is XML based, like XPath, the DOM, or an XML-based API.

Today, almost all databases are XML enabled, but few are native XML. Both types serve a distinct purpose and are useful for specific types of applications. For example, an RDBMS is useful for storing a large financial database, and the XML database is useful for storing the most used dataset or tables from the financial data. The XML database could easily store the account balances dataset.

dbXML

dBXML is an open source initiative, and its information is found at `http://www.dbxml.org`. It follows the XML:DB XML Database API initiative for developing XML databases. API information is found at `http://www.xmldb.org`. dbXML is written in Java and provides access APIs for Java programmers.

XML:DB is a specification definition for APIs for XML databases. The API enables the construction of applications to store, retrieve, modify, and query data stored in an XML database. These capabilities enable the construction of applications for any XML database that claims conformance with the XML:DB API. The API is considered generally equivalent to technologies such as ODBC, JDBC, or Perl DBI.

The database provides the capability of storing and retrieving XML documents as a whole or in parts. It allows querying the documents using keys, similar to an RDBMS. The database offers the XPath query language for interaction. Consider the following XML document stored in the dbXML database:

```
<?xml version="1.0"?>
<product product_id="1234">
   <description>XML Database Server</description>
</product>
```

Query the database using the following XPath query:

```
/product[@product_id="1234"]
```

This would give the result shown in the following:

```
<product product_id="1234" xmlns:src="http://www.dbxml.org/NodeSource"
      src:col="/db/data/products" src:key="1234">
   <description>XML Database Server</description>
</product>
```

To describe a query from the dbXML command line tool, the query for the preceding example would look like the one shown here:

```
dbxml xpath_query -c /db/data/products -q /product[@product_id="120320"]
```

The string uses dbXML's command line program to query the database.

In programming terms, the collections form the basis for handling all documents in the database. Once the collection is retrieved, it can be queried using XPath to retrieve the results, as shown in the following code:

```
String driver = "org.dbxml.client.xmldb.DatabaseImpl";
Class c = Class.forName(driver);

Database database = (Database) c.newInstance();
DatabaseManager.registerDatabase(database);

col = DatabaseManager.getCollection("xmldb:dbxml:///db/root/ocs");

String xpath = "//test[text()='Hello']";
XPathQueryService service =
            (XPathQueryService) col.getService("XPathQueryService", "1.0");
ResourceSet resultSet = service.query(xpath);
ResourceIterator results = resultSet.getIterator();
while (results.hasMoreResources()) {
      Resource res = results.nextResource();
      System.out.println((String) res.getContent());
}
```

The code follows a workflow, in terms of sequence, similar to the normal database query mechanism in Java/JDBC.

Ipedo XML Database

Ipdeo XML is another native database storing XML files as-is. You can download the fully-functional evaluation version from `http://www.ipedo.com`. The latest production version is v2.0.

During installation, note the sample database name and its default port number. The port can be changed if there is a conflict with an existing use of the port on your system. The name and port are needed later for adding a database server.

After starting the application console, the database server can be added by opening the Server menu and selecting Add. This shows a dialog box for entering the server name, host, and port number. If the application is local, the proper entries are `IpedoXMLDB`, `localhost`, and `18080`. Ensure that the port number is identical to the one you previously assigned.

After it is added, connect to the server. Once connected, the view is the same as that shown in Figure B.3.

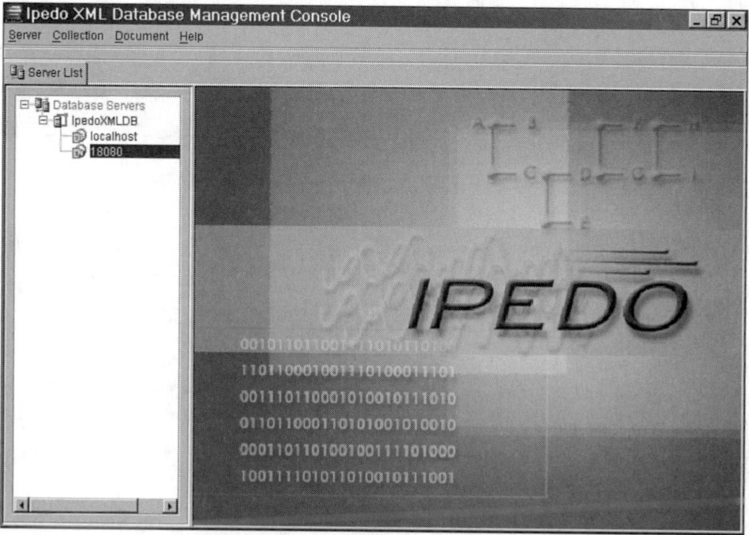

FIGURE B.3 Ipedo XML Database Management Console view.

Ipedo is organized, or structured, around collections. It uses the concept of documents (XML and DTD/Schemas) grouped together to form a collection. The documents might be indexed on any element. A single database can have multiple collections and indexes. Figure B.4 shows how the collection looks when a single XML DTD is added.

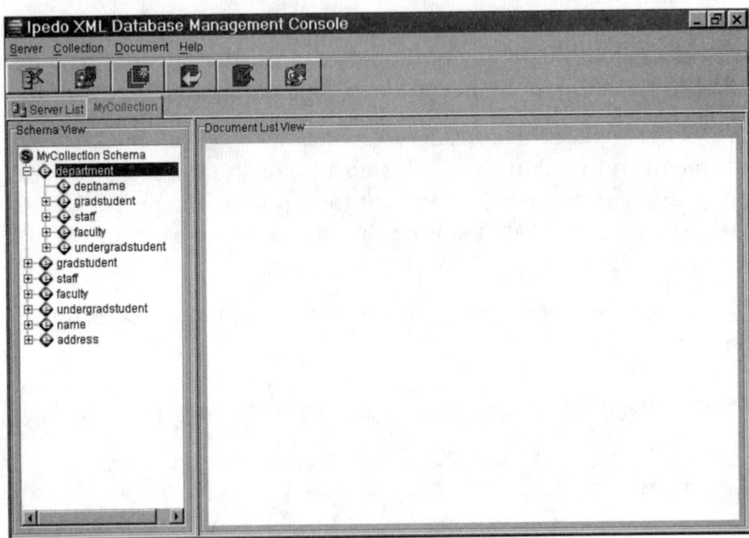

FIGURE B.4 Collection view in the Management Console.

In theory, the database uses the concept of session versus connection, as used in the JDBC world. The following fragment shows typical Java code that connects to a database and gets a specific collection:

```
' create a session and connect to the database server
Session someSession=IXClientSessionFactory.getSession("192.168.168.67", 18080);
' create the database object
Database db = someSession.getDatabase();
' get the collection
Collection someCollection = db.getCollection (CollectionName);
```

To get all the collections, use the `Collection` names enumeration as shown in the following:

```
Enumeration allCollectionNames = db.getAllCollectionNames();
```

Similarly, create a collection by specifying a DTD file pointer as shown in the following:

```
Collection somecol=db.createCollection(someTypedCollectionName, "d:/mypo.dtd");
```

Alternatively, specify the root element name while creating the collection as showm in this example:

```
Collection somecol=db.createCollection(someTypedCollectionName,
➥"root_element", "d:/mypo.dtd");
```

Each collection is composed of XML documents. A document can be added using the addDocument method. A document can be retrieved if its name is known, as shown here:

```
//Retrieves the document mypo.xml and returns it
//as a DOM document object
Document xmldoc = somecol.getDocument("mypo.xml");
```

A collection can be indexed on elements in documents. The following code creates an Index, called phoneIndex, on a collection. The index object is created from the com.ipedo.xdi.Index package. Please note that element location is specified by using XPath query syntax.

```
TextIndex index = new TextIndex("phoneIndex", Index.INDEX_ELEMENT, "phone",
➥"/department/faculty/phone");
someCollection.createIndex(index);
```

Finally, the interface allows execution of queries on a set of collections. The following code queries the departments collection to retrieve phone numbers of all faculty:

```
Session session=IXClientSessionFactory.getSession(server, port);
XPathStatement stmt=session.createXPathStatement();
XMLResult result=stmt.executeQuery("departments", "/department/faculty/phone");
```

Summary

As shown, many resources and options are available for using XML-enabled databases. The XMLDataManager, presented in Chapter 13, follows the same principles described here, although XMLDataManager was not a fully-formed database.

C

Component-X

IN THIS CHAPTER

- Component-X

Integration products are the customizable middleware components that allow you to XML enable a system. This middleware might also offer integration services libraries that allow the close coupling of an application with typical Web services as well as implementing XML libraries for other common uses.

Perhaps the most widely talked about integration standard is *ebXML (Electronic Business Extensive Markup Language)*, which is common to the B2B type of integration. `http://www.ebxml.org` offers complete information. Currently, OASIS at `http://www.oasis-open.org` manages the ebXML project.

The ebXML initiative was intended for standardizing a business messaging service framework that enables the interoperable, secure, and reliable exchange of messages between trading partners. Also, it allows registering and storing business process and information meta models for reuse.

Component-X

CX-Studio is Data Access Technologies' drag-and-drop component assembly tool for Component-X. CX-Studio implements the "Component Collaboration Architecture" as its own component architecture, but is specialized for XML use.

Component Collaboration Architecture (CCA)

The *Component Collaboration Architecture (CCA)* is a key part of the *Enterprise Collaboration Architecture (ECA)*, a response to the OMG Request For Proposal for a UML profile for

Enterprise Distributed Object Computing (EDOC), and is referenced by the response to the OMG RFP for a UML profile for *Enterprise Application Integration (EAI)*.

A component, in this sense, is something capable of being a component or part of an assembly. CCA components are processing components, ones that collaborate with other CCA components within a CCA composition. CCA components can be used to build other CCA components or to implement roles in a process, such as a vendor in a buy-sell process. The CCA concepts of component and composition are interdependent.

In a simplistic way, the specification states how to define components and combine various components to form composite components. The interesting aspect of this specification is the approach to the design of simplistic components as well as combining them to form a complex component. It also highlights the use of the adapter mechanism you learned about in a previous section of this book. The ability to express the system in terms of components and then to combine these components is very useful for component reusability, maintenance, and rapid application development.

Component-X

You can download a free version form of Component-X from `http://www.enterprise-component.com`. Data Access Technologies maintains the Component-X development news and related product review information.

The Component-X studio allows you to design both simplistic and composite components by combining simple components. Though the studio is still under development, it is useful for productive work and for learning how component architectures can evolve into the next generation's design approach.

Component-X components have the following attributes: They conform to the Component-X architecture based on UML-CCA.

- They can be used within CX-Studio.
- They have ports that produce and use XML initiated by Java events.
- They can have properties that can be configured in CX-Studio and are stored in XML configuration files.
- They have a base implementation in Java and expose specific Component-X interfaces.
- They are executable.

System Design Using Component-X

Let us jump-start into Component-X by designing a small component. After you start the Studio, the default screen appears as shown in Figure C.1.

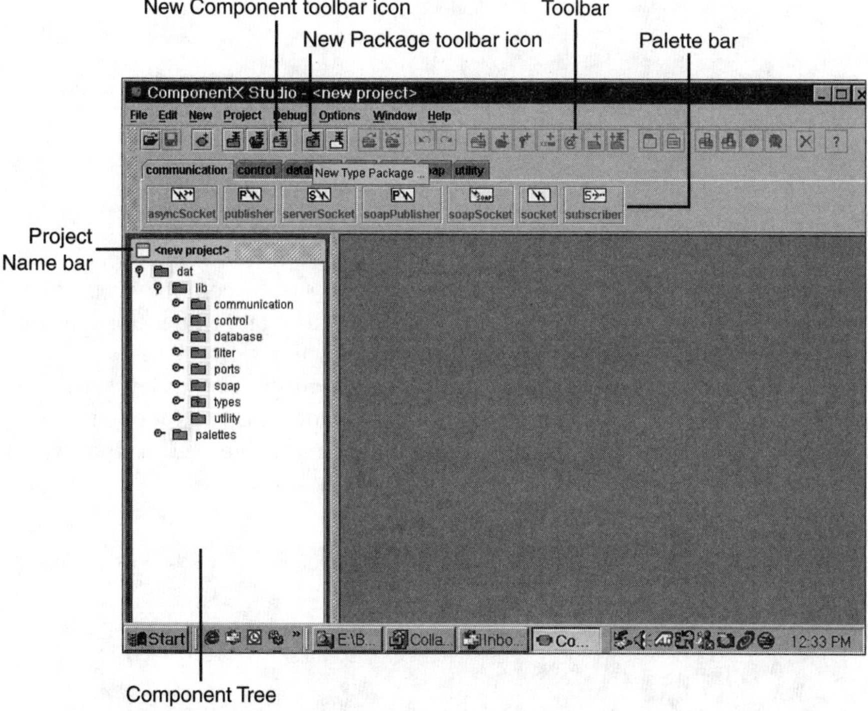

FIGURE C.1 The ComponentX Studio default start screen.

Figure C.1 shows the major options provided by Component-X. Once in Component-X, click the New Package icon and type '`proj`' in the new package name area. Again, click on New Package and then create a package called '`helloPackage`' as shown in Figure C.2, with `proj` selected, which indicates that we need to open this package under it.

The package names appear in the Component View pane on the left side. Note that the `helloPackage` would appears under `proj` main package. To create a component under this package, click the Create component icon and double-click on `proj` package in the top window to show the `helloPackage` we created before. In the dialog box that opens, type in the name of the new component as **`helloApp`**.

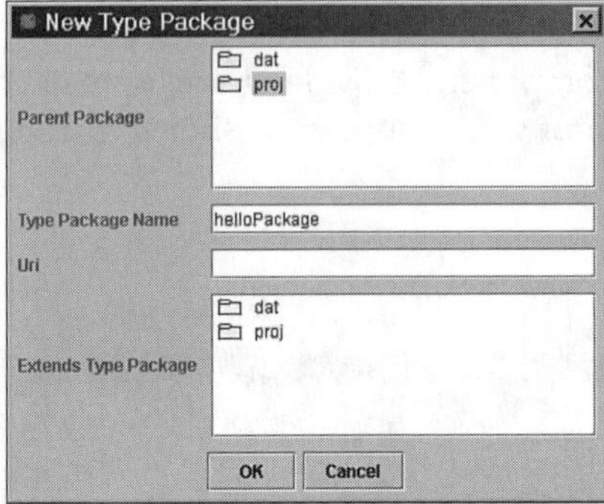

FIGURE C.2 The Package and Component View pane.

To see how we could create a composite component, let's put a component in this existing component. Go to the palette and select the Utility tab. Under this tab you will find a 'dialog' component. Drag and drop the component on the `helloApp` component. Notice that this component provides an input port on its left side, which accepts an XML document. It is important to mention that all message feeds across all the components, designed using this suite, are in XML. The resultant workspace appears as shown in Figure C.3.

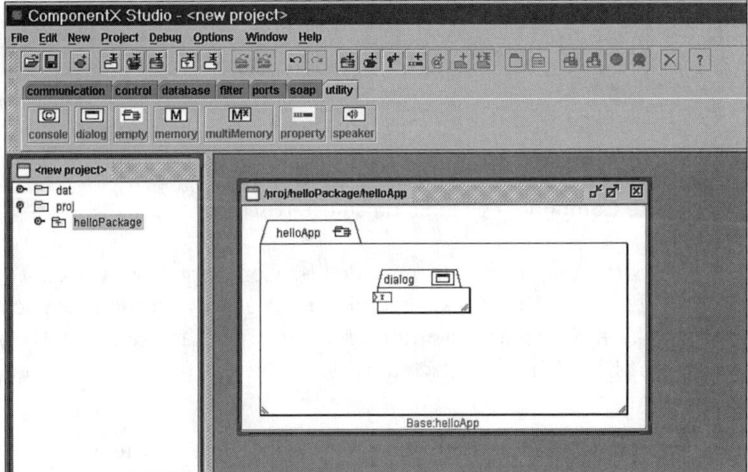

FIGURE C.3 The component workspace.

Now, to demonstrate that this is a working application, let's feed something to the input of this dialog box. Double-click on the input port to open an XML editor. It opens up in the default tree view, so select the Text View icon from the toolbar in this editor window. Enter `<hello/>`, a simple XML string, in this window. Click on the Send icon in the toolbar, and the dialog component responds by showing a message box with the entered string value, as shown in Figure C.4.

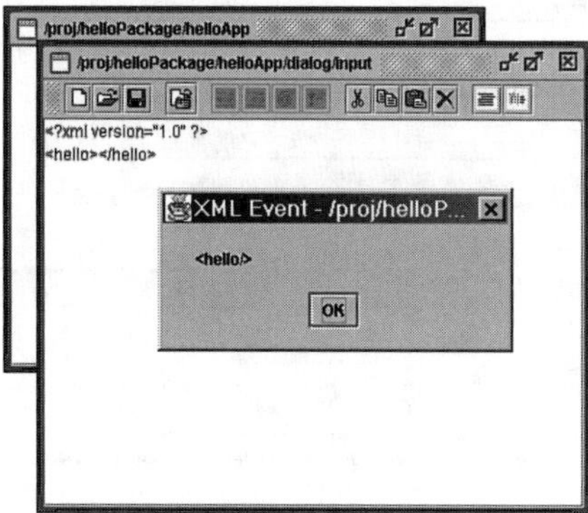

FIGURE C.4 Assigning values to XML variables.

Let's try another procedure: Again, create a component called `Person`. The new component is shown in a separate window. From the component tree on left hand pane, drag the `Person` component and drop it on helloApp to create an instance. Create a second instance so that you get two `Person` class instances in `helloApp`. Rename them as **`Nita`** and **`Anju`**. Remember, these are two instances of the base class Person.

Now let us try to define some ports for our components.

> **NOTE**
>
> One important thing to note is that for changing the derived class, all you need to do is change the base class.

Select the `Person` base class window and go to the Ports tab of the Component Palette. Pick up the input port and drop it on the left side of this class, and similarly pick up the output and drop it on the right side. The instances reflect the changes in the base class components instantly.

Because we are dealing with an example, let's say that all the `Person` class would do is pass whatever is at the input to its output, as-is. So, on the `Person` class click on the input port and, with the left mouse button down, draw a "wire," or line, to the output port. This would tell the application that the component conveys the input to output, as-is, for now. The completed screen shot at this point appears as shown in Figure C.5.

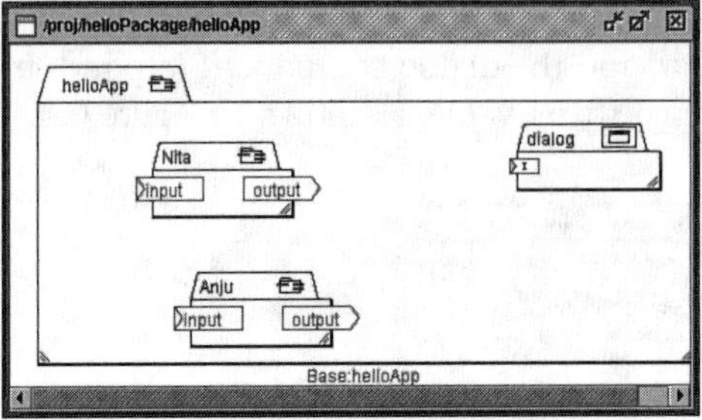

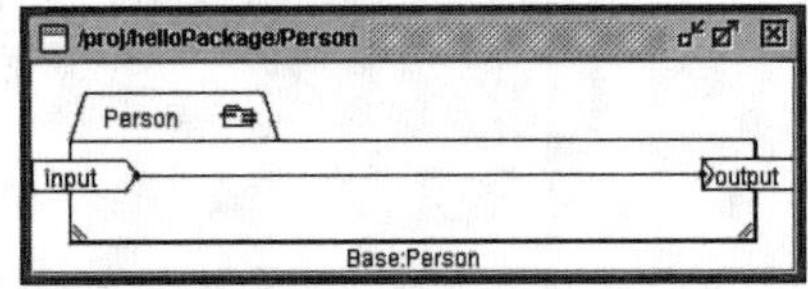

FIGURE C.5 Workspace view with component internal layout.

Now, in the `helloApp` window, similarly draw lines between `Nita`'s output port and `Anju`'s input port. Also, connect `Anju`'s output port to the dailog box's input port. The connection model specifies that the input fed to `Nita` be passed to `Anju` and then to the dialog box. To try our simple application, double-click on `Nita`'s input port, which will invoke the XML Editor. Type the string **`<hello>Hi!</hello>`** in it and click Send. You should see the dialog box showing the message. The screen shot displaying this is shown in Figure C.6.

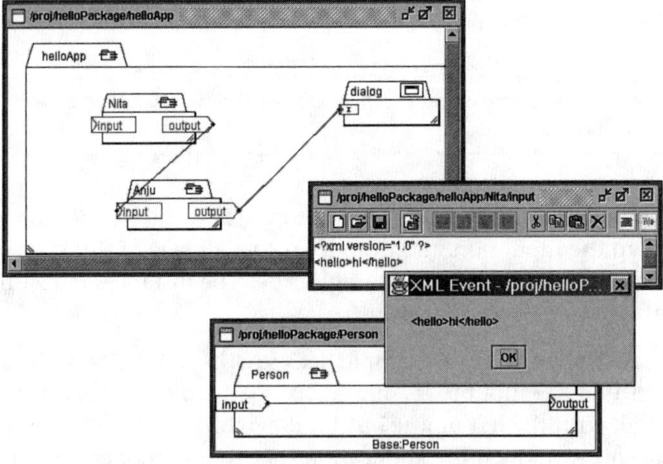

FIGURE C.6 The sample application in action.

Summary

Component-based modeling has a definite advantage for most system design in use today. Our generic systems modeling approach, which we dealt with throughout this book, is easily achievable using this approach.

Component design models are important for designing and devising most generic, reusable systems. Component-X, and products in same line, combine industry standards like ebXML and SOAP to provide ready-to-use components that act as wrappers. This allows the use of simpler systems when designing and modeling.

D

BizTalk Server

IN THIS CHAPTER

- BizTalk Orchestration Designer
- Mapper
- Messaging and Tracking
- Using BizTalk

Microsoft BizTalk 2000 Server is an important enterprise modeling system. The useful aspect of this system is the graphical interfaces it offers to model and create enterprisewide systems. It uses modeling tools like Microsoft VISIO to create the business workflow and generate template program structures directly from the model.

BizTalk Server 2000 is the Microsoft implementation of the BizTalk framework specification. BizTalk is "powered" by XML and uses it extensively for process definitions and connectivity. Besides this, XML provides interoperability with public domain standards like EDI. BizTalk uses XLANG directives to specify the schedules. This schedule controls the workflow and hence the flow of information within the application as well as outside it. The server provides gateway services for document interchange via TCP/IP.

Combining Messaging Services with support of the .NET development platform could really leverage common business process knowledge to create powerful applications.

Communication with a BizTalk server uses XML as the message format. BizTalk uses a SOAP 1.1 XML message format. The BizTalk-friendly XML message is rather a SOAP 1.1 XML message with additional business-specific tags to comply with the BizTalk Framework specification.

BizTalk Orchestration Designer

BizTalk Orchestration Designer is a Visio 2000-based design tool that enables the creation of business process drawings that can be compiled and run as XLANG schedules. As mentioned previously, XLANG is an XML-based language. An XLANG schedule describes the business process and the binding of that process to application services.

Various business processes can be identified, defined, designed, and interconnected through this process. This makes the visualization of design easier; therefore creating an application becomes easier.

You could design the high-level definitions for workflow using many "moving parts." Those moving parts could take the form of a message queue, COM component, BizTalk Channel, file, e-mail message, or HTTP-based service.

Orchestration Designer provides a way to create loosely-coupled business processes that might, in some cases, be long-lived. With the Orchestration Designer, analysts can participate in the development of business rules by using the designer in VISIO to construct the business flow. Once designed, developers can implement the design.

There are three key object categories in the business process page of the Orchestration Designer: flowchart shapes, ports, and implementation shapes. The business analyst would uses the flowchart shapes to create the process flow. The flowchart shapes support basic constructs such as if-then-else decisions, looping while a condition is true, branching and rejoining execution, and defining transactional boundaries.

You can implement application functionality in four basic ways: COM+ components, Scripting components, MSMQ (Microsoft Messaging Queue), or BizTalk Messaging. The object that binds the business process to the implementation code is the port.

Ports are named locations where messages are sent and received. Ports can be defined initially as unbound or bound.

One primary use of the unbound port is to import an XML document and define the fields of the message to be passed. Note that unbound ports are less useful than bound ports for defining message flows, especially flows that are bi-directional.

Binding a port provides the ability to define precisely what will travel through the port, both in and out. This is because the target implementation is known when the binding is created.

It is preferable to use the process of Orchestration only at the middle or high levels; for example with COM/COM+ components that support major business data processing aspects. On top of this, there is a high-level COM/COM+ component, which uses these business data processing components and defines the workflow. It is advisable to replace the workflow COM component using the process, instead of the data processing components.

Another important aspect is that the XLANG schedules, which are created by the process of Orchestration, can be accessed from the code as objects. This enables the business components to access the process models and initiate the workflow pattern.

The VISIO interface allows you to define the business processes in the left-hand pane, using typical flowchart elements. The right-hand pane has implementation elements, in the right-hand tool palette, which can be dragged and dropped in the right-hand designer pane and related to the flow chart elements. This allows a clear view of design and implementation in same interface.

Mapper

The BizTalk Mapper allows the visual mapping of the data between two distinct data sets. It allows easy drag-and-drop methods to map one data set to another.

The map file is stored as an XML stream that can be used by any application. This allows easier middle-tier design, especially for system data integration.

Extending an existing system, which provides data in some proprietary fashion, can be done using mapping functionality. The use of mapping allows existing applications to be used as-is by simply creating the map file as a data mapping to a standard extension. For example, an indigenous internal PO in an organization can be mapped to standard ebXML or OAG format to provide organization-wide PO as its output.

Additionally, simple data mapping can be supported with a transformation base using functions, or "Functoids" as they are called. For each entry mapped between two data sets, the user could initiate a Functoid palette that allows defining or setting suitable functions to the mapping, hence representing transformation rules. The palette offers a choice of pre-built functions categorized into Strings, Mathematical, Logical, and so on.

The important aspect of Functoids is that they allow a source data set's multiple fields to be combined to generate or represent a single data field in a result data set.

Messaging and Tracking

BizTalk supports wizards that allow easy message routing to many other vendor products. The message security level can be set and the transformation can be specified.

Tracking is another important aspect desired in a critical business environment. The tracking interface allows you to choose the fields for tracking, and you can query the track interface easily. The track result provides a simple report view for audits and analysis.

Using BizTalk

There are numerous ways for the use of a design tool like this, but we will focus on some important abilities and aspects.

Typically, a designer would like to leverage the existing application without additional investment and introduce new capabilities to it. BizTalk, combined with MSMQ, provides such a framework.

A business expert or analyst specifies the business model in the form of flowcharts. The developer provides a list of existing components and proposed interfaces needed to implement the new system. The process of Orchestration combines the flowcharts and the implementation, which are then stored as workflow maps in XLANG.

At times you would be in a situation where old components would not provide the ability to interact over MSMQ, and you would create simplistic object wrappers to extend the functionality. The messages can be routed on multiple queues within the system so that they are served accordingly. Besides, the components can be coded so that they know where to forward a message of a specific type. This typically follows the query engine/adapter design presented in this book.

External data interfaces would require the specification of a data interface that can be through any e-mail or Internet protocol mechanism. The packet definition can be specified using Messaging services. The conversion mechanism can be implemented using data mapping services that can also offer transformation.

Hence, BizTalk provides easy-access tools in a single framework that can be used to synthesize an enterprisewide system.

Summary

By providing cross-language integration through COM/COM+, Microsoft made it evident that it wants to operate all its development platforms in a common environment. By introducing .NET, it has created a common serving environment for all these languages and simplified shifting from one coding environment to another.

By offering the BizTalk server framework, it further ensured that the applications can communicate over the Internet easily and leveraged the existing modeling tool to provide an intuitive solution. BizTalk server has many functions, which would require a separate book to explain. But, the major highlights in this chapter provide a simplistic view for a Systems Designer and Architect point of view.

E

JMS—Unified Message Model

IN THIS CHAPTER

- Messaging Frameworks and JMS
- Key Features of JMS
- JMS Messages
- Publish/Subscribe Messages
- Point-to-Point Messaging

As information routing requirements grew, especially for information exchange between diverse systems, the messaging systems requirements became more evident. Messaging was given serious consideration, and many frameworks were introduced to supply the growing need for integrating diverse systems in distributed environments. JMS (Java Message Service) formed a solid framework for messaging supporting major messaging concepts and requirements.

Messaging Frameworks and JMS

The requirement of a messaging framework is not only to support system data interaction, but also to function in a robust manner. For example, when a message is sent over the network, there is no guarantee that it will be delivered to the destination. Under such circumstances, the messaging infrastructure becomes the most essential requirement. The systems offer reliable message delivery by providing a polling capability, causing the message to persist until it is delivered!

JMS offers an API and a set of semantics that prescribe the interface and general behavior of a messaging service. The underlying wire protocol is not specified by JMS. But, in practice, Java messaging is often performed over TCP/IP. Java messaging solutions that conform to the JMS specification provide the implementation of JMS behavior over these protocols.

Key Features of JMS

The key features of JMS can be classified into these categories:

- Major messaging aspects—JMS supports two major messaging paradigms: publish/subscribe and point-to-point.
- Resilience—JMS offers message persistence and a guaranteed message delivery framework.
- Event-based mechanisms—Message sending and receiving is synchronous or asynchronous.
- Transaction support—The broker holds the message until the client application confirms the transaction or rollback.
- Subject based routing and filtering—Messages can be filtered based on user-defined settings in the message header.

JMS Messages

JMS Messages are composed of three parts, as specified here:

- Header fields—Contain values provided by the client and JMS specific values for the routing of messages.
- Properties—JMS-specified or user-defined fields, like message type, as name/value pairs that can be used for message filtering and selective routing. Values can be `boolean`, `byte`, `shorts`, `int`, `long`, `float`, `double`, and `String`.
- Body—Contains an application-specific message. Types of messages can be `BytesMessage`, `MapMessage` (name/value pairs with primitive Java data types), `TextMessage` (`java.util.StringBuffer`), `StreamMessage`, or `ObjectMessage` (serialized Java object).

Note that the body can contain a message in XML format similar to the generic message packet that I have shown in various examples. This allows the use of the framework for communicating the XML messages. The message type for using XML message would be `TextMessage` for the body.

A connection concept used by each client for connecting to the message broker. Within this context, the client application establishes one or more sessions, with suitable transactional characteristics.

Publish/Subscribe Messages

Each session publishes, or subscribes, to one or more topics. An authorized publisher produces messages through a specified topic, and authorized subscribers receive messages by subscribing to that topic. This model promotes the independence of producers and consumers.

When publishing a message, the publishing application specifies the quality of service to be used. Factors involved here include the message's delivery mode, time-to-live, and priority, as well as whether the subscriber requests a reply. Here's an example:

```
publish(Message message, int deliveryMode, int priority, long timeToLive)
```

- `message` is a `javax.jms` message.
- `deliveryMode` is either NON_PERSISTENT or PERSISTENT.
- `priority` is between 0 and 9, with 0 being the lowest and 9 the highest.
- `timeToLive` is between 0 and *n*, with 0 being infinity and any other positive value of *n* being *n* milliseconds.

Subscribers can filter the messages they receive by qualifying their subscriptions with message selectors. Message selectors cause the JMS provider to evaluate message headers and properties prior to sending messages to the client application.

The following message selector might filter a subscription on a topic to retrieve requests, requiring a reply, for high-priority prices.

```
Property_Priority > 6 AND Property_Type='Price' AND Property_Reply is NOT NULL
```

The following code example creates a subscriber subscribing and a publisher publishing the same message.

```
String APP_TOPIC = "my topic";

//Use the session method to create the topic.
javax.jms.Topic topic = session.createTopic (APP_TOPIC);

//The subscriber uses the session object to create a subscriber and
//subscribe to it.
javax.jms.TopicSubscriber subscriber =
   session.createDurableSubscriber(topic, user);
```

```
//Set the listener to topic for the subscriber.
subscriber.setMessageListener(myListener);

//Use the session method to create a publisher.
publisher = session.createPublisher(topic);

// Publish a message stream to the topic.
private void jmsPublish (String strMessage)
{
   try
   {
      javax.jms.TextMessage messagestream = session.createTextMessage();
         messagestream.setText( user + ": " + strMessage );
      publisher.publish( msg );
   }
   catch ( javax.jms.JMSException jmse )
   {
      jmse.printStackTrace();
   }
}
```

Point-To-Point Messaging

Each session object sends, or receives, through one or more queues. The consumers either get the message in the same sequence in which they are queued or browse through all the messages in the queue without destroying the messages.

JMS specifies the queue browser mechanism. A queue browser allows authorized clients to examine queues without destroying the examined messages.

Summary

This is a simple introduction to a readily-available messaging framework that can be easily used to implement a design. Though sophisticated frameworks can be designed with more work, JMS provides a good starting point for realizing distributed architectures.

F

Online References

IN THIS CHAPTER

- System Modeling References
- Online Java References
- XML References
- XML-Based Standards

The following is the concise list of online references. Note that the web is in a state of constant flux and addresses might become obsolete over time.

System Modeling References

- Adapter Architecture for Distributed Web services: `http://www.enterprise-component.com/docs/AdapterWhitePaper.pdf`
- UML Reference: `http://www.omg.org/technology/uml/`
- The WebKB set of tools—a common scheme for shared WWW Annotations, shared knowledge bases and information retrieval: `http://meganesia.int.gu.edu.au/~phmartin/WebKB/doc/papers/cgtools97/`
- Fine tuning provides links to distributed programming and related resources on Web: `http://www.fine-tuning.com/distrib.html`
- Article on Resource Description Framework (RDF): `http://www.xml.com/pub/a/2000/09/06/distributed.html`
- XML-RPC home page: `http://www.xmlrpc.com`
- Integrating Object and Relational Technologies: `http://www.rational.com/products/whitepapers/296.jsp`
- A Reference Model for Trader-Based Distributed Systems Architectures: `http://www.icc3.com/ec/architecture/traderbased.html`

Online Java References

- JavaSoft's information page for JMS, including API documentation: `http://java.sun.com/products/jms/index.html`
- jGuru page: `http://www.jguru.com/`
- Extensive information site for messaging in general: `http://www.messageq.com`
- JavaWorld Topical Index: `http://www.javaworld.com/channel_content/jw-topical-index.shtml`
- Java Boutique: `http://javaboutique.internet.com/tutorials/`
- Jini Home: `http://www.jini.org/`

XML References

- XML.org: `http://www.xml.org`
- XML.com: `http://www.xml.com`
- Microsoft's XML site: `http://www.microsoft.com/xml`
- Apache's XML: `http://xml.apache.org/soap/`
- XML Cover Pages: `http://www.oasis-open.org/cover/sgml-xml.html`
- XML Magazine: `http://www.xmlmag.com`
- XML Zone-DevX Zone: `http://www.xml-zone.com/`
- XML Database products: `http://www.rpbourret.com/xml/XMLDatabaseProds.htm`
- Sun XML Developer Connection: `http://www.sun.com/software/xml/developers/xlink.html`
- Open Source-DevX: `http://www.devx.com/sourcebank/`
- Open Source-Source Forge: `http://www.sourceforge.com`

XML-Based Standards

- W3C: `http://www.w3.org`
- ebXML home: `http://www.ebxml.org`
- Standards and other links: `http://www.enterprise-component.com/products/standards.htm`

- XML-EDI group: `http://www.xmledi-group.org/`
- XEDI—An approach to XML-EDI: `http://www.xedi.org/`
- XML Standards Reference: `http://www.webreference.com/xml/reference/standards.html`
- Rosettanet—XML Standard formats for cross industry application integration: `http://www.rosettanet.org/`
- iFX—XML Standard formats for cross industry application integration: `http://www.ifxforum.org`

G
Book References

IN THIS APPENDIX

- XML and Other Standard References
- Systems Analysis and Design References

The following is a list of XML-related books and other references useful to the developer. Note that books might go out of print over time, and become unavailable for purchase.

XML and Other Standard References

- *The Price Waterhouse Edi Handbook* by Thomas P. Colberg (Editor), Nicole Willenz Gardner, Phillip W. McLaunhin (Contributor), Dennis M. McGinnis. Publisher: John Wiley & Sons; ISBN: 0471107530
- *SOAP: Cross Platform Web Services Development Using XML* by Scott Seely, Kent Sharkey. Publisher: Prentice Hall PTR; ISBN: 0130907634
- *Professional XML Web Services* by Vivek Chopra, Zoren Zaev, Gary Damschen, Chris Dix, Patrick Cauldwell, Rajesh Chawla, Kristy Saunders, Glenn Olander, Francis Norton, Tony Hong, Uche Ogbuji, Mark A. Richman. Publisher: Wrox Press Inc; ISBN: 1861005091
- *Professional XML (Programmer to Programmer)* by Mark Birbeck (Editor), Nikola Ozu, Jon Duckett, Andrew Watt, st Mohr, Oli Gauti Gudmundsson, Jon Duckett, Andrew Watt, Stephen Mohr, Kevin Williams, Oli Gauti Gudmundsson, Raja Mani, Daniel Marcus, Peter Kobak, Evan Lenz, Mark Birbeck, Brian Hickey, Zoran Zaev, Steven Livingstone, Jonathan Pinnock, Keith Visco. Publisher: Wrox Press Inc; ISBN: 1861005059

Systems Analysis and Design References

- *Systems Analysis and Design Methods, Fifth Edition,* by Jeffrey L. Whitten, Lonnie D. Bentley, Kevin C. Dittman. Publisher: McGraw-Hill Higher Education; ISBN: 0072315393
- *Applying UML and Patterns: An Introduction to Object-Oriented Analysis and Design and the Unified Process* by Craig Larman. Publisher: Prentice Hall PTR; ISBN: 0130925691
- *Design Patterns* by Erich Gamma, Richard Helm, Ralph Johnson, John Vlissides. Publisher: Addison-Wesley Pub Co; ISBN: 0201633612

Index

Symbols

A

B

C

D

E

H

I

J

K-L

M

N

O

P

Q

R

S

T

U

V

W

X-Z

hey, you've got enough worries.

Other Related Titles

Enhydra XMLC Application Development
0-672-32211-0
David Young
$39.99 U.S./$52.95 CAN

Pure Corba
0-672-31812-1
Fintan Bolton
$49.99 U.S./$74.95 CAN

BizTalk Unleashed
0-672-32176-9
Susie Adams and Charlie Kaiman
$49.99 U.S./$74.95 CAN

XML and Web ServicesUnleashed
0-672-32341-9
Ron Schmelzer and Travis Vandersypen
$49.99 U.S./$74.95 CAN

Strategic XML
0-672-32178-5
W. Scott Means
$34.99 U.S./$52.95 CAN

SAMS

www.samspublishing.com

XML Internationalization and Localization
0-672-32096-7
Yves Savourel
$49.99 U.S./$74.95 CAN

Building Web Services: Making Sense of XML, SOAP, WSDL, and UDDI
0-672-32181-5
Steve Graham and Simon Simeonov
$49.99 U.S./$74.95 CAN

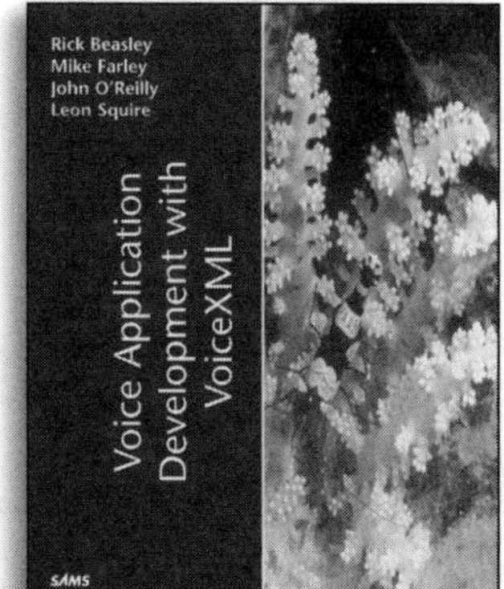

Voice Application Development with VoiceXML
0-672-32138-6
Rick Beasley, Mike Farley, John O'Reilly, Leon Squire
$49.99 U.S./$74.95 CAN

All prices are subject to change.